Wingless Eagle

★Wingless Eagle

U.S. Army Aviation through World War I

HERBERT A. JOHNSON

The University of North Carolina Press

Chapel Hill and London

© 2001
The University of North Carolina Press
All rights reserved
Set in New Baskerville and Gill types
by Keystone Typesetting
Maps by William Nelson
Manufactured in the United States of America
The paper in this book meets the guidelines for
permanence and durability of the Committee on
Production Guidelines for Book Longevity of the
Council on Library Resources.
Library of Congress Cataloging-in-Publication Data
Johnson, Herbert Alan.
Wingless eagle: U.S. Army aviation through World
War I / Herbert A. Johnson.
    p. cm.
Includes bibliographical references and index.
ISBN 0-8078-2627-8 (cloth: alk. paper)
1. United States. Army—Aviation—History—20th
century. 2. Aeronautics, Military—United States—
History—20th century. 3. World War, 1914–
1918—Aerial operations, American. I. Title.
UG633 .J47   2001
358.4′00973′09041—dc21   2001027328

05 04 03 02 01   5 4 3 2 1

In memory of

HARRY O. JOHNSON

(1895–1966)

Sergeant, Quartermaster Corps,

United States Army,

1918

Contents

Illustrations

Tables and Maps

Preface

This book has aged with me over the past quarter-century, and we have both changed in the process. On October 30, 1972, I received an Air Force Reserve mobilization assignment to the Historical Research Division at the Albert F. Simpson Historical Research Center. To familiarize reservists with the archival resources at the center, it was customary to assign each one to a research topic. Thus, one of my tasks was to conduct research on a monograph that would describe the manner in which public opinion shaped the development of U.S. Army aviation prior to 1950. The overall research plan was established by James N. Eastman Jr., then chief of the Historical Research Division. Dr. Maurer Maurer, then director of the center, provided valuable guidance from his extensive knowledge of the earliest period of military aviation. Much of Dr. Maurer's work on the First World War was published in *The U.S. Air Service in World War I*, 4 vols. (Washington: Government Printing Office, 1978–79).

My assignment to the Simpson Historical Research Center terminated on August 1, 1980, but I was reassigned as a historical officer on June 30, 1983, to work at the Office of Air Force History, Bolling Air Force Base, Washington, D.C., as a mobilization assignee to the deputy chief of Air Force History. In the course of this assignment, which terminated on April 1, 1984, I was able to continue my research and begin writing an initial draft that covered the years 1907 to 1914. These early efforts provided a basis for a preliminary inquiry into conceptual thought, entitled "Seeds of Separation: The General Staff and Military Aviation before World War I," published in *Air University Review* 39 (Nov.–Dec. 1982): 29–45. A revised version of this article appears as chapter 4 of this book. Another article covered the early history of the Aero Club of America and its role in early army aviation; this was published in *New York History* 65 (1985): 374–95, and a revised and expanded version appears in this volume as chapter 1. Finally, my initial work on the Wright patent controversy appeared in an article in *Air Force Journal of Logistics* 9, no. 2 (1985): 2–6; a much revised and expanded version comprises chapter 5 of this book. I am grateful to the editors of these journals for their editorial assistance and for their kind permission to reprint portions of these articles.

In December 1981 the Army War College Foundation appointed me a visiting research scholar at the U.S. Army Military History Institute, Carlisle Barracks, Pennsylvania. This provided access to useful materials on Army–Air Service relationships during World War I, and permitted me to examine the memoirs of military aviators who served during the war in Europe.

Subsequent to my retirement from the Air Force Reserve in February 1987, the project has changed in two ways. First, the chronological period has been shortened from its original 1950 termination date, and this has permitted me to concentrate on the years before Armistice Day, 1918. Second, the study has been redesigned to provide more comprehensive coverage of air-power doctrinal development, the adequacy of American industrial and tactical development, and the critical interplay between civilian and military groups. The book has thus moved inexorably in the direction of a monographic study that may begin to explain why the United States Army was so poorly prepared for entry into aerial warfare in World War I.

My appointment as a center research associate at the Simpson Historical Research Center in the summer of 1990 provided me an opportunity to review the air force archives from this new perspective, and to gather information from oral history materials. The University of South Carolina's Committee on Creative Research and Scholarship awarded me a grant in 1989 to complete work at the National Archives and the Library of Congress. Most recently, the University of South Carolina School of Law provided summer research support in 1996, 1997, and 1998. I spent this time studying the court-martial of Lt. Col. Lewis E. Goodier Sr., evaluating general staff and military attaché work dealing with military aviation abroad, tracing the evolution and impact of the National Defense Act of 1916, and explaining the Air Service's participation in World War I. My understanding of the complexities of the Wright patent litigation was deepened by two successive trips to consult the Wright Brothers Papers at the Library of Congress. The papers of Capt. Washington Irving Chambers, U.S.N., at the Library of Congress are a gold mine of information concerning early aviation. Although they are of tangential value to the main subject of this book—army aviation—they and the Capt. Mark Bristol Papers, also at the Library of Congress, provide many helpful insights into the politics and psychological aspects of government aviation from 1911 through 1915.

Earlier drafts on some topics discussed in this book were read and critiqued by James N. Eastman Jr., R. Cargill Hall, and Richard H. Kohn, all present or former historians with the Air Force History Program. Their suggestions resulted in substantial improvement of the drafts and added to my understanding of aviation history. However, subsequent to their review, the book has taken a very different focus. This acknowledgment should in no way be construed as identifying them or the United States Air Force with the author's current views or interpretations. More recently, Professor Irving B. Holley of Duke University has been most generous in reviewing an earlier and more lengthy draft of the epilogue, and he has saved me from several inaccurate statements and conclusions. Dr. Leonard Bruno, a specialist in the history of science in the Library of Congress's Manuscript Division, has been most generous in sharing with me his extensive knowledge about early aviation source materials. Two anonymous readers for the University of North Carolina Press have provided thoughtful and painstaking critiques, which have corrected many errors and suggested new source materials to enhance my understanding. Whatever errors remain, either of fact or interpretation, are my sole responsibility — and I would be the last to claim "Zero Defects" for this book.

I am grateful to countless archivists and librarians who have made materials available to me. First and foremost, the staff at the Coleman Karesh Law Library and the Thomas Cooper Library, both at the University of South Carolina, have assisted in many ways — handling interlibrary loan requests, providing government documents, facilitating my work with microfilm, and guiding me through a vast number of printed sources. Similarly, present and past historians and archivists at the Air Force Historical Research Agency, formerly the Albert F. Simpson Historical Research Center, have patiently and cheerfully put up with numerous requests for assistance. Among the many other institutions to which I am indebted, I must include the Library of Congress, the National Archives, the U.S. Army Military History Institute, the Earl Gregg Swem Library at the College of William and Mary, the United States Air Force Academy Library, and the Air University Library at Maxwell Air Force Base.

The staff at the University of North Carolina Press has also made a substantial contribution to the accuracy and content of this book. Lewis Bateman, former executive editor at the Press and a valued colleague for twenty years in the field of legal history, encouraged me to persist with still another draft of this study. His gentle suggestion that it needed to be shortened by 25 percent is, I am compelled to admit, the reason why this is a better book. Suzanne Comer Bell has been a careful and conscientious copyeditor, helping to identify the inconsistencies and omissions that are inevitable in any work that has been so long in both research and writing. They, and all of the others at the Press who have helped me along the way, have earned my sincere gratitude and my appreciation for their skills and concern.

My wife, Jane McCue Johnson, has patiently read each chapter to eliminate inelegancies of style, incomprehensible expressions of foggy thought, and spelling errors that escaped spell-check. Readers owe her special thanks for any grace, style, or clarity that the final text may possess. She has also been tolerant as the book has evolved through a series of changes, and has never flagged in her faith that it would ultimately appear in print.

Herbert A. Johnson
Franklin, North Carolina
July 2000

Wingless Eagle

Introduction

In the early 1970s the United States Air Force launched a campaign to increase efficiency and the quality of performance in regard to both personnel and equipment. The upbeat name assigned to the effort was "Zero Defects." While mankind has always been intrigued with the idea of achieving perfection, most close observers of human nature and mechanical functions would point out that "Zero Defects" may be an inspiring goal, but it is rarely, if ever, attained. "Zero Defects" in a military environment can be self-defeating. It is one thing to make a mistake; it is worse to refuse to admit that what has been done actually *was* an error. History may not repeat itself, but those who refuse to learn from the past are bound to appear foolish.

The early history of the United States Army's aviation has suffered from a "Zero Defects" mentality, and virtually all studies to date have ignored a very basic question: why was the United States so poorly prepared, in equipment and personnel, to engage in aerial combat in World War I? While foreign inventors were not far behind the Wright brothers in 1903, the fact remains that the first successful powered flights were made at Kitty Hawk, North Carolina, and Dayton, Ohio. Yet American airmen in the First World War flew European-designed aircraft because American products were woefully inadequate for service on the Western Front. American airframe manufacture had not evolved to permit assembly-line production. Postwar investigations of the shortcomings of the Aircraft Production Board provided grim proof that American industry was never capable of carrying out President Woodrow Wilson's ill-advised commitment to deliver a vast number of war planes to the Allied powers.

The situation in regard to World War I flying personnel was even more depressing, but it, too, has been shielded from historical recall. Lack of scholarly discussion may well be due to a wish to venerate the memory of the brave army aviators who pioneered military aeronautics during its first fifteen years. There is also a disturbing tendency to ignore biography when writing air force history. Unfortunately, human personality traits can have a significant impact upon the development of institutions and ideas. Ignoring this dimension can blind-side any historical writing, but it is particularly dangerous when applied to the study of military aviation from 1907 through 1918. The personalities of the aviators, and their interrelationships with each other, are critical aspects of this history. Biography helps us to understand how they interacted with the other arms and branches of the army, how they responded to command authority, and how they joined with civilian aviation groups to influence Congress and to shape Signal Corps and army decisions concerning aeronautics in the military.

While this study is intended to be neither revisionist nor judgmental, it will doubtless be accused of being both. Unquestionably, it casts early army aeronautics in a new light. However, its critical analysis cannot detract from the undoubted achievements of army aviation in this early period. Young flying officers in pre–World War I aviation became the instructors of pilots in the First World War, advocates of air power in the interwar years, and commanders of air units in World War II. Focusing upon their early years should not cast any shadow upon their future contributions to the military service or to aeronautics.

The Complex Story of Early Army Aviation

Although the following chapters appear in a rough chronological order, there has been a competing and more pressing need to discuss topics exhaustively and completely once they have been introduced. Several chapters overlap each other in their time sequence, and the reader may well be overwhelmed by "flash-backs" which, although artistically justified in novels, tend to confuse scholarly works. The timeline in the Appendix will assist readers in coordinating the sequence of events discussed in several chapters and in different contexts.

It has been necessary to focus upon events and situations occurring well beyond the narrow scope of army flying activities. Most proximate have been matters arising within the other arms and branches of the army, and specifically within the command structure of the Signal Corps and the staff procedures of the General Staff Corps. Some attention has been given to the War Department and the influence of the presidents. Much more space has been devoted to the Congress, and the impact of public opinion and lobbying upon the fate of army aviation in the legislative process. Throughout the text there is the *leitmotif* of civilian aeronauts and their impact upon army aviation, be it negative or positive. Necessarily, the isolation of any one topic for discussion places all others in the background, even though the close interrelationship of these factors persists.

Again and again, and in various contexts, it will be necessary to refer to what has been denominated the "aeronaut constituency." Initially a powerful ally in the development of army aviation, the Aero Club and its related societies and associations fell victim to irresponsible publicists and self-designated aviation experts. By 1916 the positive contributions that knowledgeable aviator members made to the Aviation Section were outweighed by the disruptive influence of the publicists upon congressional attitudes and military discipline. Having regularly cried "wolf" repeatedly at early army indifference to aeronautics, the "aeronaut constituency" lost both credibility with Congress and the public.

On the other hand, the American public's enthusiasm for the "Winged Gospel" kept aviation in the forefront of information media attention. Aware of this fact, the Aeronautical Division cultivated media coverage, and participated in national historical exhibitions, aeronautical meets and contests, and dangerous and counterproductive exhibition flying. Even after the army officially abandoned high-risk exhibition flying in 1913, the death rate among army pilots escalated, raising serious doubts in the public mind and undermining confidence in Signal Corps administration of military aviation.

Domestic consideration of military aviation took place against the background of aerial warfare in North Africa and Europe. Newspaper and attaché reports of aviation progress provided an incentive for creative conceptual thought by army aviators, and at the same time triggered congressional inquiries by the Hay Committee during 1913 and 1914. Contrary to earlier scholarly impressions, the United States Army and its General Staff Corps was well informed concerning foreign aviation. It was presidential and congressional reluctance to adequately fund army aviation that retarded progress, and not lack of awareness on the part of the army high command.

The congressional investigation of army aviation in 1913 and 1914 concluded with the enactment of the so-called Hay Bill in July 1914. This legislation reorganized the Aeronautical Division and renamed it the Aviation Section of the Signal Corps. It also ended an effort to separate aviation activities from Signal Corps oversight. On the other hand, the legislation authorized expansion of the new Aviation Section and liberalized certain rules concerning the qualification and status of military aviators.

Despite the improved situation of the new Aviation Section, there was still uncertainty—and thus heated debate—over the role that aviation would play in warfare. Initially the army's experience with captive balloon reconnaissance in the Civil War and Spanish American War led the General Staff to favor lighter-than-air aeronautics. Doubtless that tendency was reinforced by the army's financial support for Langley's unsuccessful heavier-than-air experiments. However, by 1912 field maneuvers in the United States and abroad demonstrated the value of aerial observation for the direction of field and coastal artillery fire. It was in these areas that cooperation between the Signal Corps and its aviation component was most productive. On the other hand, there was firm and highly placed opposition to the proposal that airplanes be used to attack enemy troops or aircraft, or as bombardment vehicles.

The threat of Zeppelin attack on London, which actually materialized in 1915, formed the background for discussion of aerial bombardment. Since the United States was a signatory to the Second Hague Convention against aerial bombardment, the army high command and the executive branch hesitated to endorse this aspect of military aviation. However, in November 1915 the General Staff modified military policy to include an offensive role for army aviation. At that time, military doctrine was amended to justify offensive aerial action for the purpose of facilitating aerial observation and artillery-fire direction.

More than conceptual theory was involved in the question of combative roles for airplanes. There were real political and administrative stakes in the military policy debate. Signal Corps control of aviation was linked to continuing aeronautics as an auxiliary to the Signal Corps mission of collecting and communicating intelligence. Once an aerial offensive role was conceded, arguments for separating aviation from the Signal Corps became much more persuasive.

In addition, the General Staff and the army high command were committed to the development of a "New Army" marked by professionalism, unified command through the chief of staff, and elimination of legislative lobbying by the various arms and branches. However, army aviators had close ties with civilian aviation groups, and with congressmen who held positions in their state National Guard units. Ultimately some of these organizational issues would be resolved by the enactment of the National Defense Act in 1916, but these intraservice conflicts and civil-military relationships continued to play a significant role in army aviation even after 1916.

Army aviation was badly hurt by the Wright patent litigation, which began in 1909 and continued throughout the prewar years. When the U.S. Circuit

Court for Western New York declared the Wrights to have achieved pioneer status in their design for an airplane control system, it ostensibly conferred a monopoly on the Wright Company. However, American manufacturers unlicensed by the Wrights continued to design and build airplanes that in many cases were superior to Wright Company products. Building a superior machine could be accomplished only by attempting major mechanical changes in the control systems that might defeat a Wright infringement lawsuit. A substantial portion of airplane manufacturing costs was involved in this engineering effort and in funding litigation to defend the results.

Despite army Signal Corps complaints, Wright aircraft remained antiquated in design and defective in workmanship, and the Wright Company's legal campaign against contest flying isolated American designers from observing European innovations and improvements. Some European nations like Britain obtained Wright licenses to produce war planes in their government factories. The German Empire, because of its patent office ruling that the Wright patent was voided through prior disclosure, was unrestricted by any Wright claims.

Patent litigation continued in the United States for at least two decades, and the damage done to U.S. Army aviation by the Wright monopoly is incalculable. The army was circumspect enough to halt its transition to Curtiss-built airplanes, and to retrain its Curtiss-qualified pilots on Wright controls. Since the two systems called for virtually opposite piloting movements, the transition caused serious accidents, and perhaps several of the 1913 fatalities. Nationally, the rapid rise in airplane manufacturing orders due to the European war resulted in a rapid decrease in the production of quality American airplanes and parts.

The Stormy Prewar Years

If things looked bad for the Aviation Section after 1914, they would deteriorate even more in 1915. In October 1915 the court-martial of Lt. Col. Lewis E. Goodier took place in San Francisco, resulting in his reprimand for inciting military aviators to press charges against their commanding officer at the Signal Corps Aviation School. Ostensibly, one judge advocate officer was court-martialed; as a practical matter, Signal Corps administration of the aviation program was exposed and found badly wanting. These revelations, confirmed by a General Staff investigation, resulted in a reprimand for the chief signal officer, Brig. Gen. George P. Scriven. Col. Samuel Reber was reprimanded and relieved from duty as chief of the Aviation Section.

The Goodier court-martial provided clear evidence of favoritism toward certain flying officers, usually holding commissions in the Signal Corps. Since most military aviators were assigned from line regiments for training and duty in aviation, the threat of having Signal Corps officers assigned as their superiors was disheartening and demoralizing. In the wake of these disclosures, the new secretary of war, Newton D. Baker, seriously considered separating army aviation from Signal Corps supervision but took no action.

After August 1914, American military attachés sent extensive reports concerning military aviation in the First World War, and the General Staff recognized the value of military aeronautics and modified its "Military Policy" accordingly in November 1915. The war demonstrated the need to dominate air space over the front lines and over lines of supply. To a lesser extent, the Allies' experience illustrated the feasibility of using airplanes for bombardment of transportation facilities, troop assembly areas, and supply and munitions dumps.

By way of contrast to these lessons learned from the European war, the American people and military professionals witnessed the disastrous performance of the First Aero Squadron in support of the Mexican Punitive Expedition. Briefly, the underpowered and dangerous Curtiss JN-3 airplanes were unable to fly over the high mountains in northern Mexico. As a result they were unable to scout ahead of General Pershing's troops for signs of Villa's presence. Neither were the airmen able to facilitate communication between the two advancing columns in the American force. As the First Aero Squadron began to lose its airplanes to accidents, the War Department imposed a blackout on news from Mexico. However, reporters and others got the facts out of northern Mexico and into the press. On April 19, 1916, the last operational airplane of the First Aero Squadron crashed, effectively ending aerial support for Pershing. Destruction of the squadron's last airplane triggered vastly expanded appropriations for aviation, but supply and production difficulties hampered any substantial aviation assistance to the expedition prior to its withdrawal in February 1917. Ironically, President Wilson confirmed the Goodier court-martial sentence on April 17, 1916; two days later the last operational airplane of the First Aero Squadron crashed into history on the sands of northern Mexico.

Enactment of the National Defense Act of 1916 completed the trilogy of humiliations that hung over the Signal Corps and its Aviation Section in 1916. At first the pending bill contained no provision for increase of the Signal Corps, due to the pendency of investigations concerning the Signal

Corps aviation program. Representatives and senators were expansive in their caustic comments about army aviation and its inadequacies. Quite obviously both the Goodier court-martial record and the performance of the First Aero Squadron in Mexico were matters of widespread knowledge and concern. Ultimately, the National Defense Act provided a substantial increase in personnel for the Aviation Section, and added new incentives for officers willing to volunteer for flying duty. Although the legislation came too late to stimulate aircraft production in the United States, it went a long way toward preparing for mobilization in the event of war.

When the United States declared war in April 1917, the lack of preparedness could not be offset by wartime effort or monetary appropriations. There was a need to train large numbers of pilots, and this effort was only partially successful. American industrial firms manufactured some reconnaissance and would-be bombardment aircraft from European designs, but never in sufficient quantity to meet Allied needs. Hampered as they were, U.S. Army pilots made major contributions to Allied victory in the air. An almost superhuman effort resulted in a resurrected Balloon Corps, rendered necessary by the stable fronts of trench warfare, and the need for economy and pinpoint accuracy in the direction of field artillery fire. Yet the war ended before some of the more advanced concepts of strategic bombardment could be tested. The war was thus both an epilogue to the struggles and troubles of the first decade of army aviation, and a prologue to the struggle for long-range bombardment and separation from the army as a distinct and coequal air force.

National Policy and Military Force

Despite all of the factors complicating the history of early army aviation, the predominant theme was a chronic lack of funding for military aeronautics. To a degree the organizational tensions, conflicting professional views, and extensive civilian-military interaction contributed to this legislative neglect. However, they played a minor role in congressional disregard for the U.S. Army as a whole, and army aviation shared in this underfunding. American public attention, governmental defense planning, and federal appropriations were focused on the development of a large dreadnought fleet. Since the oceans provided relative isolation from the rivalries of Europe and the rapidly rising power of Japan, naval defense seemed to offer the best alternative to the maintenance of a landed defense force. The teachings of Capt. Alfred Thayer Mahan, stressing the place of the oceans in national development and their role in defense policies, found a particularly receptive audience in the United States.[1] National preoccupation with naval construction and preparedness on the high seas drew attention away from the U.S. Army and its needs.

The demoralized state of the army and the popularity of the navy in American public opinion gave rise to a peculiar paradox in regard to aeronautics. An unusual sequence of events lodged scientific and technological study within the army Signal Corps. Along with experiments in cable and wireless communications systems, the Signal Corps had maintained an interest in aerial navigation since the days of the American Civil War. Not surprisingly, it was the army that encouraged early experiments with heavier-than-air flight, and the Signal Corps was charged in 1907 with the conduct of aeronautical activities for the army. By way of contrast, the U.S. Navy, by far the service more attuned to scientific and technical work, did not enter aeronautics until 1910, and the infant naval air arm barely survived the antipathy of the battleship admirals.[2] Is it not possible that the lack of navy support for aeronautics caused public doubts concerning the value of air power in the conduct of warfare?

Finally, it is necessary to note that the rise of American air power took place at a time when international politics was seeking to establish standards for "civilized war" even while world powers were jockeying for advantage in the arms race. Two Hague Conventions sought to draw lines of distinction between belligerent and nonbelligerent aspects of national life. Provisions in both conventions prohibiting aerial attack of undefended and nonbelligerent towns and cities were to prove particularly troublesome to Americans studying the use of airplanes and dirigibles in warfare. It is significant that all of the world powers (except the United States) who had any possibility of developing an effective air arm, refused to ratify those clauses in the Hague Conventions.[3]

A Comfortable Myth and Some Grim Realities

In the past, early army aviation has been cast in a romantic, even nostalgic, aura of achievement and success against the intransigence of the General Staff Corps and the army high command. Considered objectively, this is something of a historically created myth. The army establishment was *not* unaware of European developments in air power, nor was it hostile to the pleas of army pilots or their civilian proponents. It properly resented the flying officers' proclivity to appeal to Congress, and their resort to the public press when army resources proved inadequate for their purposes. Those breaches of decorum and discipline, which at times bordered upon insubordination, continued into the time of active service in World War I.

On the other hand, the efforts of the Signal Corps to control and manipulate flying activities within the army proved to be counterproductive. Punitive measures against flying officers fueled resentment against the Washington Signal Corps staff and led to the aviators' conviction that those who were promoted or who received command positions were subservient to Signal Corps wishes. At the same time, flagrant disregard for the safety of army pilots, coupled with a blind loyalty to unstable Wright Company aircraft, demonstrated the inadequacy and duplicity of Signal Corps leadership. These difficulties led to a long-honored rule that only rated officers should command flying units. Ultimately, the disaffection bred from these experiences converted army aviators into advocates for separation from the Signal Corps and, finally, independence from the army.

The history of military air power in the United States might well be quite different if it began in the eras of Grover Cleveland or Warren Harding. Progressivism made a particular mark on American life. With its encouragement of personal valor and its nationalism, it lent strength to the aspirations of army aviators. Leaders in the progressive era were likely to have broad, and at times unrelated, interests, and many were united in their support for aeronautics as a new form of human endeavor. It was popular to maintain life-long contact with one's military or naval service, either through the National Guard, the Naval Militia, or a number of private voluntary military groups. On the other hand, for all of its bombast, the progressive era was not marked by an adventuresome fiscal policy. Taft brought the national budget under tighter control, and Congress demanded more specific justification for proposed expenditures and programs. The army budget continued sharply subordinated to that of the navy, and neither service was without its attackers. Government tax revenues in those years before the federal income tax, were severely limited; and after the introduction of a moderate income tax in 1913, few additional dollars were made available for national defense.[4]

In the long run, lack of U.S. government purchases of airplanes and airships resulted in atrophy of the manufacturing industry. Coupled with the interminable patent litigation and the depressing impact the Wright patents had upon aeronautical development, these economic factors were most significant in American lack of preparedness to fight World War I in the air. The years from 1907 through 1918 were a time of failure — failure to prepare for war, failure to exploit an American invention for national defense purposes, failure to build a harmonious and functioning flying unit, and failure to establish effective discipline and organizational structure within the Aeronautical Division, Aviation Section, and Air Service. Undoubtedly, many of those who failed had the best of intentions, but in the cold retrospect of history, their shortcomings can scarcely be considered either a justification or a valid excuse.

I ★ Aeronautics in Embryo
The Aeronaut Constituency

One of the best ways to enter the complex history of early army aviation is to consider the Aero Club of America, a New York–based private club first established to advance competitive racing with free-flying hot air balloons. Organized under the auspices of the Automobile Club of America, the Aero Club not only occupied an influential place in aeronautical activities, but it also gained quasiofficial status as the international agency for the licensing of airplane pilots and for authorizing flying contests.[1] Its wealthy membership provided both material and moral support to the Aeronautical Division of the Signal Corps after the division's organization on August 1, 1907. The club also had excellent access to the communications media, and many of its members were political leaders in the states and the federal government. In addition, a significant portion of the club's membership belonged to militia organizations or to volunteer-staffed military, naval, or flying groups. As the primary civilian proponent of aviation before 1910, the Aero Club of America may well be considered the midwife of military and naval aviation in the United States.

The Prehistory of the Aeronautical Division

Military aviation, like a newborn human infant, underwent a prenatal period. During the American Civil War, stationary reconnaissance balloons made a strong impression upon Union generals as a reliable source of tactical intelligence.[2] Although the spherical balloons and their gas generators were cumbersome, and their civilian observers proved resistant to military discipline, the Balloon Corps amply demonstrated the value of aerial reconnaissance.[3] After the surrender at Appomattox, army interest in lighter-than-air navigation waned, but its occasional use did lead to the development of improved balloons, and to doctrinal thought concerning their military applications. An abortive reconnaissance attempt to use a captive spherical observation balloon was made during the 1898 battle of San Juan Hill. Not only was there difficulty in controlling the balloon near a moving front line, but the presence of the observation balloon drew Spanish fire to the American headquarters location.[4] Thereafter government economies, combined with this unfortunate experience in combat, resulted in limited expansion of army aeronautical activity. Despite these disappointments, the army continued its interest in the value of aerial flight as an adjunct to military operations.[5]

Between 1898 and 1903, the army's Board of Fortifications and Ordinance provided financial support to the heavier-than-air experiments conducted by Professor Samuel P. Langley, the secretary of the Smithsonian Institution. Langley's work was also supported by the Smithsonian Institution, but it was army disenchantment with the Langley experimental failures that had a negative impact upon military aeronautics. After achieving a modicum of success with gliders, Professor Langley moved forward to construct a large engine-powered machine, widely acclaimed as *the* aircraft that could carry man aloft in controlled, powered flight. Unfortunately its much publicized first flight from a house boat on the Potomac resulted in a dramatic crash immediately after takeoff. Down with it went Langley's dreams and the U.S. Army's financial encouragement for any heavier-than-air flight.[6] Ironically, just a few days later, on December 17, 1903, the Wright brothers flew their powered aircraft over the dunes at Kitty Hawk, North Carolina. Because of Langley's failure, the Army Board was totally disinterested in the Wrights' invention until early in 1907.[7]

Langley's failure had little impact on the Aero Club, since virtually all of its members were sport balloonists. Sport ballooning involved contest flying of free spherical balloons, the object being to increase the distance the balloon traveled or the speed it achieved. The Aero Club's intrepid men, and a few women, inflated their balloons either with hydrogen gas or with hot air generators, and drifted with the wind across the skies of rural America. To encourage this competitive ballooning, and to maintain adequate records of their achievements, they organized the Aero Club of America in 1905. Ultimately the club would serve as a center for information on aeronautics, it would stimulate nationwide interest in sport ballooning, and it would become the national coordinator of flying competitions and exhibitions until the eve of the First World War. The Aero Club's size and prestige rapidly established it as the international point of contact for foreign aviation agencies and clubs. As aviation moved out of the restricted sphere of sport ballooning, the Aero Club continued to play a significant role in popularizing aviation and at the same time encouraging the scientific study of aerodynamics, meteorology, and aeronautical engineering.[8]

Because of its size and membership, the Aero Club of America was the most prominent organization in what one may conveniently label the aeronaut constituency. This group consisted of those individuals and organizations that not only manifested an interest in manned flight but also were willing to apply continuous pressure upon Congress and governmental agencies for the advancement of aviation. When the Aeronautical Division was organized in 1907, and particularly after it received its first airplane in the autumn of 1909, the Aero Club of America was quick to join forces with army flyers in their campaign to advance military aviation.

The Aero Club of America

Modeled after the German Balloon Society organized in 1881 and the Aero Club of the United Kingdom founded in 1901, the Aero Club of America brought together a group of inventors, sportsmen, and others interested in ballooning and aeronautics in general. Eventually, it accepted the responsibility for certifying aviators.[9]

A group of Automobile Club of America members launched the Aero Club of America in 1905, focusing upon the conduct of sport ballooning and secondarily looking toward the promotion of aviation through contests and scientific study.[10] Significantly, the first purpose set forth in the club's 1910 charter of incorporation was that it was to be a social organization of persons who owned "aeronautical inventions for personal or private use."[11] This social aspect of the Aero Club of America should not be overlooked by emphasizing its early scientific activities and its public relations work for aeronautics. Members were those, both young and old, who could afford the luxury of balloon ownership or who were connected by family or friendship to those who were so affluent. Common bloodlines, parallel financial interests in mercantile and industrial affairs, and records of achievement in a broad range of human enterprises and activities united the Aero Club of America into a strong, coherent social organization. Men joined the Aero Club because it was fun. It was in keeping with their social status, and they enjoyed taking the risks of early sport ballooning in the company of close friends and like-minded acquaintances.

When the Aero Club spoke through its officers, it represented the views of a large and influential segment of America's men of affairs, who were able to influence public opinion not only by what they said but by who they were. Even cursory study of the membership of the Aero Club of America and its affiliates suggests the pervasive influence of the club in American life. The first printed membership list for the Aero Club of America dating from 1907 is most helpful. It lists 240 active members and five honorary members. Among the honorary members were Lt. Frank Purdy Lahm of the U.S. Army, who won the 1906 James Gordon Bennett ballooning trophy in Paris. Active members included Capt. Charles deF. Chandler, a Signal Corps officer active in military balloon activities. Beyond these military members, the 1907 Aero Club membership ranged broadly over a number of occupations and among men of different ages. For the most part the active members were individuals already marked as men of accomplishment, although only thirty-three of them would be listed in *Who's Who in America* for 1910–11.[12]

With some accuracy it has been commented that the Aero Club provided an association between young airplane fliers and old balloonists. From the club's 1907 organization until 1910, this would be an accurate description of the membership. Balloonists Thomas S. Baldwin, Alberto Santos-Dumont, and Leo Stevens were members, as were Wilbur and Orville Wright, Glenn Curtiss, and Octave Chanute. However, age did not make a clear division between heavier-than-air enthusiasts and those who continued in the development of balloons and dirigibles. Yet Roy Knabenshue, a relatively young member of the Aero Club and one of the Wright Company's test pilots, persisted in experiments with the dirigible well beyond 1910, when his colleagues had shifted their enthusiasm to the "flying machine." Lieutenant Lahm was among the first army aircraft pilots and certainly not an old man even though his fame as a balloonist dated from 1906 and his interest in balloon navigation persisted into the First World War. Lahm's participation in ballooning was encouraged by his balloonist father, Frank S. Lahm, who was also a member of the Aero Club.[13]

The thirty-three Aero Club members in *Who's Who in America* show the catholicity of the group and its social and political importance. The material wealth of the membership is demonstrated by those who described themselves as "capitalists"—John Jacob Astor, Charles J. Glidden, Pierre Lorillard Jr., and Harry P. Whitney. One member, Thomas B. Clarke, listed himself as an art collector. Three appeared in *Who's Who* as bankers—John E. Borne, Colgate Hoyt, and Jefferson Seligman. Sport ballooning was an expensive activity as well as a hazardous one, and the appearance of wealthy men on the Aero Club's membership lists is not surprising. However, in the Horatio Alger world of early-twentieth-century America, the populace venerated men of great wealth. The club's appeal for the rich "captains of industry" gave it both respectability and publicity.

No less distinguished on the 1907 membership list were the inventors, scientists, and even journalists and writers. They included Alexander Graham Bell, the Wright brothers, physicist Michael I. Pupin, meteorologist A. Lawrence Rotch, electrician Charles P. Steinmetz, and astronomer David P. Todd. Octave Chanute, William J. Hammer, and Peter Cooper Hewitt represented the engineering community. Journalism was the occupation of members George G. Bain and George O. Shields. Gutzon L. M. Borglum and A. S. Anderson were artists, and lawyer John J. Rooney was better known as a poet. The age was one of rapid scientific progress, particularly in applied science and mechanical invention. Precision and certainty of mathematical computations appealed to the popular mind, and the individuality and virtuosity of the inventor was praised by all groups in society. Writers and poets were treated with deference, and their works were perpetuated in multivolume editions of their literary output. Each of these members brought public esteem to the Aero Club and its activities.

Several members of the Aero Club of America are identifiable despite their failure to reach public notice through the 1910 edition of *Who's Who in America*. Capt. Homer W. Hedges, the first president of the club, was also president of one of the largest advertising agencies in the United States. Robert J. Collier, who joined in September 1909 and served as president in 1911–12, was the publisher of *Collier's Weekly* and a personal friend of the Wright brothers. Cortlandt F. Bishop, a charter member of the club and its president in 1906–7 and again in 1909, was in the real estate business, and George B. Chamberlain was a real estate lawyer. James C. McCoy, a copper-mining magnate, was intermittently president and vice president of the Aero Club in the years 1908–11.[14]

Other significant connections existed between the Aero Club and the centers of political and economic power in the United States. When Lieutenant Lahm won the Gordon Bennett Cup in 1906, his aide in piloting his balloon was Henry Blanchard Hersey, former major in President Roosevelt's Spanish War regiment, the 1st U.S. Volunteer Cavalry.[15] The "Rough Rider" officer joined the Aero Club in April 1907. As affiliated Aero Clubs were established throughout the United States, other men of prominence across the nation joined the program. Judge Elbert H. Gary, head of U.S. Steel, joined an affiliated Aero Club and was among those who backed the Wright brothers' corporate organization in 1909. The Milwaukee Aero Club had Col. Gustave Pabst, the brewer, as a member. It was Pabst who gave that club a first-class balloon. The Aero Club of Seattle counted within its membership M. Robert Guggenheim of the American Smelting and Refining Company.

Cortlandt F. Bishop, president of the Aero Club of America, 1906–7 and 1909. It was during Bishop's second term as president that the schism in the Aero Club took place. The group of socialites who were ballooning enthusiasts remained with the Aero Club, while active pilots and aircraft builders formed the Aeronautical Society of New York. (*Aerial Age Weekly*, December 11, 1916, 329)

Aero Club affiliates functioned as geographical outposts of aeronautical activity throughout the United States and abroad. By October 1909 affiliated clubs were meeting in St. Louis, North Adams (Massachusetts), and Seattle, along with regional or statewide clubs in New England, Ohio, California, and Indiana. New groups were forming in Mississippi and in the Northwest. There was even a short-lived affiliated club in Argentina.[16]

Through the affiliated aero clubs in the United States and its monthly magazine, the Aero Club of America maintained nationwide contact with aviation enthusiasts. Aero Club delegates convened in St. Louis for a national convention in January 1910. They recommended that Congress establish a National Aero Commission to coordinate flying activities, and also passed a resolution calling for larger governmental expenditures in support of aeronautical work. Strangely, this was the only national meeting to be held. Thereafter the major contact between the New York–based Aero Club of America and its affiliates was through the monthly magazine, *Aeronautics*.

Lt. Frank P. Lahm and Maj. Henry B. Hersey after winning the 1906 James Gordon Bennet balloon race in Paris. This was the most prestigious international balloon race, in which the winning team traveled the greatest distance from the launch point. Lahm was an army officer whose father's business was located in Paris; Hersey was a businessman who formerly served as major in Theodore Roosevelt's "Rough Rider" regiment during the Spanish-American War. (*Collier's Weekly* 38, no. 5 [1906]: 17)

The journal began publication in 1907, carrying the title *American Magazine of Aeronautics*. In February 1908 the masthead was changed to *Aeronautics*. So thoroughly comprehensive was the reporting in *Aeronautics* that it soon became the basic vehicle for transmitting news, both technical and otherwise, concerning ballooning and heavier-than-air navigation. Under editor Ernest L. Jones it became a forceful advocate for aeronautical progress and a factor in the continuing education of an entire generation of airmen.[17]

Valuable though its contributions were to the interchange of aeronautical information and specifications, *Aeronautics* was even more visible as a sounding board for air-minded individuals who sought to influence federal and state policies concerning aviation. It published Albert F. Zahm's plea for the establishment of a federal aeronautical laboratory. An *Aeronautics* editorial pointed out that such a laboratory might be more quickly established if appropriations for military aviation were increased. Supporting this position, the magazine inaugurated a regular section on "Army News" in its 1908–9 volume. In September 1908 and January 1909, it urged readers to write to Congress demanding increased appropriations for the newly established Aeronautical Division, and in 1910 it repeated a suggestion from the British Aerial League—that candidates for legislative office take positions concerning military aviation.[18]

On January 31, 1909, the *New York Times* reported that Aero Club members were jubilant over the House of Representatives' approval of a $500,000 appropriation for Signal Corps aviation. It also noted that Congressman Herbert Parsons had visited New York City before the House voted on the bill, and while there he obtained the recommendations of Cortlandt F. Bishop, president of the Aero Club of America. The biographer of Secretary of War Newton D. Baker claims that Baker decided to send airplanes to France as a part of America's effort in the First World War because he felt that it was the most dramatic step he could take—all Americans had been made aviation-conscious by the prewar efforts of the Aero Club of America.[19]

Among the most enthusiastic Americans were young men who took part in the Junior Aero Club's activities. These included the construction of model airplanes and kites, and competitions with unmanned "pilot" balloons to determine which flew the farthest from the point of release. Grover C. Loening, a future pioneer in aeronautical engineering, attributed his life-long fascination with aviation to his experiences with Aero Club model airplane construction. He went on to study aeronautical engineering at Columbia and organized a university Aero Club. Probably because of Columbia's proximity to the New York City headquarters of the Aero Club of

America, it was the first institution of higher education to boast such a club. The Columbia club soon was duplicated at Harvard, Cornell, Notre Dame, the University of Virginia, Amherst College, and Johns Hopkins University. Like the Junior Aero Clubs, these collegiate activities were important to future public support of aviation, but their lasting contribution was in the attraction of talented young scientists and future political leaders into the cause of aeronautical experimentation.[20]

Exhibitions and Flying Contests

Public enthusiasm for aviation was enhanced by a variety of aeronautical events and contests. The first exhibition held in connection with the James-town Exposition of 1907 was planned by the Committee of Aeronautics of the Aero Club of America. A Wright biplane flew from Governor's Island to Grant's Tomb as part of the 1909 Hudson-Fulton Exhibition. Former president Theodore Roosevelt took his first airplane ride at the St. Louis exposition the following year. There were rumors that President William H. Taft would be a passenger at a flight to occur at the 1910 Harvard-Boston Aero Meet, but, considering his weight, Taft wisely declined to fly even though he was an interested bystander.[21]

Less dramatic in their public impact were the numerous contests organized by the Aero Club. Initially these emphasized balloon ascensions, but soon airplane records were established and broken at these contests. Military and naval aviators, with full support of their superiors, played an active role in contest flying and judging. For example, the Fourth International Gordon Bennett Airplane Meet, held at Chicago in mid-September 1912, drew heavily upon Signal Corps flying officers as contestants and officials. Maj. Samuel Reber chaired the Aero Club of America Contest Committee at that time; Capt. Charles de F. Chandler was the official starter; and Lts. Henry H. Arnold and Thomas deW. Milling were in charge of the barographs.[22] At a later 1912 contest, Lieutenant Arnold won the Clarence H. Mackay trophy for airmanship, drawing favorable comment for this achievement in the chief signal officer's report for 1913.[23] However, by August 1913 the novelty of aviation meets and exhibition flying had played itself out. Brig. Gen. George P. Scriven, the chief signal officer, told Congress that in his opinion the future progress of aviation would depend upon the military and naval aviators and their routine, ongoing work rather than on exhibitions and contests.[24] Yet in the interval from 1907 through 1913, Aero Club of America activities had kept aviation in the public eye and helped to sustain congressional interest in military flying at a critical stage of its development.

The Army–Aero Club Interface

Since the Signal Corps had long been the primary army service corps for scientific experimentation, it was natural that its officers would have close contacts with the civilian scientific community. Maj. George O. Squier was a prominent inventor in the fields of radio, cable telegraphy, and aerial photography. Squier, who would become chief signal officer during the First World War, held a Ph.D. degree in physics. In 1910 and 1911, Lt. Paul Beck had drawn favorable British comments for his work on radio transmission from airplanes. As experiments progressed in communications and in aviation, these and other Signal Corps officers reported their scientific findings to the Aero Club of America and other scientific organizations. Such information exchange frequently served as an opening wedge for policy discussions with civilian members of the Aero Club. *Aeronautics* promptly reported Brig. Gen. James Allen's April 1911 speech to the Aero Club of New York, in which he, as chief signal officer, expressed the need for $125,000 to purchase new airplanes and to train thirty officer pilots.[25] Subsequently, it drew attention to the "startling statistics" contained in the 1912 report of the House Committee on Military Affairs that detailed the degree to which European nations had surpassed the United States in military aviation. In July 1912 *Aeronautics* featured the report of Signal Corps major Charles McK. Saltzman, who visited the French military aviation center at St. Cyr and recommended American purchase of the Nieuport monoplane and a Breguet biplane.[26] A consistent theme on the prewar editorial pages of *Aeronautics* and *Flying* was the lack of American preparedness, the vital need for larger Aeronautical Division appropriations, and the advocacy of political action by Aero Club members to achieve more rapid growth of the military air arm.

Two factors propelled army flying officers into the inner circle of the Aero Club. One was the scientific interests that the officers and other club members shared, and the other was a common military tradition kept alive through volunteer-regular contacts initiated in the Spanish-American War, and also fostered by the existence of a strong militia tradition within the United States. Beginning with the climactic 1912 New York–Connecticut National Guard maneuvers, there was growing civilian and Aero Club pressure for the establishment of National Guard aviation units. Most of the persuasive arguments were made by members of the Aero Club of America. In a 1913 article published in *Flying*, Henry Woodhouse suggested that army wartime requirements for pilots could best be satisfied by permitting the state National Guard units to participate in military flying activities. In

April 1914 an *Aeronautics* editorial advocated that the U.S. Aviation Reserve, a civilian volunteer group, be integrated into army and navy flying activities. Eventually air units were established in the National Guard elements located in New Jersey, Pennsylvania, Illinois, and Missouri, but the first unit to participate in aerial flight was that from Missouri.[27]

The Aeronautical Society of America and Other Splinter Groups

The pandemic aspirations of the New York City–based Aero Club of America — to embrace under its auspices the work of all other Aero Clubs, and to include within the club all groups and individuals interested in aviation — were doomed to early failure. The first secession occurred in 1908, when a group of members termed "practical aeronauts" left the Aero Club of America, claiming that their attempts to do experimental work within the programs of the Aero Club were blocked by the club's officers. The seceding faction formed the Aeronautical Society of New York, dedicated to experimental and flying activities.[28] Litigation broke out between the officers and dissident members in March 1910, and by April of the same year the editors of *Aeronautics* deemed the survival of the Aero Club of America to be "uncertain."[29] Commencement of the Wright patent litigation caused a further division: an anti-Wright contingent seceded and became the American Aeronautical Association when the Aero Club agreed not to sanction contests in which Wright patent rights were not compensated.[30] The final schism took place after the 1917 Annual Dinner of the Aero Club. Henry A. Wise Wood, in the course of introducing former ambassador to Germany James W. Gerard, launched into a one-hour tirade against the Wilson administration. As a consequence, the Aero Club divided into two opposing political camps and its demise seemed well at hand.[31]

Although schisms within the Aero Club of America and its gradual decline after 1910 removed a most effective military aviation lobby from the scene, they also generated new civilian groups that would continue the Aero Club's advocacy on behalf of the Aeronautical Division. The concentration of scientifically minded members in the new groups meant that Aeronautical Division officers had the benefit of association with scientists and aviators who shared their concerns about continued progress in the development of aviation technology, about careful weather prediction, and about studying the physiological impact of speed and altitude. In 1912, navy captain Washington I. Chambers encouraged Robert G. Skerrett to join the Aeronautical Society because "it is the nucleus of the principal body that will get into the

Henry A. Wise Wood in 1917. An active publicist on behalf of the Aero Club of America, Wise Wood was also an avid member of the Republican Party. In 1917 he succeeded in dividing the Aero Club into Republican and Democratic Party factions by an hour-long denunciation of President Wilson's preparedness policies. With outspoken friends like Wise Wood, the army aviators didn't need enemies. (*Flying* 4 [September 1918]: 662)

aeronautical problems from a scientific standpoint. Most of the active members are young engineers. . . . [A]s aviation first ran into the hippodrome or sport phase they are temporarily tripped by the Aero Club of America."[32] By 1913 Aero Club dinners were sparsely attended and a pilot who was present at that year's annual dinner reported that of the seven members present, he was the only active flyer.[33]

In 1911 a group of aircraft manufacturers formed the Aeronautical Manufacturers' Association under the presidency of Ernest L. Jones. This group led industry through encouraging the exchange of technical construction data, and managed to achieve a modicum of standardization in a field bedeviled by eccentric engineering.[34]

The splinter groups that were established from 1910 through 1914 were indicative of the growing number of aviation enthusiasts, and they also demonstrated the degree to which aeronautics had come of age. Military aviators retained close contact with the new organizations, and the civilian input to military aeronautics continued unabated.

Unfortunately the continued existence of the Aero Club, and its understandable struggle to retain members and to influence aviation development, had serious negative impact upon aeronautics in general and military and naval aviation in particular. One such development was an unfortunate alignment of the Wright brothers, the Aero Club, and the army aviators against Glenn Curtiss (and all of the other manufacturers), the Aeronautical Society of America, and the U.S. Navy's aviators. When the Wrights sued to enjoin Curtiss and others from infringing upon their patents, the Aero Club entered into an agreement with the Wright Company that it would sanction only those meets held in accordance with proper financial arrangements with the Wright Company.[35] The Aero Club also used its pilot licensing power to the disadvantage of naval aviation, and club members in 1915 urged manufacturers not to bid on navy seaplane contracts.[36] When the Wright patent litigation was in preparation, army lieutenant Benjamin D. Foulois assured the Wright brothers that he would be glad to do whatever was legitimately possible to assist them.[37]

Army favoritism toward the Wright brothers did not go unnoticed. The editor of *Aeronautics* magazine informed U.S. Navy captain Chambers that Lt. Col. Samuel Reber of the Aeronautical Division was such a strong partisan of the Aero Club that it was impossible for his magazine to get any information about army aviation.[38] Colonel Reber's behavior in withholding information from the Aeronautical Society magazine is also symptomatic of the severe competition that existed between rival aviation publications. In March 1913 the Aero Club's magazine, *Flying*, published an advance copy of a presidential commission's report recommending that a national aeronautical laboratory be established. Henry Wise Wood, one of the more flamboyant publicists in the Aero Club and a member of the commission, was accused of this impropriety. One of the scooped editors commented, "He's a typical Aero Club member, it's obvious."[39] In fairness to the magazine editors, it should be recognized that all were faced with rapidly falling circulations as the number of specialized aviation societies increased, dispersing former Aero Club members and undermining journals intended for a broadly based readership. By November 1913, *Aerial Age* and *Fly* had stopped publishing, and *Aeronautics* was on the verge of a similar fate.[40]

The Mixed Blessings of the Aeronaut Constituency

The Aero Club of America and its spinoff groups formed an aeronaut constituency that was of vital importance to the future growth of military and naval aviation in the United States. Well placed in the political, economic, and social hierarchy of the nation, the members of these societies made Congress and the American people aware of army aviation. While this did not result in any marked increase in annual appropriations, it did ensure that Congress knew something about the potentialities and benefits of aeronautical development.

Aside from occasional speeches in Congress favoring an expanded military aviation budget, the most telling evidence of congressional concern was the appointment of investigatory committees by the House of Representatives.[41] A proposal to increase the pay and allowances of military aviators, denominated the Hardwick Bill, sparked a brief investigation into foreign military practices for the encouragement of flying officers. Introduced in January 1912, the Hardwick Bill was followed by a resolution of March 26, 1912, demanding that information on military aviation be submitted to the House. In the intervening time Congressman James Hay, chairman of the House Military Affairs Committee, scuttled increased army aviation appropriations by pointing out inconsistencies in the chief signal officer's aviation budget, as well as the fact that the 1912 appropriation was as yet not fully expended. Undaunted by their defeat in securing a $125,000 appropriation, Hardwick Bill supporters used attaché reports from Europe to show how far American army aviation had fallen behind the major world powers. The Hardwick Bill passed the House of Representatives on August 5, 1912, but it died in the Senate Military Affairs Committee and made no lasting impact on army aviation.[42]

However, once having utilized the investigatory device, pro-aviation congressmen returned to the fray in the next Congress to introduce the Hay Bill on February 24, 1913. Containing provisions for flying pay and death benefits, and authorizing an increase in the size of the Aeronautical Division, the legislation went through many revisions and had to be reintroduced in the subsequent congressional session. When it finally passed on July 18, 1914, the Aviation Section of the Signal Corps was created and the Aeronautical Division was terminated.[43] With the organizational title change, there came an enlarged personnel roster and a substantially increased budget.

While the full implications of the Hay Bill legislation can safely be postponed to later discussion, the extensive hearings held in August 1913 provide strong evidence of close relationships between army aviators, members of Congress, members of the Aero Club, and officers in the National Guard and other citizen-reserve units. General Scriven, the chief signal officer, provided extensive information concerning the Panama Canal's vulnerability to aerial attack. However, the Committee on Military Affairs quickly changed the subject and inquired why Lt. Benjamin D. Foulois had been relieved from aviation duty.[44] Foulois happened to be a poker-playing associate of the committee chairman, James Hay. In his off-duty hours, Foulois had rendered yeoman service to the Signal Corps, and his contacts helped to ensure its continued supervision of the aviation program. The original

Hay Bill, introduced in the prior session of Congress, provided for the separation of army aviation activities from the Signal Corps. Scriven and his staff were distressed and worked to defeat this portion of the bill when it was reintroduced in 1913. Foulois and all other flying officers, with the single exception of Capt. Paul W. Beck, testified against separation during the committee hearings. In addition, Foulois was active behind the scenes. With General Scriven's permission, he persuaded Congressman John Q. Tilson to vote against separation when the matter came to a vote within the Committee on Military Affairs. Tilson was a colonel in the Connecticut National Guard, and Foulois probably met him through his assignments to the army's Division of Militia Affairs. It is also likely that Foulois dissuaded Congressman Hay from insisting upon separation in the final version of the bill.[45]

Although the pilots testified that separation was premature, it became abundantly clear from their testimony and from submitted newspaper articles and military attaché reports that army aviation was in a sorry state. Reporting the bill to the full House, the Military Affairs Committee recommended a $300,000 appropriation for the Aviation Section, not to bring the United States up to the programs of other major powers but to ensure the continued development of the flying program. Reporting the Hay Bill, the committee commented, "[I]t would be most unwise to continue the parsimonious policy which the Government has pursued with regard to military aviation." On June 2, 1914, the Senate Military Affairs Committee concurred, "[I]f this branch of the military service is to be made effective every opportunity ought to be given for its development." Aeronautical engineer Grover Loening reported how favorably impressed he was by the "sound interest" that the Hay Committee members showed in military aviation, and that he saw encouraging signs that there might be a large appropriation for flying activities in the following year.[46]

Unfortunately, while Congressman Hay was interested in military aviation, he was even more dedicated to conservative governmental budgets. By July 1916 when Hay was appointed a federal district judge, Henry T. Allen, then on duty with the Mexican Punitive Expedition, wrote to his wife that all of the officers were delighted that the appointment had removed Hay from the Military Affairs Committee chairmanship.[47]

Overall public interest in army aviation, and congressional attention to its needs, would have a beneficial effect from 1914 through 1916. Yet the existence of the Aero Club and the other organizations in the "aeronaut constituency" would prove a mixed blessing in at least two ways. First, the climate of public opinion was no longer receptive to activities that brought army officers into close social contact with the captains of industry and finance who increasingly dominated the Aero Club's meetings. As a reform movement, Democratic party progressivism adopted a grim view of "captains of industry." Woodrow Wilson's political support came from a coalition of middle-class citizens who viewed themselves as the "consumer," the "common Man," and "the taxpayer."[48] Such an emphasis gave the Wilson era an aura of egalitarianism that did not bode well for army officers who spent their time and some of the taxpayers' dollars in company with the socialites of the Aero Club.

Secondly, civilian influences in army aviation introduced new problems in military discipline and public relations. For the most part, the U.S. Army in 1900 was a small and isolated segment of American society, stationed in small detachments scattered among western forts. It was rare that army officers came into contact with highly placed civilians, but fliers in the Aeronautical Division did so on a daily basis. Indeed, military aviators learned to fly from civilian instructors, and their airplanes and dirigibles were dependent upon civilian manufacturers for vital supplies and for major maintenance. Their public relations and high visibility with the American public was largely due to the work of the Aero Club of America and its successor civilian organizations. As a consequence army aviators, even at this early stage of military aeronautics, were subjected to influences that differed sharply from those familiar to their army contemporaries in other branches. Their ready access to congressmen and others in high governmental positions made them a threat to the stability and command relationships in the rest of the army. After the Hay Committee hearings, it was public knowledge that the army was censurable for its conduct of military aviation activities, and that discomfort added to the alienation between the aviation officers, the Signal Corps, and the General Staff.

It was civilian interest and influence that precipitated the Hay Committee hearings and the altered approach to army aeronautics that developed after 1914. Within the formal structure of the army, no group of junior officers could possibly have achieved such a change without powerful political backing. Although General Scriven felt that he had capitulated to the "demands" of his aviators, neither he nor his director for aviation affairs, Col. Samuel Reber, was able to escape censure in the wake of a 1916 congressional probe of military aviation. Throughout these rifts with the chief signal officer and Colonel Reber, the military aviators would enjoy the full support of the Aero Club of America.[49]

Enthusiastic and well-meaning civilians could be a source of embarrassment to naval aviation, and we may assume that similar awkward situations developed in regard to army aeronautics. In an undated letter from the 1911–13 time period, navy captain Washington I. Chambers wrote aviation editor Henry A. Wise Wood that government officials were as interested in furthering aviation as the editors were. He pleaded with Wood to "Pat them on the back if you will, but don't attempt to hold them up to ridicule or suspicion that you know more about their business than they do. . . . [T]hey have to get the sinews of war from a lot of haymakers of two opposing parties."[50]

Chambers worked diligently in an effort to control Aero Club initiatives. In March 1914 he informed Henry Woodhouse that the navy had decided not to request an aviation appropriation until Congress ceased to be apprehensive that the latest tariff would not yield sufficient revenue. Two years before, Chambers cautioned the Aero Club that the continuing deficiencies in appropriations for naval aviation should not be appealed to the people above the head of Congress. When Aero Club criticism of Congress reached new heights in the spring of 1912, Captain Chambers protested that no good would be served by attacking the legislators, and Lee S. Burridge sympathized with his position, commenting that the Aero Club had always been a "knocking" organization. It was, in Burridge's view, "a grievous error to knock our politicians at this time because they will all the more be adverse to our cause. I think it was the very points that you raise in your letter, that lead some of us to begin in the militia in hope that a general diffusion of interest and activity throughout the country would bring forward good results."[51] Arnold Kruckman, the general secretary of the Aeronautical Society of America, agreed with Chambers's alarm by the fact that some of the pro-aviation pressures on Congress were motivated by self-serving private financial interests.[52] Although army aviators and their Signal Corps superiors may have been exerting the same moderating influence exhibited by Chambers, there is no documentary evidence that they did so. What we do know is that beyond the very earliest stages of military flying, the Aero Club would have been a balky partner in dealing with Congress.

As we shall see in later chapters, the new air arm of the army was already beginning to develop along lines that diverged from the ground forces. At first this manifested itself in a form of individualism that produced new attitudes toward the use of aerial weapons. It created a close camaraderie among the flying officers that permitted them to withstand pressures from their own commanders and from the rest of the army. Ultimately the support of public opinion and the aeronaut constituency would make it possible for military aviators to advocate separation from the Signal Corps, and to champion a related emphasis upon offensive uses of air power rather than an exclusive emphasis upon reconnaissance activities.

2 ★ Army Aviation in the Media Fishbowl

Aeronaut constituency enthusiasm triggered the American people's fascination for aviation, and military aviation made a significant contribution through the 1908 acquisition testing of the Wright brothers' invention. Not only did Americans become "air-minded," but they did so with a religiosity that equated aerial flight with spiritual power. Professor Joseph Corn asserts that this was a secular equivalent of evangelical religion, and that many air-minded Americans viewed mechanical flight as an omen of an imminent messianic age. The airplane promised "a wondrous era of peace and harmony, of culture and prosperity. This was the promise of the winged gospel."[1]

Public awareness of the Wrights' success was focused by the army aircraft trials held in September 1908 at Fort Myer, Virginia. Several new records were established during the tests, which ended tragically when a crash injured Orville Wright and killed army lieutenant Thomas E. Selfridge.[2] Thereafter aviation would remain in the fishbowl of communications-media observation, and army flyers would be deeply involved in public relations.

In the decade preceding World War I, a number of magazines and newspapers provided a forum for publicizing the exploits of aviators, balloonists, and inventors. Metropolitan dailies carried regular feature sections on aviation, and some sponsored special flying contests or exhibitions with the intention of increasing their paid circulation. Crusading journalism became the hallmark of the age, and "muckraking" magazines were essential parts of burgeoning reform movements. The business practices of the Rockefellers were exposed to public scrutiny, and the unsanitary conditions prevalent in the meat-packing industry were reported in sickening detail. Predictably these journals triggered electoral pressures to restrict unfair competition and to provide legal protection for the health and welfare of the American consumer.[3] Americans relied on newspapers and magazines to provide information on world affairs, and to serve as sources of reliable information concerning political and economic issues. Before the advent of radio or television, the news of the day was carried in printed form, and there was always space for special news of national progress — including the great strides being made in aeronautics.

Military Aviation in Newspapers and Periodicals

Daily reporting of army flying activities, followed by pro-aviation editorial commentary, did much to whet the public's appetite for even more aviation news. As early as July 1908, John Trevor Custis's one-half page aviation column appeared in the Sunday edition of the *Philadelphia Inquirer*. In 1910 the *New York Times* began devoting an entire page of its Sunday edition to military aviation, replete with photographs and other illustrations. Three Washington newspapers stationed reporters at the army's College Park, Maryland, flying school in June 1911. Each newspaperman was expected to provide a newsworthy article every day.[4] For the army this was a mixed blessing. Although it was a proud moment to release news of achievement, there was deep chagrin involved in acknowledging the inevitable failures, injuries, and deaths.

Coverage in individual newspapers was broadened and enriched by the newly established system of nationwide news services. This meant that local articles on military aviation were distributed to a vast network of national newspapers. Significantly, Jerome Fanciulli of the Associated Press wire service was a charter member of the Aero Club of Washington.[5]

Aviation also was a forum in which to make news, as well as to simply report it, and some of the larger city newspaper sponsored aeronautical events. While providing entertainment for the public, these exhibitions and contests helped to increase goodwill for the newspaper involved, and hopefully might boost its circulation. An airship overflight sponsored by the *Philadelphia Inquirer* added to the excitement of the October 1910 Founder's Day parade in that city. During the 1909 Hudson-Fulton exhibition, the *New York World* offered a $10,000 prize to an aviator who would fly an airship up the Hudson from New York City to Albany, following Hendrik Hudson's route. Glenn Curtiss won that prize with his airplane, and six months later provided the *World* with additional copy by conducting bomb-dropping experiments at their request. His success triggered newspaper speculation about how airplanes might destroy battleships through aerial bombardment.[6]

The major magazines were quick to exploit aviation news. *Collier's: The*

National Weekly is typical of the magazines that took a special interest in aeronautics. Published by Robert J. Collier, an active member of the Aero Club of America, *Collier's* was in an expansive mode when army flying began. In 1909 its paid circulation per issue ranged from a low of 454,000 copies to a high of 545,000 copies. In April 1913 the newsstand price was cut from ten to five cents per issue in an effort to attract more readers.[7] *Collier's* editors exposed Interior Secretary Richard Ballinger's coal lease manipulations, and subsequently they supported Gifford Pinchot, a member of the U.S. Forest Service, when he was improperly dismissed by Ballinger. These events were major scandals of the day, causing the 1912 political rift between incumbent President William H. Taft and his predecessor, Theodore Roosevelt.[8] With a large and influential readership, *Collier's* boasted a reputation for crusading in reform causes. It was a formidable factor in the politics of its day.

Aviation notices appeared with regularity in *Collier's*. Before March 1908 there were fewer than ten aviation citations in a six-month period; from March 1908 to March 1910, the total increased to approximately 15; thereafter, until the outbreak of the First World War, the aviation mentions and articles averaged about 25 in every six-month period.[9] The article-length treatments were bound to hold the reader's attention. Hudson Maxim's March 1910 article on "The Flying Machine" summarized the current state of aeronautics, and, lest his warnings be ignored, Frederick Palmer's article four months later reemphasized the danger of aerial bombardment: "Every foggy morning, . . . the commuter starts for London, which he knows may sink before his eyes under a shower of dynamite from an aerial flotilla secretly made in Germany."[10]

In July 1910 reporter Arthur Ruhl provided details on the Wrights' flying activities at Dayton, and George Fitch's facetious accolade to the Wrights followed in September: "In the summer of 1908 it was suddenly discovered that the Wright brothers of Dayton, Ohio, had been doing cross-country work in an airplane for five years. . . . This clinched the success of the aeroplane. The Wrights demonstrated that it was as easy to go up as to come down. What was more important, they proved that it was as safe to come down as to go up."[11] Fitch's article, entitled "The Aeroplane: The Annals of Aviation in the Attempt to Fly Lengthwise Rather than Downward," was no doubt a reference to the ill-fated Langley experiments of 1903.

The volume and accomplishments of aviation in Europe overwhelmed the more modest news of American flying. A November 1910 *Collier's* editorial pointed out that France then had 100 airplanes in its army and the

United States had but one, which was out of repair most of the time.[12] The point had already been made in countless full-page pictorial accounts of European flying contests, in photograph captions, and in the ominous lack of news from the Signal Corps' Aeronautical Division. Sir Hiram Maxim's September 1911 article on aviation, subtitled "The Aeroplane Is the Greatest Power for Destruction Invented since Gunpower," stressed the long-range aerial bombardment capability of airplanes, the vulnerability of coastal areas to airborne attack, and the superiority of airplanes to dirigibles as bombardment and defensive aircraft. British aviation writer A. C. Graham-White published an article in the October 7, 1911, issue of *Collier's*; he noted Germany's diversification of its air fleet to include airplanes as well as lighter-than-air dirigibles and rigid airships.[13] Readers of *Collier's* were assured current news and careful analysis of worldwide developments in military aviation.

Even *Collier's* advertisements emphasized aviation themes. On March 12, 1910, the A. P. Warner Instrument Company of Beloit, Wisconsin, announced that it would spend its advertising dollars to publicize aviation, and printed as its first insertion a scene from the aerial meet at Los Angeles. Warner Instruments' advertisements continued for several subsequent issues, ensuring that the Warner Auto Meter and Warner Aero Meter came to the attention of flying enthusiasts. Even men's haberdashery was impressed with an aeronautical stamp. The November 1910 *Collier's* offered for sale two styles of Silver Band collars: one that was 2 ⅛ inches high was named the Biplane; the taller collar, 2 ⅜ inches high, was denominated the Monoplane. As an incentive, the Silver Band company offered to send a free aviation booklet to *Collier's* readers. An Adler-Rochester Clothes ad featured a male model posed at the open door of an airplane factory, presumably discussing flying with another well-dressed aeronaut who, strangely, was holding an airplane propeller.[14] Apparently it was not considered odd for men in three-piece suits and starched collars to be inhabiting an aircraft factory—did not the Wright brothers always appear formally dressed while working on their machines? The most ingenious use of an aviation motif was probably the advertisement of the International Correspondence Schools, America's largest mail-order educational institution. Their 1913 advertisement depicted a flying airplane to which was appended the slogan, "Nothing Is Impossible to Men with Ambition."[15]

Although *Collier's* stands out in publicizing early aviation, it was not alone among magazines for the general public that highlighted aeronautics. From 1906 through 1914 *Century Magazine* printed sixteen items of aviation interest.[16] Despite its generally pacifist editorial positions, *Century* published a 1908 article by Edmund C. Stedman which argued that the German Zeppelin fleet threatened British naval supremacy. A few months later a rare article by Wilbur and Orville Wright described their airplane. When August Post completed a record-breaking balloon flight from St. Louis to Lake St. John in Quebec, *Century* published his account of the voyage that won him the 1911 Bennett trophy.[17] By way of contrast to *Century* and *Collier's*, *Atlantic Monthly* published only two articles of aviation interest from 1907 through 1914, and *Harper's* published one such item. Nevertheless, in a 1911 issue of *Atlantic Monthly*, Katherine F. Gerould comments, "It would be a platitude, at the moment, to say that the human imagination is immensely taken by the notion of flying; for at the moment the human imagination seems to be taken by nothing else."[18]

Robert J. Collier and like-minded periodical editors and publishers were responsible for fueling the fire of public airmindedness. They made strenuous efforts to acquire news of foreign aerial achievements, and reported them to American readers. Coverage in *Collier's* made aeronautical progress a matter of general knowledge, increasing public support for all flying activities and vastly increasing the exposure of aeronautics well beyond the relatively small scientific community.

Of course, the scientific and engineering magazines helped to keep aviation professionals current with new technical developments in the field. *Scientific American* actively reported aviation progress and experimentation. Samuel Yale Beach, its aviation editor, provided unstinting support to the aeronautics community from the earliest days of flying. A member of the Aero Club of America, Beach did much to direct editorial policy in a pro-aviation direction. When Congress rejected a 1909 military aviation budget of $200,000, *Scientific American* protested vigorously.[19] Undoubtedly, the most valuable service that *Scientific American* performed was the promulgation of technical data to the aeronautical field; its next service, scarcely less helpful to the army aviators, was keeping the scientific community aware of aeronautics and stressing aviation as a legitimate branch of scientific study. Despite the relatively small circulation of *Scientific American* in comparison with *Collier's*, it played an important role in advancing the interests of army flying.

Strangely, the *National Geographic Magazine*, with a 1912 circulation in excess of 107,000 subscribers, did not emphasize aeronautical items.[20] The magazine, and the society it served as house organ, was under the direction of Alexander Graham Bell, the inventor of the telephone and an experimenter with gliders and tetrahedral kites. After founding the Aerial Experiment Association with headquarters at Baddeck, Nova Scotia, Bell continued his active interest in aeronautics while serving as the National Geographic Society's president. From 1908 through 1916, a few *National Geographic* articles detailed Bell's work with kites and explained the tetrahedron concept of construction. However, with the exception of reporting a 1911 society dinner honoring the Wright brothers, there is a notable scarcity of items on aeronautics or army aviation.[21]

A change in editorial policy, perhaps attributable to Gilbert Grosvenor, the new editor and Bell's son-in-law, moved the magazine into the popular and widely circulated periodical it is at the present. Before 1910, *National Geographic* utilized a rather technical format, appealing to the tastes of its small and select scientific readership. By 1912, not only had the society's membership grown, but its interests had diversified. *National Geographic* began to feature travel and adventure articles, relegating the scientific research reports to separate printings by the society. However, even aeronautics did not appeal to the editor and his advisers as a matter of great public interest. Another explanation for the neglect may be that Bell and his colleagues, having invested considerable time and money in the Baddeck experiments, found it difficult to report the successes of the Wrights and their army officer students. As we shall see, by 1912 the Wright patent rights were under litigation, and Bell supported Glenn Curtiss in that struggle.

Professor Corn's thesis about a "winged gospel" appears to be valid when the "air-minded" newspapers and periodicals are examined in isolation. Authors, editors, and most readers were consumed with a missionary zeal for aerial navigation. Yet the "winged gospel" was far from a universal, and certainly not an established, religion. Lukewarm legislative support suggests that there was limited voter concern about airplanes or dirigibles.

Science Fiction and Aeronautics

The literary world's fascination with aviation predated the establishment of the army's Aeronautical Division. Rudyard Kipling's novel, *With the Night Mail*, was published in London in 1905 and issued in an American edition in 1909. Previously serialized in the United States in *McClure's Magazine*, the book described an airship's ill-fated London-to-Quebec journey, and a remarkable rescue of the crew with the modern aerial equipment available in 2000 A.D. While Kipling emphasized that skill and daring would characterize the era of trans-Atlantic flight, he hastened to assure readers that aerial travel would be no more risky than a steamship crossing. Finally, the author discounted possibility of war in the air, asserting that commercial growth by 1967 would create a world in which war was unprofitable and hence was declared illegal in international law.[22]

H. G. Wells's novel *The War in the Air* dealt with a more threatening scenario of airships as terrifying weapons of a new age. Written in 1907 for serialization in *Pall Mall Magazine,* the book received wide and immediate attention throughout Britain. It was advertised in the United States through *Aeronautics* magazine, and thus was well known to aviation enthusiasts as early as January 1909. Few books of science fiction have had a more profound impact upon military aviation and public opinion. Wells clearly believed flying machines and airships had already altered modern warfare. He was convinced that aerial warfare would lead to social disintegration, and, used alone, air power could not achieve victory.[23]

Burt Smallways, the hero of *The War in the Air,* stows away on a Zeppelin-type airship that, unbeknownst to him, is to participate in a trans-Atlantic bombardment of the United States. Because the United States is expected to be the most likely nation to mount an effective defense, the German commanders elect to make a surprise attack. They plan to "fling a great force across the Atlantic heavens and bear America down, unwarned and unprepared."[24] En route, the German airships destroy the American Atlantic Fleet by aerial bombardment. Arriving over New York City at twilight they begin their attack, and shortly after the bombs begin to fall the city surrenders. Unfortunately for both sides, the dirigibles do not carry sufficient combat troops to enforce the surrender terms, and confusion on the ground denies control to the remaining American authorities who are powerless to surrender. The German commander, in a rage at being denied the fruits of his aerial victory, orders renewed aerial bombardment until the city is destroyed. Wells opines that military unpreparedness and widespread cynicism among the people were the proximate causes of American defeat and suffering. He comments that "so discredited were the newspapers of that period, that a large majority of New Yorkers, for example, did not believe the most copious and circumstantial accounts of the German air fleet until it was actually in sight of New York."[25] However, in spite of its weakened condition, the United States launches a few military airplanes which disable the dirigible carrying Burt Smallways. It drifts to Greenland and lands on the icecap. In company with the few survivors, Smallways listens to radio news broadcasts which report that in the aftermath of worldwide warfare, Japan and China have emerged as the two major aeronautical powers.

Unlike Kipling's book, which was set in the distant future, *The War in the Air* dealt with events that were quite plausible, given aeronautical development in 1908 and 1909. At this time there was growing concern among Britain's high-ranking military and naval officers that the range and lift capacity of the German Zeppelin fleet was a genuine threat to the British Isles. Wells, through his membership in the Coefficient Dining Club, had access to Richard B. Haldane, then secretary of state for war in the British Cabinet.[26] This connection might well have raised doubts among those who read *The War in the Air*: Was this really fiction, or was it based on current British intelligence assessments of German military aviation?

American reactions to *The War in the Air* were quite varied. In July 1908 the *New York Times* noted the book's publication but incorrectly reported that it dealt with a German aerial attack on Britain. The notice also described the plot as resting upon a "fantastic scheme." However, by March 1909 new reports on German Zeppelin capabilities caused the *Times* to reconsider. The author of a feature article entitled "Looking Forward to War in the Air" surmised that Wells's novel might actually demonstrate what future aerial warfare might bring. American military professionals were not inclined to so quickly abandon their skepticism about Wells's plot. Stung by the novelist's depiction of the loss of the Atlantic Fleet, the *United States Naval Institute Proceedings* in 1910 cautioned, "Let us not be carried away by the highly colored imaginings of the writer of 'War in the Air' and his host of imitators."[27]

Historical hindsight demonstrates how accurately Wells was able to predict both the military value and the limitations of Zeppelin airships. Within a short period of time, German airships did achieve trans-Atlantic range, and in World War I they were used for aerial bombardment of London but not New York City. Wartime London provided grim evidence that aerial bombardment, from Zeppelins at first and later from airplanes, could wreak extensive destruction on civilian communities and disrupt logistical and political support for the war effort. Airships also proved to be vulnerable to airplane attack, and many operational Zeppelins fell victim to adverse winds and harsh weather conditions.

Yet subsequent events should not obscure the plain fact that in 1908 Wells was considered a visionary and alarmist by many Americans. Scientist and inventor Octave Chanute, in the spring of 1908, noted, "The popular mind often pictures gigantic flying machines speeding across the Atlantic and carrying innumerable passengers. . . . such ideas must be wholly visionary."[28] Given what Americans knew about airships and airplanes in 1908, they were probably willing to concede Chanute's point. The rickety wood and cloth contraptions that were called airplanes had already taken their toll in deaths, and their instability and vulnerability to high winds made trans-Atlantic flight seem impossible. The old spherical balloons were sturdy, but even uninformed citizens dismissed them as the expensive and hazardous toys of rich sportsmen. Semirigid airships, just coming into use in the United States, seemed the most promising of all three, but to project this bizarre collection of aircraft into a future of trans-Atlantic flight seemed preposterous. On the other hand, as historian Alfred Gollin has shown, the twelve-hour flight of a Zeppelin on July 1, 1908, raised serious concern among British military strategists about that island nation's vulnerability to aerial attack. It was a fear that might well spread across the North Atlantic, increasing pressure for air power in the United States.[29]

Public Relations in the Army Air Arm

A mere two weeks after the establishment of the army's Aeronautical Division, Capt. Charles deF. Chandler suggested to the chief signal officer that a press release about the new organization might be appropriate. His appended note stressed the need for the division to encourage future cooperation with the Aero Club of America and the editors of its magazine, *Aeronautics*. Chandler wrote, "The new periodical, American Magazine of Aeronautics, should be encouraged and assisted as far as possible. The editor has asked to send him news items for publication."[30] Chandler was not alone among Signal Corps officers who were anxious to exploit media attention to benefit military aviation. Another was Maj. George O. Squier, whom aviation pioneer John F. Victory considered a "spark plug" for aviation progress, based upon the major's lectures and writings devoted to army flying.[31]

When Brig. Gen. James Allen, the chief signal officer, returned from a 1908 tour of Germany and France, he optimistically told *New York Times* reporters that "the public mind of America, thanks to the exhaustive attention our newspapers are now giving aerial navigation, has become thoroughly interested in the subject. I believe a very influential body of public opinion favors providing the War Department with the money necessary . . . for aerial experiments."[32] Given the fact that Congress continued to reject budget proposals to advance military aviation, the general's confidence in newspaper support seems to have been misplaced. On the other hand, both he and his subordinates believed that publicity was the highway to legislative attention and fuller governmental funding. However, when army aviation news was bad, as it was following a spate of aviation accidents at the San Diego flying school in 1913, Capt. Benjamin Foulois, as head of flying instruction, ordered press releases to cease. In retrospect, Foulois claimed that an unnecessary number of these early accidents occurred when pilots took risks to gain newspaper notoriety.[33]

Signal Corps officers were indefatigable in their speeches and magazine articles. Speaking to the International Aeronautical Congress on October 28, 1907, Major Squier emphasized the need for coordination and control of army combat elements. Predictably, he identified aerial navigation as a source of "perfect lines of information and control." Capt. D. J. Carr of the Signal Corps told newspaper reporters that the Wright brothers deserved the same support that Germans had given Count Zeppelin after his airship crashed at its first trials. The Germans never wavered, and neither should Americans withdraw their support for the Wrights. Carr's statement, issued immediately after the fatal crash of the Wright biplane during its September 1908 army trials, demonstrated the Signal Corps' determination to advance the image of military aviation even in its darkest hour. In December 1908 Major Squier called upon Americans to fund military aviation proportionately to the appropriations of foreign nations, just as the U.S. Navy warship construction budget kept pace with that of the other major powers.[34]

The Role of Exhibition Flying

Yet deeds rather than words made the strongest impression upon the American public. Since taking risks and flirting with danger were associated with robust manhood, the human daring of flying exhibitions and contests riveted the nation's attention on the skies. Politicians recognized the value of being associated with aviation. Immediately after being involved in an airplane crash as a passenger, the mayor of Richmond, Virginia, appeared on the speaker's platform of the 1910 Virginia State Fair. He assured the crowd that if another airplane were available, he would fly again.[35]

With or without airplanes, the army's flying officers were regular attenders at historical and aviation exhibitions. The Signal Corps had an aviation exhibit at the 1907 Jamestown Exhibition, but of course no flying equipment was on hand. Three years later Glenn Curtiss piloted one of his planes at the aviation meet held at Sheepshead Bay. Lt. Jacob E. Fickel fired four shots from the plane and managed to hit a target on the ground two times. During the same meet a radio message was transmitted from the

Senator Black with Lt. Thomas DeW. Milling in a Wright B Flyer, 1911. The passenger, presumably a state senator, was given a ride by Lieutenant Milling at the army's flying field, then located at College Park, Maryland. Many prominent politicians and other civic leaders were flown by army pilots as a part of the Aeronautical Division's public relations program. (Ernest L. Jones Collection, Air Force Historical Research Agency, Maxwell AFB, Alabama)

Curtiss airplane to a receiver in the grandstand. The radio transmission demonstration, and an exercise of bomb dropping, was provided by army pilots at the January 1911 Los Angeles flying exhibition.[36]

Sometimes even routine flying activities became a spectacle. On July 10, 1911, two army fliers flew over the city of Washington at a height of 2,400 feet, and their presence caused Congress to adjourn and, together with all of the staff personnel, rush outside to look aloft. Harry N. Atwood, a civilian aviator, was in the course of attempting a cross-country flight from Massachusetts to Washington, and the army airplane was mistakenly identified as being his. Unaware of the congressional adjournment they had inadvertently caused, Lts. Henry H. Arnold and Roy C. Kirtland calmly returned to the College Park, Maryland, flying field. Atwood actually flew into town four days later, landed on the White House lawn, was presented an Aero Club medal by President Taft, and then took off immediately to return to Boston. An even more significant "fly-over" took place above the West Point parade ground in 1912, although it received little publicity at the time. Cadet Carl Spaatz, a future chief of staff of the U.S. Air Force, and several of his classmates decided then and there to make a career in military aviation.[37]

Despite the public relations benefits of exhibition flying, military aviation pioneer Benjamin D. Foulois criticized "[a] policy which became customary in the early days of Army flying when one of our primary jobs called for our attendance at County Fairs, Aviation Meets, etc., etc., in order to 'sell' a generally hostile public both military and civil, that aircraft had potentialities in addition to its use as a new mechanical toy."[38] Foulois, a former enlisted man, was one of the rare army pilots who stressed careful preflight inspection of aircraft. He considered precaution and good mechanical knowledge to be the keys to successful and safe flight. Willing to back his beliefs with action, in May 1911 he pressed charges against his commanding officer, whom he considered negligent in causing the death of Lt. George M. Kelly.[39] When Foulois himself was in command of flying units, he specifically prohibited both exhibition flying and the issuance of any statements to the press.

At first, danger provided additional glamour to the feats of pioneer aviators, but ultimately the carnage had a negative impact upon the American public. As is often the case, a macabre sense of humor cloaked growing concern and apprehension. A 1907 issue of *Aeronautics* quipped that "the secretary of the new Aeronautique Club of Chicago is an undertaker, and he is accused of joining the organization for mercenary reasons." By 1914 the death toll among army aviators was no longer a laughing matter, if it ever had been. Between the 1908 death of Lieutenant Selfridge at the Wright trials until 1914, Ernest L. Jones counted eleven accidents which killed fourteen Signal Corps aviation officers and one enlisted man. One officer from another branch and one civilian paid with their lives for flying with the army. Jones blamed the Wright B–type airplane for the carnage. Its engine placement behind the wings created a dangerous tendency for the plane to nose-dive in the course of descents. On February 24, 1914, the Aeronautical Division belatedly declared the Wright B and Wright D pusher-type aircraft unsuitable for military use.[40]

The rising level of public concern over army aviation deaths is reflected in the aviation coverage of *Collier's Weekly*. In 1908 and 1910 the magazine viewed flying deaths as "tragic" but the inevitable cost of progress. In September 1911 one of its articles analyzed the record of death by flying and pointed out two deficiencies in the Wright biplane: (1) when it nose-dived, there was nothing for the pilot or passengers to hold onto; and (2) when it crashed, the rear-mounted engine was likely to fall upon the occupants. However, in the same September 1911 issue there appeared a reassuring article by Hudson Maxim, claiming that technical improvements in aircraft would decrease the aviators' fatality rates. Praising the Wright brothers, *Collier's* November 1911 editorial page noted the inventors' avoidance of publicity, but also commented that when risk was necessary to achieve real progress, the Wrights did not hesitate to take the risk.[41] By October 1912 the magazine's editors again became somewhat defensive about the flying deaths: "however much we deplore the loss of these men of action, we are moved to admiration, . . . for every man who drops by the way, twenty spring forward to take his place, until at last man has triumphed."[42] Despite the renewed bombast and praise for the Wrights, the time of reckless flying and public support for risk taking was drawing to a close.

As a consequence of Colonel Reber's 1913 investigation of flying accidents, the Aeronautical Division stopped exhibition flying in January 1914. Transmitting the new policy, Reber stated that adverse reactions in Congress and in the public at large required this step. The navy had taken similar action nearly two years before, and the policy had long prevailed in Britain's Royal Flying Corps. Foulois's safety-oriented policies were vindicated, and the Aeronautical Division settled down to the business of learning safe flying.[43]

Conclusion

While army aviation's achievements and failures were matters of considerable public concern, neither these events nor efforts to publicize them seem to have influenced either legislative or executive action in favor of military aeronautics. In 1911 former balloonist Lt. Col. William A. Glassford commented that exaggerated claims about the future capability of army aviation, "instead of facilitating appropriations for defense, . . . impedes them."[44] He was quite correct. Despite its public relations initiatives, the army air arm before 1914 had limited success in mustering widespread public support, and little progress in securing congressional appropriations.

Before 1914, army aviation barely survived a parsimonious congressional attitude toward flying in the military. As European wars and mobilizations became known to the American people and their legislative representatives in Washington, there were more and larger surges of concern for an adequate military flying program. This would result in some major reorganization of army flying, and a more active concern on the part of Congress in aeronautical activity.

3 ★ European Military Aviation and the Hay Committee Hearings

After 1912, the future development of army aviation was shaped by official and unofficial reports of the wartime applications of air power in Europe. That impact was manifested in two ways. First and foremost, it generated growing public and congressional concern that, should the United States become involved in war, its military air arm would be inadequate. While H. G. Wells's novel, *The War in the Air*, had raised some genteel speculation among aviation enthusiasts, attaché reports and newspaper accounts now provided a firm factual basis upon which to criticize the government's neglect of military aeronautics. Events of the day thus reinforced the pressure being brought upon Congress by civilian aeronautical clubs and organizations. Ultimately, widespread public concern and alarming factual reports caused Congress to initiate a comprehensive investigation into the Signal Corps flying program. Conducted under the chairmanship of Congressman James Hay of Virginia, this inquiry examined at length the information received from European battlefields, and recommended reorganization of the Aeronautical Division into an Aviation Section to be administered by the Signal Corps.

The second American response was the army's increased attention to revisions of official doctrine that would incorporate the new uses of aircraft in war. Although the Aeronautical Division engaged in conceptual thought since 1907, it now became necessary to mold those concepts into an official doctrinal position. Conceptual thought is useful, but it must be refined by practical experience with weapons systems before it can form the basis for sound doctrine. Significantly, the development and enunciation of army doctrine was the responsibility of the General Staff Corps, and not the official concern of the Aeronautical Division or its successor, the Aviation Section of the Signal Corps.

Before April 1914, the army considered its aviation branch as a "service of information" that gathered and transmitted intelligence to army combat units. This doctrinal position provided the rationale for placing army aviation within Signal Corps command structure. Since military aeronautics was limited to reconnaissance, field artillery fire direction, and carrying messages between ground units, it belonged within the Signal Corps organizational structure. However, intelligence reports from Europe supplied ample tactical evidence of both the value and the limitations of aircraft as instruments of combat. Army Field Service Regulations issued in April 1914 recognized that airplanes were valuable offensive and defensive weapons. Writing in 1915, Brigadier General Scriven drew upon the reports of American attachés and observers to report on the new status of aviation in Europe. In addition to the information-gathering activities, he noted that airplanes were used for attacks upon enemy personnel and materiel. Airplanes provided defense against incursions by enemy aerial units, and, in conjunction with airships, they were vital to effective coastal defense.[1] Despite Scriven's admission against the Signal Corps' interests, the General Staff moved only slowly toward adopting relevant Aeronautical Division conceptual thought and applying it to military intelligence reports from Europe.

The army's slow reaction to European developments was not due to a lack of good military intelligence. As far back as the Turco-Italian and Balkan Wars of 1910 through 1912, there had been a steady flow of information, and this had been followed by reliable reports concerning European preparations for World War I. Neither the General Staff nor Congress was unmindful of the need to rethink the role of airplanes in modern warfare. On the other hand, army aviators were best qualified to resolve the practical and technical questions concerning airplanes and their military applications. That was true whether the activity involved reconnaissance, observation, information dissemination, or aerial combat and bombardment. Unfortunately, no army aviators had served with the General Staff prior to 1913, and only William "Billy" Mitchell served a three-year General Staff term after that date.[2]

Military Air Power in European Conflicts, 1910–1913

In the autumn of 1911, Italy became involved in war with the Ottoman Empire concerning the Sultan's sovereignty over Tripoli and Libya. While our historical knowledge of this war is much more specific than the information contemporaneously available to U.S. Army officers, it is apparent that they knew about the widespread use of aircraft by the Italian forces. Army aviators knew that the Italians used aerial reconnaissance and were experimenting with airborne direction of field artillery fire. Italian prewar maneuvers at Monferrato in August 1911 demonstrated Italian aviation capabilities and tactical applications. They used airplanes and semirigid airships for aerial observation, and these aircraft also performed well as couriers between separated ground units of the command.[3]

Immediately after landing Italian troops at Tripoli, army and navy commanders launched reconnaissance flights to locate oases and Turkish camp areas. On November 1, the main Turkish camp at Ain Zara, a short distance south-southeast of Tripoli, was attacked with aerial hand grenades, followed by some four-pound aerial bombs. As ground forces made contact, some clumsy attempts were made to direct Italian artillery fire from the air. However, the absence of air-to-ground radio communication frustrated this effort. By November 30, 1911, the airmen conducted far-ranging reconnaissance south and southeast of Tripoli. When the Italian army marched toward Ain Zara in December 1911, its flanks were scouted by the aviators, who were instructed to fly figure-eights above the threatened Italian troops. After the defeat of the Turkish forces at Ain Zara on December 4, Italian military aviators observed their withdrawal and verified that the oasis area had been abandoned.[4]

Despite initial success with combat reconnaissance, the Italian aviators soon had opportunity to experiment with a variety of other tactical applications of air power. In January 1912 they prepared sketch maps for the use of ground forces, and in late February the aviation commander developed a photographic camera for use in a primitive form of aerial photo reconnaissance. In March and April the airmen learned the capabilities and limitations of their dirigibles. Two airships reconnoitered Turkish positions at Zuara, refueled from warships nearby, and then returned to Tripoli for a flight totaling twelve hours in duration. This significant achievement was offset by the discovery that ground fire prevented airship observation at altitudes less than 4,000 feet. Aerial bombardment was also tested in the winter and spring of 1912. At first grenades were dropped by hand, with considerable danger to the pilot who also served as bombardier. The death of the inventor of the Cipelli grenade by an accident with his own invention caused the Italian flyers to defer further aerial bombardment until they developed a bomb-dropping box that armed bombs only as they left the plane. Considerable effort was made to develop a mechanical bomb that would explode upon impact, thereby achieving maximum fragmentation against personnel. That effort was partially frustrated by the softness of the desert sands. Similar ordnance problems blocked the Italian attempt to destroy submerged naval mines by aerial bombardment. The projectiles exploded on striking the water surface, inflicting no damage upon the targeted mines and torpedoes.[5]

The sand that swallowed the explosion of Italian aerial bombs also raised havoc with airplanes. Coupled with the wind that impeded airship navigation, sand threatened to destroy the combined air arm of the Italian army and navy. It made landing so hazardous that the airmen were compelled to build a one hundred–foot wooden runway, rather than relying upon packed sand. In addition, sand infiltrated mechanical equipment and made engines less reliable than they should have been. In May 1912 one airplane was totally destroyed in a sandstorm and the remaining machines were damaged.[6] Aviation publicists seized upon the Turco-Italian War as a portent of future air warfare. Henry Woodhouse wrote in *Flying* magazine for February 1913 that every army needed aerial eyes, and that "the explanation of the quick end and the economy of the Tripolitanian campaign is . . . the aeroplane."[7] On the other hand, the official history of the war points to the advantages of aerial attack on troops and equipment occupying desert camps or moving on desert landscape. When the scene of conflict shifted to Cyrenaica and the Turks occupied trenches around Benghazi, the military situation changed and the airplane lost much of its value as a combat weapon.[8] Turkish units encamped or moving on exposed areas of desert had no shelter from aerial attack and were easily spotted from the air. Once entrenched Turkish troops were shielded from aerial attack other than direct bombardment, and their numbers and preparations for offensive action were far better concealed than they would be on the open surface of the desert.

The Turco-Italian War is important because the history and tactical evaluation of the campaign was prepared by a young Italian Army major, Giulio Douhet. Assigned to study the campaign by the Ministry of War, Douhet completed his work in late 1912. Despite the apparent lack of effectiveness of aerial bombardment, Douhet contended that airplanes would be most effectively used for offensive purposes — for aerial bombardment and for attacks on enemy aircraft. His report also stressed the value of airplanes and dirigibles in both tactical and strategic reconnaissance.[9] Douhet's study had great impact on Italian air-power thought and conceptual development in the years before the outbreak of World War I.

Contemporary American public reaction to the Turco-Italian War was blunted by strict censorship imposed by the Italian military, but newspapers and periodicals reflect appreciation for the new developments in air-power tactics. *Scientific American* noted that the war had greatly strengthened Italian interest in airplanes for reconnaissance and aerial combat. The *United States Naval Institute Proceedings* reprinted an article from *Engineering* magazine that claimed troop movement could no longer be concealed from an enemy equipped with airplanes and dirigibles. *Flying* magazine, in an article by Congressman Henry Woodhouse, asserted without much support for the speculation, that Italy's air arm had saved nearly 20,000 lives and five billion dollars during the course of the desert war.[10]

Shortly after the end of the Turco-Italian War in North Africa, a movement for independence occurred in the European tip of the Ottoman imperial crescent. Greek and Slavic peoples in northern Greece, Macedonia, and Bulgaria revolted against Turkish authorities, precipitating the First and Second Balkan Wars. The surviving evidence concerning military aeronautics in the Balkan Wars is elusive and unreliable, but there is no doubt that one-plane aerial attacks occurred on the fortress town of Janina, or Yanina, in northern Greece, and on Adrianopole. *Aeronautics* magazine reported that a Russian aviator flew over Janina, dropped six bombs, and reconnoitered the fortress. On the basis of his information, it was decided to launch an immediate infantry attack, and the fort was taken a few days later. In regard to Janina and also in connection with the Adrianopole bombing, it was claimed that panic among the defending troops facilitated the ground victory. The principle American historical account on the Balkan Wars does not mention these aerial adjuncts to the ground action.[11]

Military Aeronautics and Preparations for World War I

Prior to 1911, intelligence concerning European military aviation was not collected on a regular basis. In August 1909, the chief signal officer, Brig. Gen. James Allen, tasked military attachés in Paris and Berlin to attend aviation meets held that year at Rheims and Frankfurt am Main. A year later, Capt. Charles deF. Chandler attended a Brussels flying exhibition, and may also have reported on military aviation in France and Germany.[12] However, in late 1910 the London military attaché began to provide detailed information concerning British efforts to develop both airship and airplane capabilities.

In September 1910, British military airships were used in maneuvers, and demonstrated potential as observation vehicles; they achieved a speed of fifteen miles per hour and traveled 700 miles on a single flight. A month later, the War Office purchased a Lebaudy airship from the French manufacturing firm for £18,000. Following the German practice of encouraging public subscriptions to develop new aircraft, the British government raised £6,000 by means of a public subscription toward the airship's purchase. The contributors were gratified when the Lebaudy dirigible crossed the English Channel at a speed of 41 miles per hours, travelling the 246 miles at altitudes ranging from 650 to 1,000 feet. By February 1911, two smaller military airships joined the British air arm after construction in government factories. The British then turned to construction of a medium-sized airship. In addition, during 1911 and 1912 a number of naval airships were acquired by the Royal Navy, including German-built Parsevaals and French constructed Astra-Torres dirigibles. By August 1913, plans were in place to construct five naval airships of the Parsevaal type at the British plant of Vickers Ltd. Public enthusiasm for airship construction resulted in a proposal to create a Britannia Airship Trust, designed to raise a subscription that would permit the construction of a large airship for naval service at a cost of approximately £15,000. Despite extensive military experimentation with airships, the army announced in January 1914 that its dirigibles would be transferred to the navy and that, thereafter, the army would concentrate on heavier-than-air airplanes.[13]

The British army also advanced rapidly in developing tactical uses for the airplane. In August 1910 an airplane was employed in observing troops, and photographs were made of trenches and other emplacements. Shortly thereafter, unsuccessful efforts were made to hit ground targets with sandbags dropped from airplanes. Undeterred, the military flyers continued bomb dropping experiments, and by May 1911 they demonstrated that accurate delivery was possible, and that the release of a heavy object did not disturb equilibrium in flight. In September 1912 the American military attaché reported that special efforts were being made to develop a larger biplane that could carry a Maxim machine gun in flight. Significantly, the British government was the only major purchaser of aircraft at the time, suggesting that no reserve of civilian-owned aircraft would be available in the event of hostilities.[14]

British interest in military aviation resulted in growing parliamentary appropriations and increased organizational independence for the flying units. From March 1911 through March 1914, yearly expenditures increased from £133,000 (about U.S. $718,200) to £717,000 (U.S. $3,885,000). In June 1911 the Army Council announced that the air battalion provided the most useful method of reconnaissance, and in March 1912 the king approved the redesignation of the air battalion as the Royal Flying Corps.

Divided into a Military Wing and a Naval Wing by May 1913, the Royal Flying Corps then consisted of 145 officers and 967 noncommissioned officers and enlisted men. As of October 1912 thirty-six airplanes were in service and four were under construction.[15]

In addition to routine attaché reports from Britain, the army received some valuable reports from Maj. George O. Squier, a Signal Corps officer earlier assigned to the Aeronautical Division. Ordered to attaché duty in London commencing on June 15, 1912, Squier attended the International Aero Exhibition held in London on February 14–23, 1913. He reported that only one army dirigible was exhibited at the event, but Britain was making great progress with airplanes, particularly seaplanes. According to his report, the British government purchased almost all of the airplanes on exhibit. The Grahame-White Aviation Company demonstrated a biplane that carried a Colt quick-firing gun mounted for offensive tactics. An astute observer of the British aviation program, Squier anticipated by several months the official announcement that thereafter Britain intended to concentrate upon airplanes rather than large dirigibles.[16]

A respected scientist in his own right, Squier was privy to some closely held information about British army aviation. In May 1913 he advised the War Department that the Birmingham Arms Company was in active negotiation with U.S. Army colonel Isaac N. Lewis concerning Lewis's machine gun, which had been rejected for aerial use at home. Two Lewis guns had already been ordered for trial use by British aviators, and by November 1913 the aviators reported great accuracy in firing the Lewis machine gun from an airplane in flight. Squier was also able to obtain confidential scale drawings of two new British reconnaissance planes in April 1914. The plans were made available to him by Brig. David Henderson, then head of the British army's aviation activities.[17] Brigadier Henderson also suggested that the U.S. government follow the British lead and operate its own airplane manufacturing plants rather than acquiring them from private builders. While that suggestion fell upon deaf ears at home, Henderson's views about the value of the Advisory Committee on Aeronautics may have encouraged army efforts to establish the National Advisory Committee on Aeronautics some two years later.[18]

Military intelligence from the German Empire was less readily available, but Capt. Samuel Shartle, the military attaché in Berlin, kept the War College Division reasonably well informed concerning German aeronautical progress. He took particular pains to provide details concerning the large rigid airships known as Zeppelins. In a 122-page typewritten report prepared in June 1910, he noted the increased speed and range of newer Zeppelins, suggesting that, while Zeppelins would be of value in defending fortified areas and for long-range reconnaissance, they would be less adaptable to assist mobile armies in the field. Two years later, his August 1912 report reaffirmed the Zeppelins' limitations in conducting short-range reconnaissance, but urged that the United States develop a rigid airship for coastal-defense purposes. Shartle stressed that private firms would have to be subsidized by the government, not only to build large rigid airships, but also to ensure the survival of lighter-than-air manufacturing firms. He confirmed the bomb-carrying capacity of Zeppelins, and noted that the large airships were able to achieve great heights, travel long distances, and remain in the air much longer than other airships and airplanes.[19] In September 1912 Shartle noted that representatives of the Schutte Lanz and Parsevaal airship companies were traveling to the United States to determine whether they should erect factories there. His recommendation was that such a step should be encouraged, since this would make available to the United States the results of ten years' development of these larger airships.[20]

Although German military interest in Zeppelins continued unabated, after April 1912 Shartle and his colleagues noted increased efforts to develop new airplanes designed for military purposes. The German government purchased a British Sopwith and White seaplane, and instructed their firms to produce a better seaplane. At this time German conceptual thought was alert to the airplane's potential as an offensive weapon. In June 1913 Capt. A. W. Bornstad reported to the War College Division that Zeppelins were equipped with machine guns for defense against airplane attack. The vulnerability of the rigid airships was accentuated in October 1913, when a German naval Zeppelin exploded in the midair as a consequence of escaping hydrogen gas being ignited by an engine spark. Twenty-seven crew members died in the disaster.[21]

This admittedly limited survey of American attaché reports in the years 1909 through the summer of 1914 suggests that both Britain and Germany were aware of the value and the disadvantages of long-range rigid airships in warfare. Both appreciated the superiority of airplanes in terms of speed and cost of construction. As a consequence these powers, and other European nations as well, were engaged in the simultaneous development of both lighter-than-air and heavier-than-air aerial weapons. What was particularly impressive was the magnitude of their effort compared to limited American progress in military aviation.

1912: The Year of the Maneuvers

In the summer of 1912 the U.S. Army held an ambitious maneuver which drew upon organized militia units from New York, New Jersey, Connecticut, Massachusetts, Maine, and Vermont. A total of 15,007 men from the organized militia participated in the exercise, and they were supplemented by 2,324 regular army troops, including one aviation section. For the first phase of the exercise, the aviation section was attached to the headquarters of the chief umpire. Presumably its reconnaissance functions were utilized to judge the effectiveness of ground action and to evaluate the training accomplished during this instructional phase. During the final phase of the maneuvers, the aviation section was assigned to the Blue Force, which was given a defensive role. According to the opening scenario, the offensive Red Force had already overrun Boston and was moving toward Albany. Their immediate objective was to occupy New Haven and Waterbury in Connecticut, prior to moving against the New York City water supply in Westchester County. The New York, New Haven and Hartford Railroad was vulnerable to bombardment from Blue naval forces located in Long Island Sound, hence the inland route selected for the Red advance. In scouting the Red Force advance, the aviators were instructed to observe from a minimum altitude of 2,000 feet, and fly at greater altitude when they crossed the Red lines. Barographs were mounted in each plane to ensure that the minimum altitude rules were followed, and to check on the accuracy of observation at these heights. It was assumed that this limitation on low flying would protect the airplanes from ground-troop rifle fire.[22]

The Connecticut maneuvers proved that airplanes were valuable adjuncts to the normal processes for gathering and disseminating intelligence concerning enemy positions and intentions. Even more ambitious were French army maneuvers staged in November 1912, in which both competing armies had aerial reconnaissance capability. One dirigible and 72 airplanes were assigned to each command for reconnaissance purposes, and additional airplanes were utilized for artillery spotting. Despite heavy rains and wind, the airplanes were in flight almost constantly. Each plane flew an average of 600 miles; five were damaged and one was destroyed. Lt. Col. T. Bentley Mott, the U.S. military attaché in France, concluded that the aviation units had made an excellent showing. To test the best method of utilizing aircraft, the competing forces used differing control systems. According to Colonel Mott, the best method of reporting findings was to relay aerial observations directly to the general controlling the unit, rather than filtering the information through the staff components of the army. On the

A Wright military flyer at the 1912 summer maneuvers. The 1912 maneuvers involved the New York and Connecticut National Guards. Pilots from the Aeronautical Division provided aerial observation for one of the armies and proved the value of aerial reconnaissance. They also succeeded in preparing some sketch maps of the enemy's advance. In the photograph the Army pilots are explaining the flyer to military attachés from Mexico and Russia who were official observers during the maneuvers. (*Collier's Weekly* 49, no. 24 [1912]: 22)

other hand, it was not conclusive that this form of direct control and reporting was the most effective use of aviation resources.[23]

Presidential and Congressional Attitudes up to 1912

Reports of military flying in Libya and the Balkans awoke some political concern in the United States, and were partially responsible for a modest increase in army aeronautical appropriations. Intelligence reports from Europe provided additional reason for concern. Finally, the French and Connecticut maneuvers of 1912 provided undeniable evidence that aerial observation and scouting would play a critical role in any future armed conflict. Despite the efficient and dedicated work of army intelligence, congressional appropriations for military flying remained substantially below any aviation budget for the other major powers. Presidential and congressional inaction, despite Aero Club prodding and alarming intelligence reports, is remarkable, and the intransigence requires some explanation.

President Theodore Roosevelt's impact on air power was minimal. He was anxious that the U.S. Army be "up-to-date" with the other armies of the world, and he and his family had been involved with army aviation at its earliest stages. Roosevelt's son and the president's military aide accompanied Capt. Charles DeF. Chandler on a 90-mile balloon flight, and the *New York Times* commented on the president's enthusiasm for army flying.[24] However, Roosevelt left the White House before the army accepted its first Wright airplane in June 1909. Roosevelt's support for things military could be ambivalent; Dr. Greenwood suggests that after sending a blue-ribbon contingent of military observers to study the Russo-Japanese War, Roosevelt subsequently squelched any possibility that their recommendations might be given serious consideration.[25] The "New Army" was Roosevelt's creation, and the General Staff Corps was established during his presidency. The Aeronautical Division's lobbying in Congress, joined by the Aero Club and the National Guard, might well have alienated him from the army aviators' cause.[26] Nevertheless, the aeronautical press considered Roosevelt a strong supporter of military aviation, and it openly supported his 1912 reelection campaign.[27]

William Howard Taft, Roosevelt's hand-picked successor, previously served as governor of the Philippines and then as secretary of war. Necessarily, he had much more contact with military aviation, since army flying only commenced in earnest after Roosevelt left the White House. Despite this, Taft's attitude remained equivocal. He consented to the use of the White House for ceremonies honoring Wilbur and Orville Wright in June 1909, and he authorized the one-month trial of the second "flyer" they had built for acceptance by the army. In September 1910, Taft and his military aide, Maj. Archie Butt, traveled to Boston to attend an aviation meeting. Charles J. Glidden, an Aero Club official, introduced the airmen to their president, who was gracious in his praise. On the other hand, at the same event Taft vetoed the wishes of Mrs. Taft, their son, and Major Butt, all of whom wished to experience aerial flight as passengers.[28]

In terms of army organization, Taft was no more predictable than Roosevelt. He retained Maj. Gen. J. Franklin Bell as chief of staff when he took office, permitting that officer to serve a full term. He then appointed Maj. Gen. Leonard Wood to serve as chief of staff, but felt that Wood was attempting to reorganize the army too rapidly and objected to Wood's following "Prussian" models.[29] Like Roosevelt, Taft experienced troubles with Marine Corps "politicking" and let it be known to his army military aide that if any marine officers were discovered currying favor with Congress they would soon find themselves in the Philippines or in Guantanamo Bay, Cuba.[30] From this we may assume that the "Old Army" political ties of the Aeronautical Division were as much a disadvantage during the Taft administration as they would have been under Roosevelt.

President Taft was suspicious of military points of view, and this feeling had been deepened by his service in the Philippines, where he clashed with Gen. Arthur MacArthur. Taft did not read newspapers that criticized him, or those that differed with him in their editorial policies. Major Butt, who served Taft faithfully for three years, commented, "[P]ugnacity of any kind was distasteful to President Taft." These personality and political distinctions between Roosevelt and Taft suggest that the trend in presidential leadership and inclinations was away from sympathy for things military and toward greater concern with political pragmatism.[31] Taft was in many ways a transitional figure, delicately poised — given his weight, figuratively but not literally — between the jingoism of Roosevelt and the neutrality of Woodrow Wilson.

On the eve of Taft's leaving the White House, the editors of *Flying* magazine commented that, with the exception of George von L. Meyer, secretary of the navy, and Postmaster General Frank H. Hitchcock, "it cannot be said that Mr. Taft and his Cabinet have displayed more than the most elementary knowledge of . . . modern aeronautics. . . . While fundamental changes in armaments abroad were afoot, they sat supinely still in inexcusable ignorance and disbelief."[32] The editors of *Flying* hoped that the incoming Wilson administration would do better; four years later, *Aerial Age Weekly* printed in each issue a black-bordered caption, stating that the only hope for military aviation was another Theodore Roosevelt administration.[33] Until well into 1916, President Wilson seemed destined to follow in the footsteps of his Republican predecessor.

Congress likewise proved to be a stumbling block to aviation progress, despite the fact that a number of members were flyers themselves or, at the least, active members of aeronautical organizations. At no time before 1916 were the supporters of aviation able to secure adequate funding for army aeronautics. Certainly some early legislative reticence can be attributed to the highly publicized 1903 failure of the Langley experiments. Even after the Wrights proved flight to be attainable, the aircraft themselves were so fragile that great imagination was required to see them as weapons of war. Many congressmen may have been suspicious of the veracity, or the motives, of the army aviators, which was reflective of a growing distance between "professional" military men and the general public. Perhaps most significant was a profound ignorance about modern military science and world diplomacy. At its base, this indifference rested upon sublime confidence in America's isolation from the rest of the world, and particularly upon the invulnerability of the United States to European attack. Given this attitude, Congress deemed it unwise to invest in military airplanes until their utility for defense of American territory could be demonstrated, and their operational value proved beyond any question.

These fundamental attitudes toward military aviation did not change before 1916. However, some limited progress was made in alerting Congress to the need for an expanded flying program in the army and the navy. From 1912 until 1914, air-minded members goaded the House of Representatives into a series of investigations of army aviation. Gradually the annual appropriations for military flying activities began to grow, although at no time before 1916 was the sum adequate for even a modest program. In 1911–12, Britain, France, and Germany each expended no less than $1 million for expansion of their aerial forces. Imperial Russia allocated $900,000 for the same purpose. Mobilizing for the Turco-Italian War, the Italian government appropriated $2 million for aeronautical work. For the same time period, the United States increased its army aviation budget to $125,000.[34] After a U.S. Navy flying program began in 1910, there was a brief spurt of support for naval aviation work, but it soon dried up, leaving the seamen in as bad a state as their army counterparts.

Shortly after the 1907 establishment of the Aeronautical Division, Lt. Col. William Glassford told the International Aeronautical Congress that the U.S. Congress would no longer be influenced by its unfortunate experience with Samuel P. Langley's "flyers." This overly optimistic pronouncement was destined to be refuted time and time again. Glassford was correct in his claim that "many in Congress . . . have observed the progress of the world in flying machines."[35] What he neglected to mention was that there were even more congressmen who were steadfast in their doubts concerning aeronautics. Representative John A. T. Hull, chairman of the House Military Affairs Committee in 1908, actively supported an airship procurement effort. He even took his plea to President Roosevelt in hopes of obtaining an adequate appropriation in that year.[36] Two months later a proposed $200,000 appropriation for military aviation was killed in the Senate by Senator Stephen B. Elkins of West Virginia. The *New York Times* quoted an army officer's 1908 opinion that "Congress . . . thinks aeronautics is an idle Summer amusement, instead of a science that in the next war may change the geography of the globe."[37]

Congressman Hull returned to the fray in the 1909 budget battle. Even before the House Appropriations Committee acted, the *New York Times* reported that it was obvious that the members felt that aviation was still too experimental to warrant public support. When the bill was reported out of committee, Hull pointed out to the House that none of the other great powers had signed the Hague Convention against aerial bombardment, and consequently their dirigibles could destroy shipping and property of enormous value in American coastal cities. Not content to rely upon Congress's knowledge of international treaties and the law of war, Hull took pains to insert in the *Congressional Record* the reports of American military attachés concerning European progress in aviation, with particular attention to the Zeppelin airship.[38]

As chief signal officer, Brig. Gen. James Allen criticized American lack of preparedness and the nation's failure to keep pace with world aviation progress in his October 1909 annual report: "All first-class powers except the United States are providing themselves systematically with aerial fleets, Germany and France being notably in the lead. The United States does not at the present possess a modern aeronautical equipment, and it is believed that a systematic plan of development of this modern auxiliary for national defense should be inaugurated without delay."[39] How did this plea for adequate funding appeal to Congress? Chairman Hull knew his duty and included $500,000 for military aviation in the October 1910 draft of the appropriation bill. As the legislation moved through committees, it became obvious that many congressmen and senators had serious doubts concerning the need for military air power. During this session a Washington newspaper reporter claimed to have heard a congressman ask, "Why all this fuss about airplanes for the Army? I thought we already had one."[40]

Clearly General Allen's 1909 and 1910 annual reports had left no impression upon members of the lower house! He outlined the rapid development of the airplane abroad, and how the United States was already far behind, not only in obtaining modern equipment but also in training personnel.[41] Yet a recurring theme in subsequent congressional debates involved the alleged durability of aircraft operating in field conditions and during routine training activity. The general legislative view was that procurement of an airplane added a permanent resource to the army flying program that would not need to be replaced or updated. Regardless of future changes in aeronautical design and technology, the existing inventory of one obsolete airplane was more than adequate.

Despite congressional misunderstanding and confusion, the 1911 military aviation appropriation increased by a modest amount. With support from Representative Richard P. Hobson and but mild opposition from Congressmen James Mann and Joseph W. Keifer, Chairman Hull succeeded in obtaining an appropriation of $125,000 for military aeronautics. This appropriation was enacted into law on March 3, 1911, and some twenty-five years later an army flyer reminisced that this law marked "the real beginning of progress in Army aviation."[42]

Army pilots might bless good fortune in 1911, but the aeronaut constituency and its following in Congress remained restive. In February 1913 the *Congressional Record* reprinted an article by Alfred W. Lawson which claimed that days after it declared war on the United States, Germany could have ten huge "armor-clad airships" and one hundred airplanes over the United States. Inserted in the *Record* at the request of Representative William G. Sharp of Ohio, Lawson's article pointedly reminded Congress of the great aeronautical progress being made in Europe. In March 1913 Henry Woodhouse, writing in *Flying* magazine, commented that ". . . with Congress practically all of the opposition to advancing military aeronautics in this country is caused by lack of knowledge of the tremendous development of military aeronautics abroad in the last eighteen months."[43] Despite Woodhouse and Lawson, Congress decreased the 1913 army aviation appropriation to $100,000, voting an additional $10,000 to support the small naval aviation program. In 1914 the army's aviation budget returned to the 1911 level of $125,000. However, by that time Germany had an aeronautical budget of $5 million. Surprisingly, in 1914 there was a sudden peak in funding for naval aviation, which then declined to, or below, army levels until mid-1916. In December 1914, Representative Keifer remarked to the Military Affairs Committee that since aircraft had "proved worthless to a very large extent," the United States could be considered gainers by not having expended much upon them.[44] At that time the European war was already five months old.

The Shift to an Activist Congress

In spite of continued congressional intransigence, the events of 1912 proved to be turning points for army aviation. As we have seen, attaché reports on French military maneuvers in the summer of 1912 were confirmed by the encampments and maneuvers of the Connecticut and New York National Guard units in the same year. Thereafter, it was clear that airplanes were invaluable for reconnaissance and field artillery fire direction. The Aeronautical Division flyers and airplanes were ordered to Fort

Riley, Kansas, in October and November 1912 to conduct additional experiments with aerial direction of artillery fire. The General Staff Corps, following French practice, asked that the planes operate between 2,000 and 3,000 feet in altitude, and that the artillery fire be directed so that it surrounded the target within a distance of 200 yards.[45] Like the aerial work with artillery during the National Guard maneuvers, the Fort Riley tests demonstrated the value of aerial fire direction.

Goaded by the aeronaut constituency and the communications media, Congress began to take an interest in army aviation. At first Congress's exertions were limited in scope and short in duration. Representative Thomas W. Hardwick of Georgia introduced a bill in January 1912 providing for an expansion in the number of Signal Corps aviation positions and allowing incentive pay for flying officers. The secretary of war objected that the number of personnel then assigned to army aviation was quite adequate, and the bill, after a series of amendments, died in committee. Although Hardwick's bill never reached the House floor, the Senate Military Affairs Committee solicited the opinion of the secretary of war concerning its terms. Not surprisingly, the secretary restated the objections he earlier had provided to the House.[46]

The Hardwick bill represented the first of a series of legislative efforts to expedite progress in army aviation in spite of executive branch opposition. Frustrated by an uncooperative House Military Affairs Committee, airminded Congressmen used Congress's investigatory power to expose weaknesses in the Signal Corps aviation program. The first step was House Resolution 448, introduced by Representative William G. Sharp on March 8, 1912, requesting that the secretary of war submit information concerning military aeronautics.[47] Significantly, the House Committee on Military Affairs, newly chaired by Congressman James Hay, a Democrat from Virginia, amended Sharp's resolution by deleting some diplomatic language from the original. Instead of "respectfully requesting" documentation from Secretary of War Henry L. Stimson, it simply "directed" the secretary to provide the information requested. Hay's committee also deleted Sharp's conclusory words that the information requested be supplied "if not incompatible with the public interests."[48] In this form the resolution passed on March 26, 1912, demanded details concerning aviation in foreign countries, the extent of government expenditures at home and abroad, the nature of training given to both American and foreign officers, and the U.S. government's plans for increasing present army flying equipment. The motivation for House Resolution 448 is to be found in its recognition of the "great impor-

Congressman William G. Sharp of Michigan. Representative Sharp was among the strongest congressional advocates for army aviation and witnessed the successful 1909 trial of the Wright Army Flyer. In September 1914, President Wilson appointed Sharp as ambassador to France. (*Flying* 3 [October 1914]: 125)

tance and necessity of a practical knowledge of aviation as it relates to warfare. . . . [Some foreign nations] are spending large sums of money in equipping their armies with various kinds of aircraft as a means both of attack and transport. . . ."[49]

In requesting access to the army's intelligence assessments of foreign military aviation activities, the House for the first time evidenced its mistrust of the management of army aeronautics. Probing into areas of foreign intelligence collection, it moved not timidly, as Sharp had intended, but boldly as the Hay Committee amendments indicated. This was the beginning of a dramatic wrestling match over things military and "preparedness," which would have broader implications and generate great political heat in the next four years. The aeronaut constituency and Aeronautical Division public relations had a great deal to do with awakening congressional interest. However, once the battle lines were drawn between supporters of the president and the General Staff on one side, and supporters of the House of Representatives, the Aeronautical Division, and the National Guard lobby arrayed on the other, the flying officers themselves lost control of the movement.

The War Department's report was a straightforward presentation of attaché reports and other materials on world military aviation. The magnitude of foreign flying programs compared to those of the United States made an immediate impression. As Lt. Colonel T. Bentley Mott later observed, the years from 1905 through 1911 were times when the American military attachés in Paris and Berlin lived in a world where aviation was a "burning actuality"; at home it was a matter of mere academic interest. This came through in the reports. Mott's dispatches from Paris told of vast expenditures and vigorous training for an elite corps of French aviation officers. Government-sponsored contests among manufacturers sought the fastest and most modern aircraft for army and navy use. Universities were engaged in technical and engineering training and experiments designed to facilitate aeronautical development. By December 1912 France hoped to have twenty-seven squadrons for the use of its field armies, five squadrons to help in the defense of fortified places, and another four squadrons assigned to cavalry units.[50] Capt. Samuel G. Shartle, attaché at Berlin, had less detail to report. Although Germany had begun to work on airplane design, the number of airplane squadrons was not large, and he lacked information concerning the Zeppelins. From London, Maj. Samuel L'H. Slocum reported modest British airplane construction that resulted in seven operational squadrons. He also noted that the British were thinking of uniting all of their flying activities into a separate military service that would combine both army and navy flyers, and draw upon civilians for a variety of services.[51]

Against this background of American inferiority in military aviation, Secretary of War Henry L. Stimson assured the committee that funding for the three squadrons requested in his department's March 1912 draft appropriation would be sufficient. His confidence is puzzling, since at that very time the War Department was revising squadron organization and manning, and, having finally declared Wright bi-planes obsolete, it was looking for an improved airplane. The report containing foreign military intelligence, along with Secretary Stimson's comments on appropriations for army aeronautics, was submitted in the spring of 1912. That summer, the French military maneuvers thoroughly demonstrated the airplane's value in modern warfare. Germany immediately began a vigorous airplane construction program, and other European powers vastly increased their overall aviation budgets. Unimpressed by the War Department's 1912 submission, Congressman Hardwick on January 16, 1913, commented that "today this country is behind, woefully behind, every other civilized country on earth, every other great power on earth, in this great matter of aviation."[52]

The Two Hay Bills and an Independent Air Service

The strong and dominant personality of incoming Military Affairs Chairman James Hay, shown by his mandatory language in House Resolution

448, was to play a significant role in aeronautical funding and policies from 1913 until the United States declared war in 1917. The two pieces of legislation that bear his name (H.R. 28728, introduced on February 11, 1913, and H.R. 5304, introduced on May 16, 1913) were to generate debate in Congress over army aviation. They also gave rise to extensive committee hearings in August 1913, and ultimately H.R. 5304, much amended, became law on July 18, 1914, and created the Aviation Section of the Signal Corps.[53]

In the seventeen months of hearings, army aviators had an opportunity to push for an aerial unit that would be separate and distinct from the Signal Corps. Congressional dissatisfaction with Signal Corps management of the aviation program might easily have facilitated such an organizational change. However, the flying officers hesitated in their encouragement of the separation effort. Two factors seems to have influenced them. Nearly all of the flyers, like Benjamin Foulois, felt that separation from Signal Corps oversight was "premature." They were probably correct, since all of the army aviation officers were young and held ranks no higher than first lieutenant. The Aeronautical Division was simply too young in establishment to be staffed by experienced senior officers with a flying background, and would have been disadvantaged in dealing with other branches and the General Staff.

The drive for autonomy from the Signal Corps may also have been compromised by fear of public reaction to an increasing number of flying deaths. These tragic events may have been viewed as emanating from poor leadership in the Aeronautical Division. The General Staff remained in strong opposition to the airmen's concept of air power, favoring a "reconnaissance-only" role for the airplane. Gathering information and its transmission to ground commanders should be the mission of a single branch — in this case, the Signal Corps in conjunction with its Aeronautical Division.[54] Congress's seeming friendliness to army aviation was difficult to assess, but the low level of appropriations coupled with the persistence of strong opposition by influential House and Senate members made it likely that no bill providing for separation of the aeronautical activities from the Signal Corps would be approved. When Representative Henry Woodhouse, as cosponsor of the first Hay Bill (H.R. 28728), introduced it in the House, he himself felt that its provisions were "radical." Since they reportedly had been drawn up in consultation with Capt. Paul W. Beck, they very likely had the same reputation among the other army pilots.[55]

A board of army pilots, including Lts. Henry H. Arnold and Thomas DeW. Milling, met at Washington on February 24, 1913, pursuant to the call of Col. George P. Scriven, then acting chief signal officer. While the group favored portions of the proposed legislation, they agreed that the creation of a separate Air Corps as an organization in the army line was not appropriate. This determination, coupled with more general War Department opposition to the bill, caused the death of H.R. 28728 before the House Committee on Military Affairs.[56] It was reintroduced in modified form on May 16, 1913, as H.R. 5304.

Although Representatives Hay and Woodhouse accepted the defeat of an Air Corps form of organization, they nevertheless persisted in their desire to create a distinct organization responsible for military aeronautics. H.R. 5304 provided for the creation of an Aviation Section in the Signal Corps, to be expanded in size to 60 officers and 260 enlisted men.[57] Even in its amended form, the bill drew War Department disapproval, and hearings were scheduled before the House Committee on Military Affairs and held in August 1913.[58] Among the committee membership, in addition to James Hay, were Representatives S. H. Dent Jr. of Alabama and Julius Kahn of California,[59] both strong supporters of aeronautics.

Committee hearings began on August 12 with testimony from recently promoted Brigadier General Scriven, Chief Signal Officer, and Acting Secretary of War Henry Breckinridge. Both objected to Hay Bill provisions that made aviation activities separate from the Signal Corps. They felt that attention to military aeronautics was commendable, and Scriven endorsed the view that it was unwise to "rely upon a few machines and a few trained men." Secretary Breckinridge emphasized his belief that 99 percent of the value of military aviation was in the reconnaissance and courier fields. On the other hand, he conceded that dirigible bombardment of England was within the realm of possibility. Shortly after his testimony, Secretary Breckinridge wrote to Congressman Hay officially stating that, upon recommendation of the War College Division of the General Staff Corps, he could not accept the provisions of the Hay Bill calling for separation of aviation activities from Signal Corps supervision.[60]

Lt. Col. Samuel Reber, a son-in-law of retired Lt. Gen. Nelson A. Miles (the last commanding general of the army), supported the secretary and General Scriven in their belief that aviation activities should remain in the Signal Corps. He felt that the second Hay Bill would not add to the efficiency of army aviation. General Scriven returned for further testimony on August 14, at which time he ventured the opinion that aviation should be permanently assigned to the Signal Corps.[61] This was in opposition to the testimony of Captain Beck, who testified that nonflying officers should not command aviation units, and that separation into an independent branch or arm of the army was desirable.[62] Scriven emphasized the scientific progress achieved by the Signal Corps, and stated that scientific knowledge was more important in aeronautics than flying experience. The following day, Maj. Edgar Russell testified that if aviation should develop combat capabilities it should then be transferred to a separate arm, but in the meantime it should remain under Signal Corps supervision. Lieutenant Foulois informed the committee, "We have just gotten to the point . . . where we are beginning to learn something about aviation; we have not yet gotten to the point where we know what our organization ought to be. . . . it looks to me like swapping horses in the middle of a stream."[63] Capt. William Mitchell and Lt. Henry H. Arnold shared his opinion. Only Captain Beck held out for separation of aviation from the control of the Signal Corps.[64]

While the House Military Affairs Committee proceeded with its consideration of the Hay Bill, General Scriven began work on his 1913 annual report. Submitted on October 10, the paper forcefully stated the Signal Corps position.

> It is no time now to make experimental changes, whatever the future may develop in regard to the organization of a separate corps. . . . It is to be remembered that the science of the air requires the best efforts of the most highly trained men. . . . [T]rained and experienced men in or beyond middle of life are required in the development of the science of aeronautics of the future. . . . [T]he pilot of the airplane . . . is the man behind the gun; but from the nature of things he must be a young, venturesome officer, generally without the knowledge of administrative and technical matters which can only come with years of experience.[65]

The immediate future of military aviation rested with the Signal Corps. So he concluded, and ultimately so Congress decided. When the second Hay Bill was enacted into law, the Signal Corps continued to supervise the activities of its Aviation Section.[66]

Although the congressional campaign for separation suffered a setback, the Hay Bill[67] created a subordinate Aviation Section of the Signal Corps, and thus facilitated the submission of quantitative reports on flying activities. While the new statute limited aviation officer appointments to lieutenants, and required that lieutenants assigned as student aviators be unmarried and not over the age of thirty, it did permit the immediate redetail of proficient military aviators to fill vacancies in the Aviation Section. This ameliorated the impact of the detested Manchu law, which required two years of service with an officer's line regiment before redetail.[68] In effect, it eliminated the preferred position that Signal Corps officers were seen to enjoy over their fellow aviators detailed from line regiments. The statute also established standards for rating junior military aviators and military aviators, and required that future certificates for those grades be issued upon the recommendation of an examining board of three flying officers and two medical officers.[69] It increased the allowance of flying pay to student aviators, junior military aviators, and military aviators; another provision awarded a lump-sum payment of one year's salary to the estate of any flying officer killed in the course of duty.[70]

Enactment of the Hay Bill into law evidenced a renewed congressional interest in army aviation, and it may have served to encourage aircraft manufacturers to seek new orders from the army. It also alerted senior Signal Corps officers that, while separation of aviation from the Signal Corps had been averted, they would be watched closely in their administration of the newly designated Aviation Section.[71]

Conclusion

The modification of the Hay Bill before its passage into law preserved Signal Corps supervision of flying in the army; to a limited degree this ensured the continuance of "business as usual." But the glare of publicity altered a number of relationships in the years from 1912 to 1914. While aviation officers rallied to the defense of the Signal Corps, they continued to feel alienation from the leadership of that branch and resented their subordination to nonflying officers. The ill will was to a degree based upon fundamental differences in concepts of air power that, in turn, had bearing upon the organization of military aviation. Since the Signal Corps viewed offensive applications of air power as arguments for the separation of the aeronautical activities from its overview, it would continue to see combat applications through a dark-colored glass.

However, in a broader sense the army aviators for the first time had been exposed to the heady atmosphere of a congressional investigation, and the mixed blessings of being directly under the critical eye of Congress and an anxious public. In the spring of 1913 the combined strength of the aeronaut constituency, the communications media, and concerned members of Congress threatened to control military aviation's destiny. Larger national interests were involved, including the burning question of relying upon the National Guard for reserve military strength, and how military aviation would fit into that or some other reserve program.[72] With the outbreak of

Col. Charles B. Winder of the Ohio National Guard at the controls of a Wright Flyer, 1911 or 1912. With the permission of the army chief of staff, Colonel Winder was taught to fly in 1909. Several state National Guard units were anxious to participate in the aviation program, but the War Department was not enthusiastic about the idea until the approach of American entry into World War I. The Signal Corps encouraged National Guard interest in military aviation, and unofficial connections with the National Guard and its officers may have alienated the Executive Branch and the General Staff from supporting Aeronautical Division initiatives. (Ernest L. Jones Collection, Air Force Historical Research Agency, Maxwell AFB, Alabama)

the First World War in Europe just two weeks after Congress enacted the second Hay Bill into law,[73] the hearings before the Hay Committee took on additional significance in the public mind. Never again would the alignment of political forces be simply "anti-aviation / pro-aviation." These camps continued to exist, but after 1914 they formed but one of the many alliances that worked either for preparedness or against it, either for a strong Regular Army or for a revitalized National Guard.

4 ★ Tactical Thinking, Army Politics, and Congressional Confusion

Few periods of air-power thinking have been as productive as the years from 1907 through 1914.[1] For the most part, conceptual formulations were highly speculative and tentative, given the primitive level of development that was characteristic of American airplanes and ancillary flying equipment. To the extent that army doctrine ignored the value of the dirigible and the stationary balloon, it was also narrow in its scope. Nevertheless, virtually all of the basic principles of aerial warfare (with the exception of current missile-employment theory) were enunciated in an embryonic form by July 1914. It was but a matter of time before technology could catch up with the military aviators' evolving concepts of aerial reconnaissance and the more controversial applications of airplanes as combat weapons.

The Development of Air-Power Doctrine

The army's involvement with aerial flight went back to the use of observation balloons during the American Civil War, and this had a formative impact upon early views concerning military applications of the airplane. The new mechanical flying device offered an improved alternative to captive balloon observation, which was flawed by vulnerability to hostile ground fire and more recently developed balloon guns.[2] While the airplane's speed, maneuverability and smaller target area made it superior to the balloon or dirigible, its inability to hover over a given point placed greater demands upon the pilot or his observer to gather intelligence rapidly and accurately. As a consequence of this historical association of aerial flight with intelligence gathering, the army long persisted in a narrow view of the airplane's potential.[3]

While army pilots rejected traditional doctrine that restricted military aviation to reconnaissance and artillery fire direction, they nevertheless developed proficiency in those activities. We have already noted their demonstration of aerial observation in the August 1912 National Guard maneuvers in the vicinity of New York City and Bridgeport, Connecticut. The aviator's assistance was deemed to be most advantageous to the ground troops they supported.[4] In early 1913, during field maneuvers near Texas City, an officer in an airplane sketched an eighteen-foot strip map of the ground below.[5] Between January 1911 and the summer of 1915, the Aeronautical Division developed aerial photography and prepared the first aerial mosaic photograph for military use.[6] By November 1915 official army policy recognized that airplanes would supplement and perhaps even replace cavalry as the army's approved method of strategic reconnaissance.[7]

Remarkable success attended experimentation with aerial direction of field artillery fire. Again, there was precedent in Civil War experience. Professor Thaddeus S. C. Lowe had directed Union artillery fire from a stationary balloon, aiming a cannon by messages transmitted to battery by telegraph.[8] Speaking to the 1907 International Aeronautical Congress, Lt. Col. William A. Glassford noted that newly developed long-range field artillery made aerial observation necessary to locate camouflaged targets. In 1910, Lt. Col. George P. Scriven's study alerted the army to the vulnerability of the fortress of Corregidor to balloon-directed artillery fire from the Luzon mainland. Reports from American military attachés in Europe, written in 1912 and 1913, emphasized the efficient manner in which the French army directed artillery fire from the air.[9]

Aeronautical Division airplanes participated in field artillery maneuvers at Fort Riley in November 1912, and extensive tests were made in aerial observation and fire-direction techniques. Radio communication with the ground, developed in Signal Corps laboratories with the aviators' assistance, greatly facilitated communications with rapidly moving airplanes. After these trials, Lt. Thomas deW. Milling claimed that the tests "proved conclusively that airplanes could be used most effectively" in field artillery fire direction.[10] The ease with which communications problems were solved is a tribute to the army's wisdom in locating aviation functions within the Signal Corps. By the time hostilities broke out in Europe, the army and its aviators had made major progress in field artillery fire control.

Aerial reconnaissance and artillery-fire direction flourished in an atmosphere of cooperation between the army flyers and their Signal Corps superiors. Aeronautical Division technical requirements dovetailed with ongoing Signal Corps basic research into photography and radio signaling. This partnership was bearing a rich harvest of technical progress and conceptual development. It was the pride of three successive chief signal officers, and merited the 1915 General Staff endorsement of aerial reconnaissance and artillery-fire direction from the air.

However, controversial alterations in existing doctrine were demanded when the broader combat implications of military aviation were considered. Both dirigibles and airplanes were potential weapons for attack upon troop concentrations, matériel depots, or lines of communication and transportation. Given increased lift capacity, as Germany's Zeppelin program showed, aircraft could be used for long-range bombardment of enemy cities and industrial areas. These concepts required revolutionary changes in army thought patterns.[11] Military aviators differed sharply with the General Staff Corps and their Signal Corps superiors regarding the offensive applications of air power. They viewed aerial combat as a necessary means to achieve aerial superiority. An enemy air arm could nullify aerial observation or artillery-fire direction. Thus, one of the aviator's first priorities was to gain and maintain dominance in the airspace over the battlefield. That could be done only by using the airplane as a combat weapon.[12]

By far the most controversial application of air power was the concept of long-range bombardment of cities, factories, and rail and sea terminals. As we have seen, this alarm had been sounded by novelists in England and it was early repeated in the United States. Actual experience with aerial bombardment — during the Turco-Italian and the Balkan Wars — was reported in American newspapers and formed a focal point of the 1913 Hay Committee hearings. Even more alarming were November 1913 reports that the German war ministry had sponsored bomb-dropping contests.[13]

Since 1910 the Aeronautical Division had been involved in developing an accurate bombsight. Army pilots entertained the public with their proficiency at dropping sand bags on ground targets in 1910 and 1911. The emphasis upon accuracy was a significant departure from the indiscriminate bombardment of troops and matériel in Libya. Even at this early date, American conceptual thinking dealt with aerial bombardment as precise utilization of explosives to destroy specific targets of military value. During the summer of 1911, Riley E. Scott, a former army officer, experimented with a bombsight of his design, using the facilities of the army's College Park flying field. Those tests continued through 1913, interrupted only by Scott's trip to France, where in January 1912 his bombsight was awarded the Michelin prize of $5,000.[14]

There is substantial evidence that the Signal Corps high command encouraged these early efforts at precision aerial bombardment. One example is Brig. Gen. James Allen's May 1910 comment concerning the need for defense against foreign aerial attack: "[I]t is entirely practicable today, with a single dirigible balloon or a few aeroplanes, to destroy by means of explosives, and particularly with incendiary mixtures, *the shipping* of any of our large cities, as well as property of enormous value" [emphasis added].[15] Here one can find the mustard seed from which would grow the shrub of daylight strategic bombardment—that targets should be selected with care and attacked with a concentration of accurate firepower continuously applied. Indeed, the use of aerial bombardment against targets of paramount importance to the enemy had occurred to Wilbur and Orville Wright shortly after their successful powered flight. They believed that the airplane, through the threat of aerial bombardment of capital cities, would render war less likely. For the first time in history the national leaders who declared war would find themselves within the range of the enemy's destructive power.[16]

Two official Signal Corps studies also evidence interest in aerial bombardment even before its use in Africa and the Balkans. A 1909 report by Maj. George O. Squier that small dirigibles might be used to attack front-line troops, suggests the value of close air support and interdictional bombardment. Squier allocated strategic longer-range bombardment tasks to larger dirigibles. Although limited to dirigibles, the Squier report represented a substantial advance over American military doctrine of its day.[17] The other report, written in 1910 by Lt. Col. George P. Scriven, deals with possible aerial attacks on Corregidor. Prepared during Scriven's tour as chief signal officer in the Philippines, it ranks as one of the most farsighted staff studies of its day. Scriven pointed out that enemy airplanes and dirigibles could locate exposed supplies and destroy them, either by directing field artillery fire or by aerial bombardment. Again, the emphasis was upon precise location of the target most critical to the enemy, and its destruction either by field artillery or precision bombing.[18]

Squier's 1909 report anticipated Capt. William Mitchell's testimony before the Hay Committee in August 1913. Mitchell informed the congressmen that aerial bombardment of dockyards, bridges, and storage facilities was more effective than similar attacks on front-line troop concentrations.[19] French intelligence reports concerning the war in Libya, and that nation's growing interest in bombsights, persuaded American army aviators to continue their experiments leading toward precision bombing of vital enemy targets. These new innovations in air-power thought surfaced before the public in the Hay Committee hearing transcripts.[20]

American army aviators approached the question of aerial bombardment with three limitations on their conceptual thought and operational planning. First and foremost, the planes owned by the army and constructed within the United States in the years 1907–14 lacked lift capacity to accommodate a load of bombs, fuel, the pilot, and a bombardier. Second, the United States, as a signatory of the Second Hague Convention against aerial bombardment of unfortified towns and villages, was reluctant to engage in the development of bombardment aircraft while the treaty remained in effect. Third, even within the Aeronautical Division there developed sharp differences of opinion regarding the effectiveness of aerial bombardment.[21]

Aerial supremacy also played a vital role in the evolution of American air-power doctrine. Since observation aircraft required protection from enemy attack, the Aeronautical Division turned its attention to armament for offensive and defensive purposes. Lt. Benjamin D. Foulois's 1907 thesis at Fort Leavenworth argued the necessity of arming dirigibles and airplanes that would precede the ground troops into battle. Once aerial supremacy was established, extensive aerial reconnaissance could be used effectively against a "blind" enemy.[22] In 1910 army aviators began experiments with firing rifles and machine guns from airplanes in flight. Two years later they tested a new machine gun developed by retired army colonel Isaac N. Lewis, achieving moderate accuracy and confirming once more that the weapon's discharge would not disturb the stability of a flying airplane.[23] Unfortunately, the Lewis machine gun fell victim to a feud between Major General Crozier, chief of army ordnance, and Chief of Staff Leonard Wood. Consequently, it was not approved for army use. The only army-authorized machine gun was unsuitable for aeronautical use because its ammunition feed system interfered with wing struts and control cables.[24]

Army Aviation versus the General Staff

Like the Lewis machine gun, the airplane also was enmeshed in intraservice animosities. From an early date in the history of army aviation until the establishment of the Army Air Corps during World War II, there was tension and misunderstanding between the army aviators and the officers of the General Staff Corps. This greatly impeded any rational discussion of army air power, but by April 1914 the scope of conflict had narrowed appreciably. From an earlier position of accepting aviation only for purposes of reconnaissance and artillery-fire direction, the General Staff progressed to limited acceptance of the principle of aerial supremacy. *Field Service Regulations* issued in April 1914 recognized the offensive and defensive combatant roles of military aviation. In amending its military policy statement in November 1915, the army underlined the need to maintain control of the air.[25] Thereafter, the major doctrinal differences between the General Staff and army aviators centered upon the single issue of long-range aerial bombardment of strategic targets. This was the segment of air-power thinking most remote from current capabilities in the years from 1914 through 1917. The lift capacity of army airplanes prior to 1918 was totally inadequate to carry the weight of a pilot and bombardier, along with a modest payload in aerial bombs. Current aircraft in army flying units were also deficient in altitude capacity and range.

Viewed in terms of the Second Hague Convention, army doctrines advocating long-range bombardment of cities raised serious questions in international law. American ratification of the treaty did not bind the army to refrain from bombardment of military targets in population centers, since the treaty included only *unfortified* cities within its protection. In addition, the convention specifically provided that if a signatory went to war with a nonsignatory, either as an ally or an enemy, the provisions concerning aerial bombardment would be inapplicable. Doubtless these subtleties escaped the notice of all but the most careful students of military affairs and international law.[26] The American people viewed the convention as a national commitment against the use of all aerial bombardment, and this reinforced national inclinations concerning arms limitation and pacifism. Considering the poor quality of army airplanes, the nature of American public opinion, and the lukewarm attitudes of the president and Congress toward military flying, the General Staff Corps disapproved of strategic long-range bombardment as a legitimate field for Aeronautical Division planning.

Despite the American public's preference for air power as a virtually bloodless mode of warfare, the General Staff Corps realistically (and correctly) believed that victory was won on the ground. They called attention to the inadequacy of aerial bombardment lest the American people pressure Congress to unbalance army appropriations in favor of an untried and inadequate weapon.[27] Public enthusiasm, followed by hasty army action, had produced the Langley aerodrome fiasco; what might it do now that the Wrights had demonstrated the practicality of heavier-than-air flight?

The position of the General Staff in regard to military aviation was not static. From 1907 to 1915 they moved from "reconnaissance and artillery-fire direction only" to accept a limited combat role to protect American aerial observation activity, as well as to ward off attacks on artillery-directing planes and balloons. *Field Service Regulations, 1914* gave tacit recognition to aerial combat as a means of denying air superiority to enemy aircraft and observation planes. On the other hand, the General Staff was unable to accept as doctrine the use of airplanes for the bombardment of military, industrial, and political targets well behind the enemy's front lines. Significantly, despite the substantial advancement of foreign military aviation during the First World War, the General Staff did not modify the aviation sections of its *Field Service Regulations, 1914* prior to July 1917.[28]

Even within the Signal Corps there was indifference or hostility to the concept of long-range strategic bombardment. Brig. Gen. George P. Scriven, chief signal officer from 1913 through 1916, endorsed the observation role of army airplanes in December 1914, but he, like the General Staff, questioned the offensive value of military aviation.[29] Scriven's attitude dominated the War Department's testimony before the 1913 Hay Committee. Separation of army aviation from Signal Corps direction was hotly debated at that time, and it mirrored the conflicting views of the aviators and the Signal Corps over long-range strategic bombardment. To the extent that Signal Corps officers could restrict aviation to a "reconnaissance and artillery spotting only" position, they were able to assert a claim to continued authority over the Aeronautical Division. However, the disagreement provided new impetus to the aviators' quest for separation from the Signal Corps, and recognition as a new combat arm of the army.[30] Although some pioneer military aviators gave credit to the Signal Corps high command for their willingness to "buck the War Department General Staff on Capitol Hill,"[31] the Hay Committee hearings revealed to pro-aviation congressmen that the aviators did not acquiesce in the doctrinal views of their Signal Corps superiors.

Two other factors created tension between the General Staff Corps and the Aeronautical Division. One was the disagreement over who should develop doctrine for military aviation. As the principal organization for conceptual development in the army, the General Staff Corps claimed occupancy of the field. Yet before sound doctrine could evolve, General Staff officers needed familiarity with the technology and the capability of the airplane as a new and largely untried weapons system. They also needed to acquire familiarity with the technical limitations on airplanes and airships, as well as the relative advantages of both heavier-than-air and lighter-than-air apparatus. Finally, any sound doctrine would have to deal with the conduct of warfare in a new, and third, dimension. The aviators felt that they, as the army officers best acquainted with aeronautical technology and applications, were the individuals best qualified to develop concepts and doctrine for army aviation. They argued persistently for offensive applications of aerial weapons, and, closely related to that view, they contended that control of army aviation by ground commanders would cripple air power.

Even without disagreements over doctrine, the Aeronautical Division and the General Staff Corps would have found themselves on a collision course. Cooperation was hindered by: (1) the close relationship between flying officers and the aeronaut constituency, and (2) the supportive contacts between army aviators and the National Guard and Naval Militia establishments. Both connections oriented the Aeronautical Division, and after July 1914 the Aviation Section, toward ties with the civilian community and the "citizen-militia" component of military infrastructure in the United States. These relationships facilitated access to airminded congressmen and located army aviators within the "Old Army" camp. The "Old Army" dynamic was characteristic of the command situation before 1903 in which powerful army bureau chiefs lobbied Congress for their pet projects, to the detriment of army organizations that lacked similar congressional influence. Undermining the command authority of the commanding general and the secretary of war, the "Old Army" system had not died with the establishment of the General Staff Corps in 1903. Rather, it lingered on until the First World War. Successive chiefs of staff constantly struggled for their primacy over well-ensconced bureau chiefs. Army aviators were plunged into this organizational tempest more by the force of circumstances than from any documented personal convictions. Yet once the Aeronautical Division and its civilian supporters engaged in congressional lobbying, it and they became a threat to the "New Army" and its professionalism, typified by the General Staff.[32]

At a different point in time, it is possible that the chief of staff's "New Army" advisers might have taken a more benevolent view of the Aeronautical Division and its political involvements. But from 1911 to the first months of the Wilson administration in 1913, the position of the army chief of staff, Maj. Gen. Leonard Wood, was precarious. From the outset he clashed with Maj. Gen. Frederick Ainsworth, adjutant general of the army and the "Congressman's best friend." Ainsworth's hostility, in concert with other bureau chiefs, had driven one of Wood's predecessors to the indignity of an open break with Ainsworth. Another chief of staff went to the hospital to recover his health and mental equilibrium. By February 1912, Wood prevailed and Ainsworth resigned from the service in lieu of a court-martial. However, since Wood had been appointed by Republican president Taft, the outcome of the forthcoming November 1912 election cast another shadow over his path. When incoming president Wilson retained Wood until the end of his statutory four-year term in December 1913, it then became clear that the "New Army" forces had prevailed.[33] As long as the Ainsworth affair was pending and Wood's reform programs were threatened by "Old Army" forces in Congress, the Aeronautical Division presented a hostile threat to the General Staff Corps.

The Militia Tradition, the General Staff, and Military Aviation

One other intraservice consideration contributed to the tension between the General Staff and the chief of staff, on one hand, and the Aeronautical Division on the other. This involved the status of the National Guard in army organization and planning, as well as the influence that various State National Guard officials could bring to bear upon the deliberations of Congress. Publicly, General Wood was strong in his support for National Guard and militia training. In 1909 he urged Congress to consider the needs of the National Guard and advocated cooperation between Regular troops and their militia counterparts. In regard to the army's flying activities, the 1912 and 1913 reports of the chief signal officer submitted under Wood's authority were strong in arguing for the extension of flying training to officers of the National Guard, and alternative possibilities for the creation of a reserve flying corps.[34] Under Wood's direction, President Taft's creation of the Army Reserve was carried forth; and it was with General Wood's approval that Lt. Col. Charles B. Winder of the Ohio National Guard received flying training at the army's Augusta, Georgia, aviation field.[35]

Why, then, was there animosity between congressional supporters of the National Guard and General Wood, the chief of staff, who ostensibly had the same goals in mind? The explanation would appear to be in the means each advocated to secure those ends. While Congress wished to see a National Guard directed by the states with a modicum of responsibility to federal officers, the General Staff Corps looked toward a National Guard trained to high federal standards and subordinated to federal policies. Ultimately the General Staff Corps lost this fight, for the National Defense Act of 1916, drafted by Congressman James Hay in consultation with retired Major General Ainsworth (General Wood's nemesis), provided for a stronger National Guard along traditional state lines.[36]

Beyond these training and command issues, the contestants recognized the National Guard as a separate and powerful force in American politics and military circles. The guard was a reserve force subject to direction by Army Regulars in time of war, yet it was also a state-oriented organization that had a life of its own, quite independent of the army. In many ways the National Guard played the same role in national politics that volunteer fire companies did at the local level. A meeting place for men from all walks of life, the guard was a valuable place to garner votes and recruit new political allies. Appealing to civilians with military interests, the guard nurtured the ideal of the citizen-soldier among men who were sincerely interested in preparing themselves for service in the event of war. Guard units served as focal points for military discussion outside the Regular Army, and had the potential to launch creditable and damaging criticism of national defense policy. When "New Army" professionalism began to threaten guard autonomy, tensions began to mount.

The Aeronautical Division was drawn into the National Guard–"New Army" battle through its connections with the Aero Club of America and other organizations in the aeronaut constituency. Before 1914, National Guard interest in army aviation tended to be spotty, but even this occasional attention alerted the General Staff Corps to the possibility that National Guard influence might be mustered in favor of the insubordinate aviators in the Signal Corps. The independence of the guard, by virtue of its state orientation and its civilian membership, cast doubt on whether the guard's support for military flying would manifest itself within the Regular Army organization (thereby supporting army requests for congressional appropriations), or outside the command channels of the Regular Army (through direct appeals to Congress to build military aviation by support of air units in the guard). On balance, the historical evidence seems to indicate that the General Staff was correct in prophesying the future development of National Guard–Aeronautical Division relationships: they would be outside official command channels and the guard would become a counterweight to the General Staff in appropriation hearings before Congress.

State National Guards were prompt in organizing unrecognized Aero Squadrons. Encouraged by the Aero Club of St. Louis, the Missouri Guard engaged in ballooning in 1908. The California National Guard staged its first balloon ascension in 1909. Based on these facts, the Missouri National Guard is considered to be the first American militia unit that engaged in aeronautics. However, the Missouri group did not receive official sanction until 1911, when Lt. Benjamin D. Foulois lost $75 in a poker game with the adjutant general of Missouri, but won that officer's promise to work for federal recognition. The New York National Guard had valuable contacts with the Aero Club of America, but delay in obtaining legislative authorization postponed official organization and recognition until 1913.

The Aero Club of America and its affiliated clubs played an important role in introducing military aviation to the National Guard. The Missouri Guard relied on the Aero Club of St. Louis for its equipment and training. Capt. Homer W. Hedge of the New York National Guard, and also an officer of the Aero Club of America, took an active interest in promoting general participation in military flying. After Hedge's death in 1909, the secretary of the Aero Club, Augustus Post, handled lecture assignments before the would-be military aviators. Lt. Frank P. Lahm, although assigned to flying duties in the Aeronautical Division, found time to instruct his New York National Guard friends in ballooning.[37] When Lt. Benjamin Foulois was assigned to the Division of Militia Affairs in 1912, he made good use of his opportunity to advance the guard's aeronautics.[38] These ties between the guard's aeronautical units, the Aeronautical Division, and the local affiliates of the Aero Club of America were productive of a strong alliance between military officers, militia reservists, and civilian aeronauts, all dedicated to expanded use of the airplane and balloon in the U.S. Army and the National Guard.

The most formidable civilian organization to emerge from this period of militia interest in aviation was the U.S. Aeronautical Reserve Corps, established on September 8, 1910. The organization's parentage was checkered. On one side it was born of the First Provisional Aviation Corps, headed by Mortimer Delano.[39] This group was something of a mail-order aviation organization, and *Aerial Age Weekly* felt bound to alert its readers against what appeared to the editors to be a flim-flam operation. Such skepticism was justified. Despite his lack of military experience, Grover Loening was offered appointment as a major in the Ohio organization. He declined, probably on the basis of comments by Lt. Col. Samuel Reber, who suggested that the main organizer of the Aviation Reserve and its successor, the U.S. Aeronautical Reserve, Mortimer Delano, was motivated by the need to justify his own rapid "promotion." There certainly was evidence to support that conclusion, for Delano, a sergeant in the New York National Guard, had promoted himself to a major in charge of the First Aero Squadron of New York and, through expansion to a multistate regiment or military division, might become a colonel or general within the year![40]

The other line of reserve flying organizations had much more respectable ancestry, since it traced its genealogy to the Aero Club of St. Louis by way of Albert B. Lambert, the respected former president of that organization.[41] Formed in Boston, the U.S. Aeronautical Reserve boasted Glenn H. Curtiss, Wilbur Wright, Augustus Post, Charles J. Glidden and Capt. Thomas F. Baldwin among its charter members. John H. Ryan was its first president and Richard R. Sinclair was the first general secretary. With offices not far from those of the Aero Club of America in New York City, the Aeronautical

Reserve by November 1910 claimed no less than 3,200 members, including President Taft. The group had not neglected the need to cultivate War and Navy Department cooperation. Even before the organization of the Aeronautical Reserve, Gen. Leonard Wood as army chief of staff was consulted and his cooperation secured. When Aeronautical Reserve member Harry S. Harkness began experimenting with wireless transmission from airplanes, the navy's Point Loma, California, Wireless Station was directed to cooperate with him. The spring of 1912 found the Aeronautical Reserve erecting hangers and conducting their flight experiments at the army's flying field at College Park, Maryland. When the Wilson administration became involved with Mexican problems in April 1914, the Aeronautical Reserve promptly offered the services of forty-four aviators to the navy; included in the offer was the loan of twenty airplanes owned by the volunteering aviators.[42] The offer was declined, but the fact that it could be made at all would indicate the strength and capabilities of the organization. The U.S. Aeronautical Reserve was destined to play a significant role in the preparedness controversy of 1916, particularly in regard to the revival of naval aviation which had been sorely neglected after 1914.

There were smaller voluntary flying organizations with a military emphasis; they included the Wisconsin National Aeronautical Society and Signal Corps, and the National Association for the Promotion of Military Aeronautics, established by officers in the District of Columbia National Guard. The latter organization disbanded when its members joined the Aeronautical Reserve.[43] Taken in the aggregate, these associations and quasimilitary flying organizations indicate the commitment that many air-minded citizens felt to military and naval aviation. Like the unofficial National Guard flying groups, they relied upon the Aero Club of America and Aeronautical Society of America for assistance and encouragement.

The alacrity with which military aviation was adopted by National Guard units deepened suspicions between the Aeronautical Division and the General Staff Corps, just as it solidified army pilots in their persuasive relationship with Congress. Whether by choice or under the pressure of expediency, army aviators found themselves strongly within the "Old Army" camp and at odds with the General Staff Corps and the army high command.

The Airship-Airplane Weapons Choice and Its Consequences

Unfortunately, the army's decision between heavier-than-air and lighter-than-air weapons was dictated more by expediency and economy than it was by sound consideration of the two weapons systems and their differing missions. Given the high cost of rigid airships and the shrinking industrial basis to support this technology, the army by 1911 had made its choice for the airplane. That decision ignored the possibility of trench warfare, and the need for stationary balloons to direct artillery fire. It also overlooked the navy's need for aircraft that might hover over a slowly moving fleet, or detect and destroy surface vessels and submarines along the American coast.

While premature and shortsighted, the army's election of the airplane was made with tactical knowledge of the value of balloons and dirigibles. During the Civil War and the war against Spain, it became apparent that stationary balloons were awkward to move as front lines changed, and they also revealed the presence of troops and drew enemy artillery fire. Vulnerability to ground fire, technical problems in air-ground communication, and the natural threats of wind, rain, fog, or snow rendered the stationary balloon of questionable value — until the development of fixed trench warfare in the First World War.[44]

In foreign wars, observation balloons and free-flying balloons continued to play a significant role in military operations. In 1871 free balloons were used to transport people, goods, and messages out of the besieged city of Paris. During the Russo-Japanese War, artillery-fire direction from stationary balloons had been very effective. When Lt. Col. William A. Glassford, a Signal Corps officer long active in ballooning activities, addressed the 1907 International Aeronautical Congress on the requirement for aerial observation in modern artillery tactics, he pointed out that registering long-range guns upon distant and concealed targets would be impossible without high-level balloon observation. In December 1908 Maj. George O. Squier told the American Society of Military Engineers that Zeppelins would pose a serious threat to American seacoast cities, and in 1909 Brig. Gen. James Allen, the chief signal officer, stressed the danger of aerial bombardment and authorized a study by Major Squier to consider the defensive uses of dirigibles against foreign aerial attack.[45]

Army concerns about lighter-than-air attack appear graphically in the 1910 report prepared by Lt. Col. George P. Scriven, then serving as chief signal officer for the Philippines. This document demonstrated the vulnerability of Corregidor to artillery and aerial bombardment from the Luzon mainland. Scriven concluded that under constant attack from night-flying dirigibles, with daytime bombardment by balloon-registered artillery, "most things uncovered and destructible upon this island will be broken to rubbish and the nerves of the harassed garrison reduced to fiddle strings."

Scriven's memorandum was so convincing that, at some point shortly before World War II, a clerk decided that its contents were vital to national security. The copy in the Air Force Historical Research Agency until 1978 bore the classification mark "Top Secret," presumably because American officers in 1940 feared that Scriven's analysis would provide encouragement to the aerial forces of the Japanese empire![46]

Lt. Benjamin D. Foulois's student thesis at the Signal Corps School in Fort Leavenworth was entitled "The Tactical and Strategical Value of Dirigible Balloons and Dynamical Flying Machines." Foulois identified the dirigibles as the most likely aerial combat vehicle, since the flying machine lacked lift capacity and sufficient altitude capability to be effective. He anticipated that airships would contact enemy aerial forces before the ground troops met, and the relative strength of the two air arms would determine the effectiveness of their reconnaissance. Aerial observation would be invaluable, since dirigible reconnaissance of enemy troop movements would assist in planning strategical advances by friendly forces. Mounting searchlights on the airships would make it possible to illumine enemy trenches at night, and thus minimize the possibility of secretly massing infantry for an early morning attack.[47] In a 1968 memoir, Foulois recalled that he was sent on a tour of France as a reprimand for advocating the army's abandonment of lighter-than-air experimentation. However, on August 15, 1913, he complained to the Hay Committee that the army was neglecting lighter-than-air experimentation, since "that is going to be one of the most useful things we will have in the art of war."[48]

Regardless of Foulois's personal views, it is apparent that army aviators' affection for lighter-than-air navigation began to wane as early as December 1907, and that by 1913 there was widespread agreement that the airplane was the aircraft of the future.[49] Chandler and Lahm, both balloon officers before they became airplane pilots, recalled that between 1911 and 1913 the army flyers became disenchanted with their primitive dirigible and heartened by airplane improvements. Unfortunately, this was one time that the War Department seems to have given weight to the aviators' views. As a result, the War Department wrote off lighter-than-air craft as no longer useful for military purposes. Decreased army interest in balloons and dirigibles is apparent from *Aeronautics* magazine's September 1913 report. At that time, the Aeronautical Division had sixteen airplanes on hand and seven more were scheduled for October delivery, but there were only five free balloons and one captive balloon in army inventories.[50]

Once made, the decision for the airplane was irrevocable, since American balloon and dirigible factories depended upon government orders for their survival. When the United States entered World War I, it had no observation balloons and no airships. Worse yet, it lacked any industrial capacity to build lighter-than-air craft, and would find it impossible to procure semirigid dirigibles abroad. As we shall see, the airplane equipment was both antiquated and dangerous, but that situation was due to Wright patent litigation and the lack of congressional understanding of the need for military aviation.

The American Decision for the Airplane

The two pre–World War chief signal officers of the army were equivocal in their support for lighter-than-air navigation. Returning from the 1908 International Balloon Races in Paris, Brig. Gen. James Allen was enthusiastic about Germany's Zeppelin II, which had remained aloft for thirty-six hours, carrying twenty-six passengers over a distance of nine hundred miles. General Allen, even before his European trip, had shown interest in lighter-than-air flight.[51] Lt. Frank P. Lahm's July 1908 recommendation that the army should immediately acquire three airships encouraged Allen to include dirigible construction budgets in his 1908 and subsequent reports to the secretary of war.[52] He also asked Major Squier to consider plans for the utilization of airships. Squire recommended that small dirigibles be used for bombing bridges, supply depots, and enemy forces near the front or near the American seacoast. Heavier dirigibles should be used against dry docks, arsenals, ammunition depots, railway centers, and storehouses.[53]

Yet General Allen was not consistent in his support for airship development. On June 28, 1908, before his trip to the Paris balloon races, he stated to newspaper reporters that if Congress would not appropriate funds for dirigibles, the army would gain a few years by continuing its development of flying machines. In May 1910 he seemed to contradict himself by contending that military authorities agreed that the only way to protect American seacoasts and cities against airships was to build defensive airships.[54]

Allen's successor, Brig. Gen. George P. Scriven, fresh from his Philippines tour and authorship of the report on aerial attacks on Corregidor, also seems to have favored the airship over the airplane. In his first annual report, General Scriven told the secretary of war, "[I]t seems probable . . . that the day of the dirigible as an aerial cruiser is just about to dawn." The following year's annual report, submitted after the outbreak of war in Europe, recommended that the United States continue its reliance on the airplane. The ambivalence inherent in these conflicting statements mirrored British official policy which varied from strong support for lighter-than-air development to a wish to enhance airplane engineering through an official government experimental and manufacturing program.[55]

The American Drift to the Airplane

The equivocations of both chief signal officers may be some explanation of their difficulty in funding balloon and dirigible programs. When their requests for airship construction money were denied, both Allen and Scriven were content to praise the airplane as an alternative. Yet to find the cause of congressional neglect in the actions of the Signal Corps leadership is to overlook a more fundamental factor. This was a time in American history when the United States was only beginning to awaken to its new responsibilities as a world power. The Spanish-American War had been a short and successful conflict that qualified as a "bully little war," but the duty of policing Cuba, suppressing the Philippine Insurrection, and building the Panama Canal were more sobering realities of world-power stature. Despite these demonstrations of need for an enlarged Regular Army, the nation clung to its tradition of isolation behind the shield of the U.S. Navy. Although this was expensive in terms of dollars spent on large capital ships, it was more compatible with the constitutional and popular suspicion of a standing army and conformable to a national strategy that eschewed the commitment of large bodies of troops to ground combat. Emerging from the Indian Wars and garrison duties in the insular possessions, the army itself possessed a self-imposed modesty concerning its status and potential. Of the two services, the navy was the favored child of Congress, and the army was a victim of neglect, if not outright "child abuse."

William Howard Taft's accession to the presidency in 1909 exasperated the already difficult financial situation in the army. His biographer, Paola Coletta, notes that "one might assume that because . . . Taft had been secretary of war, as president he would take special interest in the army. This was not the case. Rather than increasing the size of the army, he wished to economize in government spending."[56] In his budget submitted on December 7, 1909, Taft cut $45 million from the army appropriation for 1910, thereby halting for the entire fiscal year all progress in military matters. Again in the 1911 budget, President Taft made further reductions in the overall military and naval budget, with a net decrease of $53 million. However, this may not have reflected a considered policy against military preparedness as much as Taft's singleminded determination to institute a new form of budgeting in the federal government. The budgets for 1910 and

1911 were predicated upon Taft's advising Congress what "we can get on with," but Congress, following earlier practice, routinely cut presidential budget estimates by 20 percent. The fiscal year 1910 budget was a disaster; deficiency bills were required to continue vital governmental functions. With the 1911 budget, some groundwork was laid for the new budgeting system.[57] These fiscal and budgetary adjustments came at the very time when American military aviation was most in need of continued and substantial support, and when the Signal Corps was deciding the fate of lighter-than-air navigation.

From their weak bargaining position, army chief signal officers found themselves asking for a dirigible program in keeping with that of the other great nations of the world. The magnitude of that undertaking far exceeded the willingness of Congress to fund *any* army program, no less the proposal of a new and relatively obscure branch of the Signal Corps. The third Zeppelin model, begun in 1909, cost $112,000 and was designed to achieve aerial supremacy for the German Empire. By late 1912 the chief signal officer's report estimated that the newest German Zeppelins, with their hangers and equipment, would cost no less than $640,000 each. Small wonder that Grahame-White and Harper surmised that the high cost of maintaining a Zeppelin fleet would be entirely out of line with the additional benefits the airships would have over the cheaper airplane.[58]

In addition to congressional limitations on army aviation expenditures, national neglect of dirigible development found theoretical justification in a flawed comparison of the cost effectiveness of the dirigible and the airplane. Originally published in *Blackwoods' Magazine* for April 1912, the estimates of aeronaut T. F. Farman were that thirty-five airplanes could be constructed for the cost of one dirigible. While that dirigible could carry from five to six tons of high explosives, the thirty-five airplanes could carry a total of ten tons of bombs. In addition, the airplanes had advantages of speed and maneuverability in mounting an attack upon a dirigible. Farman's article was quoted with War Department approval in testimony before the Hay Committee in 1913.[59]

Farman's cost-effectiveness analysis found ready acceptance in both British and American military circles, but naval officers were less persuaded of the airplane's superiority over its competitor. Several writers touched upon the difficulty of accurate bombardment from a rapidly moving airplane, and the advantage of an airship that could cut its engine and drift almost motionless while taking careful aim on targets below.[60] For all practical purposes, the two forms of aerial locomotion were not at all interchangeable in terms of military and naval tactics. The frailty of the airplane, its load limits, and its restricted ceiling made it inferior to the Zeppelin in long-range reconnaissance and aerial bombardment. Altitude limitations of contemporary airplane engines made it impossible for interceptor airplanes to operate at the high altitudes already achieved by German dirigibles.[61] It was pointless and inept to compare the two weapons systems upon the presumption that they had the same military and naval applications.

To recognize the preeminence of the dirigible Zeppelin in the years before the Great War is not to overlook its obvious limitations. The immense size of the airship, which provided it with a large carrying capacity, a high rate of climb, and exceptional operating attitudes, also made it cumbersome while moored on the ground. Surface winds made landings and ascents extremely dangerous. To facilitate ground handling and storage, the Germans constructed large movable sheds mounted on turntables. These permitted a launch into the winds prevailing when the ship was next needed. Size also made the dirigible vulnerable to balloon guns and small-arms fire when it operated at normal observation altitudes, and also contributed to the likelihood of successful airplane attack at low altitudes or while the dirigible was on the ground. Coupled with this was the explosive quality of the hydrogen used in the gas bags, and the development of incendiary ammunition for use against war dirigibles.[62] Even if these weaknesses were conceded, the fact remained that before 1914 the dirigible military and naval airship was the most formidable aerial weapon for offensive attack upon enemy troops, fleets, and cities.

Based on these factors, it can be seen that while army aviators argued for long-range bombardment and offensive tactical use of air power, their embrace of heavier-than-air navigation and their neglect of airships limited, if not completely negated, the validity of their conceptual thinking. Furthermore, the vacillations in statements by the chief signal officers created confusion in the mind of the public and Congress. On balance, however, the decision against lighter-than-air navigation was strongly influenced by the Signal Corps' recognition that no appropriations for dirigibles would be forthcoming. The weapons choice was driven by short-sighted budgeting decisions by the president and Congress rather than vigorous military conceptual thought.

One additional factor should be mentioned, in justice to the political leadership of the United States. While it is frequently forgotten, there is need to mention the extremely narrow federal tax base that existed prior to the enactment of individual income taxation in 1913 and its vast expansion to fund World War I in 1918. Most revenue collected by the U.S. government was derived from customs collections, supplemented by excise taxes on some retail sales and financial transactions. The point is that even if Congress was willing, the Treasury was inadequate.

Diplomacy and the Zeppelin Threat

American complacency about the dirigible airship's military threat was not shared by the other nations of the world. Shortly after Germany began construction of the first Zeppelin in 1898, the world powers negotiated the Hague Convention which prohibited aerial bombardment of undefended cities, and this provision was perpetuated by the Second Hague Convention of 1907. The United States ratified both conventions, but the two major powers with airship fleets, France and Germany, did not ratify. Ostensibly, the United States, lacking the capacity to build any rigid airship, no less a Zeppelin, gave up nothing by its ratification.[63] However, it did lend an aura of self-righteousness to the subsequent American decision against a lighter-than-air construction program. American statesmen could argue that failure to build dirigibles was clear evidence of the nation's pacific intentions.

The pious arms limitations of the 1907 Hague Convention did not assuage the fears of either British or American experts. Writing in the *Daily Mail* in October 1907, Harry Harper identified the German Zeppelin as a dire threat to British security. In the same year the *New York Times* speculated that if the Zeppelin then undergoing trial flights were successful in navigating 1,600 kilometers safely, it would prove to be a most fearful weapon. Philip Crutcher in the August 1908 issue of *Scientific American* informed readers that, contrary to the magazine's editorial opinions, there was great likelihood of aerial bombardment directed not only at troops and front-line cities but also against railroad bridges, railroad stations, and cities to the rear, designed to slow the movement of troops into battle areas. German sources made light of British concerns, terming a Zeppelin invasion of England a "childish idea." Yet that idea caused an acrimonious vote of censure debate at Westminster in March 1909, and by the early months of 1910 British military authorities began to make plans to counter the threat of Zeppelin attacks on the British isles.[64] In February 1913 the *Congressional Record* published a report of the exploits of German commercial Zeppelins. After eleven months of operation, in 1912 the dirigibles had carried 10,291 passengers, operated 308 out of 334 days, and spent a total of 1,167 hours in the air. No life had been lost.[65]

Germany's refusal to ratify the 1907 Hague Convention assumed grim significance, as its Zeppelin fleet grew and increased in range. While both British and American theorists might sing the praises of the airplane, the fact remained that the most reliable and most efficient vehicle for aerial bombardment continued to be the war dirigible of Zeppelin design. No mere paper guarantee, even if Germany had given one, would be adequate to counterbalance the superiority in weaponry and psychological power that rested in the hands of the German emperor.

The Neglected Observation Balloon

Miserly military budgets compelled the army to abandon dirigible development, but shortsightedness was responsible for neglect of the stationary observation balloon. Again, this was not for lack of familiarity or a dearth of military thought concerning their use. The captive balloon, the sole aerial reconnaissance vehicle in the American Civil War, rapidly lost favor in the Aeronautical Division after 1908. In 1890 Lt. William Glassford was sent to Europe to study foreign progress in the use of captive balloons, and he subsequently purchased a balloon for the army that was installed at Fort Logan for future experimentation and use. Benjamin Foulois in his 1908 Signal Corps School thesis mentioned the use of balloons in siege situations and particularly the French use of free balloons to move mail, men, and supplies over the encircling Prussian Army and into the city of Paris. A similar analysis of the value of both captive and free balloons appeared in a 1908 *Aeronautics* magazine article, written by an army officer.[66] Yet Maj. George Squier, in his December 1908 address to the American Society of Military Engineers, did not include spherical observation balloons in the list of aeronautical equipment that would be needed by a modern army.[67] After an unnerving experience with stationary observation balloons in the Spanish-American War, Theodore Roosevelt wrote that they were "worse than useless" in the conduct of the war. By 1903 the German high command had given up its enthusiasm for the captive balloon, principally because of the difficulty of maneuvering it when the ground situation changed.[68]

American Industry and Lighter-Than-Air Navigation

If the American airplane industry was anemic for lack of government orders, makers of balloons and dirigibles had an even more precarious existence. In July 1910 the *New York Times* commented that the airplane-manufacturing industry in New York City had grown from two builders in 1908 to fifteen in 1910, and that there were several agents of French firms selling airplanes in the metropolis. By contrast, there was only one balloon manufacturer — Leo Stevens. Two years later the report of the chief signal officer stressed the lack of industrial firms competent to construct dirigibles in the United States, a theme picked up in the Hay Committee hearings the following year.[69]

The army's procurement of its first airship in August 1908 was to end its dirigible acquisitions, and by October 1912 the chief signal officer reported the deterioration of that airship beyond the point of economical repair. From the very beginning the press commented upon the small size and limited capabilities of Signal Corps No. 1, comparing it unfavorably to European dirigibles. By 1913 it was known that the British had attempted to build a Zeppelin-type dirigible, and that they had failed. An American writer suggested that the United States would also fail in such an attempt, leaving it as helpless before the world powers as the Philippine guerrillas had been against the modern weapons of the U.S. Army.[70]

The dearth of domestic sources for observation balloons and modern dirigibles was to daunt the United States as it entered World War I. This was due to two factors — the decline of interest in sport ballooning, and the failure of the military and naval authorities to maintain a steady flow of orders to the existing balloon manufacturers. This neglect of the industrial base for lighter-than-air navigation occurred at a time when the worldwide industry was receiving great stimulus from foreign government orders for military purposes. In Germany and France the technology of balloon design and manufacture was reaching high levels of sophistication, while the United States placed its reliance upon the airplane, which it also failed to support by an ongoing procurement program.

The "Hot Air" of Public Opinion

Given the lack of congressional interest in aeronautics in general (and dirigibles in particular), the airplane enthusiasm of the Aeronautical Division fliers, and the lack of industrial capacity for airship construction, it is doubtful that public opinion played a major role in the U.S. Army's attitude toward the dirigible. However, it should be noted that newspaper editorials and congressional opinion were strongly against the developments of dirigible balloons for military use. The *New York Times* consistently championed the airplane and denigrated the dirigible on its editorial pages, calling the Zeppelins "bubbles" and suggesting that the dirigible appealed more to the imagination than the intelligence. These attitudes indicate that American advocates of dirigible balloons faced problems similar to those of the French authorities, who also had to contend with a public devoted to airplane development.[71]

Lighter-than-air military aviation also suffered from public ignorance concerning the capability of the German Zeppelins, or the differing uses for airplanes, dirigibles, and stationary observation balloons. Acrimonious debate between self-proclaimed "experts,"[72] coupled with German secrecy regarding Zeppelin developments, went far to convince many Americans that few people knew the true facts about the dirigible — including the army high command and the Signal Corps Aeronautical Division.

Imprecise and prejudiced thinking also dominated congressional debates over the role of the dirigible, the observation balloon, and the airplane. One example of the confusion is the 1908–9 debate over the Signal Corps request for $500,000 to be used for the development of military aviation in the army. Based upon General Allen's observations in Germany in the summer and autumn of 1908, he returned home determined to revive the lagging interest in lighter-than-air navigation. The War Department endorsed his request for $500,000 to launch a program of both lighter-than-air and heavier-than-air flying. After General Allen and Lt. Frank P. Lahm, winner of the 1906 James Gordon Bennett trophy, testified before the House Committee on Military Affairs, an appropriation was reported by the committee, only to be defeated in floor debate by the strenuous opposition of Congressman Tawney and his associates. The essence of the argument against the appropriation was that there were already spherical observation balloons available in the army inventory. Congressman Hitchcock argued in vain that there was a difference between spherical balloons and dirigible airships. Tawney and his colleagues were equally unimpressed by the contention of Congressman John A. T. Hull of Iowa, who pointed out that the army without both forms of aerial balloon was at a severe disadvantage in the conduct of modern warfare. Confusion, more than a misguided choice of weapons systems, determined legislative action in that session of Congress. To add insult to injury, two years later, it was noted in debate that in 1908–9, General Allen had requested $1 million for war balloons. Not only was the amount wrong, but Congress had apparently still been unable to distinguish between spherical balloons and dirigibles.[73]

Congressional misunderstanding was heightened when the army shifted its emphasis to the airplane. During the January 1911 debates on the aviation appropriation, Representative Fitzgerald pointed out that the provision of $250,000 for airplanes was "preposterous." Just two years earlier, the War

Department had been equally insistent upon the appropriation of $500,000 for a lighter-than-air machine — a balloon. Legislative skepticism remained despite Congressman Hull's assurances than in the past six months there had been a remarkable change of opinion concerning the military uses of the airplane.[74] These various incidents would suggest that in making comparisons between the airplane, the dirigible, and the spherical observation balloon, both Congress and the American people were hampered by a lack of clear knowledge of the three forms of aerial transportation. To the extent that the aviation officers of the Signal Corps could give objective guidance, they were ignored as mere army officers or as individuals who had a vested interest in large appropriations for weapons of untested capability. Indeed, the aviators and their senior officers in the Signal Corps (who were not flying officers), differed as to the relative value of the airplane and the dirigible, and enthusiasm for the dirigible and spherical balloon was short-lived after the establishment of the Aeronautical Division in 1907. The War Department's shift of emphasis in 1911 was viewed as evidence of confusion and inefficiency, rather than a reflection of the trend in military aviation that was triggered by the 1910 and 1911 French maneuvers and that had already altered the course of both German and French aerial experimentation and development.[75]

Conclusion

In this, as in other questions relating to aeronautics, American public opinion and official action was to reflect more the heat of emotion than the light of sound knowledge. Ultimately, the dirigible as an adjunct to ground warfare was to prove ineffective. In that regard the U.S. Army's commitment to the airplane was rendered a wise choice by the hindsight of history. However, its attitude toward the spherical observation balloon and stationary balloon surveillance of a stabilized front was to prove an expensive mistake in World War I. When the United States entered the war, it had to build anew a corps of balloon pilots and observers and to relearn the skills of balloon construction. World powers usually cannot afford to gamble on the eventual obsolescence of a weapon system; the wiser choice in 1910 and 1911 would have been to continue development of both heavier-than-air and lighter-than-air vehicles for aerial navigation. Fortunately for the United States, its commitment to the airplane proved, in the long run, not to be a strategic disaster, and its allies were in a position to assist it in recovering proficiency in lighter-than-air flying.

5 ★ Patents, Production, and Progress

   The Hay Committee hearings graphically brought to public attention the fact that American military aviation lagged the progress of European armies. While inadequate congressional appropriations and increasing numbers of army airplane crashes played a role, there was still another
reason why American aviation was in such a sorry state—chronic patent
litigation. Indeed, the casual observer must have concluded that everyone active in aeronautics was suing everyone else for patent infringement.
Charles K. Hamilton, a Curtiss company exhibition flyer, noted wryly in
1911, "A man has to have ten years in law school before he has a chance of
becoming an aviator."[1] It is ironic that Wilbur Wright echoed this sentiment
in January 1912: "It is much more pleasant to go to Kitty Hawk for experiments than to worry over lawsuits."[2]

The Wrights began the outbreak of suits and countersuits, and their
primary role as designers and manufacturers of airplanes was sorely neglected in their singleminded determination to protect their original patent
from infringement. The madness for litigation soon spread through the
aeronautical community, which polarized into pro-Wright and anti-Wright
factions. A wrestling match for legal advantage rather than cooperative efforts for scientific progress dominated the critical years from 1909 through
1917. Arguably the Wrights won, but at the cost of their manufacturing
capability. Military and naval aviation shared with their civilian counterparts
both the responsibility for, and the consequences of, the tragedy of patent
litigation.

The Aeronautical Art and the Wright Invention
As the nineteenth century drew to a close, European and American engineers stood on the brink of solving the problems of powered aerial flight.

Nearly five centuries of ostensible failure has provided valuable guidance, but rising engineering professionalism played a major role in encouraging the exchange of data and the increased accuracy of scientific measurement. Among other achievements, the development of light-weight and relatively high-powered gasoline combustion engines was most significant. The study of aerodynamics provided better appreciation for the lifting capacity of air foils. Yet the maintenance of stability in powered flight continued to elude even the most careful and perceptive aircraft constructors. From 1900 to 1903, several promising experiments were in progress while the Wrights accomplished their major work, but the brothers' closer attention to aerodynamic theory and their precise observation of aircraft dynamics and control were responsible for their success.

As a result of Wilbur and Orville Wright's experiments with gliders, they reduced the camber of the wings (from 1:12 to 1:22) and inserted on the trailing edge a series of control connections that allowed the wings to be warped simultaneously in opposite directions. This control system provided effective three-axis control in roll, pitch, and yaw. Unlike later Curtiss aircraft, which were provided with movable ailerons mounted between rigid biplane wings, the wings on the Wright brothers' gliders and their first models of powered airplanes were flexible. While the idea of twisting wings came to the Wrights early in their experiments, it was not until 1902 that they decided to build the wings with a rigid front edge and a movable trailing edge (every Wright airplane and glider thereafter was so constructed). To supplement the control function achieved by wing-warping, the two brothers developed a vertical tail arrangement which served to balance the forces that worked upon opposite sides of the aircraft while in flight. Thus, they achieved not perfect inherent stability, which they considered unattainable, but, rather, a control system that would easily restore stability whenever equilibrium was disturbed.[3]

The patent litigation cannot be understood without some attention to the nature of the Wrights' invention, which was not a mechanical improvement but the simultaneous use of several control elements to produce lateral stability in flight. Movable wing surfaces were not unique to the Wrights' flyer; nor was the use of a vertical tail. Their application of these mechanical systems did, however, vary from those of earlier experimenters. What was creative and innovative about their work was the combination of these elements into a control system that worked effectively and permitted level flight of a powered heavier-than-air craft for an extended period of time. The *combination* of these elements, and not the mechanical contrivances themselves, was what formed the most defensible part of the Wright patent when it was issued.

Secrecy and Premature Disclosure

While the Wrights were not unaware of the risks inherent in premature publicity concerning their invention, they nevertheless vacillated between the extremes of total secrecy and naive disclosure. In 1906, they asked Octave Chanute to recommend a remote Florida island from which they could make flights unobserved. They also declined to fly in exhibitions, fearing that it would expose the nature of their invention. Their fear of industrial espionage was heightened by an incident that followed the fatal army flyer acceptance tests in September 1908. Shortly after the crash that resulted in the death of Lt. Thomas E. Selfridge and serious injury to Orville Wright, Alexander Graham Bell and other members of the Aerial Experiment Association were discovered in the shed containing the wrecked airplane, measuring the camber of the wings. At the time, Bell was still conducting powered flight experiments with his tetrahedral kite, and the Wrights properly resented this intrusion at such a tragic time.[4]

Of course, this incident followed other attempts by competing aeronautical experimenters to obtain specifications for the Wright flyer. Since these activities followed the 1906 issuance of the U.S. patent, they could have no negative impact on the Wright brothers' legal entitlement. On the other hand, disclosure prior to the patent's issuance posed a serious threat to its enforceability.

One damaging prior disclosure was that of their experiments viewed by Augustus Herring in 1902. Herring was permitted to observe Wright gliding flights at Kitty Hawk, and, based upon the details purloined at that time, he subsequently attempted unsuccessfully to coerce the Wrights into a partnership. As we shall see, it was Herring who later maneuvered Glenn Curtiss and Cortlandt Bishop into joining him in forming the Herring-Curtiss Aeroplane Company, which would become the first defendant in the patent litigation.[5]

The Aerial Experiment Association (AEA), which Alexander Graham Bell formed in October 1907, along with its predecessor experimental groups, played a significant role in early aviation, but its relationship to the Wrights is unclear. Fred Kelly, the official Wright biographer, claimed that it was only after future association members met with the Wrights that they formed the new experimental group.[6] On the other hand, a Glenn Curtiss biographer asserts that when Lieutenant Selfridge, secretary of the AEA, wrote to the Wrights for information in 1908, he "met with a curt refusal."[7] Despite this statement, it is apparent that, either through British publication of Wright data or through contact with those who knew the details of the Wrights' work, the AEA by March 1908 had a very good idea of the aerodynamic principles that were the basis for the Wrights' success.[8] Glenn Curtiss was among the active members of the AEA. It would be Curtiss's innovative approach to airplane design, as well as his work on flying boats, that would provide the greatest threat to Wright predominance in American airplane manufacture.

In January and February 1909, the Aerial Experiment Association was dissolved and a commercial enterprise, the American Aerodrome Company, was established with Glenn Curtiss as its manager. AEA members were the principal stockholders of the new corporation. However, Curtiss's association with the American Aerodrome Company was short-lived. Bell's tetrahedral-powered kite failed to fly in February 1909, and Curtiss joined business financier Cortlandt Bishop and a self-proclaimed inventor, Augustus Herring, in incorporating the Herring-Curtiss Company. In March 1909 Herring-Curtiss announced that it had been awarded a $5,500 contract to build an airplane for the Aeronautical Society of New York. The control system of the proposed aircraft was based upon movable ailerons mounted between the upper and lower wings. Unfortunately for Curtiss and Cortlandt, they failed to investigate Herring's misrepresentation that he held airplane patents prior in date to that of the Wrights. By August 9, 1909, Glenn Curtiss discovered that August Herring never had any airplane patents, and that Herring's only income came from building and selling toy model airplanes. The corporation's precarious legal situation was obvious to all. Shortly after successful army trials of the Wright flyer in June and July 1909, the Wright brothers sued Herring-Curtiss for infringement of their patent. The Herring-Curtiss Company filed for bankruptcy prior to 1911, and Glenn Curtiss continued in business, at first as the Curtiss Aeroplane Company and subsequently as the Curtiss Motor Company.[9]

Although Herring's underhanded activities triggered litigation between the Wright and Curtiss interests, Octave Chanute's disclosure of the Wright control systems prior to the 1906 issuance of the American patent also posed a serious threat to the Wrights' legal position. In the spring of 1903, Chanute lectured on the Wrights' glider control system at a banquet in France. Later published in various European scientific magazines, the Chanute statement hindered the issuance of their German patent, and, even after Germany recognized their invention, Chanute's disclosure was held in German courts to preclude any infringement action based upon wing-warping alone.[10]

Throughout the early years of aviation, the figure of Octave Chanute cast a large shadow — if not an ominous cloud. He maintained contact with most groups and individuals experimenting with aerial flight. In the case of the Wrights, he was the generous provider of data and other information not readily available to them in Dayton. On the other hand, it was Chanute who introduced the wily Augustus Herring to the Wrights and encouraged the brothers to admit Herring to the 1902 Kitty Hawk encampment. In 1909 Chanute admitted this "impolicy" to Ernest L. Jones, the editor of *Aeronautics* magazine. Likewise, it was Chanute who, having obtained structural details on Wright gliders in early 1903, relayed this confidential information to French aeronautical circles by means of a speech and an article in the *Revue des Générale Sciences*. Those facts were used in the future development of French aviation, usually without attribution to the Wrights.[11] Indeed, when Wilbur Wright visited France in 1910, it was generally accepted that he and Orville were Chanute's protegées.[12] Wilbur's agitation at this falsehood was heightened by his awareness of how Chanute jeopardized their patent claims by his 1903 speech.

In 1906 the Wrights learned that Chanute had revealed the camber ratio of their glider wings, as well as the general principles of wing-warping control. Subsequently, in March 1912, the German patent office, while the American patent litigation was pending, held the Wright patent applications null and void because of Chanute's 1903 disclosure. While the German patent examiner later retreated from this position, the German courts held that the prior disclosure of wing "torsion" precluded an infringement action based upon wing-warping. Therefore, in Germany the Wrights were restricted to infringement actions based upon the use of the aircraft rudder.[13] The warm friendship between Chanute and the Wrights cooled rapidly as the full impact of his disclosures was realized.

The Wrights' American and Foreign Patents

The basic U.S. patent covering the Wrights' control system was applied for after the successful 1902 glider experiments. Few inventions faced more obstacles in gaining patent recognition. The March 23, 1903, application covered only their glider control systems. After the patent examiner rejected their invention as "inoperative" and termed the Wrights' twisted bicycle tire box exhibit as being of "no assistance," the brothers decided that professional help was required.[14] Their local attorney, John Kirby, suggested that they contact Henry (Harry) A. Toulmin of Springfield, Ohio, who in January 1904 undertook the further processing of the patent application.[15]

Toulmin's first effort in what would become two decades of trials and settlements, was to amend the original patent application to have its terms refer to a powered airplane as well as a glider. By May 1905 the examiner did concede that the application "disclosed patentable matter," even though he rejected it. A December 1905 amendment produced an examiner's holding that the application applied to a powered flying aircraft rather than a glider. Toulmin had argued that the invention applied to both types of aircraft. Eventually, in March 1906, the new matter was withdrawn, with a careful reservation of rights that might otherwise be precluded from a subsequent application by a "file wrapper estoppel." The danger was that when Toulmin withdrew the powered-airplane provisions from the application, it might be held that the Wrights had by inference admitted it did not apply to aircraft with motors. In patent law practice, the files and records in the Patent Office constitute the principal documentary evidence in a subsequent infringement action. The patentee's admission during the application procedure may estop him or her from offering contrary testimony at trial. Furthermore, once a patentee has been granted a patent, he cannot claim that a subsequent patent on the same invention is valid.[16] Ultimately, the U.S. patent was held to be a "pioneering" patent, and as such was broadly construed to include gliders as well as powered airplanes. In addition, it was held to cover both wing-warping and an alternative control system based upon rigid wings and freely operating ailerons between the wings.[17]

However, even as the effort to obtain an American patent was nearing success, the proceedings in the German patent office were jeopardized by Octave Chanute's prior disclosure. Wilbur Wright observed, "We had been congratulating ourselves that this had been overlooked by them. We fear it may interfere with our being granted a broad claim on twisting the wings." Thereafter, they hoped that the different meaning of "distort" and "twist" might work to their benefit, and Wilbur ruefully predicted success: "I think we will [succeed] unless the German examiner is unreasonable and stubborn." Apparently, he was both "unreasonable and stubborn," because he rejected the application. Toulmin and German patent counsel managed to gain a partial reversal of that decision, but German courts persisted in following a narrow construction of the Wrights' German patent.[18]

British law required that patents be used or be revoked; as a consequence the British Wright Company was established early in 1913, and to it Orville

Wright assigned his rights under British patent 6732 AD 1904. The British government purchased a manufacturing license for £15,000, and Orville Wright received a shareholder's portion of that settlement amount.[19] In return, the Crown was authorized to engage in experimentation and aircraft construction free from the dangers of a patent infringement action.

French patent 342,188 was issued on March 22, 1904. Eventually it formed the basis for Wright Company litigation in French courts against the major French manufacturers — Voison, Breguet, Caudron, Morane-Saulnier, and Spad. In 1920 the newspapers estimated that several million dollars would be payable in settlement of this litigation. For the assignment of their rights to the German Wright Company, Flugmaschine Wright Gesellschaft, the Wrights received 200,000 marks in cash, a block of stock, and 10 percent royalties of all machines marketed in Germany, Luxembourg, Turkey, Sweden, Norway, and Denmark.[20] Securing these patents required expenditure of substantial legal fees, both in the United States and abroad. On the other hand, the lucrative proceeds for license sales reinforced the Wright brothers' determination to prosecute infringers vigorously.

The Patent Litigation

Detailed consideration of all infringement cases filed by the Wrights would expand this study to an unacceptable length.[21] For present purposes, reviewing the principal American litigation will clarify the legal questions that recurred in a seemingly unending array of proceedings which extended well into the 1920s. At the same time, readers should be cautioned that virtually identical cases were being heard in Europe and that the American litigation was but a small portion of all Wright patent lawsuits.

Early in airplane development, there was an American effort to raise sufficient funds to place the Wright invention within the public domain. In 1908 the Aero Club of America launched an unsuccessful effort to purchase U.S. patent rights, and Wilbur Wright indicated willingness to release the brothers' interests if a sum of $100,000 were secured. The arrangement failed when a mere $11,000 was collected within the first six months of solicitation.[22]

Despite the Wrights' initial willingness to negotiate, there is no question that Glenn Curtiss and the AEA on one side, and the Wrights on the other, were well prepared to litigate the Wright patent's validity. During the March 1908 test flight of the AEA Red Wing, Alexander Graham Bell emphasized the need for a complete photographic record, both to aid future designers and to forestall possible patent complications. In July 1908 Orville Wright wrote to Curtiss concerning a newer AEA model, the June Bug, noting that the AEA had used adjustable wingtips, and offering to negotiate license terms. However, once Curtiss advised him that he did not expect to use the June Bug for commercial purposes, the Wrights dropped their demand that the AEA obtain a license. Only after the June Bug was used for compensated exhibition flying did they renew their demand. Bell's patent attorneys entered the picture shortly after the successful flight of the June Bug in July 1908.[23]

Curtiss's success in prize competition during the summer of 1909 triggered the first patent action against the Herring-Curtiss Company, formed three months earlier by Glenn Curtiss and Augustus Herring. *Wright v. Herring-Curtiss* proved crucial to the Wrights' impregnable legal position. Wright pretrial motions in late 1909 asked the federal court to issue a preliminary injunction against Herring-Curtiss, Glenn Curtiss, Augustus Herring, and several others active in the Herring-Curtiss enterprise. Such an order for injunctive relief would prevent Herring-Curtiss from manufacturing airplanes until patent rights were determined. On January 3, 1910, U.S. district judge John R. Hazel, sitting in the Western District of New York, issued a preliminary injunction and wrote a strong opinion upholding the Wright patent. Four months later, the Circuit Court of Appeals for the Second Circuit reversed Judge Hazel and dissolved the injunction on a procedural technicality. However, the substantive basis for Judge Hazel's district court decision — that the Wright brothers had discovered a method for controlling lateral roll and that in doing so they had made a pioneering contribution to state-of-the-art aviation, would set the stage for subsequent litigation. In essence, the holding that the Wrights were pioneers entitled them to a liberal interpretation of their patent claims.[24]

Within three years, Judge Hazel's broad construction of the Wright patent was ratified when further proceedings took place in *Wright Company v. Herring-Curtiss Company*. Predictably, Judge Hazel's ruling again was favorable to the Wrights and most encouraging to their chances for future success. As before, he stressed the pressing need to solve the problem of ensuring lateral stability of airplanes in flight. Conceding that Samuel Langley, Otto Lilienthal, Octave Chanute, and Hudson Maxim had made great progress in this task, the judge pointed out that all of these experiments ended in failure. Even the published theories of Chanute "were not sufficiently definite to suggest the later improvements by the patentees." From the Henson patent issued in Britain in 1842, to the most recent European patents, the specific combination of wing-warping features and a vertical rudder was not present as a unified proposal for controlled aerial flight. An 1868 British patent demonstrated the inventor's grasp of the mechanics of air in controlling a flying machine and incorporated some of the features later used by the Wrights. However, as Judge Hazel pointed out, the "assertions and suggestions were altogether too conjectural to teach others how to reduce them to practice, and therefore his patent is not anticipatory."[25]

Since the Curtiss airplanes used a separately controlled vertical rudder, there was considerable legal argument over the originality of their modification of the Wright vertical rudder which was linked to the wing-warping controls. In this instance, Judge Hazel held that the vertical rudder was an essential part of the Wright invention and was used in connection with the wing-warping system to secure lateral stability. However, in the Wright airplane the use of flexible wings, which permitted the wing angle of attack to be altered (or warped), was also an essential part of their machine. It did not matter that the Herring-Curtiss wings were rigid, and another method was utilized to alter the angle of incidence. "The employment, in a changed form, of the warping feature or its equivalent by another, even though better effects or results are obtained, does not avoid infringement."[26]

Judge Hazel found the vertical rudder a valid subcombination within the overall Wright scheme for obtaining stability in flight. Although it was not identical in form or function to Curtiss's movable ailerons, it was shown by testimony to have at least an occasional use in countering aerodynamic forces generated by changing the angle of incidence of one wing surface. Testimony concerning the use of the Wright and Curtiss vertical rudder was provided by both army and navy aviators, including Lt. Thomas DeW. Milling, who had flown both types of airplanes.[27]

In this 1913 opinion, Judge Hazel again held the Wrights to be "pioneer inventors in the aeroplane art." He observed that the Wrights' "concept was practical and their combination of old and new elements meritoriously advanced the operatives of aeroplanes of this type from which astonishing flights have resulted." With an eye toward the confused legal definition of a "pioneer inventor," he then commented that "even if the patentees were not strictly pioneers, . . . they nevertheless strikingly surpassed their predecessors . . . and are entitled to a liberal construction of their claims in controversy."[28] A pioneer invention was defined as one that covered a function never before performed, through the creation of a wholly novel device, or one of such novelty and importance that it marked a distinct step forward in the progress of the art. It could not be a mere improvement or perfection of what had gone before.[29] Judge Hazel was affirmed by a brief per curiam opinion that expressly held the Wrights to be pioneers. Following this decision, Orville Wright correctly observed: "This will give us an absolute monopoly."[30] For Orville and his sister, Katherine, it was a Pyrrhic victory. Their beloved brother, Wilbur, overworked by managing the patent litigation as well as attending to corporate matters, was broken in health and died of pneumonia in 1912.

Related Infringement Actions against Aviators and Manufacturers

With their success against the Herring-Curtiss Company, which included all affiliated inventors and manufacturers, the Wright interests pressed their advantage in a series of actions directed at exhibition aviators on one hand, and additional manufacturing firms on the other. The most daring exhibition flying usually was rewarded by a monetary prize, and as the aviators' international reputation grew their gate receipts increased. Since the Curtiss firm built many exhibition aircraft and also sponsored its own exhibition pilots, the Wright Company asked for injunctive relief and damages against these pilots as alleged infringers. By stopping contests between European and American aviators, the Wrights incurred sharp public criticism. Denying the American aviation community any direct observation of European designs virtually destroyed the possibility of any competitive development in American aircraft designs. Success in this litigation would ensure the Wright Company a virtual monopoly on all powered airplane manufacture in the United States.[31]

The Wrights experienced difficulty in obtaining service on non-U.S. exhibition pilots, and the Wrights and Toulmin had some serious problems determining which federal courts would have jurisdiction of the cases, since exhibition flyers traveled from state to state. This difficulty was solved by suing the American promoters and sponsors as an effective alternative.[32] However, tactical advantage sometimes is a strategic mistake — in law as well as in war. The moneyed interests that backed exhibition flying, although less in the public eye than the pilots, had a much more influential place in American life. Alienation of this group may have hurt the Wrights far more than minor inconveniences they encountered in serving process on exhibition pilots.

One of the major exhibition pilot cases was that brought against French aviator Louis Paulhan in the U.S. Circuit Court for the Southern District of New York.[33] After initial success in obtaining a preliminary injunction, the Wrights lost this advantage when the grant of injunctive relief was overruled by the circuit court, pointing to inadequate proof that this extraordinary relief was necessary. However, the opinions are important because they addressed, not a variant method of altering the airfoil angle of attack, but, rather, the use of a rudder to maintain control. District judge Learned Hand held that there were mechanical differences, but he asserted that the Wright patent involved more than mere mechanics; rather, it was the concept of obtaining lateral equilibrium through alterations in the angle of incidence of the airfoils and balancing deflections of the rudder to the left or right. As Judge Hand observed, "[T]he invention is not of a machine, it is not an invention of this means of so turning a rudder, but it is an invention of a combination of which this action of the rudder is a part." Paulhan's counsel argued that the Wrights' invention was a mere improvement over the existing state-of-the-art. As a consequence, Judge Hand devoted considerable attention to that argument in his opinion. He conceded that Clement Ader of France came close to anticipating the Wright invention, but he rejected the idea that Ader was entitled to priority. The mere suggestion that a rudder might aid in maintaining lateral control was insufficient. Echoing Judge Hazel's opinion, Judge Hand reasoned that it was the use and combination of previously discovered techniques that resulted in the Wrights' pioneer discovery.[34]

Exhibition flying was so widely practiced that it would have been impossible to sue every aviator, promoter, and sponsor. The Wrights realized that bringing a small number of suits would impel most would-be infringers to obtain licenses before staging their exhibitions. The key element was secrecy and surprise, and this tactic kept the aviation world in suspense. Even when an exhibition group wished to comply with the law, the Wrights struck a hard bargain. In some cases their settlement for an exhibition license was based upon their receipt of one-third of the gate proceeds, and they insisted that their contractual claim take priority over that of sponsors who provided capital to launch the exhibition.[35]

The same hard bargaining went into construing manufacturing licenses. A post–World War I instance of this intransigent stance is the infringement action against the British firm Handley Paige. Although Handley Paige held a license under the Wrights' British patent, it had built aircraft in the United States as well as in Britain during the war. The Wrights sued for infringement of the U.S. patent, pointing out that the aircraft were built in America and not in England.[36] Well before the war, the American Signal Corps, mindful that some of its aircraft were Curtiss-built, asked the Wright firm whether they might procure spare parts from Curtiss without subjecting the government to an infringement action. Despite the cordial and supportive relationships that existed between Orville Wright and the military aviators, Wright suggested that he would not grant such a license. However, if he brought suit and recovered, the government would be able to collect its damages from the bond that the Curtiss interests had posted to indemnify the United States against such actions.[37]

Patents and Production

Even limited investigation of the Wrights' litigation to protect their patent rights demonstrates that this was a costly endeavor. The cost of legal services alone is evidenced by Harry Toulmin's January 22, 1910, letter to Wilbur Wright. Toulmin suggested that a more economical approach would be for the Wright Company to enter into a retainer arrangement with his firm. A retainer of $12,000 per year for the following two years, and $10,000 per year for the next five years, would be acceptable. It would release him to devote most of his time to the Wright litigation. The Wrights rejected the proposal two days later, but the fact that such a substantial sum was proposed indicates that the patent litigation had become a major aspect of Wright Company business.[38] In December 1920 the Wright Aeronautical Company indicated that less than 19 percent of its revenues had been obtained from patents, and that in the years since 1917, less than 8 percent of income was derived from patents. At the same time, the Wright Aeronautical Company asserted that since 1917 it had been the largest American manufacturer of aircraft engines.[39] Significantly, it did not comment upon its airplane construction business.

Preoccupation with patent litigation punctuated the declining airplane manufacturing role of the Wright Company. After 1910 the Wrights seem to have neglected further development of airplane design or control systems.[40] Grover C. Loening, a Columbia graduate in aeronautical engineering, was associated with the Wright Company from June 1913 to the fall of 1914. He left to accept a position at the Signal Corps flying field on North Island near San Diego. Loening's correspondence reflects the Wright Company's failure to provide a flying boat for military use. His efforts to produce a flying-boat design were, according to him, frustrated by Orville Wright's insistence that the plane not resemble that of the Curtiss Company. The Wrights moved slowly in developing tractor airplane designs, despite Loening's advice that pilots preferred the engine mounted in front of the wings rather than behind it. By January 1914 Loening conveyed army discontent with defective six-cylinder Wright engines.[41] Naval aviators were strongly

Grover C. Loening, one of the nation's first university-trained aeronautical engineers. After obtaining his engineering degree from Columbia University, Loening was briefly employed by the Wright Company but found it difficult to work with Orville Wright. He then worked for about eighteen months at the San Diego Signal Corps Aviation School before leaving to start his own manufacturing company. (*Aerial Age Weekly*, February 7, 1916, 496)

prejudiced against Wright aircraft, and in December 1915 Lt. Victor D. Herbster referred to "my old mankiller Wright machine."[42]

Loening earned the displeasure of Orville Wright for carrying the bad news of the Wright Company's declining reputation, but direct complaints from Signal Corps headquarters confirmed widespread discontent with Wright aircraft performance. Col. Samuel Reber cited five military aviator deaths in the Wright C flyer by November 1913, usually through stalling while diving the airplane. Orville Wright and other company officials temporarily convinced Reber that poor training and pilot error were to blame. However, by January 1914, both army and navy pilots were afraid to fly the Wright pusher-type aircraft. In February 1914 Colonel Reber reported difficulties with the long-awaited, but overweight, tractor airplane developed by the Wrights.[43] Aviation executive John D. McCurdy asserted in January 1915 that neither the army nor the navy had any wing-warping planes in use, and that the army had no intention of buying more. Flying officers of both

The College Park Army Flying Field, with a Wright B, Wright C, and two Curtiss planes. The Wright B is the first aircraft on the left; next is a Wright C; the two planes to the right are the Curtiss aircraft. Since the photograph is identified as having been taken at the College Park flying field in 1911, it is clear that Curtiss aircraft purchases continued despite the pendency of Wright patent litigation against Glenn Curtiss and his company. (Ernest L. Jones Collection, Air Force Historical Research Agency, Maxwell AFB, Alabama)

services considered wings constructed on the warping principle to be structurally defective.[44] A half century after these events, army flyer Frank P. Lahm recalled that the Wright C flyer was aerodynamically unfit for flight. Even though it had higher horsepower than earlier models, the engine cylinders were subject to cracking while in flight, and a seaplane version was incapable of rising from the water.[45]

The switch from pusher aircraft to tractor-type airplanes in 1914 sharply reduced the army's pilot fatalities. Nine out of fourteen pilots had been killed in the period 1909 through 1914. In 1914 only one of twenty-nine pilots on duty was killed in a crash. According to Grover Loening, the earlier deaths were caused by stalling. An additional problem may well have been the controls of the Wright C flyer. All of the earlier models were operated with two levers that were widely separated. The Wright C had four levers situated directly in front of the pilot, increasing the possibility of pilot error.[46]

Design defects, coupled with army and navy aviators' growing fear of Wright aircraft, undermined whatever consumer demand remained. There was an immediate reduction in Wright Company aircraft production, and discontent ensued among the employees. Grover Loening had done extensive experimentation with "aeroboat" fuselages before he joined the Wright Company in July 1913. The predecessor of the future "flying boats," aeroboats were of particular interest to the navy, but the Wrights could not satisfy navy requirements that aircraft be capable of flying from the decks of warships and landing on water. However, Curtiss had provided a catapult launcher for aircraft by January 1911, his first flying boat was flown in San Diego in January 1912, and by May 1914 the navy had purchased four flying boats, three of them of Curtiss's manufacture.[47] Shortly after the federal court's decision of the Herring-Curtiss infringement case, Loening received a letter from aviator Ladislas D'Orcy commiserating with Loening that the Wright Company was claiming Loening's early flying-boat designs as being their invention (March 1914). In June 1914 Loening wrote to Lt. Thomas DeW. Milling that he was leaving Wright Company employment as of July 15, 1914. Loening explained: "I cannot agree with some of his [Orville Wright's] policies, and if he is going to run the factory over my head, he certainly does not need me. He seems most unappreciative and is most decided in his views."[48] Loening considered Orville Wright "a great genius, but a troubled one." He chronicles his experience at the Wright Company as finding Orville unable to make decisions and acting indecisively. Still suffering from his 1908 injuries sustained at Fort Myer, Wright experienced great pain when riding in railroad trains and was unable to stand for long periods of time. He and his sister increasingly dwelled on the patent litigation's progress, which Loening believed that Orville had brought for purposes of revenge and prestige.[49]

Knowledge of the Wright Company's deficiencies spread throughout official Washington. The navy's director of aviation, Capt. Washington I. Chambers, reported in May 1912 that "congressmen [were] . . . actually hysterical over the number of accidents," and that aeronautical appropriations were threatened. Col. Samuel Reber reminded Orville Wright that the original army flyer killed Lieutenant Selfridge; the Wright B machine killed Lieutenant Rockwell; and from its 1912 acceptance up to November 1913 the Wright C aircraft had killed five other army pilots.[50]

The Impact upon American Aviation Progress

Successful infringement actions against Herring-Curtiss Company and foreign exhibition pilots like Louis Paulhan depressed American aircraft production and hobbled experimentation and production with limits imposed by the Wright-dominated licensing system. After 1914 Glenn Curtiss and his associates spent extraordinary amounts of time on research attempting to develop control systems that would not infringe upon the Wright patent. This largely unsuccessful effort persisted until the formation of a patent pool between Curtiss, the Wrights, and other inventors, in 1917.[51]

Resolving the legal impasse was complicated by the understandably belligerent attitude of Orville Wright, the surviving brother of the partnership. During the litigation following the 1913–14 case of *Wright Co. v. Herring-Curtiss Co.*, Curtiss interests decided to attack the "pioneer" status of the Wright flyer. This was done through reproducing (with some major modifications) the old Langley aerodrome. Not only had the Smithsonian Institution authorized the reconstruction,[52] but it also paid Curtiss to complete it, and then sent Dr. Albert Zahm to represent the institution at the test. Zahm testified against the Wright interests, asserting that the Langley machine would have flown but for an accident with the launching apparatus. Actually, the original Langley flyer was rebuilt in many subtle ways, but the modifications did not escape the sharp eyes of Orville Wright, who explained them to Grover Loening. Floats were fastened under the wings, but in such a way that the wings were greatly strengthened. The rudder control was altered. A more powerful modern engine was installed, with an improved carburetor. All in all, thirty-five changes were brought to Loening's attention by Orville. Loening characterized the Smithsonian Institution's activity as "something very shameful . . . in American science."[53] Although the testimony had little impact on the pioneering status of the Wright patent, the Smithsonian earned the enmity of Orville Wright for nearly three decades. As a consequence, the original Wright flyer was sent to Great Britain, and not returned to the United States for exhibit in the Smithsonian Institution until 1948. The Herring-Curtiss litigation also strained relations between the Wrights and Octave Chanute, who had advised them against filing the first infringement actions in 1909, and who subsequently gave testimony damaging to the Wright interests. Although the break with Chanute was not complete, Orville Wright, and Wilbur before his death in 1912, were suspicious and hesitant in their friendship with Chanute.[54]

The Wright patent litigation also isolated American aviation from European developments and the exhibition flying of foreign pilots. The experience of Louis Paulhan is indicative of the extent to which American courts protected the Wright position. Notified of the existence of the Wright patents, he reworked the controls of his aircraft to avoid similarities to the wing-warping mechanism of the Wrights. Both of his airplanes crashed as a consequence, but he was still sued by the Wrights for an alleged infringement of their patent. Paulhan's treatment at the hands of the Wrights virtually stopped all European participation in U.S. exhibition flying. Only the good offices of the Aero Club of America secured an agreement between the club and the Wrights, by which they agreed not to sue aviators on the basis of contest appearances.[55] The distinction, of course, was that contests were not commercial in the sense that they did not produce entrance fees from the spectators. However, there might be prizes awarded to successful competitors, and thus a Wright infringement action was possible.

In December 1914, Israel Ludlow, a New York attorney active in the Aero Club of America, wrote to navy captain Washington I. Chambers that the patent litigation had stagnated the commercial development of the airplane in the United States, and that fear of infringement litigation had made it impossible to attract investment capital into aviation. Wright biographer Fred Howard accurately and succinctly described the situation: "[I]n the years before World War I . . . it seemed as if the infant aviation industry was being strangled by its umbilical cord — the Wright patent."[56] These statements, and the general state of anti-Wright public opinion, should not be accepted as fully descriptive of the situation. It is obvious that, for a variety of reasons, government appropriations for military and naval aviation were totally inadequate and far below the amounts spent by European nations. It is also true that the Aero Club, and other organizations in the aeronaut constituency, alternated between condemning Congress and extolling the "progress" of American aviation. Finally, the Signal Corps abandonment of lighter-than-air aviation at a time when German Zeppelin achievements were the greatest, cast some doubt upon army ability to wisely utilize even the small appropriations provided by Congress. Given these variables, perhaps the Wright patent litigation should be considered a catalyst for unpreparedness in the air rather than a fundamental cause.

A 1989 biography of the Wright brothers by Dr. Tom C. Crouch may provide deeper insight into what happened within the Wright Company after the patent litigation. At the beginning stages of the Wrights' aeronautical work, Wilbur Wright seems to have been the moving party, with Orville drawn into the project as Wilbur became more deeply involved. In addition, Wilbur was more outgoing in personality and assumed leadership in the business aspects of their work. Significantly, most of Wilbur's time and energy immediately before the onslaught of his final illness was dedicated to the prosecution of the Curtiss infringement suit. Lacking direct evidence, Dr. Crouch does not speculate on what the death of Wilbur Wright meant, both to the Wright Company and to his brother, Orville. He does note, however, that Orville lacked his brother's restless ambition and drive to succeed, and he quotes Grover Loening's judgment that the falling prospects of the Wright Company after 1912 were due to Orville's delays in decision making and also to his lack of vision. At least part of Loening's frustration may have been due to Orville Wright's refusal to move forward, either on airplane design and production or in regard to continuing patent litigation, until he could acquire the shares of the Wright Company and sell the company to a new group of investors. In this he succeeded, but the Wright Company under new management continued to lose money until 1916, when it was merged with the Martin Aeroplane Company.[57]

Dr. Crouch notes Loening's observation that revenge against Glenn Curtiss was the reason for Orville's behavior.[58] Is it not possible that Wilbur's death, while Wilbur was heavily engaged in managing the Wright-Curtiss litigation, may have caused Orville to blame Curtiss for his brother's death? That would seem far more likely to generate such a singleminded devotion to the litigation than would simple business rivalry. It might even trigger a willingness to sacrifice the profitability of the Wright Company. Family ties were unusually strong in the household of Bishop Milton Wright, particularly between Wilbur, Orville, and their sister, Katherine.[59] Orville Wright might well have focused upon the patent litigation as a form of vengeance, or perhaps as a sacred duty that he owed to his deceased brother. The net result was the same — the Wright Company lost both leadership and business after 1912.

Military-Industrial Complexities and Aeronautics

The decline of the Wright Company was to prove particularly damaging for army aviation. There were close ties between army fliers and the Wright organization, and the Signal Corps had learned not to rely upon Wright indulgence when it attempted to refurbish its Curtiss-built aircraft. The general malaise in U.S. aircraft manufacturing caused foreign manufacturers to solicit business from the army as early as 1914, but the advent of the First World War eliminated this procurement source. Given the litigious character of the Wrights, these solicitations from foreign manufacturers seem to have been left unanswered as the Signal Corps continued its futile efforts to have the Wrights modernize their military airplane.[60]

Close ties existed between the Signal Corps Aviation Section and all aeronautical manufacturers. These connections served army aviation by providing access to public opinion and also by making available technical knowledge of airplane construction. Inevitably the army became involved in patent application, and manufacturers were dependent upon army aviation appropriations. In November 1910 the Glenn Curtiss Company offered to the chief signal officer the services of newspaperman E. D. Moore, in the hope that Moore's expertise would enhance congressional approval of the

Signal Corps' 1912 budget request. In February 1913 the Wrights asked the newly appointed chief signal officer, Brig. Gen. George P. Scriven, to obtain special treatment for one of their patent applications. Scriven excused himself, citing the Patent Office's ruling that only a personal appearance by the secretary of war would justify priority treatment.[61]

Archival records show that the Signal Corps actively followed the patenting activity, with special attention to aviation matters. It requested copies of all new aircraft patent descriptions for study and filing in departmental records.[62] This monitoring of aviation patents was second nature to the Signal Corps, which, for nearly a decade, had been deeply involved in developing and patenting the telegraph, radio, and cable systems that would mark a turning point in worldwide communications.

Army aviators helped the Wright Company in the patent infringement litigation, permitting Wright officials to examine Curtiss-built aircraft in operation at the North Island flying field. Lt. Thomas DeW. Milling was asked to provide testimony at the February 1912 final hearing in *Wright Co. v. Herring-Curtiss Co.*, with a special request that he measure the Curtiss ailerons and describe the operation of the "tail fin" on Curtiss airplanes.[63] This cooperation with the Wrights derived from a variety of circumstances. First and foremost, the army pilots had been trained either by the Wright brothers themselves, or by Wright employees. Secondly, the army began its aviation program in 1909 with Wright aircraft purchases and continued that practice until it became apparent that the Wright Company was lagging behind in airframe development. Thirdly, the connections between the Aero Club of America, the Wright Company, and the Aeronautical Division were close and of long standing.

Naval aviation, launched in 1910, was closely aligned with the Glenn Curtiss camp. At first the connection was dictated by Curtiss's willingness to experiment with aircraft that could land on water. The director of navy flying activities, Capt. Washington I. Chambers, was closely tied to the scientific community and had secured a number of patents for his personal inventions. It was Chambers who was instrumental in lobbying for a national aeronautical laboratory. In this he gained support from the Smithsonian Institution, by 1912 an enemy of the Wright Company in its patent fight.[64] Even after the litigation against Curtiss was under way, the navy spurned procurement of Wright aircraft. Grover Loening, while working for the Wrights in 1913, discovered that Chambers's dismissal was eminent in an interview with the new secretary of the navy, Josephus Daniels. Despite

Loening's exultant report to the Wright Company, virtually no progress was made in designing a Wright-built flying boat.[65]

When army aviation began its official existence in 1907, the Wrights had not yet filed their first patent infringement action, and the Aerial Experiment Association had not staged a successful powered flight. Naval aviation, established in 1910, found itself faced with a sharp division in the aeronautical community. Favored with even less financial support than the army's Aeronautical Division, naval aviators found the Wrights either disinterested or unable to meet their requirement for a sea-going airplane. Glenn Curtiss worked with them and designed hydro-airplanes and catapult launching devices. After 1911 the two services were drawn into two competing spheres of civilian aviation influence. In this they mirrored a schism in the aeronaut constituency between the Aero Club of America, which remained pro-Wright, and the Aeronautical Society of New York, which purchased its first airplane from the Herring-Curtiss Company. Ostensibly the army's industrial champion by 1914 had won the patent battle, but the navy's favorite could claim victory in the aircraft design and production war.

Curtiss continued to produce improved airplanes. After the final injunction was issued in early 1914, Curtiss defendants to Wright infringement actions asserted that the merits were not involved in the case. Consequently, they followed the advice of legal counsel and considered themselves at liberty to organize a successor to the bankrupt Herring-Curtiss Company and continue to build airplanes.[66] Curtiss prospered under an avalanche of foreign government contracts. His biographer claims that in December 1914, Curtiss was the only manufacturer who was geared to mass-produce airplanes. By October 31, 1915, British government contracts produced a profit of $2.5 million, and in February 1916, the Burgess Company was absorbed into the Curtiss Aeroplane and Motor Company. When the United States entered the war in April 1917, the government competed with European governments for Curtiss's output, mainly training planes in the JN series. Having retained W. Benton Crisp, Henry Ford's patent attorney, Glenn Curtiss and his associates followed Crisp's advice and developed a control system that moved each aileron separately. At the very least, this would force the Wright Company to institute a new infringement action. Crisp thus introduced into the Wright-Curtiss legal contest a programmed reliance upon the law's delays. As long as Curtiss could develop new mechanical approaches to airplane control systems, it was possible to reopen the issue of the Wright's pioneering status, and thus gain additional time to consolidate Curtiss control of the market. This tactic also deferred indefinitely the final settlement of the conflict.[67]

The Wright Company was vulnerable to such a delaying tactic. Despite its favored legal situation in the American aircraft industry after 1914, the Wright Company labored under severe limitations. The Wright brothers, and Orville after Wilbur's 1912 death, had operated with a very small capitalization, and their native caution and secretiveness prevented expanding the circle of their financial supporters. The reported defects in their military aircraft suggest that while the brothers themselves were meticulous craftsmen, they were unable to shape their attention to detail into a system of assembly-line production. The willingness and ability of French and British manufacturers to enter and compete successfully in the American market is the best evidence that the supply of American-built aircraft did not satisfy American domestic requirements. In July 1917 Congress deplored the degree to which Wright patent litigation inhibited capital investment in airplane production.[68]

Ernest L. Jones, an indefatigable chronicler of aviation in this period, maintained a running total of airplanes produced in the United States. His statistics for the years 1909 through 1918 are reproduced in Tables 1 to 4. Table 1 graphically demonstrates the rapid fall of Wright aircraft procurement after 1912, the year the deadly Wright C model joined the army inventory. On the other hand, the number of Curtiss aircraft purchases by the army remained steady and increased rapidly in 1916. Curtiss airplanes furnished in 1915 and 1916 were of the "Jennie" types. These were the "Jennies" that met disaster in the Mexican deserts during the 1916 Punitive Expedition. If the 1913 army aircraft crashes demonstrated the obsolescence of Wright pusher airplanes, the Mexican Punitive Expedition's aviation disaster in the Chihuahua desert punctuated the inadequacy of Curtiss's "Jennies."

The navy was consistent in its preference for Curtiss airplanes, as illustrated by Table 2, and in the immediate prewar years, naval aircraft procurement shifted slightly to dirigibles and other lighter-than-air vehicles. However, throughout this period the army was the primary governmental buyer of all heavier-than-air flying machines (Tables 3 and 4). This makes the army's switch from Wright to Curtiss airplanes even more significant in tracing the decline of the Wright Company into a mere patent-enforcing instrumentality. Once army support was lost, the Wright Company languished as an aircraft-designing and manufacturing entity. It is remarkable that as late as August 1911, Lt. Frank P. Lahm could report to his father that

Table 1. U.S. Army Purchases of Aircraft, 1909–1918

	Wright Co.	Curtiss Aeroplane Co.	Burgess	Burgess-Martin	Others
1909	1				
1911	3	3	1		
1912	8	1	3		
1913		3	5		
1914	1	4	1	5	
1915		11	1	8	
1916		74		2	7
1917–18		5,043		21*	

*Produced by Wright-Martin, a firm created by the merger of Wright Aeroplane Company with Martin Aeroplane Company
Source: Ernest L. Jones Collection, 168.65413-12, Air Force Historical Research Agency, Maxwell Air Force Base, Alabama.

Table 2. U.S. Navy Procurement of Wright and Curtiss Aircraft, 1911–1916

Date	Wright Company	Curtiss Companies
1911	1	2
1912	1	4
1913*	0	4
1914*	0	3
1915*	0	2
1916	0	3

*One Burgess airplane purchased per annum in 1913–15
Source: Ernest L. Jones Collection, 168.65413-12, Air Force Historical Research Agency, Maxwell Air Force Base, Alabama.

the Wright factory was very busy and behind in filling its orders. It employed 50 workmen in two buildings, turning out airplanes at the rate of one per week.[69] Three years later, army procurement of Wright aircraft had ceased.

Loss of army support can be directly attributed to Wright Company resistance to engineering and design change; it also grew out of shoddy workmanship that killed army flying officers. Army experience from 1909 through 1913 suggested that Wright planes were underpowered in comparison to those of Burgess-Curtiss, which by 1913 operated under a Wright license but surpassed the original inventors in aircraft construction and engine development.[70] Wright persistence with the "pusher"-style engine despite the safety advantages of the "tractor"-type mounting may have been

Table 3. U.S. Army and U.S. Navy Airship Purchases, 1908–1919

Date	Army	Navy
1908	1	0
1909	0	0
1910	0	0
1911	0	0
1912–16	0	0
1917	0	9
1918	0	16
1919	7	17

Source: Ernest L. Jones Collection, 168.65022-2, Air Force Historical Research Agency, Maxwell Air Force Base, Alabama.

Table 4. Total U.S. Government Procurement of Airplanes, 1909–1918

Year Dept.	Army	Navy	Other Govt.
1909	1	0	0
1910	0	0	0
1911	7	4	0
1912	12	4	0
1913	8	6	0
1914	11	4	0
1915	20	6	0
1916*	83	59	0
1917	1,807	206	0
1918	11,916	2,075	9

*Jones's notes indicate that the figures for 1916 and for subsequent years are based on poor data.
Source: Ernest L. Jones Collection, 168.65022-2, Air Force Historical Research Agency, Maxwell Air Force Base, Alabama.

partially responsible for heavy army aviation fatalities in 1913. Established in position and recognized by U.S. courts as pioneers in the field, the Wrights had little incentive to move forward aggressively in new design development. This is perhaps best illustrated by their correspondence with the chief signal officer in 1913 and 1914. After the army suggestion that they develop hand controls which would be simpler in operation, the Wrights began to

Pilot Al Welsh and Lt. Leighton W. Hazlehurst take off on the last flight of a Wright C flyer, known in aviation circles as the "man-killer." Al Welsh was a test pilot and instructor for the Wright Company. Although the photograph is undated, the Wright C flyers were "grounded" late in 1913. Several Wright C planes were involved in fatal crashes in 1912 and 1913, resulting in administrative action withdrawing the planes from army use. (Ernest L. Jones Collection, Air Force Historical Research Agency, Maxwell AFB, Alabama)

work on modifying their antiquated system of levers. Using army descriptions of foreign control systems, they evolved a new system based upon a wheel and a rim that could control both the wing-warping surfaces and the rudder and stabilizer.[71]

While part of this malaise may have been due to the 1912 death of Wilbur Wright, the success of the patent litigation and the inchoate monopoly it created sapped initiative. Orville Wright was preoccupied in correspondence with his army of attorneys defending the Wright invention throughout the world. At the same time, Orville continued to interject himself obstructively in aircraft design and production, as Grover Loening learned to his dismay in 1913–14. As a consequence the Wright firm's production capacity dropped, and its share in the aircraft market plummeted.[72]

Devoid of substantial outside financial backing before 1914, the Wright Company found itself in a difficult competitive situation, for other American manufacturers could afford to pay royalties on the Wright patents and still turn an adequate profit through production volume. Reorganization of the Wright Company in 1914 was completed through Orville Wright's purchase of virtually all of the outstanding shares. Among the original share-holders, only publisher Robert J. Collier retained an interest in the Wright Company. Then Orville, with Collier's acquiescence, sold his interests to a syndicate composed of, among others, William Boyce Thompson and Frank Manville.[73] Thereafter, the Wright Company belatedly attempted to partici-pate more actively in the mass production of aircraft.

The Formation of a Patent Pool

In spite of one informal licensing arrangement that facilitated aircraft manufacture in the United States, a "patent jam" developed that inhibited aeronautical progress well before America's 1917 entry into World War I. A "jam" is a situation in which the competing interests of adverse patent holders cause a halt in the development of the art and an inflation in the cost of the invention because of excessively high royalty demands. By 1914 the vast majority of the practical inventions used in heavier-than-air flight were in the hands of either Wright or Curtiss corporations. Eventually, the government was instrumental in obtaining the formation of a patent pool, known as the Manufacturers' Aircraft Association. The association was os-tensibly formed by private manufacturing firms voluntarily pooling their patent resources. In reality, the threat of congressional seizure of the patent rights drove the contending parties to the bargaining table.[74]

In January and February 1917 the aircraft manufacturers met and formed the Manufacturers' Aircraft Association, and by July 24, a patent pool was established with all rights to be controlled by three trustees. One of the trustees was appointed jointly by the Wright and Curtiss interests, one was appointed by the small manufacturers, and the third was appointed by the National Advisory Committee on Aeronautics. Revised and redrafted in 1928, the patent pool represented by the Manufacturers' Aircraft Associa-tion became a permanent part of American aviation financing.[75]

As a vital part of postwar American aviation, the patent pool represented a major achievement for the War Department and the government.[76] The controversy between the Wrights and the rest of the aviation industry had finally been settled under the threat of governmental action to alleviate wartime shortages. However, it was a resolution of the patent litigation that came too late to save the United States from unpreparedness in the air from April 1917 through November 1918. Consequently, American military and naval pilots fought the enemy equipped with European-designed and -built aircraft. General Patrick's *Final Report of Chief of the Air Service* acknowledged American technological deficiencies: "When we declared war there had not been manufactured in the United States a single airplane or engine considered fit for use on the western front. The manufacturers in America had no experience in the technical development since 1914, nor in the production of service airplanes."[77] Speaking to the House on July 14, 1917, Representative S. D. Fess of Ohio noted, "The tardiness with which capital launched into investments for aviation development because of the unsettled status of the invention . . . hindered the growth and development . . . [of aviation.]"[78] The patent pool came far too late to help American aircraft production in World War I. Cowed by the threat of patent litigation, denied ready access to investment capital, and subjected to limited and fluctuating governmental orders, the surviving airplane manufacturers were in no position to expand production to the levels required by modern warfare.

Conclusion

The Wright patent litigation deepened already existing divisions within the aviation community. Unquestionably the Wrights and their company were justified in insisting that their invention be protected from infringement. However, when the determination of their competitors — both in the factory and in the courtroom — became obvious, Orville Wright lacked the detachment and the foresight needed to settle the litigation and repair the damage already done to the company's productive capacity.

The patent litigation compounded the difficulties imposed upon airplane engineering and manufacture by the lack of governmental appropriations for army and navy aviation. However, the relatively limited tax base of the federal government prior to 1918 may well have made it impossible to compete with European expenditures in any event. Certainly the strident protests of the aeronaut constituency did not enhance the army's chances for favorable congressional action. The Signal Corps' failure to present a consistent picture of the national security value of aircraft and airship development blunted any effort to rouse widespread public opinion in favor of military aviation.

Ultimately, it would be in the course of military operations in Mexico, and in military attaché reports concerning European military aviation between 1914 and 1917, that alerted Congress and the people to the dangerous neglect in aircraft development.

6 ★ The Goodier Court-Martial

Even as the Wright patent litigation was taking its toll on aircraft design and production, the injury and death of army pilots depressed morale within the Aviation Section and built discord and disaffection among army aviators. Lt. Col. Samuel Reber's complaints secured some belated improvements in Wright Company aircraft, but they did nothing to assuage the pilots' resentment against the Signal Corps' lack of effective leadership. There was also division among army aviators themselves based upon their divergent loyalties to the Wright brothers on one hand, and Glenn Curtiss and his supporters on the other. This factionalism stemmed from those who had been trained to fly by the Wrights, and those who were instructed by Curtiss.[1] Grover Loening, a civilian employee at the San Diego aeronautics school in 1914, noted that banter and good-natured kidding between Wright- and Curtiss-trained pilots eventually escalated into deadly serious rivalry and inordinate jealousy and spite.[2] Still more conducive to dissension was the strong feeling that some aviators were "pro-Signal Corps," and therefore the beneficiaries of favoritism from the nonflying Signal Corps high command. All that was needed to trigger a major explosion from these elements of discontent was a single spark — and that was provided by the Goodier court-martial.[3]

Despite its complexities, the Goodier court-martial is of vital importance to the history of early army aviation; it goes far to explain discord that extended into American participation in World War I. The testimony ranged far beyond the narrow issues raised by the charge and the three supporting specifications. Because the prosecution elected to allege that Colonel Goodier acted with malice, the court permitted the defense broad latitude in rebutting that accusation. In doing so, Goodier's attorneys laid bare Signal Corps mismanagement of army aviation. They showed flagrant disregard for flying safety, and a concerted pattern of misrepresentation, concealment, and deceit, on the part of Lt. Colonel Reber, the chief of the Aviation Section. Testimony under oath showed the pathetic inadequacy of army airplanes, and a command policy of nondisclosure in regard to higher army authority, Congress, and the general public. It was also shown that discipline among the aviators was enforced by the practice of immediate relief from aviation duty, sometimes within a few days' time from the purported offense.

The Goodier court-martial was as important to Aviation Section personnel policies as the Wright patent litigation was to industrial preparedness for war in the air.

Background Events

Seeking a warm-weather seacoast location for army aviation training, the Signal Corps moved most of its flying training to North Island, near San Diego, late in 1912. Capt. Arthur S. Cowan, an officer who later qualified for an aviator's rating under suspicious circumstances, was placed in charge of the San Diego school immediately prior to the tragic accidents of 1913. At this time the Wright B flyer was being phased out of operation, and the Wright C, ostensibly a modernized version, was added to the airplane inventory. The Wright C promptly began its deadly career of killing army pilots. For a time Colonel Reber in Washington accepted the Wright Company's assurances that the accidents were due to overenthusiastic and inexperienced army aviators. Finally, the Wright C planes were grounded, but in the interim, Reber and Cowan were engaged in an effort to minimize the public relations impact of the crashes and to reassure the aviators that the planes were safe.[4]

Ironically it was not a fatal crash which brought on the crisis, but rather a crash that resulted in severe injuries to a pilot, Lt. Lewis E. Goodier Jr., who was a passenger and official observer in a test flight being conducted by a civilian pilot. Ned Goodier suffered painful injuries to his legs, was rendered unconscious by the impact, and remained in a coma for many days. During the course of his hospitalization at Letterman Army Hospital in San Francisco, he received regular correspondence from fellow pilots expressing their grievances against their commanding officer, Captain Cowan. Ned shared these complaints concerning Cowan's flight pay with his father, Lt. Col. Lewis E. Goodier. The elder Goodier was the army judge advocate for the Western Department, assigned to its headquarters at the Presidio in San Francisco.

In response to the aviators' request that he help them with the formalities of drawing up charges, Colonel Goodier provided some legal advice and drafting assistance. Through correspondence, he and the aviators at North

Island prepared and served charges against Captain Cowan, accusing him of fraudulently drawing flight pay, of obtaining a junior military aviator certification for an unqualified officer, and of dishonestly claiming credit for a piloting achievement actually accomplished by someone else.

Following Goodier's advice, the aviators served a copy of the charges on Captain Cowan only after they had mailed a copy to the Headquarters for the Western Department in San Francisco. Despite this precaution, Captain Cowan and Colonel Reber succeeded in getting the charges referred to the judge advocate general of the army. Once that transfer of jurisdiction was completed, the judge advocate general's office found the charges unsupported and dismissed them.

Instead of bringing Captain Cowan to trial, the army court-martialed Colonel Goodier. Captain Cowan charged him with violation of general articles, then numbered 60 and 61, which prohibited conduct that undermined discipline, or which brought a commanding officer into contempt among his subordinates. In retrospect, this would prove to be a grave mistake, despite the fact that Goodier was convicted, was reprimanded, and shortly thereafter resigned from the army. The revelations brought to public attention by Goodier's defense ultimately resulted in administrative censures of Brigadier General Scriven, the chief signal officer, and Colonel Reber, who was also relieved from command of the Aviation Section. The court-martial directed public attention to discontent rampant throughout the Aviation Section.[5]

The Goodier Court-Martial

Convening on October 18, 1915, under the authority of the commanding general of the Western Department, the general court-martial tried Colonel Goodier on one charge: conduct to the prejudice of the good order and military discipline of the army. There were three specifications. The first cited a letter Colonel Goodier sent to Lt. Townshend F. Dodd, a pilot at the flying school. It provided information obtained from Captain Cowan's pay vouchers, and it also advised that more than one officer might sign the charges. Given the aviators' distrust of Capt. Benjamin D. Foulois, Colonel Goodier suggested that it would be unwise to bring the charges to his attention, since he might take them to Captain Cowan prematurely.[6] The second specification alleged that Colonel Goodier, with malice directed against Captain Cowan, sent a letter to another army aviator, Lt. Byron C. Jones, enclosing charges amended to allege that Captain Cowan had not been assigned to aviation duties in his orders appointing him to command the

Signal Corps Aviation School, and thus was not eligible for flight pay. This letter also referred to a ceremonial visit to a naval vessel made by a flying boat, concerning which Captain Cowan filed a report that made it appear that he had piloted the aircraft. Colonel Goodier commented in reply to this incident that "no decent man" would claim credit for an achievement to which he was not entitled. Finally, this letter directed Jones to mail a copy of the charges to Brig. Gen. Arthur Murray, commanding general of the Western Department, with a note saying that the original had been given to Cowan. The third specification was based upon another letter to Lieutenant Dodd, referring to charges that Goodier was preparing against Cowan, and suggesting that perhaps if several pilots would sign the charges, it would show that they were standing together.[7]

To obtain a conviction, the prosecution bent its efforts toward proving that Colonel Goodier had either incited or encouraged the aviators to bring charges, and in regard to specifications two and three, the government's attorneys attempted to show that malice motivated Colonel Goodier. In addition, the prosecution asserted that Goodier's official position as principal legal adviser to the commanding general, required him to remain impartial since, in the event of Cowan's conviction, he would be advising the general concerning the court-martial's decision. Simply put, the charges against Goodier also involved what today would be called "conflicts of interest," and violations of professional ethics.

If the aviators' testimony is to be believed, resentment against Captain Cowan long preceded Colonel Goodier's connection with the matter. The first witness, Lt. Roy C. Kirtland, who had been relieved prematurely from duty as the flying school's procurement, supply, and transportation officer, claimed that Captain Cowan, rather than he, was responsible for the overcommitment of Aviation School funds. Prior to this assignment, Kirtland had been on the best of terms with Cowan, and had been an usher at Cowan's wedding. However, Kirtland testified that Cowan had a very quick temper, and he knew that when an officer incurred Cowan's anger, he was immediately relieved of aviation duty by the Signal Office in Washington.[8]

More to the issues raised by the court-martial charge, on cross examination Kirtland testified that in December 1913, Capt. Benjamin D. Foulois mentioned to him that it was peculiar that Captain Cowan received flight pay even though he could not fly. According to Kirtland, Cowan's lack of familiarity with aviation led him into serious errors in dealing with the aviators. For example, he cited Cowan's demand that Lt. Thomas S. Bowen pay for damages to an airplane, despite the fact that Bowen had been cleared of negligence in the accident. In Kirtland's opinion this showed how an officer who was not himself a flyer could not understand a pilot's natural instinct to exercise care for his own protection. This and other incidents generated discontent with Cowan's leadership, and resulted in a meeting at which Kirtland and Lt. Byron Jones were authorized to draw up charges against Cowan's improperly drawing flight pay. Since they did not know the proper legal terminology, they wrote to Ned Goodier asking that he get some informal advice from his father.[9]

Kirtland's testimony also revealed that late 1913 or early in 1914, Captain Cowan announced that General Scriven was coming to San Diego to get their views concerning his assignment of Signal Corps officers to the Aviation Section. It was Cowan's suggestion that they follow the procedure they had adopted while in Texas City earlier in 1913. At that time all of the aviators threatened to request relief from flying duty as a protest against General Scriven's wish to move the Aviation School to Fort Sam Houston. This would have eliminated all qualified pilots from the Aviation Section. The proposed move was canceled as a result of this protest, and North Island near San Diego was selected as the alternative site. What Cowan had suggested in regard to the general's expressed wish to assigning additional Signal Corps officers was itself a conspiracy to undermine discipline, the very charge Cowan now presented against Goodier.[10]

The next witness called by the prosecution was Lieutenant Jones, who had been given the first of Colonel Goodier's letters when Kirtland was relieved from duty at the school at Cowan's request. It then fell to Jones to continue their task of preparing charges against Cowan. Jones testified that neither he nor Kirtland had any doubt concerning the truth of the charges, but to ensure they were in proper form, they referred them to Colonel Goodier. As one of the eight or nine flying officers who attended the meeting at Lt. Townshend F. Dodd's home in early March 1915, Jones was asked to review Cowan's pay vouchers maintained at Fort Rosencrans. The group had already decided that the best way to proceed was to prefer charges.[11] Finally, Jones testified that he did not talk to Foulois concerning the charges because Foulois was interested in "feathering his nest" by catering to the Signal Corps and getting command of the First Aero Squadron. If Foulois learned of the charges, he would have been frightened and reported it to Captain Cowan.[12]

The judge advocate, Captain Greer, was stopped by the court president during Jones's testimony, and asked to explain the relevance of the questions. He explained that he was seeking to prove that Colonel Goodier's letters made the aviators disrespectful in their feelings toward Captain Cowan, or improper in their conduct toward him.[13] When Goodier's counsel cross-examined Jones, the witness unequivocally asserted that Goodier's letter could not possibly have caused him to disrespect Cowan, because "I had lost that [respect] long ago."

Another strategy by the prosecution revealed a deficiency in the defense's case, but also cast doubt upon Signal Corps procedures. On redirect, Jones was examined by the judge advocate and admitted that Captain Cowan never attached to his station reports any certificates that he was on actual flying duty. Ostensibly, this corrected Jones's surmise on direct examination that Cowan must have made such a certificate, which would be sent to Washington to be reviewed by Colonel Reber and General Scriven before payment.[14] The correction exonerated Cowan from having made a false official statement, but indicated that the Washington Signal Office was either negligent or indulgent in permitting Cowan to collect flying pay without the appropriate certification.

The next witness was Lieutenant Dodd, who had been in charge of the Aviation School's machine shop during the period in question. He stated that a student received aviation pay as soon as he started instruction, and that he personally had qualified as a junior military aviator six months after his first flight. In Dodd's opinion, Colonel Goodier's letters in no way caused the aviators to present the charges. However, the colonel's examination of the pay vouchers that Dodd and two other officers discovered at Fort Rosencrans made it possible for Dodd to draw up more detailed specifications. When Dodd located a War Department special order that assigned Cowan to the San Diego school as an administrative officer and not as a pilot or student, this conformed with what General Scriven had told the House Military Affairs Committee a year before. The printed transcript of the general's statement was reported as follows: "Captain Cowan, also of the Signal Corps, is in charge of the school at San Diego, but is more of an administrator than anything else, but is not a flier; but he never orders a man to go up in the air and fly, so far as I know, nor does any other man of intelligence."[15]

On cross examination by Goodier's counsel, Lieutenant Dodd stated that he had found no record of Captain Cowan flying a plane alone from January 1, 1914, through April 24, 1915, the date the charges were served on him. Dodd further stated that he did not ask for an inspector to look into Cowan's flight pay, because Lieutenant Willis had attempted to get an inspector and nothing happened, and that then-Lieutenant Geiger had been removed in an unfair way for requesting an inspection. To claim flight pay, an officer had to make two certificates: (1) that he was an actual flier of heavier-than-air craft and detailed to aviation duty by the secretary of war, and (2) that he was on flying status, citing the special order appointing him to that status. Finally, Lieutenant Dodd asserted that he had trouble believing that Captain Cowan understood he was entitled to flight pay.[16]

Captain Cowan followed Dodd on the stand, and testified that his understanding with Colonel Reber was that he would do a certain amount of flying, but that the amount of hours in the air would be left to his own, that is Cowan's, discretion. On cross examination, Cowan admitted that because engines were erratic in operation, he did not accomplish much flying in his instructional period. He also asserted that in the year before the charges had been filed against him, that is, from April 1914 to April 1915, he had flown an airplane alone on a straight course for a distance of seventy-five to one hundred feet. He admitted that he knew of no other officer than himself who had been certified as a junior military aviator without demonstrating the ability to turn an airplane in flight. On the other hand, "One does not have to be a professional flier to run a risk of breaking his neck up in the air." Shortly after Cowan's purported solo flight, he received a letter from Colonel Reber, stating that Reber had been involved in quite a row with Congressman James Hay over Cowan's receiving flying pay, and that Reber planned to take the matter up with the comptroller general.[17]

When the questioning turned to the certification of Capt. William L. Patterson as a junior military aviator, Cowan claimed that Patterson's training was unusual since he had been sick for a good part of the time and required hospitalization. When Patterson was healthy enough to be trained, no airplanes were available. However, Lieutenants Foulois, Milling, and Taliaferro stated that they felt Patterson would be able to fly, so Cowan telegraphed the chief signal officer to certify him. The new rating requirements enacted in 1914 by the Hay Bill provided a two-month grace period during which student aviators might qualify under the old statute. Cowan and Reber exchanged letters concerning Patterson's situation, since they wanted to retain him on aviation duty. To satisfy the statutory deadline, they rushed his training, only to have him fail to make progress after he was certified. In December 1914, Colonel Reber wrote to Cowan that it was embarrassing to have a junior military aviator who had no current flying hours to his credit, but "Luckily, nobody has noticed this fact so far and no explanation has been asked." In May 1915, Reber wrote Cowan that he intended to put Patterson in command of the aviation squadron to be sent

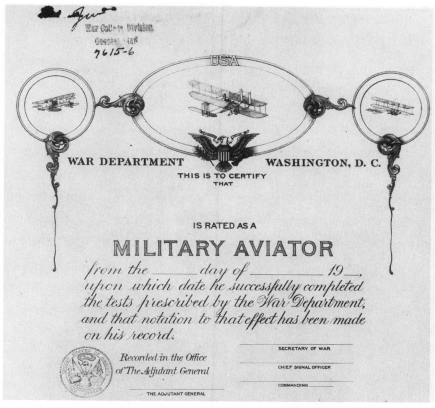

WAR DEPARTMENT   WASHINGTON, D. C.

THIS IS TO CERTIFY
THAT

IS RATED AS A

MILITARY AVIATOR

from the _____ day of _____ 19__,
upon which date he successfully completed
the tests prescribed by the War Department,
and that notation to that effect has been made
on his record.

Recorded in the Office
of The Adjutant General

SECRETARY OF WAR

CHIEF SIGNAL OFFICER

COMMANDING

THE ADJUTANT GENERAL

A military aviator's certification—easy to get if you knew the right people. Before the Goodier court-martial and the army inquiries that followed, there was considerable favoritism in the awarding of pilot certifications. Congress altered the situation radically with the National Defense Act of 1916, requiring that pilots be involved in the licensing process and that accurate records be kept of training and actual flying time. (National Archives)

to the Philippines, but insisted that Patterson learn to fly before he boarded the January 1916 transport for Manila.[18]

In cross-examining Cowan, the defense made effective use of the correspondence between Cowan and Reber, which it held in its possession and introduced into evidence. Much of this documentary material touched upon the charges that the aviators had filed against Captain Cowan, and thus had relevance to the issues before the court-martial. Furthermore, defense counsel successfully argued that since the charges against Colonel Goodier accused him of malice toward Captain Cowan, the correspondence was admissible to show the conditions existing at San Diego, and that Colonel Goodier was motivated not by malice, but, rather, by a sincere concern

Capt. Arthur S. Cowan's "triple threat": Lts. Lewis E. Goodier Jr., Joseph E. Carberry, and Walter R. Taliaferro at the San Diego Signal Corps Aviation School, 1913. It was Goodier's crash at the San Diego flying school that persuaded Taliaferro and others to bring charges against Captain for the welfare and dignity of the army. Once the correspondence was held admissible, the judge advocate demanded that Colonel Reber be summoned to appear before the court-martial. He pointed out that since the letters were in evidence, the author should also be called to testify as a witness for the prosecution.

How the entire correspondence file ended up in the hands of the defense attorneys remains a mystery, but it is likely that Cowan had earned the enmity of enlisted personnel or civilian clerks in the Washington office. Cowan asserted that these were personal letters taken from his private files. The defense quickly pointed out that all of the correspondence was mailed postage free under a government franking privilege — which, if the letters were shown to be private correspondence, would violate postal regulations. On the other hand, use of the franking privilege evidenced the fact that Reber and Cowan considered the letters to be official. It did Cowan little good to protest how the letters were obtained by the defense; they were held admissible and proved damaging not only to the prosecution's case, but also to the reputations of Cowan and Colonel Reber. They cast serious doubt concerning the Signal Corps' administration of the aviation program.[19] Ultimately, the contents of this correspondence file precipitated an army inspection into the Signal Corps Aviation School, and a full-scale congressional investigation was barely avoided.[20]

Cowan's testimony showed that he and the aviation officers disagreed on matters of military discipline. He felt that the pilots considered themselves exempt from the army's ordinary rules. Cowan was particularly disturbed by the banter and rivalry between officers trained to fly Wright airplanes and those trained by the Curtiss company. He felt that Lt. Ned Goodier had taken a leading role in this activity.[21] Cowan described in some detail his difficulties with Lt. Robert H. Willis Jr., who persisted in wearing a "riding uniform" when on duty and when traveling to the Aviation School from San Diego. The "riding uniform" mixed authorized uniform parts with civilian clothing, and was allowed to facilitate freer movement when mounted on a horse. Undoubtedly it may have also been more convenient in an airplane,

---

Cowan, asserting that he took flight pay without being qualified to fly and that he showed favoritism to Signal Corps officers attempting to fly. All three officers had been subjected to disciplinary action by Captain Cowan, who, among other things, objected to their informal "riding" uniforms. The fourth officer, identified only as Reasoner, was not involved in bringing charges against Cowan, nor did he testify at the Goodier court-martial. (Ernest L. Jones Collection, Air Force Historical Research Agency, Maxwell AFB, Alabama)

but such use was not officially authorized. When Willis reacted angrily to Cowan's correction, he was relieved from flying status by the Washington Signal Corps office.

Subsequently, Colonel Reber testified that Lieutenant Kirtland was one of the ringleaders in Texas City during the 1913 confrontation with the Signal Corps high command, and that Kirtland was "considered a political schemer." In Reber's view, when Dodd and Taliaferro became involved in pressing charges against Captain Cowan, "they certainly lost their usefulness if they conspired against their commanding officer. . . . Discipline and conspiracy do not go together."[22]

There is no question that the San Diego military aviators were a most unruly lot of army officers. However, the Reber-Cowan correspondence reflected far more adversely upon their commander and higher headquarters than it did upon them. There was evidence of favoritism. Both Cowan and Patterson were beneficiaries of Colonel Reber's protection. Reber wrote Cowan that General Scriven wanted two Signal Corps officers assigned to aviation duty, William Mitchell and another officer named Hartmann. Reber had "fought this hammer and nail," and the general had compromised, permitting another officer named Gibbs to be assigned in Hartmann's place. However, Cowan need not worry since Reber would make sure that when the new majors were announced, Cowan would be senior to Gibbs in date of rank.[23]

Clearly, it was fatal to an aviation career to be on Captain Cowan's list of delinquents. Lieutenant Goodier fell into this class. Colonel Reber wrote after the young man's second accident that he should be declared medically ineligible for further aviation duty. Reber contacted Letterman Hospital to ensure that the doctors made such a recommendation. Lieutenants Kirtland, Jones, and Dodd testified that it was common knowledge at the school that Captain Cowan was "nagging" young Goodier and did not like him. When the disfavored Lt. Walter R. Taliaferro established a new flying record on September 18, 1914, Colonel Reber wrote to congratulate him, and at the same time wrote Cowan, urging that someone else be encouraged to break Taliaferro's record.[24]

Even more damaging to Reber's reputation was the evidence the letters contained in regard to the disposition of the aviators' charges against Cowan, as well as the decision to let the Goodier court-martial proceed in San Francisco. When the charges against Cowan were forwarded to the Washington Signal Corps office, Colonel Reber was in charge in the absence of General Scriven. Despite his personal involvement in the subject matter of the charges, Reber took it upon himself to begin an investigation and wrote Cowan that "I think I am going to get one or two scalps before I get through." On his return, General Scriven made a personal call on Maj. Gen. Hugh Scott, the army's chief of staff, but General Scott refused to take the Goodier court-martial out of Brig. Gen. Arthur Murray's hands and direct that it be considered in Washington. Thus the court-martial of Colonel Goodier, as well as the potential investigation of the Signal Corps Aviation School, remained within the jurisdiction of General Murray, as commander of the Western Department.[25] Apparently, in the world of Cowan and Reber, riding uniforms were disciplinary issues, but perverting the course of military justice was not. In closing argument, Colonel Goodier's civilian attorney aptly characterized Reber's "pernicious activity" as being "grossly indecent."[26]

Flying-Safety Revelations

Part of the defense's strategy was to emphasize command neglect of flying safety in San Diego. Against the background of frequent deaths in 1913 and 1914, this was perhaps the most inflammatory aspect of the case as far as the general public was concerned. Over the objections of the prosecution, the court-martial permitted the introduction of evidence concerning the state of airplanes at the Signal Corps Aviation School. Lieutenant Dodd testified that new airplanes assigned to the First Aero Squadron in September 1914 already had been condemned as dangerous by the navy, and that the navy's official report had been forwarded to Reber and Cowan. The army's engineering specialist, Capt. Virginius Clark, stated unequivocally that "these machines are dangerous." Although Dodd took the navy message to Captain Cowan's quarters immediately after it was received, he heard nothing further. In subsequent testimony Captain Cowan stated that since the Curtiss JN-2's were no longer at the school, he was not responsible for sending the safety information on to Captain Foulois, the squadron commander of the First Aero Squadron, which had received the JN-2s. Cowan ignored Lt. Edgar S. Gorrell's request that they send a telegram to Washington, asking that use of the JN-2s be discontinued throughout the Aviation Section. Cowan believed that such a request would cause the younger fliers to panic and that, since the squadron was outside his command, he should not interfere with their work.[27]

While these flying-safety incidents might seem to be isolated examples of command indifference, they must be evaluated against the fact that an investigation by a Western Department inspector conducted from February to May 1914 resulted in all Wright airplanes being scrapped. Some Curtiss equipment was condemned at the same time. The investigating officer, Col. John L. Chamberlain, who was inspector general for the Pacific Division, reported to the General Staff that of fourteen fatal accidents, only one could be attributed to mechanical malfunction, and stalling was a common cause of accidents. It is not without interest that the initial testimony in the Goodier court-martial indicated that there was a critically narrow angle of attack in aircraft flown at the Aviation School. Should a pilot depart from that safe angle, the airplane would stall. Technically, this was not mechanical error, but it was a design defect that made flying hazardous.[28]

Colonel Chamberlain's 1914 report recommended that the army secure the services of a qualified aeronautical engineer, and that, as the first step in flying training, officers be sent to an aviation factory for familiarization with airplane construction and design. He also noted that while he had referred specific criticisms to the chief signal officer, General Scriven "answered only in the most general terms." The endorsement urged that the army chief of staff take note of the state of affairs in the Aviation Section, "with a view to the application of remedial measures." Unfortunately, few of the recommendations were implemented, and no action was taken by higher headquarters to rectify the errors in administering the training program or following accountability requirements for government property and funds.[29]

A complaint which may have helped initiate the 1914 Chamberlain investigation was filed by Lt. William Nicolson after Lieutenants Moss Love, Hugh Kelly, and Eric Ellington were killed while making their transitions from flying Curtiss airplanes to gaining familiarity with Wright aircraft.[30] This retraining was necessitated by the army's decision to fly only Wright airplanes, because of the U.S. Circuit Court's judgment in the Wright patent litigation. In the case of Lieutenant Post, Nicolson had reportedly complained to Lieutenant Foulois, the squadron commander, that the Wright airplane involved had a weak engine section. Foulois said the machine would have to be flown, and Lieutenant Post was killed in the subsequent crash.[31]

Against this background of negligence and command indifference, the defense built a strong case against the bona fides of Colonel Reber and Captain Cowan. In his closing statement, Goodier's military counsel argued that "our aviation service is in a deplorable condition; drastic measures are necessary to afford relief. Colonel Shanks . . . recommended a field officer to be placed in charge of the school; that was vetoed by Colonel Reber; an incompetent flier, Captain Patterson, is to go to Manila to command the aero squadron there. Trouble is absolutely certain to follow." William Penn

Humphreys, who served as civilian defense counsel, termed the San Diego situation a "great running sore, caused by a lack of straight forwardness, that threatened to become a national scandal." Not only had the prosecution failed to prove Colonel Goodier's influence over, or incitement of, the aviators, but the prosecuting judge advocate had avoided mention of school conditions much as "the average man avoids a rattlesnake."[32]

The Court-Martial Sentence and Its Sequelae

On November 18, 1915, the court-martial found Lieutenant Colonel Goodier guilty of the first and second specifications, based upon his letters of advice to the aviators. In doing so, they also found malice in his conduct toward Captain Cowan. The court also found Goodier guilty of the third specification, based upon Goodier's letter suggesting that several pilots join in signing the charges. However, the court acquitted him of malice in regard to that specification. Upon the finding of guilty as charged, the court imposed a sentence of reprimand, which was upheld upon review by the judge advocate general, the secretary of war, and President Wilson.[33]

Transmitting the reviewing documents and transcript of trial to the president, Secretary Newton D. Baker noted that a reprimand was entirely justified, and that this was "an essential part of the plan for clearing up the whole aviation question and making a fresh, and I trust a better, start."[34] In subsequent correspondence with Goodier's attorney, William Penn Humphreys, Secretary Baker refused to release the report of the separate investigation into conditions at the Signal Corps Aviation School. President Wilson confirmed the sentence of reprimand on April 17, 1916.[35]

Counsel for Lieutenant Colonel Goodier succeeded in placing the Signal Corps on trial as part of the defense's strategy. A substantial part of the correspondence between Col. Samuel Reber and Captain Cowan was submitted in evidence and survives in the record of the court-martial proceedings. These letters indicate a clear animosity by Scriven, Reber, and Cowan toward flying officers detailed to the Aviation Section from other branches, as well as an official policy of introducing more Signal Corps officers into the Aviation Section. In 1913 Colonel Reber wrote to Cowan that the chief signal officer, Brig. Gen. George P. Scriven, was anxious to put more Signal Corps officers, "particularly Mitchell," into aviation. At about the same time, Captain Cowan warned Reber not to send a new officer to command the second squadron to be stationed at San Diego. He wrote: "[Y]ou will find that if an attempt is made to send an outside officer here to command the second squadron the older officers on this detail are going to regard it as a deliberate slur on them and a positive indication that the Signal Office is not going to allow detailed officers to get into any important positions in the Aviation Section."[36] Apparently Reber preferred to have Capt. Benjamin D. Foulois placed in command of the First Aero Squadron, and had reservations about adding more Signal Corps officers to the section. Both Reber and Cowan recognized that flying officers detailed from the other arms would resent such a preference for Signal Corps officers, and this would increase their support for separating flying activities from the Signal Corps.

In their enthusiasm to position officers of their choice in the Aviation Section, Reber and Cowan were not above bending the regulations. Capt. William L. Patterson was qualified as a junior military aviator after only fifty-four minutes of training in the air and without serving in student status. Most of Patterson's time was spent in the hospital, and for the remainder of the training period, no aircraft was available for use. However, even before Patterson finished his training, Colonel Reber decided that he should command the First Company of the Second Aero Squadron, ready to depart for Manila. As Reber put it, before Patterson left, "he must learn to fly." Unfortunately, that raised a problem, for as Lt. Herbert Dargue would later testify, Patterson would never make a military aviator.[37]

Apparently Brigadier General Scriven was responsible for initiating some of these disruptive personnel actions. In February 1913, Cowan wrote to Reber that if a congressional investigation evolved concerning Signal Corps administration of the flying program, the aviation activity would be taken from the Signal Corps. Subsequent to the Hay Committee hearings, Cowan lamented that the general had apparently failed to learn that lesson. In 1915, Reber commiserated with Cowan about Scriven's acquisition of the so-called Macy stabilizer. He wrote Cowan: "About the only people that I run across who are very keen for stabilizers are the gentlemen who sit around the Aero Club of America or those who never go up in the air in anything except perhaps an elevator."[38] Scriven's initiatives, both in terms of personnel and regarding aeronautical equipment, apparently did not meet with approval from either Reber or Cowan. Neither one was willing to confront the general directly, but they were willing to permit the aviators to try to do so. Lt. Townshend F. Dodd, on the eve of Scriven's visit to San Diego in March 1915, was advised by Cowan to meet together with the other aviators and then ask Captain Foulois to represent them in expressing to the general their views concerning the assignment of Signal Corps officers to the Aviation Section.[39] It would be speculative to assess Captain Cowan's motive in making this suggestion. Perhaps he honestly believed that Foulois would be the best spokesman for the pilots, and it is possible that he, too, wanted to challenge this personnel policy but was afraid to do so. In any event, it is unlikely that the suggestion was followed, because the pilots suspected that Foulois was too subservient to the Signal Corps leadership.[40]

Flying Safety in the Signal Corps Aviation Section

It would be inaccurate to attribute army reforms of aviation entirely to the Goodier court-martial revelations. There was a long list of fatalities or near fatalities. Lt. Henry H. Arnold removed himself from flying for an extended time after his airplane in November 1912 experienced "lifting tail" and almost crashed. Lt. C. Perry Rich was the victim of a similar incident in the Philippines in May 1913, but did not survive.[41]

Worn and shoddy parts were installed in army aircraft, and Aviation Section mechanics complained bitterly of these defects. Grover Loening did as much as an engineer could do at the Signal Corps Aviation School. He grounded all "pusher"-type aircraft, and reconfigured the single plane that was a "tractor" type. These efforts turned back a rising number of fatalities, but ultimately he resigned, probably realizing that the commander, Captain Cowan, ignored his advice and acted without concern for flying safety.[42]

Even when flying safety became an issue of broad public concern, Reber and Cowan persisted in maintaining the appearance that all was under control. Protests by flying officers were resented and suppressed. Their fear of flying under these conditions was ignored. In these circumstances the Goodier court-martial simply provided a dramatic focal point around which there clustered all of the problems of nonflying officers in charge of military aviation.

The Aftermath of the Goodier Court-Martial

Congressional interest in the status of military aviation was heightened by the revelations that surfaced in the Goodier court-martial, and Senator Joseph T. Robinson introduced a resolution calling for the appointment of a joint House and Senate Committee to conduct an investigation of army aeronautics. Charging that the Signal Corps had deliberately withheld information from Congress, and that favoritism was rank in the flying program, Senator Robinson made public the correspondence that had been introduced at the court-martial hearings.[43] In support of his request that an investigating committee be appointed, the senator pointed to the Goodier court-martial record. He argued that the Aviation Section had misused appropriated funds, and that Colonel Reber was devious in concealing his mismanagement and misdoings from the War Department. Military aviators were being killed, a majority of them at the San Diego flying school, where the antiquated biplanes were both defective and dangerous. Command "incompetence and indifference had added to the dangers inherent in aviation." Following this impassioned plea, the Senate passed his resolution, but it was defeated in the House of Representatives.[44]

Although congressional action was delayed, the army did not allow the situation to lie fallow. Instead, it took the initiative to preclude the threatened legislative inquiry. On February 12, 1916, the army chief of staff, Maj. Gen. Hugh L. Scott, instructed the adjutant general to convene a board to look into matters raised by the Goodier court-martial. This was a high-level board composed of the adjutant general, the army inspector general, the president of the Army War College, and a recorder.[45] Apparently sufficient information was developed to support subsequent command action against Brigadier General Scriven, the chief signal officer, and Lt. Col. Samuel Reber. In mid-April 1916, Secretary of War Newton Baker announced that General Scriven had been censured for failing to personally supervise the administration of discipline in the Signal Corps. Colonel Reber was censured for expressing disrespect to a coordinate branch of the government, for failure to observe the legal procedures in personnel and pay matters, and for failure to keep General Scriven informed. Reber was also relieved from command of the Aviation Section of the Signal Corps. He was replaced by Lt. Col. George O. Squier, recently recalled from duties as military attaché in London, so that he might lead a reorganization of the Aviation Section.[46] Captain Cowan transferred out of the Aviation Section in 1916; Captain Patterson served in the Aviation Section throughout the First World War, and transferred out in 1919.[47]

The Kennedy Committee

To its credit, the army persisted even beyond the censure of Scriven and Reber. On April 24, 1916, the secretary of war directed that a General Staff committee be appointed under the chairmanship of Col. Charles W. Kennedy. The committee was to make a thorough study of the organization and administration of the Aviation Section, with special attention to the course of instruction and administration of the San Diego aviation school. In addition, the Kennedy Committee was directed to consider what reorganization might be appropriate for both the aviation school and the aero squadrons. At the Kennedy Committee's request, General Scriven appointed Lt.

Thomas DeW. Milling to serve as a committee consultant from the Aviation Section.[48]

Milling's appointment was criticized by Capt. Benjamin D. Foulois, who pointed out to the Kennedy Committee that Milling had not served with an aero squadron in the field, and that his views on organization should not be relied upon by the committee. Of the twenty-three aviators then on flying duty, twenty-one favored separation from the Signal Corps. Only Milling and Capt. William L. Patterson opposed separation. Foulois proposed that he be permitted to gather information from the officers who advocated separation. Replying to Foulois's suggestion, committee member Maj. John Palmer observed that since "it may not be the policy of the War Department to recommend such a separation at this time," the advocates of separation might be wise to draft an alternative plan for the best organization obtainable without separation from the Signal Corps. The committee had already received a proposed reorganization plan drawn by Lieutenant Byron C. Jones, and that plan was based upon separation from the Signal Corps. Two weeks later Foulois assured Palmer that he and the other twenty flying officers endorsed the plan prepared by Jones.[49]

The Kennedy Committee's investigations ranged widely, and both military aviators and civilian pilots submitted testimony. Lt. Herbert Dargue informed the committee that the commanding officer of a flying unit should be a flyer himself. Dargue also advocated the airplane as an economical alternative to dirigibles, and he argued that the United States needed to develop battle planes since foreign nations had combat aircraft that carried as many as four machine guns each. Lieutenant Milling urged a change in authorization of flight pay that would permit that pay to continue in the event of a flight-related injury. The Aeronautical Society of America's president urged the formation of an aviation reserve, and criticized the government for failing to support the airplane-manufacturing industry through its military and naval appropriations.[50]

A First Aero Squadron board of officers submitted a proposal for organizational change in the Aviation Service, and a training curriculum for the aviation school. The pilots recommended that primary training deal with the practical side of flying, motor instruction, airplane construction, and activities designed to eliminate the unfit and unsatisfactory from the flying program. The advanced course should include aerodynamics, construction and repair of airplanes, motor instruction, aerial topography, photography, meteorology, radio telegraphy, and aerial navigation.

A letter from Capt. Roy C. Kirtland to Colonel Kennedy emphasized the cost of poor equipment and inadequate leadership: of all the officers trained as pilots from 1911 to August 1915, 58 percent had been lost, either by death or withdrawal from flying duties. Kirtland commented that the aviation school barely produced enough aviators to meet the attrition rate.[51]

The Kennedy Committee reported that "the full development of an effective aviation service is to be secured only by forming what would practically be a new and separate arm of the service, free to draw upon the whole Army for its commissioned personnel." They pointed out that this was the practice of all the belligerent nations in the World War, and asked whether they should study such a reorganization.[52] Drawing upon reports from France concerning the successful defense of the Verdun fortress, the Kennedy Committee urged that an aerial component was required for reconnaissance, for artillery-fire direction, for aerial bombardment, and for aerial combat. They stressed the need to develop the necessary types of military aircraft, as well as the urgency of creating National Guard and other reserve units that could augment regular army aviation in time of war. Finally, they called for a central agency to direct aviation and to serve as a technical and command center reporting to the chief of staff and the secretary of war. In the opinion of the committee, "military aviation . . . can no longer be considered a minor auxiliary service. It is a new military arm, capable of decisive influence in war. . . . The development of an aviation service . . . involves the perfection of a new art, the training of a new military personnel and the development of a new engine of war practically all at once."[53]

The Kennedy Committee report was transmitted to the secretary of war, Newton D. Baker, with Maj. Gen. Tasker H. Bliss's tart comment that the committee had improperly considered the unofficial letters it received from the flying officers, and it undoubtedly was influenced by them. According to Bliss, documents submitted in connection with a previous investigation (presumably the Chamberlain inquiry of 1914) showed a spirit of insubordination among these officers. While they were influenced by a wish for improvement in the service, they were also motivated by a desire for personal aggrandizement. Much of their criticism, Bliss argued, dealt with matters that would have been resolved no differently if the Aviation Section had been separate from the Signal Corps. He concluded that the chief of the Aviation Section should be in absolute charge of its activities, subject only to the disapproval of the secretary of war or the chief of staff. This last recommendation was approved personally by Secretary Baker on July 10, 1916.[54]

When he wrote his endorsement, Bliss was assistant chief of staff of the army. A career officer with little sympathy for the military aviators, he criticized the Kennedy Committee for its willingness to consider unofficial letters from the aviators and civilian aeronauts. He was particularly incensed by the Aviation Section officers communicating directly with members of Congress, and recommended to the secretary of war that any similar activities in the future should result in immediate removal from aviation duty.[55] Of course General Bliss did not speak for the army, but his comments on the Kennedy report suggests that the army's commanding generals were rapidly losing patience, not only with the Signal Corps but also with military pilots who acted in an undisciplined and, by New Army standards, an insubordinate manner.

Ostensibly, the Kennedy Committee failed to obtain any significant change in the Aviation Section. However, the independence accorded to the incoming chief of the Aviation Section, Lt. Col. George O. Squier, meant that Signal Corps influence in the section would be sharply reduced.[56]

Longtime Personnel Implications

While in 1916 the army faced the difficult task of "making a new start" in aviation, as Secretary Baker phrased it, there were perhaps even more lasting manifestations of the troubles at the aviation school and in military aeronautics. Although the 1918 squabble between Benjamin D. Foulois and William Mitchell was doubtless exasperated by personality differences, its origins may well have been the chronic suspicions between Signal Corps aviators and other fliers detailed from line regiments.

During the Goodier court-martial, it became known that Foulois was considered to be an officer who curried favor with the Signal Corps office in Washington. William "Billy" Mitchell, fresh from success as the Signal Corps officer who established telegraph service in Alaska, had been handpicked by General Scriven for aviation duty prior to the inception of the Goodier court-martial. However, Foulois eventually took a prominent pro-separation and anti–Signal Corps position during the Kennedy Committee investigation. Then on service with the General Staff, Mitchell had supported continued Signal Corps supervision in 1914, and probably continued to do so in 1916.[57]

Following a brief time as assistant chief of the Aviation Section, Mitchell went to Europe in April 1917 as an attaché in Paris, and there studied the aeronautical activities of the Allied powers. Once war was declared, General Pershing arrived in France and established his headquarters with Maj. Townshend F. Dodd as the Air Service officer on his staff. In June 1917 veteran aviator Dodd was replaced by Maj. Billy Mitchell, who had only recently been awarded pilot's wings. Mitchell remained on Pershing's staff until November 30, 1917, when Brigadier General Foulois was appointed chief of Air Service, AEF.[58]

Foulois later recalled that while he expected some lack of organization, he was not ready for the chaos that characterized the Air Service in France. More disruption would occur when General Pershing appointed Maj. Gen. Mason Patrick, an Engineer Corps officer, to be his chief of Air Service, and placed Foulois in the principal combat position as chief of Air Service, First Army. Since this was Mitchell's position, Mitchell became chief of Air Service, First Brigade, and he and Foulois were forced to work together. Tempers flared and matters came to a head in late May and early June 1918. Foulois wrote to General Pershing that when he arrived to relieve Mitchell as chief of Air Service, Zone of Advance, Mitchell raged incoherently, refused to surrender his desk, and would not assist Foulois in learning the office routines. According to Foulois, "[Mitchell] is either mentally unfitted for further field service, or is incapable of working with me," and he recommended Mitchell's relief from duty. An inspector general's report suggested that Mitchell's position in the table of organization was redundant, and there were indications that his aggressiveness had caused much disarray in the newly constituted AEF Air Service. On the other hand, both the inspector and the unit commanders noted Mitchell's ability as a combat commander. Pershing ignored Foulois's suggestion and followed the inspector's recommendations. Foulois was assigned to a support command position in October 1918, and Mitchell was given command as chief of Air Service, Zone of Advance.[59]

Maj. Gen. Mason Patrick, after presiding over the May-to-July Foulois-Mitchell squabbles, attributed the difficulty to a clash of personalities. He saw Mitchell as "very likeable and [a man of] ability, his ego is highly developed and he has an undoubted love for the limelight, a desire to be in the public eye. He is forceful, aggressive, spectacular. He has a better knowledge of the tactics of air fighting than any man in the country."[60] Mitchell was the son of a U.S. senator, and Foulois claimed that he was not only photogenic, but also curried favor with newspaper reporters by condemning people in high places. In contrast, Foulois was a veteran of enlisted service who felt that Mitchell suffered from a lack of adequate enlisted service, which would have saved him from his later difficulties and court-martial.[61] When Foulois arrived in France with his staff, Mitchell confided to his memoirs that "a more incompetent lot of air warriors had never arrived in the zone of active military operations since the war began." Foulois, on the other hand, found the Air Service delegation in "complete chaos" when he arrived, Mitchell talking incessantly about huge aviation units dedicated to attacking deeply into enemy territory, and ignoring the lack of planes and men required to launch any sort of aerial operations.[62]

Some interesting factors in the Mitchell-Foulois imbroglio suggest this may have been the tip of a much larger iceberg of discontent in the Air Service. In Mitchell's *Memoirs*, he mentions that Col. Raynal C. Bolling was removed from virtually all of his duties by Foulois. Bolling was a civilian with management experience in aircraft manufacturing; he was commissioned directly into the Air Service at the outbreak of the war. Mitchell felt that "temporary," that is, nonregular officers, were superior to regular army men for the command of air units.[63] Townshend F. Dodd, a veteran flying officer, was in charge of the Air Service briefly before Foulois's arrival, and Pershing urged Foulois to join AEF headquarters quickly because Dodd was being given trouble by Mitchell.[64] In February 1918 Mitchell quarreled with veteran Air Service officer and championship balloonist Col. Frank P. Lahm. Lahm was a regular line officer detailed to the Signal Corps for aviation work. During the early months of American participation in the war, Lahm commanded the balloon section, and he would later be chief of Air Service for the U.S. Second Army. His quarrel with Mitchell occurred when Mitchell refused to permit Lahm to issue orders to balloonists in the Zone of Advance.[65]

The difficulty very likely was far more widespread than a simple personality clash between Foulois and Mitchell. Rather, there was a deeply divisive line between two or more factions within the Air Service. Given the testimony at the Goodier court-martial, it is apparent that in the prewar period there was tension between officers commissioned in the Signal Corps (like Billy Mitchell) and line officers (like Benjamin Foulois, Townshend Dodd, and Frank Lahm) who were assigned to aviation duties but subject to certain disadvantages.

Among the most significant problems confronting line officers was the requirement that they return to their units periodically. This "Manchu law" had been enacted in 1901 to limit the assignment of line officers to certain staff offices, including the Signal Corps.[66] Apparently, it was feared that junior officers assigned to Washington duty would scheme to remain in the seat of government, hoping to advance their careers through political contacts. For this reason, the Manchu law provided that line officers detailed to certain staff agencies, including the Signal Corps, return to their regiments after four years. Prior to the enactment of the Hay Bill in 1914, aviation officers detailed from the line were limited to a four-year tour, and were precluded from reassignment before serving two years in their line regiment.

Officers commissioned in the Signal Corps, on the other hand, did not have to serve regimental assignments, but as permanent staff personnel might remain on flying status indefinitely. While they might be assigned to Signal Corps field agencies outside the Washington area, those duties might be closely related to aviation, or involve piloting aircraft. Breaks in aviation work meant that piloting skills were lost by the line officers, and if no flying fields were accessible to the regimental assignment, flight pay lapsed.

Given the complex interrelationships that existed between the army aviators and various reserve components, personal networks were established by army aviators with National Guard leaders and members of Congress interested in army and aviation matters. This was certainly true of Foulois. Several of his assignments outside the Aviation Section were with the Directorate of Militia Affairs, the predecessor of the National Guard Bureau. In addition, as we have noted, Foulois developed a close friendship with Congressman James Hay, the influential chairman of the House Military Affairs Committee. Without exhaustive study of the backgrounds and contacts of all Air Service officers, it is impossible to tell how these contacts might have been the basis for factions and animosity within the Air Service. What we can say with certainty is that Mitchell was well situated to become a lightning rod for discontent and controversy within the ranks.[67]

In his biography of Billy Mitchell, General Hurley makes the valid comment that if Pershing had been able, he would probably have removed both Foulois and Mitchell from command positions.[68] The difficulty in doing so involved the scarcity of senior officers with an aviation background. Prior to 1916, only unmarried lieutenants under the age of thirty were eligible for flying duty.[69] This not only restricted the time that officers could serve as aviators, but it also deprived the Aviation Section and Air Service of pilots who were both mature in age and experienced in flying. Temporary promotion to higher rank when World War I was declared did not rectify this problem. Indeed, the temporary promotion program, with its uneven and arbitrary administration, may well have created new jealousies in an already highly controversial Air Service personnel system. At the highest levels of command, the Air Service of the AEF suffered from a surfeit of officers who aspired to be "chiefs," and too few willing to follow commands as loyal "Indians."[70]

Conclusion

It is likely that we shall never know the full extent of damage done by the Cowan-Reber administration of the Signal Corps Aviation School at San Diego. However, there is no question that its impact was both broad and pervasive. When President Wilson confirmed the reprimand of Colonel Goodier on April 17, 1916, the demoralizing story of the First Aero Squadron in Mexico was just becoming available to the general public. One year before the United States would enter World War I, it became abundantly clear that the army's aviation equipment was both deficient and dangerous. The Signal Corps command had proved to be unethical, devious, and insubordinate in its administration of Aviation Service personnel. At a time when congressional support was vital, the legislators were appalled to discover that army officers went to great lengths to keep Congress in the dark concerning their maladministration of military aeronautics. On the other hand, the army aviators were an unruly and undisciplined group that had strong civilian ties in Congress, in the National Guard, and in the aeronaut constituency. Secretary of War Newton D. Baker might make a new start, but could it ever be a "fresh" start?

7 ★ World War I in the Air
August 1914–April 1917

The outbreak of World War I in August 1914 focused public attention and military intelligence collection upon new systems of warfare, including the airship and airplane. An expanding U.S. Army attaché system had been in place since the Russo-Japanese War, and initial reports on the European conflict resulted in a 1915 amendment of American military policy that recognized the growing importance of military aviation. At the same time, the realities of the conflict, reported through official sources and in the newspapers, silenced most of the colorful and highly exaggerated claims of the aeronaut constituency concerning military applications of air power. Navy captain Mark Bristol, the newly installed head of the naval aviation program, commented to Adm. Albert Gleaves, "There has been an erroneous campaign of education going on throughout the world regarding aircraft. This war has been a God send for this education. The facts brought out by way of romance, newspaper grown exaggeration, the advertising of airplane manufacturers for pecuniary benefit, and the one-sided reports of operators, are also colored for military reasons. It has, and will take close study and careful investigation to separate the facts from fiction."[1] Bristol was quite correct. The bombast of aeronaut publicists began to recede, as the defense community and the public began to take a close look at what was occurring in Europe and what had become a disheartening situation in America.

As the 1915 Goodier court-martial would reveal, the Signal Corps high command willingly sacrificed pilot safety to maintain tenuous connections with the Wright manufacturing interests and to perpetuate positive public relations. Misleading reports from the chief signal officer cloaked serious problems of command mismanagement, equipment obsolescence, and aviation personnel dissatisfaction. One reason for this dissimulation was the Signal Corps' determination to control military aviation, despite the growing separatist pressure from army pilots, the aeronaut constituency, and some members of Congress.

The Wilson administration's apparent lack of interest in military aeronautics after April 1914 might at first glance suggest that the General Staff Corps failed to alert the army to the need for preparedness in military aeronautics. Nothing could be further from the truth. As we shall see, the major operational uses of air power in World War I were described and thoroughly analyzed by the General Staff, and the conceptual thought within the Aeronautical Division and Aviation Section proved to be remarkably predictive concerning post-1914 uses of air power. However, the political leadership refused to respond to the legislative and administrative initiatives necessary to bring army aviation into a modicum of parity with the known achievements in war-torn Europe.

On the other hand, the work of the General Staff and the attachés was not entirely in vain. The achievements of European military aeronautics between 1914 and American entry into the war were not only well documented; they also provided a shocking contrast to the army's inability to provide aeronautical support to the 1916 Mexican Punitive Expedition.[2] In a very real sense the opening years of the First World War showed what American military and naval aviation might have been — but clearly was not — as the challenges of modern warfare confronted the United States of America.

Changing Ground and Aerial Tactics in the First World War

The real test of military air power in all of its applications occurred in Europe after August 1, 1914. Only then did the U.S. Army have the opportunity to observe the full utilization of aircraft in a combination of tactical situations and over varied terrain. Even though there was difficulty in securing encyclopedic intelligence concerning the war on the Western or Russian fronts, the attaché network and newspaper accounts taught army planners very useful lessons in the years before American entry into the war. Virtually all of the air-power concepts that had been discussed earlier in the United States were now to be tested in Europe.

The land war on the Western Front was unique in many ways. It opened traditionally as a war of maneuver, rapid advances, and flanking movements. However, once the front stabilized, the armies froze into entrenched positions, and the war became one of artillery bombardment, massive infantry losses through desperate frontal attacks, and a gradual attrition of economic, human, and morale resources. The airplane and dirigible, supplemented by the long-neglected stationary observation balloon, were called upon to play a variety of roles in these rapidly changing tactical environments.

Aerial Reconnaissance and Scouting

Opening maneuvers on the Western Front demonstrated the limitations upon airships in supporting ground warfare, and the advantages of the airplane for both tactical and strategic reconnaissance. As German troops swept through Belgium and northern France in August and September 1914, military Zeppelins scouted the line of advance. The huge airships proved to be extremely vulnerable to enemy ground fire at the low altitudes essential for accurate tactical observation. These hazards were compounded by the Zeppelins' relatively slow rate of ascent and lack of maneuverability. In addition, the German high command's decision to use airships for daylight rather than night reconnaissance operations put lighter-than-air craft at even greater risk. Four Zeppelins were lost within the first four weeks of the war, and thereafter most German observation was performed by faster and cheaper airplanes.[3]

By way of contrast, the hard-pressed Allied armies of France and Great Britain utilized airplanes to scout and report battle conditions and to locate enemy positions along the rapidly changing front lines. Airplane observation was particularly valuable in supporting the British holding action at Mons — tracing German advances against the defenses and sounding the alarm that permitted a safe and orderly retreat when enemy forces threatened to envelop units of the British army.[4] Somewhat later, as the leading elements of the German army shifted their direction of march from the southwest to the southeast, aerial observation alerted Allied commanders. This permitted them to reposition their forces to avoid an immediate engagement and, at the same time, to threaten the German units with encirclement.[5]

After the first battle of the Marne in September 1914, the establishment of fixed entrenchments eliminated the use of airplanes for long-range strategic reconnaissance. Thereafter they were employed in aerial photography of the enemy's front-line trenches, reconnaissance work in support of limited ground action, and artillery-fire direction.[6] The stabilization of the front in northern France graphically illustrated military aviation's reconnaissance value. Fundamental to German offensive success under the modified Schlieffen plan was the speed with which the advancing columns could move and surprise defending troops and threaten them with encirclement. Allied observation from the air frustrated these goals by providing rapid and accurate intelligence, thereby giving Allied armies adequate time to respond to enemy movements and to prepare countering concentrations of troops and matériel. Though the war of movement settled into static trench warfare after the stand on the Marne, the value of aerial observation in a war of movement was no longer subject to doubt.

Reconnaissance of Troop and Matériel Concentrations

The inception of trench warfare in the early months of 1915 increased the aerial activity, even as it altered its application and objectives. Military intelligence no longer required locating the enemy or predicting imminent threatening maneuvers. Quite the contrary, the enemy's locations were obvious from the elaborate entrenchments easily detected by aerial observation and airborne photographic records. Future offensive actions were readily predictable by observing the massing of assault forces and the concentration of supplies and munitions. Frequent and close observation of enemy emplacements facilitated identification of both strong and weak points in the defensive line. These military intelligence requirements were satisfied by aerial observation, since both the stability of the front and the accuracy of entrenched infantry and artillery fire negated the use of mounted cavalry to reconnoiter the enemy.

Allied implementation of aerial photography provided maps of enemy positions and recorded permanently any significant terrain changes or adjustments in enemy-troop deployment.[7] When the British launched an offensive at Neuve Chappelle on March 10, 1915, each army headquarters possessed a complete set of aerial photographs detailing the opposing German trenches. According to Sir Llewellyn Woodward, the Oxford University diplomatic and military historian, this battle convinced the British high command of the value of aerial reconnaissance.[8] French forces defending Verdun also made effective use of their three escadrilles of observation aircraft, locating German batteries for artillery attack and mounting a full-scale survey of enemy emplacements despite heavy attacks by German aircraft.[9]

Undoubtedly the high point of successful British and French aerial reconnaissance occurred immediately before and during the battle of the Somme from June to September 1916. In the month preceding the assault, the Allies used aerial photography to maintain continuing surveillance of German entrenchments and troop dispositions. The undulating terrain of the battlefield shielded most German positions from ground observation. Therefore, the Allies directed their artillery barrage from the air. On the eve of the British assault, aerial observers noted where artillery bombardment had opened gaps in the German barbed-wire fences, thereby providing faster routes for infantry advance. Growing crops and heavily wooded areas gave defending German troops an advantage of ambush, but on numerous occasions the Allies were able to closely observe activity immediately ahead of friendly infantry units, thereby allowing them to avoid or neutralize these traps.[10] On July 1, 1916, British aerial observers noted shifts in German reserves and were able to direct artillery fire against these troop concentrations. On July 13 a British aviator spotted German troops waiting to ambush an advancing British column; he not only succeeded in drawing fire from the enemy ground troops but also mapped their location and dropped a sketch of their dispositions to his corps commander. During the third phase of the battle, on September 26, one of the most remarkable examples of ground-air cooperation occurred. A column of British infantry, advancing in support of a tank, were halted by a heavy concentration of German troops. An aircraft observer directed artillery fire against the enemy until the British infantry was too close to permit the barrage to continue. At that point the pilot strafed the German trenches, and the enemy infantry unit waved white handkerchiefs as a token of surrender. The pilot then signaled the ground commander to accept the surrender of the German unit, composed of eight officers and 362 men. The engagement had cost the British only five casualties.[11]

Allied use of air power was not restricted to close ground support and aerial mapping of enemy defenses. Through long-range reconnaissance of enemy reserve troops and concentrations of matériel, British and French airmen made significant contributions to successful Allied action on the ground. When the Germans shifted reserve units to the Goat Redoubt in front of Corcellette, British aerial observers spotted the movement and directed artillery barrages against them. In the week July 6–12, the Germans were observed shifting their reserve troops at Lille, and the British drew accurate estimates of the new troops being readied for reinforcement of the enemy front at the Somme.[12]

Artillery-Fire Direction

Aerial direction of artillery fire contributed greatly to Allied success during the Somme battle. Although German artillery outranged British and French cannon, the Royal Flying Corps and French aviation units were so accurate in fire direction that Allied artillery barrages made it possible for the infantry to advance with far fewer casualties than might otherwise have been the case. Coordination of aerial and artillery operations was enhanced by use of the newly introduced Sterling wireless set, which had the light weight and transmission range necessary for aerial use. Only as the weather turned cloudy and rain prevented flying did this effective combination cease to function.[13]

Aerial observation, photo-reconnaissance, and artillery spotting became a recognized part of military operations as a consequence of Allied experience in the battle of the Somme. However, there were also peculiar but favorable circumstances which facilitated this remarkable success in ground-air cooperation during the early years of the war. Outnumbered by Allied aircraft, German commanders restricted their airplanes to work only over the battle lines. Their pilots did not provide them with long-range intelligence behind Allied lines, and they failed to keep Allied airplanes away from German areas of troop assembly and supply. As a consequence, in the opening stages of the Somme battle, the Allies enjoyed considerable air superiority over the enemy, and this facilitated and protected aerial reconnaissance missions.[14]

Improved German fighter aircraft soon challenged Allied air superiority, yet the lessons learned before and during July 1916 determined the future course of British and French air power. Since accurate observation and artillery-fire direction required security from attack by hostile pursuit aircraft, control of the air space over the battlefield, as well as a temporary air superiority over enemy staging areas and matériel depots, was essential. Pursuit aviation developed not from theoretical abstractions but, rather, from ground commanders' needs for military intelligence — information that was only available from aerial observers and photographers.[15]

Offensive Applications of Air Power

Combat in the air served two vital functions: (1) it provided protection for friendly reconnaissance planes, and (2) it denied German observation planes access to airspace above the Allied trenches and rear areas. The success or failure of pursuit aviation activities depended upon two variables. The lesser of these was the technical developments in airframes, engines, and aerial weaponry.[16] This evolution was extraordinarily rapid in the period of 1914 to 1915. Fortunately for the Allies, the battle of the Somme occurred before the Fokker single-seater pursuits, equipped with through-the-propeller machine guns, could be employed on the Western Front.[17] Throughout the war, and even during such prolonged offensives as the Somme, technological developments were critical factors that altered the effectiveness of pursuit aviation, and hence Allied or German superiority in the air.

Even more critical than technological progress was evolution of pursuit tactics and concepts of employment. Concentration of pursuits against carefully selected targets was found to be the most effective use of aerial weapons. All available Allied airplanes were concentrated before the battle of the Somme. Initially used to destroy German observation airplanes and balloons, the Allied planes during the assault provided close air support to the infantry. Only when the Somme battle was in its final stages did the Germans organize their pursuit aircraft into fighting squadrons, the famous *Jagdstaffeln*.[18] Then German air power began to make its presence felt. The principle of concentration of forces was vital to a well-planned air-power offensive. This offensive strategy in turn depended upon the willingness of ground commanders to release airplanes from close ground support, the function most immediately beneficial to ground units. During the first two years of the war, German army commanders insisted upon a "barrage" — the constant maintenance of airplanes over the front lines. The intent was to frustrate the work of Allied reconnaissance aircraft and balloons, and to prevent the penetration of German airspace by Allied pursuits and observation planes. This not only was expensive in matériel and exhausting to flying personnel, but it also dispersed German air power and did not substantially decrease the threat of Allied aerial operations.[19]

Beyond their effort to concentrate aerial forces, the Allies also used them aggressively to project air power well behind enemy lines. A British memorandum on aerial tactics preached this gospel: "To seek out and destroy the enemy's forces must be the guiding principle of our tactics in the air, just as it is on land and sea."[20] Penetration of German supply and support areas drew enemy fighter airplanes away from the front, and took advantage of the principle of surprise.

Gradually the technological superiority of German fighters, based in part upon the engines developed during Zeppelin experiments, established its mark over the Western Front. On September 30, 1916, Gen. Sir Douglas Haig endorsed Brig. Hugh Trenchard's request to the British war office for the development of a faster, more maneuverable, and higher-ceilinged single-place fighter.[21]

While waiting for an improved pursuit airplane, the Allies continued to press the aerial offensive against German air and ground forces. Inevitably, the introduction of superior German fighters gave them an advantage, and Allied losses increased. However, Allied leaders noted that the German air forces made spectacular gains whenever the Allies abandoned their aerial offensive even for a short time. The decision was made to continue pressure on the German air arm, and to accept the increased casualty rate. At the same time, adoption of new defensive tactics provided more security against German fighter attack. Formation flying was introduced, at first for the escort of observation aircraft, but subsequently for the mutual defense of pursuit planes against attack by *Jagdstaffel* squadrons. The Allied offense also served a protective function by keeping enemy pursuits engaged while Allied observation aircraft and close ground-support units continued their cooperation with friendly ground forces.[22]

Although only limited and spotty reports of the Allied experience was known to American aviators and strategists prior to April 1917, the early years of the conflict had a profound impact upon American tactics when the nation entered the war. British brigadier general Hugh Trenchard cited the battle of Verdun as the decisive factor in the development of pursuit tactics, and there is good reason to believe that the 1915 amendments to the U.S. "Military Policy" regarding air power were strongly influenced by these Allied experiences.[23]

Aerial Bombardment

Allied aerial bombardment behind the Western Front also dispersed German pursuit aviation, drawing it away from front-line observation escort and close support of German ground forces. On the other hand, Allied success in interdictional bombardment and in bombing enemy front-line units was limited. The basic strategy had been set forth in a conference on August 7, 1915, between British and French aviation leaders. Both parties agreed to coordinate their efforts and to attempt to cut German railroad lines through attacks upon trains operating on critical lines of supply and transport. This strategy was not significantly at variance with the German General Staff's 1913 recommendation that dirigibles be used for the bombing of troop concentrations, supply depots, bridges, and railways. As a gloss upon Allied target-selection policy, the British developed the principle that bombardment was not to be done indiscriminately. Rather, special targets were to be selected with care, and then attacked continuously and with substantial concentrations of aircraft.[24]

Narrowing the selection of Allied targets to rail lines and railway stations was a natural development based upon early success against these objectives in 1914 and 1915. Bombardment of key railway stations before the British advance at Neuve Chappelle in March 1915 resulted in a three-day delay in the arrival of German reinforcements. Attacks on rail centers decelerated the German advance from Ghent to Ypres in late April 1915. However, a July 1915 survey of Royal Flying Corps bombardment activities indicated that the effect of bombing railway tracks and isolated stations had been slight, and that the best way to disable a rail line was to attack and destroy a train traveling on the tracks. The resulting wreckage, particularly if it were at a distance from repair facilities, would stop the flow of troops and material for a longer time than would be required to repair a track or restore facilities of a station. During the battle of Loos in September 1915, the Allies launched a concerted attack upon German rail facilities, wrecking five troop trains and two additional trains carrying munitions. Despite this success, German troops reached the front on schedule.[25] Bombardment from airplanes proved to be of limited effectiveness because of the small bomb-carrying capacity of World War I aircraft, and for this reason target selection and surprise played an important role in achieving success.

While limitations upon aircraft payload restricted aerial bombardment in World War I, this use of air power in an era of trench warfare offered a number of advantages. The static nature of the front required that supplies and reinforcing troops be assembled in large quantities in the rear areas, where aerial reconnaissance could observe the logistical activity even though it was beyond the range of friendly artillery. When defending units were constrained within salients, as the French were at Verdun, and the Germans were (after 1917) at St. Mihiel and later at Chateau-Thierry, the restriction of transportation and communication lines made these positions particularly vulnerable to interdictional bombardment. As a result of this threat and the danger of aerial observation and artillery bombardment, resupply of both German and Allied front lines became a nocturnal operation.[26] Improved bombsights and the introduction of larger airplanes might well have had a dramatic impact upon trench warfare on the Western Front, heightening problems of reinforcement and supply and compelling the evacuation of salient positions.

Aerial Bombardment of London

Allied air power on the Western Front diminished sharply as British pursuit squadrons withdrew to protect the British Isles against German aerial attack.[27] This campaign against British cities, factories, and military installations began in 1915 with the major effort directed at London. From May 1915 to December 1916, German naval Zeppelins engaged in a concerted program of nocturnal bombardment of the British capital city whenever atmospheric conditions and winds were favorable. Thereafter the offensive continued with long-range bombers in daylight attacks. This tactic provided greater accuracy, airplanes were less vulnerable to British defensive measures, and daylight attack had a greater psychological impact upon the civilian population.[28]

Although the Hague Convention of 1899 and the renewed agreement of 1907 prohibited aerial bombardment of undefended cities, that provision of international law was eliminated when in August 1914 noncontracting powers (Britain, Germany, and France) went to war.[29] As far as London was concerned, the presence of dockyards and military camps within the city limits made it questionable whether it qualified as an "undefended" place in any event. As a consequence, unrestricted aerial bombardment was open to both the Allied and the Central powers.

German confidence in the Zeppelin made it likely, even before the outbreak of war, that it would be used for aerial bombardment of England.[30] This aspect of the war has been discussed extensively in writings both scholarly and popular.[31] Viewed objectively, the bombing campaign achieved better results through psychological means than it did through its limited destruction of lives or property. England was temporarily paralyzed by the stoppage of railroad trains during the attacks, and her steel industry was crippled by sudden shutdowns and the destruction of production facilities.[32] On balance, however, the most serious problem was the fear generated in the British populace, and the tendency to seek shelter even when no airships had been sighted. As a historian of British air power describes it, there was an "unrelieved gloom, . . . and a brooding sense of danger."[33]

German aerial bombardment failed to have a determinative effect on British home industry because it was poorly targeted, of inadequate strength, and ill conceived. Concentration of the offense against London permitted British defenders to emphasize that sector in defense planning and to erect warning nets and airfields in the path from the Zeppelin air sheds in Belgium to London. Navigation of the high-flying Zeppelins was difficult, and British blackouts increased this problem, resulting in a number of bomb drops on provincial villages and vacant fields. As the operational ceiling of Zeppelins increased to avoid intercepting fighters, the dangers of iced controls and oxygen deprivation in open cockpits became significant. German imperial directives prohibited attacks on St. Paul's Cathedral. As a result the Zeppelin commanders were denied access to the area of the city most vulnerable to their incendiary bombs, and when the high command authorized a change to high explosive bombs, the prevailing winds were then most favorable to destruction through incendiary attack. Finally, the Naval Airship Division and German military airships were inadequately coordinated, resulting in a chronic failure to concentrate bombardment against single targets.[34]

Defense against German aerial bombardment took both passive and active forms. The institution of a blackout by British orders-in-council issued in the first months of the war did much to confuse the navigation of Zeppelins and the location of targets. Cordons of aircraft spotters, established on land, traced the airships' approach. Ships stationed in the English Channel and North Sea did the same. Searchlights and anti-aircraft artillery were installed in the London region, following French practices in the aerial defense of Paris, and a home-defense establishment of the Royal Flying Corps was recruited. At first their inability to reach the Zeppelins because of altitude limitations frustrated the pilots of the Royal Naval Air Service (RNAS); however, by the summer of 1916, the RNAS airplanes and their newly developed incendiary bullets were compelling the Zeppelins to rise to extremely high altitudes, or to risk fiery destruction over England. Closely connected to the aerial defense of the British Isles were offensive airplane attacks upon German Zeppelin sheds on the Belgian coast and at Dusseldorf, Cologne, Friedrichshafen, and Cuxhafen.[35]

Strategic long-range bombing by the Allies was delayed in two ways, by a lack of suitable airplanes and the reluctance of the high command to divert air power from the Western Front. However, by the summer of 1916 the Royal Flying Corps established the beginnings of the Independent Air Force. Its mission was the aerial bombardment of German industrial targets and military areas. The Mauser arms factory was bombed in October 1916, followed by the steel works at Volklinger and the blast furnaces at St. Ingebert. In December the iron works at Dillingen were bombed on the 24th and 27th. Gen. Sir Douglas Haig felt that long-range bombardment was a luxury that could not be afforded until Allied aerial supremacy was established on the Western Front.[36] On this basis he opposed the creation of the Independent Air Force. However, his French allies emphasized the value of such an aerial offensive. British plans for strategic bombardment, in a developmental stage at the War Office since November 1914, were finally implemented in the second half of 1916. In 1917 Brig. Hugh Trenchard told the American liaison officer, Col. Billy Mitchell, that the aim of strategic bombing was to carry the attack as far as possible to the enemy's rear, hitting his industries, supplies, and matériel depots. Whatever the merits of the concept may have been, production failures in bomber aircraft and a chronic need to replace planes lost in combat over the Western Front delayed the full utilization of the Independent Bomber Force until the Armistice eliminated the need.[37] Although Allied strategic bombardment never operated at maximum efficiency, it did cause the Germans to withdraw pursuit squadrons from the Western Front for the aerial defense of the Saar industrial complex.[38]

The American Attaché Network and Air-Power Policy Revisions

Gen. Mason Patrick, the wartime commander of American air units in France, wrote in his 1919 history of the Air Service that when the United States entered the war, "No American, in or out of the Army, properly understood the new technique of the air."[39] This is an interesting observation when one considers the comments of American aeronautical magazines on European military activities and the reports of American attachés concerning the First World War. The General Staff's supplement to its "Statement of a Proper Military Policy for the United States," issued late in 1915, bears convincing evidence of the army's awareness of European events and conceptual thought.[40] Somewhat earlier, on September 15, Brigadier General Scriven's 1915 report as chief signal officer also reflected conclusions based upon experiences of the warring powers during the first year and a half of hostilities.[41]

In retrospect, it seems obvious that General Patrick misjudged the attentiveness of the military attachés and the intelligence analysis work of the General Staff. Indeed, some contemporaries in 1915 saw this plea of ignorance as a creation of the aeronaut constituency, designed to fault the attachés and General Staff rather than the political leadership and the army aviators. Writing to Orville Wright in August 1915, Grover Loening commented that "Mr. [Henry] Woodhouse indicated to me one day that he knew more about what types of aeroplanes and dirigibles were being used than did the Departments and therefore felt fully competent to criticize and antagonize them in the name of the Aero Club, whereas those who have been on the inside like myself, know that the reports of the attachés, military and naval observers, confidential agents and official exchanges of information on new developments, between the British War Office and our War Dept, are very extensive and quite thorough."[42] Woodhouse was clearly in error. In October 1914, Capt. Washington I. Chambers sent Oscar P. Austin of the Aero Club a set of French and German reports on aerial photography. These were taken from navy files, and Chambers asked that they be returned once Austin had finished examining them.[43] In 1914 and 1915 there was political advantage in impugning the work of the General Staff; since that time the myth has misled both General Patrick in 1919 and most historians who have written on World War I aviation.

The European experience during the first year and a half of war was well known to the U.S. Army and evaluated with a fair degree of accuracy. The failure to gain increased funding was not for lack of information, but, rather, due to the army's inability to persuade Congress to commit itself to air power. There was also a surprising amount of complacency in military circles, who, by then, should have known better. The chief signal officer's 1915 report, after noting the importance of military aviation to European armies, assured the secretary of war that the Aviation Section was well prepared to perform reconnaissance and artillery fire direction duties. According to General Scriven, the Aviation Section was already in the process of taking up those combat and pursuit functions that had been shown necessary to modern warfare.[44] In actuality and as the Mexican Punitive Expedition would demonstrate abundantly, army aircraft then in use were obsolete, underpowered, and impotent even against an enemy without defensive air units.

When the German Army invaded Belgium in 1914, an American military attaché from Berlin was with the advancing troops; and from 1915 to the end of the war, U.S. Army officers in England kept a close watch on the British war effort. Of particular importance to Aviation Section preparation for hostilities were the reports of Maj. George O. Squier, filed in 1915 and 1916, on the basis of an extensive inspection of British aerial activity on the Western Front.[45]

Squier was no ordinary army officer, and his scientific contacts opened the door to eyewitness accounts of aerial operations in France. His arrival in Britain was heralded by scientific groups who held him in high esteem for his pioneering experimental work in radio and cable communications. By November 1914 he secured permission to observe British front lines in France, a privilege denied to virtually all neutral attachés in London. As he reported to the War College Division of the General Staff, Lord Kitchener, Chief of the Imperial General Staff, made special arrangements for him to "disappear" from London and to visit Sir John French's headquarters at the front. Upon his arrival in France, he dined with Sir John and the prince of Wales.[46] From that time until he returned to England and took leave of Lord Kitchener on April 26, 1916, Squier was actively studying the impact of air power on modern warfare.

Formerly a Coast Artillery officer, Major Squier was profoundly impressed by the use of the airplane for artillery spotting. Warfare on the stable front in France was largely a matter of artillery barrages designed to harass the enemy and develop weak points in his line of trenches. Consequently, it was of paramount importance to locate and destroy hostile artillery emplacements; conversely, great care was taken to conceal the location of Allied field artillery. In this duel the airplane, and for the Germans the stationary artillery observation balloon, played a critical role. Artillerymen calculated the range of their targets from coordinates established by the air observers, and thus could continue their bombardment around the clock. In conjunction with an infantry advance, it was common to utilize a "creeping barrage" in which British troops were preceded by a curtain of artillery fire controlled from the air. Accuracy of observation was absolutely essential to success. The "creeping barrage" and other forms of fire direction were optimally controlled by radio communications between ground forces and the airmen. Other methods such as panels laid on the ground were generally neglected by the infantry. A British study concluded that no army without aerial superiority could long maintain its artillery arm intact, for the flashes from firing field guns would easily attract the attention of an aerial observer and result in its destruction. Concluded Squier, "No artillery at the present moment can hope to compete with an opponent of equal strength who has superiority in the air."[47]

Counter-battery firing was also aided by aerial reconnaissance, which produced daily maps locating enemy field-piece locations. These were supplemented by detailed sketch maps and photographic mosaics of enemy trenches, which provided information concerning location, troop strength, and efforts at resupply. All reconnaissance reports were carefully analyzed by intelligence sections who prepared reports for the appropriate field commanders. Squier believed aerial reconnaissance to be "one of the greatest aids to obtaining information, which has as yet been developed."[48]

Offensive uses of aircraft also were mentioned in the Squier report. Combat planes were defended with Lewis machine guns, rifles, and pistols, and all had many bombs hung on the outside of the fuselage. While aerial bombardment was not as steady or effective as artillery fire, it was more versatile in that it made towns within a fifty-mile radius vulnerable to attack.[49] "The aeroplane as a direct means of attack for specific military purposes, is a weapon of great moral and military value. . . . The era of war in the air is upon us, whether we like it or not."[50] Less successful in gaining information concerning naval operations, Squier was cautious in his comments concerning dirigibles. "It is very necessary to keep an open mind at present in judging of the relative military value dirigibles and aeroplane, and patiently wait until the real facts of this war, as far as the use of dirigibles is concerned, may become known."[51] He did mention, however, that smaller navy dirigibles were used to escort ships to France since they could remain above the vessels, but the faster airplanes could not. In addition, he had some information indicating that on individual reconnaissance flights some dirigibles had remained aloft for twenty-two hours.[52]

Widely circulated in the U.S. Army, Squier's report had special credibility because of the reputation of its author and the quality of his sources of intelligence. He had spent long hours discussing aviation tactics with Brig. Sir David Henderson of the Royal Flying Corps, and as a consequence he suggested that a tactical bombardment role was appropriate. In the field Squire observed impressive use of airplanes for reconnaissance and artillery-fire direction, and also the beginnings of tactical and strategic bombardment. His biographer concludes that little of military value resulted from these wartime trips to France,[53] but that is far too modest an assessment of the reports Squier filed. They provided clear proof that there was a combat role for military aviation. It should also be pointed out that Squier's reports document the first instance in which a British aviation officer instructed an American army officer in aviation tactics and strategy. It was not to be the last.

Doctrinal Changes in American Military Thought

The year 1915 proved to be a turning point in the evolution of military aviation doctrine, not only because of Major Squier's observations in France, but also because the publication of the doctrinal supplement to army policy, entitled "Military Aviation."[54] Written in 1915 and printed by the Government Printing Office the following year, this statement demonstrates the degree to which army planners had accepted the lessons taught by the European war. Beginning with coast-defense considerations, "Military Aviation" pointed out that airplanes assisting coast artillery units would scout for enemy naval forces, prevent hostile reconnaissance of the coast, destroy enemy aircraft, submarines, and surface vessels, and supply fire direction for the coast artillery guns. In the maneuver of an army, each division should be equipped with a squadron of twelve airplanes, two companies (eight airplanes) for reconnaissance and artillery observation, and one company (four planes) for bomb dropping, long-distance reconnaissance, and aerial combat. This was to be "in keeping with the best practice . . . in European war."[55]

"Military Aviation" then turned to consideration of the semirigid and rigid dirigibles, as well as captive balloons. The latter had been used successfully along the Franco-German battlefront to direct artillery fire, while the rigid German dirigibles of Zeppelin design were notable for their range, duration in flight, and lift capacity. "Aeroplanes appear to be unable to cope with them at night." With perhaps a backward glance to H. G. Wells's *War in the Air*, this doctrinal statement commented that "in good weather these airships have a radius of action of from 5,000 to 6,000 miles. Moreover, they are being constantly improved, and are probably capable of crossing the Atlantic Ocean."[56] This was official policy emanating from the General Staff, and not the imaginings of novelists or the empty threats of chief signal officers and others seeking adequate funding for military aviation!

Reconnaissance activities were divided into tactical reconnaissance, to be done by ground troops or observation balloons at less than 6,000 feet, and the broader view of the battlefield and its environs, available at heights above 6,000 feet. Strategic reconnaissance was designed to locate the activities of large bodies of troops, concentrations of men and matériel, and other factors bearing upon overall characteristics of the battle. Tactical intelligence was to identify small units and provide information.

The General Staff Corps' 1915 statement in "Military Aviation" concluded that legislation was required to provide suitable airplanes for use by the army. New captive balloon units should be created, funded, and staffed, and dirigible balloons of various sizes and types should be developed and adopted for military uses.[57]

"Military Aviation" was a cautious statement of official military doctrine, based to a marked degree upon the history of the European war up to the time of its drafting. It mentioned "command in the air,"[58] but the full consequences of aerial superiority were not fully in evidence until the epic 1916 struggles on the banks of the Somme. The policy also identified the lack of captive balloons as a weakness of American army aerial activity, and it emphasized the need to reconsider the semirigid and rigid dirigible. It recognized the reconnaissance and artillery-fire direction activities of aircraft as being paramount; they continued to be so throughout the entire war. Finally, the statement gave somewhat grudging notice to aerial bombardment and other offensive uses of air power. Only in its organizational conclusions might military aviators and their supporters find ground for serious disagreement. The crucible of war had tested the speculations and imaginings of airmen and military planners alike. As a *Flying* magazine editorial commented at the opening of World War I, "The hour has struck for the testing. Innumerable theories, spun by a world at ease, have now to bear the merciless ordeal of trial. The cherished beliefs of the doctrinaire, the statesman and the militarist are all in the melting pot."[59]

A remarkably large number of the concepts worked out by the American army aviators before 1914 were proven valid in the opening years of the war, and these were accepted in 1915 by the "Military Aviation" doctrinal statement of the General Staff. Yet further endorsement was required, and Secretary of War Lindley Garrison was not convinced that the General Staff's conclusions were correct. As late as September 1916, well after the public became aware of the dismal failure of army aviation in Mexico, *Aerial Age Weekly* chastised Maj. William Mitchell for statements to the press that criticized the quality of American airplanes and aircraft engines. The editors felt that such an attitude of mind could lead to disaster![60] Apparently, the buoyant confidence and blind chauvinism of the American aeronaut constituency survived even the sobering acid test of American air power — the 1916 field operations of the First Aero Squadron in northern Mexico.

8 ⭐ Dark Clouds and a Silver Lining
The Punitive Expedition and the
National Defense Act

From 1913 through March 1917, the most pressing challenge to American diplomacy and military policy was far from a leisurely observation of European weaponry and tactics. Rather, it was implementing a consistent and effective national response to the complex events of the Mexican Revolution. By April 1914, United States–Mexican relations deteriorated to the point that American military and naval forces were utilized to protect American citizens both in Mexico and along the international border in Texas and New Mexico. Following President Wilson's lead, military intervention was seen as a way to uphold democratically elected officials and to discourage the violent factionalism that dominated Mexican national politics since the beginning of the Mexican Revolution in 1911.

South of the border, American military and naval aviation met their first tests in combat. Fortunately, this occurred in an environment that was especially tolerant of mistakes, since none of the Mexican antagonists possessed an air arm to challenge that of the United States. To the extent that American aviation proved to be at all effective, it did so in performing tasks in observation, reconnaissance, and emergency communication.[1] This experience in Mexico corroborated the doctrinal principles that U.S. military aviation had absorbed from observations in Europe. Quite possibly the U.S. Navy's limited experience during the April 1914 incursion into the Mexican seaport of Veracruz served as the final proof needed to amend the army's "Military Policy of the United States." The 1915 amendment identified reconnaissance, observation, and field artillery fire direction as primary roles for the air arm. Significantly, it downplayed offensive use of aerial weapons and provided only implied recognition to principles of air superiority.

The Veracruz Campaign

Aside from Americans resident in Mexico City, the largest concentration of U.S. citizens in Mexico was in the seaside cities of Tampico and Veracruz. These were the major terminals for oil export, and the U.S. Navy maintained a reassuring presence in both harbors for their benefit. In April 1914 Tampico was under the control of federal troops loyal to Gen. Victoriano Huerta, the titular president of Mexico. Huerta came to power through a military coup in 1913 but in doing so alienated Generals Pancho Villa, Venustiano Carranza, and Euphemio Zapata, who formed a loose coalition known as the Constitutionalists. Villa headed a large army in the northern provinces of Mexico nearest the U.S. border, and Zapata commanded a sizable army that operated in the provinces south of Mexico City. Carranza, the so-called First Chief of the Constitutionalist Party, not only commanded a substantial rebel army but also claimed authority over Villa and Zapata, neither of whom were particularly anxious to follow his directions when it did not please them to do so.

In March and April 1914 Carranza's army threatened the continued federal occupation of Tampico and Veracruz. With the First Chief's rebel forces concentrating against them, and the American navy in the harbors, Huerta's federal troops were under considerable pressure. The incident that sparked American intervention was the arrest, for a short period of time, of a whaleboat of navy sailors that had blundered into a prohibited waterfront area of Tampico. Although the Mexican commander quickly apologized, the American admiral demanded more formal, and undoubtedly more humiliating, recognition of U.S. national dignity. Unfortunately, while these punctilios of gunboat diplomacy remained unresolved, a German freighter carrying arms and ammunition was reported to be approaching Veracruz harbor in violation of an American embargo of such shipments to Mexico. Since there was no actual war between Mexico and the United States, stopping the German freighter on the high seas would have precipitated an international incident. With presidential approval and a reluctant congressional consent, the navy was authorized to intervene and seize control of Veracruz. A shore party of sailors and all available marines landed on April 21, 1914, and took possession of the Mexican custom house and the waterfront. The arrival of a U.S. Army infantry brigade on April 27 permitted occupation of the remainder of the city.[2]

No U.S. Army air units were involved in the Veracruz intervention, but a small number of navy airplanes assisted with the initial landing and in aerial observation of Mexican troops in the city. The American aviation units on duty at Veracruz and Tampico consisted of four pilots, three student pilots, and five aircraft. During a month of flying, the naval aviators located mines in Veracruz harbor, observed enemy activity in the city, and assisted Marine ground forces by spotting the location and movements of Mexican troops. Some aerial photography was utilized in the reconnaissance missions, and when the Mexicans in Veracruz fired rifles at the scouting planes, the navy learned that rifle fire was not dangerous unless it struck the pilot. In addition, the navy discovered that the hydroaeroplane, equipped with pontoons, was faster and safer than the "flying boat." Although the Veracruz land operation was quickly reinforced by army units, the Signal Corps Aviation Section was not involved, much to the chagrin of the navy.[3]

American intervention provoked strenuous protest from virtually all of the Latin American republics. In addition, President Wilson's 1913 decision that he would not recognize the government of President Huerta, since it had gained power through a military coup, created an awkward diplomatic situation. Both Huerta and First Chief Carranza insisted that the United States immediately withdraw from Mexican territory, and only Gen. Pancho Villa expressed support for the American action. The ensuing impasse was untangled in part by the resignation of President Huerta on July 16, and on November 23 American forces completed their withdrawal from Veracruz.[4]

The Rise and Decline of Pancho Villa

General Villa's support for American initiatives in Veracruz was but one manifestation of his friendship with the United States. Of course his rise in Mexican politics was directly attributable to his ability as a military strategist and a popular leader who epitomized the aspirations of the Mexican people, particularly the poor of the northern state of Chihuahua. On October 1, 1913, his Division of the North took the city of Torreon from its federal defenders, and Villa and his men moved on to the conquest of Juarez on November 13. As Villa's troops isolated the capital city of Chihuahua, the federal garrison realized its vulnerability and evacuated the city on November 29, marching across the desert to the nearest federalist stronghold at Ojinaga. Finally, on January 10, 1914, Villa stormed into Ojinaga while its defenders fled across the U.S. border and into internment at Fort Bliss, Texas.[5]

Throughout the 1913 campaign, American public opinion and the international press had been shocked by Villa's execution of captured prisoners and his threats against foreigners, particularly Spanish residents in the conquered cities. By the time the Division of the North reconquered Torreon on April 3, 1914, it was apparent that American pressure and advice had prevailed. Executions were limited to those who had been particularly brutal in their treatment of Constitutionalist prisoners, and most foreigners were treated with courtesy.[6] Despite strong anti-Wilson arguments that Villa continued to behave as a bandit, the president accorded him great respect and considered him equally acceptable as Carranza as a future president of Mexico.[7] That view was strengthened by Villa's moderate reaction to the Veracruz occupation, and the commander of the Division of the North had reached his height in power and international prestige.

However, 1915 was to be a bad year for Pancho Villa. On February 8, President Wilson appointed DuVal West as his personal representative to visit the Mexican leaders and to report who among them would best advance the interests of the Mexican people. In his reports to the president, West began to persuade him to prefer Carranza to Villa. In addition, Villa's reputation as a military strategist faded quickly as he lost the second battle at Celaya (April 15, 1915) and subsequent battles at Leon (ca. June 14, 1915), Aqua Prieta (November 1, 1915), and Hermosillo (November 30, 1915). After the Hermosillo defeat, Villa's army began to disintegrate.[8]

Diplomatically, the tide began to turn before the battle at Aqua Prieta. On June 18, 1915, Secretary of State Robert Lansing urged Carranza to make strenuous efforts to unite the warring factions, or the United States could not recognize his government. As historian Clarence Clendenen points out, this was the first hint that recognition was possible, and such a statement had never been made to Villa.[9] By early October 1915, Villa anticipated U.S. recognition of Carranza's government, which formally took place on the nineteenth. American recognition meant that the Carrancist commanders might count upon supplies from the United States, and their access to American railroad lines facilitated their concentration of forces to defeat Villa at Aqua Prieta. Villa's frontal attack on Carrancista defenses at Hermosillo failed because machine guns were used against his troops. Customs officials at the U.S. border ensured that no coal reached Villa's army, hindering his transportation by rail.[10] American diplomatic recognition meant the Carranza government had ready access to modern weapons and American tactical assistance. It sealed the political doom of Pancho Villa — almost.[11]

The Columbus, New Mexico, Raid

After the Hermosillo defeat, Pancho Villa possessed only two resources that might possibly reverse his bad fortune: (1) the lack of strong governmental control in Chihuahua made resort to banditry an easy way to secure funds and supplies; and (2) his location next to the U.S.–Mexican border meant that he could foment an international incident almost at will, thereby jeopardizing Carranza's favored position with the United States. In the summer of 1915, he began to look to extorting financial "contributions" from the mining and smelting operations in his territory, demanding a $300,000 loan in gold to support his army. Ultimately Villista involvement with American mining companies resulted in the San Ysabel Massacre of January 10, 1916. A band of Villista soldiers stopped a train carrying workmen and officials of the La Cusi Mining Company, and proceeded to execute all seventeen American managers. Although Villa disclaimed personal responsibility for any action other than seizure of the company's payroll funds, the American public was shocked at the brutality of Villa and his men. Despite American protests the Carranza government appeared to do little to capture the responsible Villista soldiers; in point of fact, they lacked sufficiently strong forces in northern Mexico to bring the Villistas to justice.

After Santa Ysabel there was no lack of rumors concerning the whereabouts of Pancho Villa and his band. When a Carrancista commander reported that Villa was on his way to cause an incident that would trigger American intervention, Brig. Gen. John J. Pershing gave no more note to this alarm than to the many others crossing his desk. However, on March 7 and 8, Villa sent scouts to report on American military strength at Columbus, New Mexico. The scouts mistakenly reported that there were only 30 U.S. soldiers, when in fact the American garrison numbered 350. Encouraged by the report, Villa decided upon an attack in the early morning hours of March 9. The Mexican forces made simultaneous mounted attacks upon the town and the army encampment. At first the Villistas were fought with anything at hand. Army cooks doused the bandits with boiling water and fought with kitchen implements. Very quickly the machine gun company mounted a gun and began to fire at the Mexican intruders. After setting fire to several buildings, Villa's men retreated. The raid was ultimately responsible for the death of nine American civilians and eight U.S. soldiers.[12]

It quickly became obvious that Villa's scouting error was to cost him dearly. Maj. Frank Tompkins and thirty-two men from the military camp pursued Villa across the border, killing thirty on the American side. Receiving authorization from his regimental commander, Tompkins continued the pursuit for an additional three hours. In the course of their return to Columbus, the Americans counted approximately 100 Villista bodies on the escape route, and an additional 67 dead were found in the vicinity of Columbus.[13] On the evening of March 10, the War Department issued orders to Maj. Gen. Frederick Funston, commander of the Southern Department, directing that a force be organized to pursue Villa. Originally the mission was described as breaking up Villa's band; subsequently, the president altered the mission statement to include the capture of Villa, which, he hoped, would make the intervention more palatable to the Carranza government.[14] Ostensibly the Punitive Expedition was to capture Villa and his headquarters staff, and in doing so, it expected to act in concert with units and civilian authorities loyal to Carranza.

The Punitive Expedition

American troops entered northern Mexico in two columns on March 15, 1916. One column, consisting of two cavalry regiments and a battery of artillery originated at Culbertson, New Mexico, and reached Colonia Dublan on March 17. The second column, made up of a cavalry regiment and an infantry regiment, arrived on March 20.[15] The expedition was under the command of Brig. Gen. John J. Pershing, who had served with singular success in the suppression of the Morro uprising in the Philippines.[16] He recognized the difficulties of military operations in northern Mexico, and sought aerial support to provide reconnaissance and search services. He also expected to use airplanes to facilitate communications between his headquarters and advancing American columns that would be separated from other units by high mountain ranges. Pershing's plan to rely upon aerial reconnaissance was in strict accordance with 1915 War Department policy, which now made aerial observation the primary source of strategic intelligence in the field.[17] It is interesting to speculate why Secretary of War Newton D. Baker specifically ordered the aviators to refrain from offensive action against enemy forces. Perhaps this was due to the difficulty of distinguishing between troops of the recognized Mexican government and Villa's men. On the other hand, it may have been based upon Wilsonian scruples concerning the Hague Convention against aerial bombardment.[18] Whatever the reason, the expedition's air arm was restricted to reconnaissance and other noncombatant duties.

When the Punitive Expedition moved south into Mexico, Americans were aware that they were witnessing the U.S. Army's first use of both the airplane and the motorized truck in military operations. The airplane particularly touched the romanticism of the American soul. "We saw them on our first day out of Columbus, five of them in a great triangle like geese. . . .

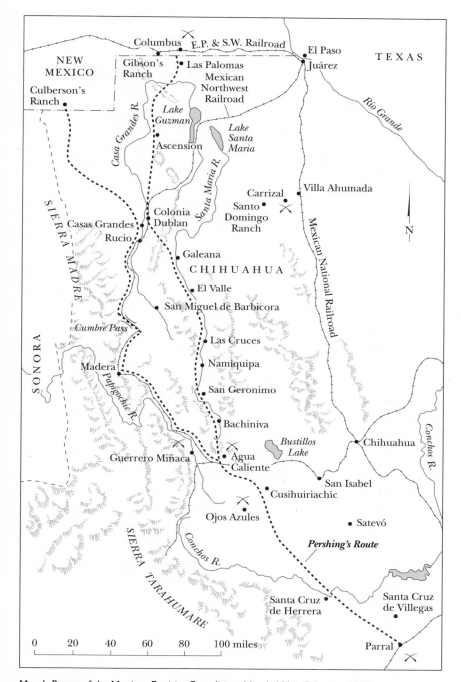

Map 1. Route of the Mexican Punitive Expedition, March 1916–February 1917.

they shimmered wonderfully in the desert air, and, watching, we thrilled with pride."[19] It was a glorious inception to what would prove to be a pathetic performance of the First Aero Squadron in Mexico.

On the other hand, the army had more than adequate evidence to anticipate that army aviation would fail the test of field service. In February 1915 the War College Division of the General Staff requested the Chief of Staff to conduct experiments with aerial direction of field-artillery fire. When the attempt was made in the summer of 1915, it was discovered that since no army aircraft were capable of carrying two passengers, observers could not be accommodated. Accurate observation of field-artillery fire, and the transmission of corrective information to the ground, was virtually impossible for the pilot alone. On the recommendation of the aviation and field-artillery commanders, Maj. Gen. Frederick Funston decided that the JN-3 aircraft were so unreliable in flight all flights should be suspended, and he so informed the adjutant general.[20] This incident so impressed Capt. Benjamin D. Foulois that he wrote the commanding officer of Fort Sam Houston on March 10, 1916, "The eight airplanes constituting the present equipment of this [First Aero] squadron are not suitable for a limited amount of cooperation with the field artillery or any other branch of the service. The limitations on their use being fixed by their inability, under certain weather conditions, to carry a pilot, observer, sufficient fuel and other necessary instruments, to a military altitude."[21] Yet three days after this letter was composed, the First Aero Squadron was moved by rail to Columbus, New Mexico. Inexplicably, on March 19, Captain Foulois ordered his squadron of JN-3s to undertake a night flight, without instruments and over hostile territory, to join General Pershing's headquarters in Mexico.[22]

Receiving Pershing's order to join the expedition "immediately,"[23] Captain Foulois ordered his pilots to fly south shortly before dusk on March 19, 1916.[24] Under normal flying conditions and over familiar terrain, night flying was hazardous. It was foolhardy when attempted over unknown and potentially hostile territory in support of a military expedition that was of questionable popularity with the Mexican people. The attempt to fly to Pershing's headquarters was foredoomed by a variety of factors, some of which were beyond Captain Foulois's control. First and foremost, the Curtiss JN-3 airplanes with which the First Aero Squadron was equipped were inadequate for field aviation work. The squadron had experienced training difficulties marked by engine failures and crashes. In late 1915, Capt. Arthur S. Cowan, commanding the flying school at San Diego, wrote Lt. Col. Samuel Reber in Washington that the JN-3s were unsafe, but he had not notified the aviators because of their tendency to panic when safety questions were raised. Harry Toulmin, an army officer who served with the Punitive Expedition, later commented that the planes were "inherently uncertain," a gross understatement concerning their readiness for flying.[25] The Curtiss factory at Hammondsport, New York, had speeded up its assembly line in early 1915 to handle European orders for training aircraft. The factory began to work overtime, and mechanics of "mixed ability" were hired. The wood used for structural members was characterized by army inspectors as being "extremely poor."[26]

Normally a cautious man, Foulois was obsessed with the need to demonstrate aerial mobility. He of all aviators should have known better. Before a California aerial meeting in December 1914, he dispatched his airplanes on a long-distance flight to the Los Angeles field that would serve as the staging area for the meet. On the way from San Diego, one plane was lost in the Pacific and the pilot drowned. One plane crashed during a forced landing, and one made an emergency landing after a fuel line broke. A year later when the First Aero Squadron was ordered from Fort Sill, Oklahoma, to Fort Sam Houston, Texas, the 350-mile cross-country flight ordered by Captain Foulois was dispersed by heavy winds. Many planes were forced to land short of their intermediate destinations, but all ultimately arrived safely.[27] Historian Herbert Mason points out that in opening the Mexican Punitive Expedition by means of a night flight over unknown territory, Foulois was inviting a fiasco. In any event, he could not have helped Pershing any more by arriving at night than if he had made a safe flight in the morning.[28] As it was, the troops accompanying Pershing's headquarters had illuminated a field studded with grass hillocks large enough to tangle with the landing gear. Had the planes arrived that night, they would have been damaged severely upon landing.[29]

Of the eight planes that began the flight at night, one turned back immediately because of engine failure; four others landed together at an intermediate point near Ascension, Mexico, where they spent the night. Lt. Walter G. Kilner landed his JN-3 at Janos, where he spent the night and flew on to Casas Grandes the next day. Lts. Edgar Gorrell and Robert H. Willis lost track of the other planes and flew about aimlessly while their unreliable compasses suffered deflection caused by iron deposits in the ground.[30] Ultimately, the two headed for a lighted area, thinking it to be Casas Grandes. Instead, it was a forest fire, and, approaching from opposite directions, they narrowly averted a head-on collision. Willis crash-landed in a rough area and his plane was completely disabled. Gorrell landed with minor damage to his aircraft and, after two days wandering without water in the deadly heat of the desert, he obtained assistance, repaired his plane, and flew on to join Pershing on March 30.[31] It was an inauspicious beginning — a beginning of the end for the airplanes of the First Aero Squadron.

Climatic conditions and the terrain of northern Mexico also added to the risks of military flying. Four-fifths of the large and sprawling state of Chihuahua was an arid plateau, and mountains rose to an average elevation of 10,000 feet in its western portion. Through the mountain passes, there were high winds and vertical air currents that made flying hazardous. The underpowered JN-3s lacked the power to fly over the mountains, and were forced to risk the turbulent air currents in the passes. Landing in the mountains was nearly impossible. Landing in the desert was a dangerous alternative because of its forbidding character. Toulmin recalled that it was sand and alkali, and that all vegetation had thorns or spines. "A hostile, harsh and desperate desert, grand only in its extent, its coloring and its forbidding aspect."[32] Gen. Henry H. "Hap" Arnold, who served as a lieutenant with the First Aero Squadron in Mexico, later recalled that "the climatic conditions were such down on the border, . . . that we spent most of our time trying to keep the planes from drying out and falling to pieces."[33] While the major problem was the warping of propeller laminates in the dry atmosphere, rain was a different but equal threat. Inadequate waterproofing of the airplane fabric leaked water onto the wooden support structure, causing rot and weakening the joints.[34]

The first day of flying demonstrated the limitations that poor equipment imposed upon the squadron's capabilities. Foulois and Lt. Townshend F. Dodd flew south on Pershing's orders to scout the line of march for the next day. As they approached a mountain range, they were unable to gain altitude, and foothill winds buffeted their JN-3, forcing them to turn back. Lt. Thomas S. Bowen suggested that he might succeed by flying without an observer. Caught by strong winds during takeoff, his plane side-slipped into a crash.[35]

Thereafter, the airmen performed few reconnaissance missions, but their work over Guerrero on March 29 showed the value of aerial observation for locating hostile forces and providing intelligence concerning them.[36] After they located a camp of Villistas at Guerrero, the Seventh Cavalry led by Col. George F. Dodd attacked the unsuspecting unit, killing thirty men, including a Villista general. As Dodd entered Guerrero from the south, Pancho Villa, with a severe leg wound, was carried out of the city to

A Curtiss JN-3 "Jenny" with the Mexican Punitive Expedition. This photograph, dated May 1916, represents an airplane sent to replace the First Aero Squadron destroyed earlier. By this time Gen. John J. Pershing had stopped his advance into Mexico and was awaiting orders to return to the United States. The airplanes were being used as couriers and to carry mail to the troops. Note the sand being blown into the air by the propellers. (Signal Corps Photographic Collection, National Archives)

the north.[37] Scouting the advance of Pershing's column was accomplished successfully on April 13, when the First Aero Squadron was able to assure the general that no large governmental force was in the vicinity of the line of advance. This was a long-range reconnaissance flight covering approximately 350 miles. Doubtless, this flight might have encouraged future use of airplanes to scout the Punitive's Expedition's line of march. However, a clash on the preceding day, April 12, occurred at Parral between Carrancista forces and a Punitive Expedition column. For diplomatic reasons, this engagement effectively halted Pershing's march to the south.[38] It was followed shortly by the crash of the First Aero Squadron's last serviceable airplane.

The limited success of most reconnaissance efforts was as disappointing to General Pershing as it was to Foulois and his air men. The general had been interested in military aviation since witnessing aerial exercises in 1908 at the Tours flying field in France. War Department instructions augmented his willingness to use the First Aero Squadron for far-range scouting leading to the location of Villa. Once the bandit chief was located, Pershing planned to use the planes to coordinate the concentration of his forces against the Villistas.[39] The unreliability and ultimate destruction of all aircraft forced

Pershing to abandon these plans. The Punitive Expedition had to fall back upon horse cavalry for advance scouting.

Given the severe mechanical limitations of the JN-3s, it is remarkable they performed as efficiently as they did in the communications and courier work assigned to them. Since General Pershing had divided his forces into two, and subsequently three, columns, effective communication became essential to the mission. Perry Nuhn, a student of the expedition, noted that "the swift movement of the campaign, driven more by rumor than valid intelligence, created a serious problem of command control for Pershing."[40] Although the General Staff advised that the expedition's airplanes be divided among the three columns, Pershing elected to retain the First Aero Squadron intact, and to have it operate from his headquarters. While this ensured that intelligence was readily available to Pershing and his staff, it denied these advantages to the other two columns. As Col. Henry T. Allen wrote to his wife from Parral, "Thus far our aeroplanes have not reached us. The mountains cause very difficult currents for such as we have."[41]

Diplomatic niceties as well as command considerations required frequent communication with subordinate units. Political considerations within Mexico made it inopportune for the Carranza government to cooperate actively with Pershing. Thus Pershing's entry into northern Mexico was merely tolerated, and offensive action against civilians or governmental units might turn the entire nation against the Punitive Expedition. The delicate international situation mandated that the American force minimize damage to Mexican citizens or property. At the same time, it was virtually impossible to determine whether an individual Mexican or a large group of Mexicans was loyal to Villa or the *de jure* government of Mexico.

So inadequate were Pershing's communications at the end of the campaign that he learned of the fatal June 21 skirmish at Carrizal from unofficial reports. That company-level engagement began when an American cavalry commander entered the town without Mexican permission, and possibly contrary to cautionary provisions in his orders. Mexican troops opened fire, and the badly outnumbered American detachment retreated after sustaining heavy casualties and killing several Mexicans. Three officers and ten enlisted men in the American units were killed; twenty-three were taken prisoner. The Mexicans lost forty-five officers and men. Mexican protests reached Pershing from Washington before Pershing's officers could report the engagement.[42]

Despite this collapse of aerial communication, earlier work of the First Aero Squadron as a courier service and embryonic airmail carrier was extremely valuable. Both activities made major contributions to command control and troop morale. Through late March and the first three weeks of April, the aviators flew several dispatch missions, and Pershing came to rely upon them for that purpose. When the last plane became inoperable on April 19, the general had to use mounted couriers to deliver his commands and obtain reports from subordinate commanders.[43] However, before that time he had adopted Foulois's suggestion that the serviceable airplanes in the squadron provide front-line courier service, leaving support communications activities to telephone, telegraph, or mounted messengers.[44]

On April 19, 1916, the First Aero Squadron's last JN-3 crashed on a photo-reconnaissance mission, destroying the newly arrived Brock aerial camera.[45] The aircraft was so badly damaged that the pilot decided to burn it rather than permit it to fall into Mexican hands. As the pilot and his passenger walked away from the wreck the underbrush ignited, starting a fire that would destroy forty miles of forest before it burned out. With that crash expired the last hope of the First Aero Squadron to make any further contribution to the Mexican Punitive Expedition.[46]

As the battle at Carrizal in June demonstrated, the loss of aerial observation capability forced Pershing to resort to cavalry reconnaissance. Because cavalry scouting elevated the danger of conflict with Carrancista units, it was both a military and a diplomatic threat to the Punitive Expedition. Aerial observation of the surrounding countryside would have offered an excellent solution to this problem. Viewed in retrospect, the Punitive Expedition proved the value of aerial over cavalry reconnaissance. However, to the contemporary observer, the patent inadequacies of the First Aero Squadron obscured the significance of this lesson.

While army flying operations persevered in Chihuahua, press interest remained at a high pitch. Despite rigid censorship of press reports, pilots talked and reporters listened. In April 1916 the *New York World* revealed the inadequacy of the expedition's airplanes, quoting Lt. Herbert Dargue's comment that it was "criminal to send the aviators up under such conditions" in "suicide bus" Jennies. *Aerial Age Weekly* quoted Lt. Thomas S. Bowen's judgment that the planes with the expedition were not powerful enough to complete their assigned tasks. Bowen's view was corroborated by his broken nose sustained in a crash at Casas Grande. Subsequently, both flyers denied making such comments, but Foulois found himself in difficulty with General Pershing, and reporter Byron C. Utrecht of the *World* was threatened with expulsion from Mexico.[47] Thereafter the War Department imposed a virtual blackout on news of the First Aero Squadron. Colonel

Allen wrote his wife about the last flights of the squadron, and then cautioned, "These things must not be given publicity." Foulois's order to his unit was even more emphatic — verbal instructions not to criticize squadron equipment had been confirmed in writing and were to be strictly obeyed. Years later, Foulois complained that the press emphasized only the First Aero Squadron's limitations, but ignored its successes, which included valuable work in keeping Pershing's columns in communication with each other.[48]

As press reports "leaked" from Mexico, the aeronaut constituency did not remain idle. Alan Hawley, president of the Aero Club of America, offered to provide civilian pilots and newer model airplanes to carry out Pershing's Air Service requirements. That offer was refused by both Brig. Gen. George P. Scriven, the chief signal officer, and Secretary of War Newton D. Baker. Less than two weeks later, *Aerial Age Weekly* reported the incredulous news that Secretary Baker declined the Aero Club offer by alleging the Punitive Expedition had "all the planes necessary" to continue its work in northern Mexico. As might be anticipated, this merely increased the public hue and cry, with large city dailies denouncing the "neglect" and "national shame" of American military aviation. Congress responded almost immediately with an emergency appropriation of $500,000 in March 1916 and an additional aviation appropriation of $13,281,666 in August of the same year. The Signal Corps and War Department also made cosmetic changes in the equipment of the First Aero Squadron. Upon its return from the border, the squadron received twelve Lewis machine guns, a weapon long requested by the aviators and long denied by the Ordnance Department. In addition, the squadron received a supply of artillery shells adapted for aerial bombardment — this despite the fact that there were no bomb-dropping devices available. The flyers presumed the War Department had provided the bombs so that it might truthfully assure the press and the American people that the squadron was ready to perform aerial bombardment missions.[49]

Participants and historians agree that adverse weather and climatic conditions, coupled with mechanical difficulties, made it virtually impossible to conduct adequate reconnaissance and courier service in Mexico. The chief signal officer's 1916 *Report* commented:

> The altitudes encountered in Mexico, up to 12,000 feet, the vast distances to be covered, and the lack of cultivated areas and resources in general made this theater one of the hardest to operate in which any

army has ever entered. The few machines were rapidly used up, although they did a great amount of flying, and rendered valuable services to the punitive expedition.[50]

General Scriven continued that "the art of aeroplane construction in this country is not satisfactory," but that the experience gained in constructing propellers resistant to heat and climatic variations was extremely valuable even though propeller failure was responsible for disabling the First Aero Squadron in Mexico. This reasoning paralleled that of Captain Foulois in his operations report concerning the squadron.[51] Finally, General Pershing was as strong in his praise of the aviators' courage as he was harsh in his criticism of the airplanes they attempted to fly.[52]

The Punitive Expedition occurred at a critical point in American history when concerns about national defense were on the rise. Congress made plans to conduct another investigation of military aviation in January 1916, and that initiative was accentuated when the transcript of Lt. Col. Lewis Goodier's court-martial was made public the following spring. It will be recalled that Goodier's court-martial brought to light some documents highly critical of the army's conduct of its flying program. These documents in turn strengthened the determination of the congressional majority which demanded a full-scale investigation into Aviation Section leadership.[53]

It was at this point in time that the failure of the First Aero Squadron in Mexico became public knowledge. Conceivably action might have occurred even if Pershing had never taken the air unit with him to Chihuahua, but the fact that he did and that it failed miserably did much to arouse public concern. As *Aerial Age Weekly* commented, "[T]he worst critic of the Army never presented a more appalling arraignment of the pitiable conditions of the Army than the Army itself has presented in the last month."[54] That April 3, 1916, critique appeared before the last JN-3 crashed in Mexico. It represented a shrewd editorial estimate of the true extent of army aviation's failure. Without the Mexican Punitive Expedition, such a sweeping condemnation would not have been possible, and even if it were printed, it would have been viewed with extreme suspicion. The pro-aviation press had cried "wolf" too often.

Nearly nine months elapsed before the collapse of the First Aero Squadron and the Punitive Expedition's withdrawal from northern Mexico. The northward march began on January 30, 1917, and concluded on February 5. The troops brought back with them some prisoners suspected of taking part in the Columbus raid. These men were later turned over to American civilian authorities for possible criminal trial. Also with the American forces were those Chinese laborers who had fled to the expedition to escape harsh labor and living conditions imposed upon them by the Mexicans. Although Villa remained at large until he was assassinated in 1923, he never again presented a threat to American border towns.[55]

The Punitive Expedition gave the army its first experience in the use of airplanes, trucks, and armored cars, and generated more systematic training and implementation of counterinsurgency skills supplementing earlier experience in Cuba and the Philippines.[56] Logistically, it demonstrated the superiority of the motorized truck to animal-propelled transport; after the First Aero Squadron's planes became operational, squadron trucks assisted in this effort. Despite the ostensible failure of the Punitive Expedition — that it did not capture Villa — Brig. Gen. John J. Pershing emerged as a determined and skillful troop leader, as well as one who could be trusted to handle diplomatic complications with tact and an even temper.[57]

The General Staff Corps lost no time in looking into the performance of the First Aero Squadron in Mexico. On April 29, 1916, Capt. Virginius W. Clark asked Foulois to gather information from squadron members concerning the proper organization of military aviation and related matters. In reply, Lt. Herbert Dargue suggested that squadrons should be composed of twelve rather than eight airplanes, and that one regiment of aircraft should be attached to each field army. Foulois stated that the airplanes taken to Mexico were in need of renovation since they had endured ten months of constant use. Among the nine planes sent as replacements, four were condemned as unsuitable. Four new and higher-powered machines had been received, and all developed serious faults. He suggested that there was a need for careful inspection at the factory before the government accepted any new airplanes.[58] Ignoring these warnings, the U.S. Army had diverted Curtiss airplanes already built to fill British orders, and these were the planes sent south to Mexico. By August 1916 they were performing some reconnaissance functions for the now stationary Punitive Expedition, nervously watched by the Signal Corps high command.[59]

A Threat of Congressional Investigation

Even before the collapse of the First Aero Squadron, events in Washington pointed toward the reorganization of the Aviation Section command. On January 5, 1916, Senator Joseph T. Robinson of Arkansas introduced Senate Joint Resolution 65, calling for the creation of a Joint Commission of

Congress to investigate the Aviation Service of the army. The resolution was referred to the Committee on Military Affairs along with Senator Robinson's specific allegations that, in addition to inefficiency in the section, there had also been an effort to mislead the War Department concerning progress being made by the aviators. In testimony before the committee, Robinson introduced evidence that Lt. Col. Samuel Reber, chief of the Aviation Section, prompted Capt. Arthur Cowan to make false reports concerning aerial training. Senator Robinson stated that the prominent aviator Lincoln Beachey had denounced the equipment and organizational management at the San Diego flying school as being "outrageously defective." Specifically, Robinson asserted that most of the army aviator fatalities from 1913 to 1915 were due to antiquated equipment. The documents and testimony were adequate to induce the Senate Committee on Military Affairs to report Senate Joint Resolution 65 with a recommendation for approval. The resolution was passed by the Senate on March 9, and taken up by the House of Representatives the next day.[60] Referred to the House Committee on Military Affairs, it was reported on March 16, with the statement that "a congressional investigation is imperative." In the course of House debate on the resolution, it was pointed out that the Joint Commission would be required to investigate below the level of heads of service, since such high-ranking officers were unable to answer the questions to be posed by the Joint Commission. Representative Caldwell stated in debate that the purpose of the Joint Commission was to pass a law that would ensure the United States would be in the forefront of military aviation. Of course, he continued, when the resolution was approved by the House in March, army aviation had been in a deplorable situation, and that had now been partially rectified.[61]

Rectification had come through the recall of Lt. Col. George O. Squier from Europe, and his appointment to succeed Lt. Col. Samuel Reber, who had been relieved as chief of the Aviation Section. Reber had played a prominent role in the effort to cover up the true state of American army aviation.[62] On April 10, 1914, Captain Cowan had written him: "[I]f our Aviation Service ever came under investigation by anyone outside our own corps it would be impossible to explain the rotten way the work has been handled."[63] Yet Reber had done nothing, and actually had condoned Cowan's failure to tell the flying officers of hazards in their equipment. On February 28, 1916, Senator Robinson singled out Reber for specific attack as the individual most responsible for the lack of efficiency in army aeronautics. "[I]t can be easily demonstrated that there is no sincere effort on the part of

Colonel Reber to improve the service; that aviation in the United States Army is contemptibly inefficient and its true condition deliberately withheld from those in high authority in the War Department."[64] Drawing upon documents uncovered by the Goodier court-martial, Senator Robinson succeeded in making it inevitable that Reber and Cowan would be removed from any further responsibility for the conduct of military aviation. In late April, Reber was censured and relieved, Brig. Gen. George P. Scriven was censured, and Cowan was relieved by Col. William A. Glassford, a veteran balloon officer who was placed in command of the North Island, San Diego, flying school.[65]

However, the removal of Lt. Colonel Reber did not satisfy the aviation journalists. In April 1916 before Reber's relief had been announced, *Aerial Age Weekly* leveled its big guns on Congress: "Congress not only is responsible for the present plight of what there is of the United States Army air squadron, but is responsible for the death of some of the officers who lost their lives in the past during their period of training."[66] Clearly the disciplining by the Signal Corps alone would not satisfy the public. To that degree the Joint Commission was sought to serve a broader purpose — the collection of information that would assist in passing army aviation legislation and appropriations in the years ahead. On the other hand, the dismissal of Reber and Cowan spiked Senator Robinson's guns for the moment.

During the Mexican Punitive Expedition, the American public was deeply concerned over the progress of the war in Europe. After the 1915 sinking of the passenger liner *Lusitania*, and through the battlefield slaughter of the spring and summer of 1916, Americans watched in dismay. Their disbelief gradually evolved into anger at Germany and apprehension of Americans fighting in Europe to defend American interests and ideals. Despite this deep concern with world events, American newspapers and magazines focused upon the debacle of American army aviation in Mexico.[67]

The Aero Club of America, among other aviation groups, would not permit the Mexican experience to be ignored. After the government's rejection of the club's April 1916 offer to sell the government two airplanes for $1.00 each, the club had the satisfaction of witnessing an outpouring of public criticism of the War Department's handling of military aviation. A June 1916 editorial in *Literary Digest*, entitled "Our Wingless Army," stated that while the situation in regard to aviation with the punitive expedition was bad, there were some private and state efforts to rectify things. The title of the editorial recalled Alan Hawley's editorial in *Flying* magazine a year before, which read, in part, "[I]f the American national bird cannot fly —

what sort of a bird is it? Surely not an eagle!"[68] Not to be outdone in ornithological satire, *Aerial Age Weekly* supplemented its article on the expedition with a cartoon of a wing-clipped American eagle. Maj. Gen. Frederick Funston, commanding the Southern Department, was pictured looking at the flightless bird, its wings marked "Clipped by Congress." The cartoon captioned the general as saying, "Perfectly good war eagle — what there is of him."[69]

In retrospect, Benjamin Foulois viewed the Mexican Punitive Expedition as a "vital milestone in the development of military aviation in this country." He believed that the experiences on the border were important to the Air Service when it got to France in the First World War.[70] There is good reason to reevaluate Foulois's assessment. He pointed out that there was no aerial opposition to the planes of the First Aero Squadron, few planes were involved, and the operational period of one month was too brief. On the other hand, he was correct that the expedition alerted the American public to the need for technical improvements in airplanes and the development of field maintenance systems.[71] Maj. Robert Sawyer, in a thoughtfully reasoned historical analysis of the lessons learned, concluded that the campaign in the air demonstrated the need for more intensive pilot training, the requirement for improved aircraft, and the need for reorganization of the Signal Corps Aviation Section.[72] Sawyer suggested that the national-preparedness political movement of 1916–17 was a product, not of the National Defense Act of 1916, but, rather, of the public outcry and military experience gained in the Punitive Expedition.[73] Of course, the National Defense Act itself was due in large degree to national and congressional reaction to the Punitive Expedition's operations.

The National Defense Act of 1916

Ten days before the punitive expedition entered northern Mexico, House Military Affairs chairman James Hay reported House of Representatives bill H.R. 12766. This bill would ultimately become the National Defense Act of 1916, a measure that had a pervasive impact upon American military affairs throughout the twentieth century.[74] Prior to reporting the bill, the House Military Affairs Committee held seven weeks of testimony concerning the military establishment in the light of current world events. Signed into law by President Woodrow Wilson on June 3, 1916, the new statute took effect eighteen days before Maj. Charles Boyd precipitated the disastrous battle at Carrizal. When the National Defense Act became law, President Wilson had just approved the court-martial sentence on Lt. Col. Lewis Goodier

A PERFECTLY GOOD WAR EAGLE—WHAT THERE IS OF HIM.

The "wingless war eagle." Its wings clipped by Congress's failure to appropriate funds, the eagle is being examined by a perplexed Maj. Gen. Frederick Funston, commander of the Western Department. General Pershing, commander of the Mexican Punitive Expedition, served directly under Funston's command. The cartoon provides a quasi-comical editorial on the failure of the First Aero Squadron during the expedition. The General Staff was not amused! (*Aerial Age Weekly*, March 20, 1916, 25)

(April 26) and the First Aero Squadron's last plane had crashed and been destroyed (April 19). For purposes of historical discussion, these events have been considered separately, but in American public awareness they were contemporaneous. Taken together, they threw dark clouds of suspicion, doubt, and anger over the Signal Corps' mismanagement of army aviation. It is not surprising that the National Defense Act, as it passed through the legislative process and as it finally became law, reflected these events occurring beyond the halls of Congress. The silver lining to the dark clouds could be found in positive statutory provisions that strengthened the organizational position of the Aviation Section, as well as important administrative changes in the control of army aviation. Finally, there were substantial increases in army-aviation appropriations.

While an exhaustive legislative history of the National Defense Act is well beyond the scope of this study, a brief consideration of the bill's legislative history reveals congressional attitudes toward military aviation and the Signal Corps in the wake of the Goodier court-martial and the Punitive Expedition.

Since the National Defense Act specifically limited the officer strength of each arm and branch of the army, debate on those sections of the law dealing with the Signal Corps is of particular interest. At an early point in the House debate on the bill, Chairman James Hay commented that while an increase in Signal Corps officers was necessary, no action was taken by the Military Affairs Committee because "the Signal Corps at present is under a cloud" and the congressional investigation should be completed before changes were made.[75] In the Senate, criticism was quite vehement. Citing the training deaths in 1913 and 1914, Senators Thomas and Works accused the army of operating defective machines and mismanaging the Aviation Service.[76] On March 29, doubtless with an eye toward reports from Mexico, Senator Gallinger commented, "I believe that we have two dilapidated aeroplanes left, but we have not a single aeroplane, and have not had a single aeroplane, that has been equipped with what France and Germany have placed on their aeroplanes, to enable them to become real instruments of war."[77] Commenting that "the Aviation Service is notoriously weak," Senator George Chamberlain of Oregon, chairman of the Senate Military Affairs Committee, noted, "Take the aeroplanes south of us on the border, . . . and I think out of four or five which undertook to cross the desert in pursuit of Villa, two went down to earth."[78] Captain Foulois's nocturnal flight to join General Pershing had apparently not escaped the senator's notice!

As if these congressional comments were not sufficiently threatening to the Signal Corps command, the issue of a separate corps for aviation was raised once more. Senator Robinson made an unsuccessful attempt to separate aviation from Signal Corps control. Asserting that the inefficiency "generally recognized" to exist in the Aviation Section could not be eliminated while the Signal Corps remained in charge of flying, he pointed out that the new secretary of war, Newton D. Baker, agreed that once aviation had a combat role, a new organization should be set up.[79] The senator's statement about Secretary Baker triggered speculation concerning the degree of separation involved. A May 17, 1916, letter from Baker to Representative Sam J. Nicholls very likely was prepared to clarify Baker's views on army-aviation autonomy. In it Baker indicated that the creation of a separate aviation bureau within the army was not contemplated at this time, since a bureau would be out of proportion to the size of the aviation service in contemplation by Congress.[80] On the other hand, despite Baker's explanation, this was undoubtedly the closest that the military aviators had come to separation from the Signal Corps prior to the First World War.[81]

The glare of publicity had indeed cast a dark cloud over the future of the Aviation Section, and deep suspicions prevailed in Congress and in the general public concerning Signal Corps mismanagement of army aeronautics. The pilot fatalities of 1913, the revelations of the Goodier court-martial, and the equipment inadequacies experienced during the Punitive Expedition — all these exposed the tangible results of a decade of mismanagement, inadequate congressional funding, and consistent media misrepresentation concerning the capabilities of U.S. Army aviation. Even in the face this accumulated evidence, the aeronaut constituency continued to publish indictments of public officials on one hand, and glorification of army aviation and American aircraft manufacturing on the other. In June 1916, shortly after enactment of the National Defense Act, President Alan Hawley of the Aero Club stated that Representative James Hay was almost singlehandedly responsible for the failure of army aviation in Mexico. Yet on April 23, 1917, the same Alan Hawley, as chairman of the Aero Club's advisory committee on aeronautics, asserted that type for type, American planes were equal to the best European products![82] Capt. Mark Bristol, then heading the navy's aviation program, commented to Charles Wolcott, secretary of the Smithsonian Institution, on April 25, 1916, "A good deal of the information disseminated through the press regarding the achievements of our aeroplanes and motors is misleading. It leads the public at large to have an exalted idea of the accomplishments of our airplanes."[83] With the aeronaut constituency as friends, military and naval aviation needed no other enemies!

The Silver Lining

As enacted, the National Defense Act provided for an expansion of the Aviation Section up to 148 officers, which included 114 first lieutenants qualified as pilots. It removed age, rank, and marital-status restrictions upon qualification for flying status. To correct the abuses revealed by the Goodier court-martial concerning flying-status determinations, Congress provided that certifications to the status of junior military aviator and military aviator were to be made by a board of five officers. Two members of the board were required to be medical officers, and the remaining three were to be military aviators. Junior military aviators were to serve a minimum of three years in that status before they were eligible for promotion to military aviator rank.[84]

The National Defense Act also provided for increased flight pay. Any aviation officer on duty "which requires him to participate regularly and frequently in aerial flights" would be eligible for flight pay. For aviation officers the increase would be 25 percent of pay; junior military aviators would receive 50 percent additional pay, and military aviators would receive 75 percent additional pay. Those officers qualifying as junior military aviators or military aviators were to be promoted to one rank higher and paid at the rate for that rank. The increase in rank and the related increase in pay was limited, since no officer could be promoted beyond the rank of captain under this provision.[85]

General Scriven had also testified in the congressional hearings that age, grade, and marital-status restrictions were hampering the recruitment of student aviators. Aviation training was restricted to lieutenants under the age of thirty who were unmarried. He pointed out that the requirement that student aviators be single did not prevent married officers from serving, and that many married after their assignment to flying duty. The age restriction meant that experienced officers would not be available to command flying units, and the grade restriction had a similar impact. Under the law as it then operated, only 668 lieutenants in the army were eligible for assignment as student aviators.[86] As enacted, the National Defense Act eliminated these restrictions.

These alterations in personnel policies were important steps toward stabilizing army aeronautics and limiting arbitrary Signal Corps control over military aviators. They indicate that Congress was determined to improve the conduct of the aeronautics program, and that while the Signal Corps retained ultimate authority over the Aviation Service, the pilots themselves would be responsible for directing their own activities.

Within the Aviation Section and the General Staff, both before and after the enactment of the National Defense Act, there were serious discussions about the removal of aviation from Signal Corps control and even of the creation of a separate cabinet department for aviation. Secretary of War Newton D. Baker pressed the General Staff for the draft of a bill to create a separate department, and this was referred to Lt. Colonel Squier, chief of the Aviation Section, for study. Baker persisted, and a three-officer General Staff committee reported in August 1916 that further legislation concerning aviation should best be delayed until the full impact of the National Defense Act could be assessed.[87] Lack of further action by Secretary Baker and the General Staff would suggest that while no one was fully satisfied with the military aviation provisions in the National Defense Act, they nevertheless recognized the substantial legislative progress that it represented in regard to army aviation. These provided a silver (and in light of the flight-pay provisions, a golden) lining to the dark clouds that surrounded army aviation in the grim years of 1915 and 1916.

A Bit More Silver

One less tangible benefit of the 1916 National Defense Act was Congress's commitment to retaining the National Guard as a primary source of wartime reserve troops and units. In this sense the act represented a victory for the militia tradition, which had been threatened by the Continental Army plan advocated in 1914 and 1915 by then–Secretary of War Lindley Garrison. The proposed Continental Army system would have utilized a system of universal military service followed by a period in an army reserve unit. All of the training would be conducted by the Regular Army, and individuals would be subject to federal recall in time of war or national emergency. The National Guard interests pointed out that the supposed inefficiencies of the guard were attributable to federal neglect, and not to a lack of commitment or professionalism on the part of the state officers. Ultimately, the majority in the Senate supported a modified Continental Army plan during the pendency of the National Defense Act. The House of Representatives held out for exclusive reliance upon the National Guard, and the disagreement was resolved by retaining the National Guard and initiating an Officer Reserve Corps and an Enlisted Reserve Corps that would ultimately become the Army Reserve.[88] The Aviation Section's relations with the aeronaut constituency, and, through it, with officers in the National Guard units, made it particularly important that the guard survive this thorough overhaul of the military establishment.[89]

In the extensive committee hearings that preceded introduction of the

National Defense Act, General Scriven and Colonel Reber testified that the only way to staff a wartime Aviation Section would be to draw upon reserve aviation units. They reported that the New York National Guard already had two pilots and one airplane, and that the Rhode Island National Guard had an airplane for its use. For these reasons, and because of the high physical requirements for aviation duty, a program to develop reserve aviation units was essential.[90] State-sponsored aviation companies and squadrons had existed for several years, but now there was statutory authority for integrating them into Aviation Section wartime planning. Both the Aero Club of America and the Aeronautical Society of America offered their facilities for the training of reserve military aviators, and the Aviation Section in July 1916 received permission to appoint reserve officers and enlisted men for training in aeronautics.[91]

Enactment of the National Defense Act did much to start the Aviation Section on its way to becoming an effective military unit. It represented the first step in bringing army aviation out of the deep troubles that beset it in 1915 and during the Mexican Punitive Expedition. Although Congress accepted many of the suggestions made by General Scriven and Colonel Reber, both officers were profoundly discomforted by committee questions that dealt with nonflying commanding officers of aviation units, unsafe army aircraft, and discontent among military aviators.[92] The revelations of the Goodier court-martial would not soon be forgotten.

The very nearness of hostilities in Europe galvanized both civilian and military leaders into acting upon the need to improve the Aviation Section. Yet only ten months remained before Congress would declare war. There were serious equipment and industrial production problems; the Wright patent issues were unresolved. The aviators mistrusted the Signal Corps, as well as each other. With more time for transition and implementation, the National Defense Act might have proved to be the salvation for army-aviation personnel stability in the First World War. But time had already run out.

Conclusion

Unquestionably, the Mexican Punitive Expedition provided strong impetus to the preparedness movement and revealed serious deficiencies in the U.S. Army's aviation activity. While European powers were using aerial weapons to determine the issue of battles, both by reconnaissance and by offensive uses of air power, the United States was unable to bring its meager air power to bear against the forces of a backward and disorganized enemy.

With the end of the First Aero Squadron's active participation in the expedition, the Aviation Section began a reconstruction of the squadron, and Congress did the same for the section as a whole. A new spirit prevailed. Following the Mexican campaign, Foulois recommended that thereafter the army test all aircraft under field conditions before accepting them.[93] This initiative in screening equipment for design defects was demonstrated in May 1916, when the aviators rejected new airplanes purchased with funds from the Urgent Deficiency Appropriation of March 1916. Condemning the planes as unsuitable for military use, the young flying officers embarrassed their superiors and infuriated the manufacturer, the Curtiss Aeroplane Company. On the other hand, they had just emerged from a period of training fatalities due to the Wright pusher biplanes and a disastrous field campaign marked by failures of the JN-3. In addition to exercising a veto over the acceptance of newly contracted aircraft, the army aviators began the establishment of manufacturing standards for airplanes and component parts. This was first manifested in their demands for improved propeller durability, and their experimentation and study of the strength-of-materials and aerodynamic aspects of propeller design. The failure of propellers in flight had been a chronic difficulty in Mexico, and shortly after the expedition the army's experimentation resulted in the adoption of more suitable laminated or metal propellers for use on military aircraft.[94]

In retrospect, the Mexican Punitive Expedition appears as a catalytic agent in the development of American air power. Previously the military aviators could count upon the support of the aeronaut constituency. They enjoyed a varying degree of support from newspapers, periodical magazines, and the authors of books on American and foreign military aviation. Yet the American public had never focused its attention upon the deficiencies of the army's Aviation Section. It took the Mexican debacle to bring on the chemical reaction of preparedness sentiment and to focus it upon military aviation.[95]

The appropriation of a vastly increased sum for army aviation in August 1916 ensured more rapid growth of the Aviation Section and improvement of its equipment. Yet money itself could not cure the diminished industrial capacity produced by a decade of governmental neglect. Indeed, since 1914 the American aircraft manufacturing industry had drawn most of its support from the warring powers in Europe. Five years earlier, a $13 million annual appropriation would have done much to foster an aircraft industry. In 1916 it merely placed the United States in competition for the outdated aircraft being produced by American manufacturers. The army and the

American people had learned from the expedition but no amount of public attention or enlarged annual appropriations could place the United States on a par with the aviation powers of Britain, France, and Germany. The disappointments of World War I, both in terms of military aviation and aircraft production, were inevitable not because the lessons of the Punitive Expedition were ignored, but, rather, because they were demonstrated too late in the history of army aeronautics. And perhaps the most significant lesson of all was the realization that modern warfare, even at the level of a border incident, depends upon a substantial amount of combat and support equipment in military hands, and a coordinated industrial supply network for the purchase of new parts and replacement equipment. The European war gave proof of the value of military aeronautics and national preparedness. The Mexican Punitive Expedition proved that the United States had neglected both.

Epilogue and Prologue
Army Aviation in World War I

General John J. "Black Jack" Pershing first saw French military aviation in June 1917 and concluded that the U.S. Army had a long way to go in aeronautics. His subsequent familiarization trips to Royal Flying Corps units operating in France provided a pointed reminder of how vastly different combat aviation in Europe was from the weak aerial support provided to the Mexican Punitive Expedition the prior year. Looking back at American entry into World War I, Benjamin D. Foulois reminisced, "In spite of what Mitchell and air-power publicists have claimed, I do not consider the World War I record of the Air Service impressive. . . . [T]he price of unpreparedness was high."[1] Unquestionably, the American Air Service had a very long way to go. Its planes were useless in the European environment. American aircraft production was badly crippled and incapable of supplying even minimal military needs.[2] Aviation officers were demoralized after a decade of struggle — for appropriations and equipment, for flying officer command of units, for General Staff acceptance of the broad range of tactical uses for airplanes, and for independence or semiautonomy of the air arm. All of the old issues resurfaced to complicate the frenzied situation of a rapid and unprecedented mobilization of the national defense establishment to fight a war that had been watched for three years but barely comprehended in its full aeronautical implications.[3]

It has been claimed that World War I was only slightly impacted by air power,[4] yet such narrowly focused criticism misses the point. Close ground support of combat troops and strategic bombardment of significant targets were both first attempted in World War I, and so were other uses of air power. In this sense, the "Great War" made it possible to test the variety of tactical applications that had been developed in the quarter-century since dirigibles and airplanes became available. For the U.S. Army, World War I was an incentive to reconsider the organizational structure of its air arm, to develop improved weapon systems, and to view modern warfare doctrine with renewed appreciation for control of the air. At the war's end, Maj. Gen. George O. Squier, who served as chief signal officer throughout the conflict, commented that more had been accomplished in the four years since 1914 than otherwise would have occurred in two peacetime decades.[5]

World War I brought U.S. Army aviation out of its neonatal stage and into full participation in the struggle for effective wartime control of the air. Indeed, the real question is not at all how much aviation mattered to the conduct of World War I, but, rather, what did American participation in World War I do for army aviation? Lee Kennett, in his comprehensive history of the air war, comments, "While the role of the air weapon in the Great War was a modest one, the role of the Great War in the rise of air power was anything but modest. . . . And the enhanced image of aviation brought with it a heightened sense of the identity, of the distinctiveness, putting the Air Service at greater distance from the rest of the army."[6] Kennett goes on to state that American military aeronautics was victimized by the fact that its partisans oversold its wartime uses, particularly in regard to the aerial-bombardment function.[7] Kennett's perceptive comments only serve to re-emphasize the degree to which the aeronaut constituency's strident claims created unrealistic public pride in a badly flawed military-aviation program. On the other hand, organizational embarrassments and disregard of discipline marked the Aviation Section's history from 1913 through 1916. These undermined the confidence that senior army commanders might otherwise have placed in their aerial units.[8]

The Transition from Peace to War

When the United States declared war on Germany and its allies on April 6, 1917, the immediate need was to assemble a large component of ground troops and to make provision for aerial support of their operations. There was also a critical need for equipment and weapons, then in short supply within the United States. That need, in turn, demanded an expanded engineering and production capacity, which would draw heavily upon the technical resources and industrial strength of the Allied powers. Finally, even though air-power conceptual thought had gone through considerable development since 1914, the Air Service needed to integrate European experience into the new weapon systems now available for use on the Western Front.

To its credit, the U.S. Army undertook a thorough reconsideration of aerial weapons as they were being used in Europe. For the first time, American officers had full access to the experiences of the Allied powers, thereby supplementing the hitherto incomplete information accessible in U.S. military attaché reports. Among the first aviation officers to arrive in Paris was Maj. Billy Mitchell, who had been dispatched even before the United States entered the war. From his inquiries and observations, Mitchell quickly realized the degree to which American aviation lagged the achievements of wartime Europe. He also met with leading French and British air commanders, including Maj. Gen. Hugh Trenchard, commander of the Royal Flying Corps in France. Trenchard had already established his doctrinal reputation. He stood for a vigorous offensive use of air power, despite heavy losses and the objections of British ground commanders. On the other hand, as Mitchell's biographer points out, Trenchard's emphasis was on what modern doctrine would call interdictional bombardment rather than the more radical dream of other British air commanders. Trenchard's views were challenged by Brig. David Henderson and Gen. Jan Christian Smuts, who viewed strategic bombardment of German cities and industrial centers as a quick route to victory.[9]

When General Pershing arrived in Paris on June 13, 1917, Mitchell prepared a report on his findings and recommendations. It urged the organization of tactical and strategic aviation units, the first to operate at division, corps, and army levels, and to provide observation aircraft and protective pursuit aircraft to ground commanders. Strategic units would be controlled by Pershing's headquarters, and would attack enemy aircraft, matériel, and troops at a distance behind enemy front lines. Subsequently a board of aviation officers, which included Mitchell, affirmed these suggestions, but General Pershing took no action. The commander-in-chief of the American Expeditionary Force (AEF) intended to move ahead cautiously. Mitchell commented in his memoirs that Pershing treated the Air Service as if it were filled with dynamite and "pussyfooted just when we needed the most action."[10] Given Pershing's Mexican experience with Air Service personnel and equipment—as well as painful recollections of Aero Club interference—his "pussyfooting" is not surprising. However, Pershing did create an Air Service for the AEF, thus recognizing aviation as a separate combat arm of his command, rather than a support branch under Signal Corps direction.[11]

Almost simultaneously, an Air Service study group under the chairmanship of Maj. Raynal C. Bolling was hard at work observing Allied airplanes at the front, and estimating the various aircraft types needed to support U.S. Army ground units. Influenced by British general David Henderson and the

Italian aviation manufacturer, Gianni Caproni, the Bolling Mission at first came out strongly in favor of strategic bombardment, only to reconsider and give priority to the manufacture of observation and pursuit aircraft.[12] The Ludendorff offensive in the spring of 1918, coupled with inadequacies of the American aircraft industry, made the Bolling Mission's report irrelevant to the American war effort. However, one of the members of the commission, Maj. Edgar S. Gorrell, went on to prepare a detailed plan for targeting strategic bombardment priorities that would later prove of value when, as Professor Holley suggests, the AEF Air Service altered its doctrinal emphasis from observation to bombardment.[13]

Gorrell's strategic bombardment plan was submitted to Brig. Gen. Benjamin D. Foulois, Chief of Air Service, AEF, on November 28, 1917. It classified aerial bombardment for the performance of three functions: (1) support of ground troops and hindering enemy troops opposing them, (2) attack of enemy troop reserves and destruction of supply depots beyond the reach of friendly artillery fire, and (3) destruction of the enemy's industrial strength through demoralization of the civilian population. Accurately predicting German technological ascendance in the struggle for air superiority by the spring of 1918, Gorrell argued for a concentrated and continuous aerial bombardment of German industrial and military targets at Dillingen, Ludwigshafen, Karlsruhe, Beechelbronn, Saarbruck, Bensdorf, and Cologne. Since only day-bombardment aircraft were currently available, Gorrell suggested that they should be used until night bombers could join them, and thereafter maintain a steady attack upon the enemy's factories and cities.[14] When in May 1918 the British established their Independent Air Force for strategic bombardment purposes, American loyalty to the overall commander-in-chief, French general Foch, precluded their full participation, as did General Pershing's objection to American units operating under British or French command.[15]

Frustrated Pilots, Too Many Cadets, and Few Airplanes

Two vital ingredients for military aviation — pilots and airplanes — were in short supply when the United States declared war. Remedying personnel deficiencies was a huge undertaking that involved establishing schools to train pilots, observers, photographers, gunners, and balloonists. Construction of these facilities and obtaining qualified staff caused a long delay in graduating combat-ready pilots. General Patrick's "Final Report" noted that only eight American-trained bombardment pilots reached the front before the armistice. No pursuit or observation pilots received all of their training in American schools. Even those trained in American schools frequently benefited from instruction by Allied officers assigned to assist in this activity. The peak of U.S. training activity at the Issoudon airfield was reached in October and November 1918, just before the Armistice ended the war.[16]

At the war's end, Col. Thomas DeW. Milling was asked to critique the American training program. He observed that school construction time was underestimated, and the army chose locations where optimum flying conditions were infrequent. Too many small schools were established when fewer but larger installations would have been more efficient. According to Milling, training on the Curtiss JN-4 airplane gave adequate basic training, and pilots should have been sent to Europe after learning to fly this plane. Instead, they were held in a training status vainly awaiting the arrival of faster and more modern planes.[17]

Once flying officers or cadets from the United States arrived in France, Milling noted, there were extended delays in receiving either basic or advanced training. Allied schools had few places available for training pilots and observers in advanced flying skills, and the Issoudon training facility was able to begin basic flying training only relatively late in the war. Col. Walter C. Kilner criticized American training methods for giving trainees little responsibility during the course and for neglecting aerial gunnery.[18] Delays in training eroded Air Service morale, and made all assigned personnel vulnerable to humorous comment at home and targets for the contempt of troops in France. One Air Service officer wrote a friend, "Why in Hell can't the people lay off the Air Service. Every time I pick up an American magazine or newspaper I see cartoons or long articles on how rotten we are. . . . [W]henever a blue-corded lad [i.e., an infantry man] salutes us disgust is written all over his face — we're the only 'cushy' job boys in France."[19] Yet pilot training, in spite of its deficiencies, was far more successful than the army's experience in preparing balloonists for combat roles.

Peacetime neglect of lighter-than-air aviation was responsible for a critical deficiency in stationary balloon pilot-observers. When Col. Frank P. Lahm arrived in France in September 1917, he found no Balloon Service organization. Some equipment had been ordered from the French and an urgent request had been sent home, asking that eight balloon companies be sent to France. However, the balloon units did not arrive until December 1917, after many American artillery batteries were sent to the front without experience in coordinating fire direction with balloon observers. Lahm, a sports balloonist in the early days of the Aeronautical Division, commanded the army's balloon units for several months in France. He believed that many later misunderstandings between the Balloon Section and artillery units were attributable to this defect in early training. At first the American balloonists were trained in French schools by French instructors. In March 1918 a separate American school was established, but it still required some French training assistance.[20]

Trench warfare made balloon direction of artillery the primary source of accurate target selection and fire control. Even airplane observation pilots recognized that they could not direct artillery fire with the same accuracy as was available from balloons. As Americans gained experience in ground combat, improved methods evolved for moving balloon units with advancing troops, and the Balloon Service became even more valuable. In his "Final Report," Major General Patrick commented that the shortage of balloon units placed a heavy burden on those in the front lines. Most of the balloon crews were almost constantly on duty and pressed to the limit of their endurance.[21]

If training Air Service personnel was difficult, airplane procurement presented an even greater challenge. Although the United States had substantial industrial capacity its aviation industry was not only small but also inexperienced in design and construction of modern military aircraft. Very few manufacturers had been able to move from customized construction into a production-line system that produced uniform and high-quality machines.

The major American contribution to airplane procurement was harvesting of raw materials in the United States, particularly spruce and other wood. At war's end Major General Squier reported on the magnitude of this accomplishment. Lumbering and processing 103,000,000 board feet of spruce engaged a total of 18,305 officers, enlisted men, and civilians. In addition, substantial amounts of Douglas fir, cedar, Central American mahogany, African mahogany, walnut, cherry, ash, and birch were harvested for the war effort. Squier's accounts showed 194,420,000 board feet of wood. The Signal Corps planted and harvested castor oil beans to lubricate Allied engine crankshafts and, unfortunately, the pilots' intestinal systems. More accurate navigational instruments were designed and put into production, and more durable and less flammable airplane fabric was developed.[22]

Aircraft production within the United States was to serve two urgent and virtually unattainable requirements: (1) equipping American aviation units for combat in France, and (2) applying American industrial capacity to augment Allied aircraft production. It was early agreed upon that the United States would not attempt to build pursuit aircraft. Realistically, American planners and their Allied counterparts felt that before American factories could be tooled for pursuit production, technological advances in Europe would make the pursuits obsolete. Instead, American procurement would stress training planes and some observation aircraft.[23]

An agreement negotiated with France on August 30, 1917, promised French delivery of 5,000 planes and 8,500 engines by June 1, 1918, with the United States to provide materials by November 1, 1917. Ultimately the French found it necessary to request American-supplied mechanics to comply with their agreement concerning pursuit planes. The mechanics finally arrived in France beginning in February 1918. By May 1918 most of the raw materials and tools required of the United States were available, and a new agreement with France, dated May 3, 1918, established a firm legal basis upon which American forces could count upon receiving French aircraft.[24]

In addition to the U.S.–French effort to supply aircraft to the AEF, there was an attempt to supply American mechanics and materials to Britain for production of 30 squadrons of the Handley-Page bomber. With Italy, the United States agreed to purchase 500 S.I.A. airplanes and 200 Caproni bombers. These procurements were terminated shortly after the Armistice halted fighting on November 11, 1918.[25]

The signal American success in airplane production involved the De-Havilland DH-4 planes received from the United States in May 1918. Despite its technical obsolescence, the DH-4, equipped with the rugged, light, and reliable Liberty engine, made a substantial contribution to Allied air power in the last six months of the war. Of the 1,213 DH-4s shipped overseas prior to the Armistice, 543 saw service on the Western Front. The Liberty engines, totaling 2,083 units, proved to be reliable power plants suitable for observation and bombardment aircraft. Unfortunately, they were not suitable for pursuit airplanes. General Patrick deemed the Liberty engine "perhaps the greatest single material contribution of the United States to aviation."[26]

The achievements of American industry, the Air Service, and the Aircraft Production Board were dwarfed by the unrealistic expectations of the American people. Even before American military missions had begun to function, the French urged that the United States establish a program to place 4,500 airplanes on the front before the campaigns were to begin in the spring of 1918. The proposal was promptly accepted by the Air Service and the Army General Staff, and was widely publicized as America's contribution to the war effort. When actual production fell far short of the French request, public opinion was aroused, leading to an extensive postwar investigation of the aviation industry.[27]

Immediately after the Armistice, "stop orders" were issued to manufacturers and Allied governments, and liquidation boards were set up to determine the amounts payable to various manufacturing firms. By May 1919 France and the United States balanced their public accounts, and the United States obtained some additional aviation equipment as a result of the transaction. Similar American missions negotiated contract terminations in Britain and Italy.[28]

U.S. Army Aviation in Combat

The long-awaited Allied offensive in the spring 1918, for which American aviators had been trained and equipped, developed in an unexpected and surprising way. Beginning on March 21, German general Erich Ludendorff launched a counteroffensive that was not halted until June 25, leaving a large salient in Allied front lines pointing directly at Paris.[29] Organized into the First Brigade under command of Col. Billy Mitchell, the aircraft were ferried from Toul to Chateau-Thierry at the end of June, with their ground and support crews preceding and following them by truck. The 140-mile transfer to the Tonquin airdrome was completed "without major mishap," according to historian James Hudson. In itself this was a demonstration that the American Air Service was fast overcoming the deficiencies marked by the Mexican Punitive Expedition just two years before. Even the threat of enemy air action and the need for immediate movement did not scatter the squadrons of the First Pursuit Group as they made a smooth transition from Toul to Chateau-Thierry.

Working in the forefront of the German advance, American pursuits and observation aircraft confronted the concentrated force of the enemy's best combat planes, including the newly developed Fokker D-VII. Flying outmoded Nieuport 28 pursuits, the First Pursuit Group took heavy losses before it was reinforced by British units equipped with newer and faster fighters. Between July 5 and early August, the group began its transition into flying new Spad XIII fighters. Despite the challenge of flying combat missions while making aircraft transitions, the Americans and their Allied pursuit squadrons maintained a modicum of air superiority over the front lines and the enemy's support areas. As a consequence, the direction of the German advance was predicted, ground troops crossing rivers were subject to strafing, and, at the request of Col. Billy Mitchell, Allied bombardment

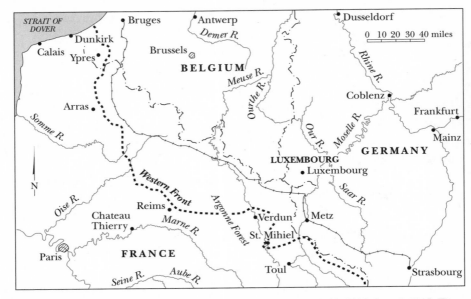

Map 2. The Western Front after the Ludendorff Offensive, March 20, 1918–June 4, 1918. The Germans' principal supply line was the railroad from Strasbourg to Bruges. American Air Service units moved from Toul to Chateau-Thierry to counter the German advance, then to St. Mihiel for an attack on the salient.

units did serious damage to a German munitions and supply area at Fere-en-Tardenois on July 16. This attack succeeded in drawing German pursuit units into defensive positions away from the front lines, and destroyed supplies vital to a further advance by the German ground troops.[30]

Although American air units began to demonstrate their value to Allied defensive tactics, the German offensive shifted Allied trans-Atlantic logistical priorities. Given the American commitment to fielding an entire army under the American flag, the initial plan was to ship troops and equipment in "phases," which would correspond roughly to a unit of corps strength. Included within that table of organization and supply were aviation troops and their equipment. However, with the German counterattack, American shipping priorities shifted in May 1918 to transport only infantry and machine gun troops, without any supply, artillery, or aviation units. Not only did this create a crisis in logistics, but it also halted the growth of American aviation. At the end of the war, Gen. Mason Patrick's history estimated that this shift in shipping priorities retarded by about four months the development of the Air Service in France.[31]

General Pershing's insistence on an independent sector for American units was responsible for the First Army's taking over the front lines surrounding the St. Mihiel salient. As two additional pursuit groups were constituted and put into combat in the Toul sector, American observation aircraft began their hazardous survey of German troop and supply concentrations in the salient and in rear massing areas.[32] Great secrecy was observed lest the Germans detect an increase in aerial activity. Patrols over enemy territory were kept to a minimum, and tactical emphasis shifted to preventing German observation of Allied front lines and rear areas. In anticipation of the attack scheduled for September 12, 1918, American observation units altered their tactics. Previously observation of enemy trenches and lines of communication had been during the daylight hours. Since most troop and supply movements were made at night, observation planes began to fly dawn and dusk flights over German lines, spotting the first and last portions of the more extensive movements at night.

Deeper penetrations into enemy territory for photo-reconnaissance demanded greater coverage than what was available in one aircraft's equipment. Previously only one plane in an observation flight carried a camera, but the new practice sacrificed dedicated escort planes so that all observation planes might carry cameras and photographic plates and some ammunition for their guns. As one aircraft's film was exposed, it moved out of the lead position to assume protective duties, and was replaced by another. It then joined the planes providing defensive cover for the flight.[33]

As Chief of Air Service for the First Army, Gen. Billy Mitchell exercised centralized control over all American air units around St. Mihiel. He also commanded an extraordinary massing of 1,481 airplanes (including some temporarily attached French and British units), compared to the 213 aircraft available to German commanders in the area. It was anticipated that one-third of the Allied air power would be utilized for ground support, with the remainder used flexibly for missions as needed. As historian James Hudson notes, the aerial blitzkrieg was frustrated by poor weather once the attack began. However, the buildup of forces in the area was successfully concealed from the Germans.[34] Normally critical of Mitchell's activities, Maj. Gen. Benjamin D. Foulois praised Mitchell for his excellent planning for the St. Mihiel offensive, and for his command and control of forty-nine squadrons, twenty-nine of which were American.[35]

Low visibility and ceiling restricted Mitchell's flyers to low-level ground support. Some valuable assistance was provided to Allied artillery in laying creeping barrages in front of advancing infantry. Panels of cloth laid upon the ground marked the lead units of American infantry, and flare signals also warned that friendly artillery was hitting them as they advanced. As German troops retreated, American fighters were able to disrupt columns on congested roads, delaying their movement. When the rain and clouds lifted on September 14, American bombardment units attacked the railroad yards at Conflans, slowing the arrival of German reserve troops at the front. Despite growing losses to German pursuit aircraft, the American bombardment campaign continued to the end of the St. Mihiel battle, supplemented by British and French night bombardment efforts. Once more, aerial bombardment drew German fighters back from the front lines, and provided some relief from pursuit attack upon Allied observation aircraft.[36]

In the Meuse-Argonne offensive, General Mitchell was again able to concentrate his aerial force. Approximately 800 aircraft were under his command when the Allied offensive began on September 26, 1918. Approximately one-third of the planes and pilots were American. Heavy fog and rain hampered first-day operations, but a number of German observation balloons were destroyed and aerial bombardment of railroad centers and bridges was helpful in isolating the battlefield from German reinforcements. Unfortunately the inexperienced American infantry were unaware of the system of signals necessary to facilitate aerial observation of artillery fire and to identify the extent of the infantry advance.

The heavily wooded terrain, particularly in the Argonne Forest, made all aerial observation difficult. In this connection the 50th Aero Squadron located the "Lost Battalion" by the dangerous scheme of drawing enemy ground fire, and plotting its location. Ultimately the area from which hostile fire did not greet the American flyers was more closely examined, and the encircled American unit was able to use cloth panels to verify its location. Ground units then fought their way into the area and freed the battalion from its trap.[37]

Long-range reconnaissance was hampered by chronically bad weather, but it was nevertheless useful in identifying German concentrations of reserve troops. American balloon observation was also exceptionally effective, and balloon units developed proficiency in making rapid advances as Allied units moved forward. At the same time, pursuit dominance of the air space over American trenches and back areas, coupled with a concerted campaign of "balloon busting" against German balloon observers, concealed American preparations from the enemy. In addition, the Air Service had learned to use long-range bombardment as a way of distracting enemy air power from the battlefront. When a motor-vehicle traffic jam risked the lives of American troops, a timely bombardment attack kept German fighters

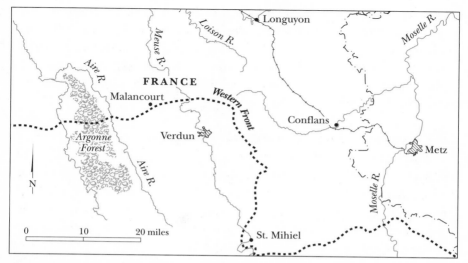

Map 3. The St. Mihiel salient. Elimination of the salient by American forces opened the Meuse to Allied use and secured the rear of Allied forces striking northeast through the Argonne Forest.

back from the threatened and congested area. These and other bombardment missions were marked by heavy concentration of aircraft, consisting of both bombardment and pursuit planes, massed for attacks on clearly identified targets.[38]

Tight formation flying by bombing and observation aircraft was further refined, resulting in sharply reduced casualties. In addition, pursuit aircraft escorted bombardment and observation planes on their missions. To assist advancing ground troops, so-called cavalry reconnaissance was developed. As the name implies, aerial observation was used to identify enemy strong points and machine gun positions. Ranging more broadly than horse cavalry, the aviators provided comprehensive and timely battlefield assessments. The drawback was that aircraft engaged in such close support of ground units were highly susceptible to enemy ground fire.[39] Cavalry reconnaissance in the air was therefore implemented only when current situation reports were urgently needed.

These campaigns in western Europe provided the U.S. Army with a valuable opportunity to test its doctrine with modern aerial weapons. They also made a substantial advance in American combat tactics and provided valuable lessons concerning the command and control of aviation resources. Historian James Hudson correctly views the war as a transitional stage in the development of the air weaponry of the United States, and he observes that while air power did not win the war, the lessons that combat taught were not lost but remained to be refined for future utilization in World War II.[40] On the other hand, if World War I was the first step toward World War II, it was also the last part of the infancy of army aviation in the United States. In light of the prewar years, World War I destroyed false optimism about America's place in military aviation even as it established realistic, battle-tested doctrine for the future of air power.

Lessons Learned: Aerial Observation and Photo-Reconnaissance

The use of aerial observation, coupled with photo-reconnaissance, proved to be an indispensable part of military intelligence during World War I. With minor variations, observation from the air was the primary source of information concerning the enemy, both in conditions of trench warfare and in times when maneuver in battle created a rapidly changing front line. In a very real sense, aerial observation replaced mounted cavalry, which was nearly worthless in trench warfare, and subject to great difficulties in communication when the battle became one of movement.

Both Allied and German armies relied heavily on aerial observation in their conduct of trench warfare. The imminence of attack across "no man's land" was signaled by the massing of troops, matériel, and medical units in the sector where the attack would occur. However, once troops were within entrenched locations, even aerial observation could not detect a buildup. Troop movements had to be identified either by personnel concentrations deep behind enemy lines, or as they were transported or marched on the highways. Since virtually all movements were conducted at night, early morning and dusk flights were the most effective way to identify troop concentrations.[41] Other signs of an offensive were the establishment of rail heads in the sector selected for launching an attack, or increased activity by observation aircraft or pursuit units attempting to establish aerial superiority.[42]

In a war of movement and maneuver, aerial observation was also critical to success. German commanders learned through aerial observation about General Joffre's counterattack from Paris in September 1914. In preparation for the attack on St. Mihiel, American observation airplanes provided continued coverage of potential routes of advance for three months prior to the assault.[43] So thorough was the aerial observation that before the initial artillery barrage, the airmen had located every German artillery piece in the salient, making it an early target for American counter-battery fire.[44] During the attack the observation squadrons were assigned the task of assessing damage to enemy field artillery. They also flew continuous observation flights to identify enemy movement of reserves into the sector. When the attack was launched on September 12, low cloud cover forced the observation aircraft to a hazardous low altitude, but the pilots were able to penetrate 60 kilometers into enemy territory. Weather continued to limit flying throughout the four-day attack. The lack of opportunity for photographic coverage and the sparsity of current and accurate topographical information was compensated for by resort to observation reports, maps, and photographs of the battle area prepared in the three-month period before the assault.[45] It was during the inclement weather at St. Mihiel that the Air Service utilized pursuit aircraft for short-range and low-level reconnaissance missions that were unsuitable for slower-moving, two-seater observation planes.[46]

The Argonne-Meuse offensive, launched on September 26, 1918, began with ideal weather conditions, but these rapidly deteriorated, with only ten days suitable for aerial observation in the month-long assault. When the weather cleared during the last three days of October, American observation planes were able to identify artillery fire objectives in German strong points. This work was accomplished in spite of heavy pursuit protection for these areas. For most of the campaign, single airplanes carried out observation missions at low altitudes. They identified the location of the advancing American units, and at times were able to penetrate 15 kilometers behind enemy lines despite German pursuit attacks.[47]

Photographic reconnaissance rapidly became an indispensable part of military intelligence. By 1914 aerial photography had progressed from its infancy, but lenses were still inadequate and the glass plates were extremely heavy for aviation use. By the time of the Armistice, new and improved cameras and lenses were available.[48] Nevertheless, the science of photography was so vital to the war effort that Maj. Kerr Riggs commented in February 1918 that aerial photographs were the most important source of Allied military intelligence. That comment was graphically proved just a month later when aerial photography permitted the Allies to identify white objects at Bullecourt as boxes of ammunition. A bombing attack promptly exploded 100 boxes intended for the front lines. Before the assault on Frappelle in August 1918, more than 25 miles of territory behind the German front lines were photographed. Both German and Allied intelligence teams used mosaics of aerial photographs to record enemy activity at the front and in the rear areas. One of the most dramatic successes of photo-reconnaissance was Allied destruction of German long-range cannon, identified by photographs taken far behind the front lines and despite German camouflage efforts.[49]

While the front lines remained stable, aerial photographs of enemy trenches and gun emplacements were prepared on a day-to-day basis. They were examined by photo-intelligence interpreters who worked on an assigned portion of the sector. Once the front changed and movements began, the intelligence interest shifted and interpreters were assigned by subject areas, to identify ammunition dumps, communications facilities, gun emplacements, and other potential targets of interest.[50] According to Lt. John L. Stewart, a British air intelligence officer examined more than 500 photographs daily and was so familiar with the front that he could identify the location depicted on a photograph without reference to its coordinates.[51] Historian Sam Hager Frank estimates that by the end of the war, one-quarter of American aircraft on the Western Front were engaged in photographic activities. Major General Squier at the end of the war commented that aerial photography was "permanently among the indispensable agencies for successful military operations."[52]

Artillery-Fire Direction

The direction of field artillery fire had long been an accepted mission for military aviation, but World War I created an environment where aerial targeting and range finding became critical. Entrenched troops and camouflaged equipment were more easily located by mobile aircraft. Increased range of cannon made balloon observation inadequate either for locating enemy targets or for spotting muzzle flashes of distant enemy cannon. However, the unique longevity in flight of stationary observation balloons made them indispensable for artillery-fire direction at the corps artillery level. Historian James J. Cooke asserts that observation balloons, along with airplanes of the observation squadrons, were the main arm of the Air Service.[53]

Prior to American air units entering offensive combat, there was some limited opportunity for training in artillery-fire direction. The 12th Aero Squadron, providing corps observation service to a portion of the U.S. 42d Division, was stationed at Baccarat and covered a relatively quiet part of the front line. In conjunction with divisional artillery, the airmen experimented with directing artillery fire on rapidly moving targets and enjoyed modest success.[54]

Unfortunately there was little time for training and liaison between most Air Service units and ground troops. This shortcoming was obvious in the opening days of the battle at Chateau-Thierry, when infantry units were hampered by their lack of familiarity with panel signaling to artillery-directing aircraft. In addition, hostile pursuit aircraft operating in the area caused failures or inaccuracy in fire direction by First Corps aviation. As the counteroffensive was launched in the Chateau-Thierry area, counter–battery artillery fire was directed successfully from airplanes, but it became difficult to determine the location of American infantry when units failed to display their panels. Aircraft descending to an altitude of 250 feet found themselves in danger from ground fire, but this proved necessary to identify the color of infantry uniforms.[55] These factors led to the postwar conclusion that artillery-fire direction from airplanes was "of comparatively small value."[56] At the end of August 1918, First Corps observation aircraft attempted to direct artillery fire in the Vesle sector by means of radio communication. The lack of reliable radio transmission and reception frustrated this attempt at fire direction, and the effort was generally considered to be unsatisfactory.[57]

The St. Mihiel offensive in September 12–16, 1918, demonstrated the same lack of coordination between artillery units and the Air Service. Pilots and observers mistakenly reported fugitive targets to the corps command post rather than to the artillery commanders, causing an unacceptably long delay and loss of opportunity. Radio calls to artillery commanders, asking that panels be displayed, went unanswered, and the pilots then failed to adopt the alternative mode of communication — dropping messages to the artillery unit. Sometimes failure of radio equipment was responsible for artillery battalions not replying, but the neglect was due to the inexperience of artillery radio operators. Finally, artillery batteries were frequently moved without notification to the Air Service liaison officer on duty at division headquarters. This meant that the airborne fire controllers plotted the location of the target but could not direct fire from an accurate firing point.[58]

Despite extensive efforts to rectify the situation, the same liaison problems that bedeviled artillery fire direction at St. Mihiel persisted in the Argonne-Meuse campaign. Surveillance of enemy artillery and direction of counter-battery fire was the most important service rendered by the Air Service squadrons. Radio malfunction, as well as failure of artillery units to respond, left more fugitive targets ample time to escape destruction. Rapid American infantry advance made consistent location of friendly batteries almost impossible, and in any event the rain and heavily overcast skies made spotting of fugitive targets virtually impossible.[59]

American aviation's lack of success with artillery-fire direction matched that of the Allies. Although Germans judged British aerial-fire direction to be very effective, British commanders themselves criticized the lack of communication between aviators and artillery batteries. This occurred even though there was a revised British manual on cooperation between the units, and a standardized system for coordinating fire. While the British used map coordinates to direct artillery fire, both German and French units ranged their artillery by making aerial photographs of the points of impact.[60] Clearly photographic fire adjustment was of no value when the effort was to destroy moving targets.

On the other hand, in ideal flying conditions and with well-trained troops, aerial direction of artillery fire was very effective in destroying hostile batteries and breaking infantry charges. At the battle of Ypres in September 1917, British field artillery broke eight charges by German infantry. Counter-battery fire at the battle of Bapaume in August 1918 was particularly precise. Over 80 percent of German artillery targets were located by aerial observation, 75 percent of the calls were answered, and German artillery was substantially neutralized. The German army took aerial observation and artillery spotting seriously. Their own observation planes were given pursuit protection, and they considered the primary mission of pursuit aircraft to be the destruction of Allied observation planes and balloons.[61]

Within the American Expeditionary Force, the seeming ostensible failure of Air Service cooperation with ground forces gave rise to strong animosity. First Lt. John H. Caulfied, an observer with the 104th Aero Squadron, commented, "Artillerymen, infantrymen, doctors, and in fact every branch of the service engaged at the front, take an unfriendly attitude toward the air service. . . . They have wholesale collections of stories as to airplane inefficiency and even cite some cases of alleged cowardice. All of such stories can be traced directly to ignorance of aerial work, and to exaggerated ideas regarding the number of American planes at the front, and the work they were expected to accomplish."[62] An operations officer assigned to the First Aero Squadron emphasized the need for ground troop cooperation if aerial observation and artillery spotting was to work effectively. "[E]xperience has proven beyond question that no matter how efficient the personnel of a squadron may be, no matter what improvement is made in type of machines, the Air Service *must* have cooperation from the ground forces in order that the results obtained will justify its future maintenance."[63] He emphasized that during war there was little time to practice coordination between air and ground units. Such work should have been done before the troops were committed to combat.

Unquestionably, there were serious technical problems in airplane direction of artillery fire. Radios did not operate reliably, and the panel system of signaling, supplemented with flares, was inadequately covered in training. Efficient artillery fire direction by airplanes simply did not occur in World War I, and to that extent prewar predictions of its value were proved overly optimistic. On the other hand, the stationary observation balloon was most effective in conditions of trench warfare, and moderately adaptable to use on a moving front. Its neglect in prewar American planning was a serious and costly error.[64]

Air Superiority

Throughout Major General Patrick's "Final Report," the term "aerial supremacy" is used to indicate that one aerial force or the other was able to dominate control of the airspace over the front lines and over the enemy's logistical support activities.[65] In point of fact, it was rare that such complete dominance existed for any extended period of time. Current doctrine would consider such temporary control of airspace to be "air superiority" rather than "air supremacy." Neither the Allies nor Germany were able to assert complete dominance of the air. In early 1918 the Royal Flying Corps was able to abandon pursuit escort for their observation aircraft, despite opposition from German pursuit squadrons. In July 1918 American reconnaissance and surveillance missions were flown successfully despite active enemy pursuit attack.[66] Both German and Allied commanders stressed the importance of what was then termed "control of the air," but it was recognized that it was impossible to deny any and all access of enemy aircraft to Allied front lines.[67]

However, at critical times a concentration of pursuit and observation aircraft within a limited geographical area could overwhelm enemy capacity to interfere with air activity. These were periods of air superiority, and when they occurred they were vital ingredients in the overall success of military operations. General Mitchell concentrated American and Allied air units in anticipation of the St. Mihiel offensive. French general Foch, the supreme commander of Allied forces, stressed the importance of air-power concentration to achieve important objectives. German practice was to centralize the pursuit group control under one commander, thereby facilitating concentration of force, and this was done even when fighters were used defensively.[68] When air superiority was gained over the front lines, it was possible to perform observation and artillery direction flying with greater efficiency. It also made possible experiments in close ground support and long-range bombardment of enemy supply depots, reserve troop encampments, transportation systems, and industrial targets.[69] To the extent that long-range bombardment drew enemy pursuit aircraft into defensive positions far behind the front lines, aerial bombardment assisted friendly air units in maintaining air superiority.

Many students of World War I aviation have suffered from viewing that conflict through World War II's glasses. Contrary to the experiences of the latter conflict, World War I aerial superiority was not based upon pursuit aircraft alone. Two-seated observation aircraft were not markedly slower than the single-seater pursuit planes of the day. At higher altitudes the larger aircraft in many cases could outrun their attackers. Formation flying by all types of airplanes made attack more difficult and had the advantage of concentrating fire power. Observation and bombardment aircraft mounted guns to fire both forward and to the rear, but pursuits were limited to forward-firing weapons.[70]

German innovations in aircraft and weapons have received great attention, and those advantages were magnified by individual combat experiences of American military aviators, as well as by those who lost their lives dealing with a better-equipped enemy. The lack of modern American fighter aircraft in American units was caused by the need to take whatever older aircraft the Allies could make available. Normally it might be expected that such a situation would trigger massive casualties and be decisive in German-American combat in the air. However, although better and faster planes gave advantages to German pursuit pilots in certain combat situations, the United States and its Allies had more airplanes and utilized systems of command that concentrated the aircraft resources to counter adequately the German threat.[71] Technological advance was important in World War I, but it was decidedly not as critical as it would become in World War II.

Allied tactical decisions emphasized the use of airplanes as weapons for attack, rather than defensive, purposes. This entailed the acceptance of greater casualties than would have been incurred with defensive tactics. However, it did keep Allied aircraft over enemy-held territory, drawing back German planes into defensive positions, and thus it denied opportunities for aerial observation and artillery-fire direction. Prior to American entry into the war, an American military observer reported German orders that their pilots not engage in combat when far over the Allied lines. The American First Pursuit Group's diary notes an incident on July 30, 1918, when an Allied bomber flight coming from Germany was harassed by nine Fokker pursuits. However, once the bombers crossed Allied front lines, the Germans turned back.[72] This raises the interesting possibility that Germany's lack of aggressive combat tactics was attributable to a quest for maximum secrecy about their aeronautical engineering achievements. By way of contrast, British and American doctrine called for sustaining the offensive, and to fight even when conditions were unfavorable.[73]

Professor Holley stresses that American doctrine giving primacy to aerial observation became one of the long-lasting legacies of World War I. However, by the end of the war American aviators had shifted their emphasis from observation to bombardment, influenced to a large degree by British conceptual thought and British establishment of the Independent Air Force, dedicated to bombardment missions.[74] For officers of the Air Service in the postwar period, the distinction was a critical one. An air *service* was dedicated to observation, and while it might have to fight in support of the observation mission, it did not seek out the enemy as a primary task. An air *force* carried out counter-air activities as its primary mission.[75] The American connection between an independent organization for aerial forces and the offensive uses of air power had solidified when the British established their Independent Force, which was to operate independently from theater commands and free from ground requirements on the Western Front. While American public opinion applauded counter-air combat as the major achievement of U.S. Army fliers in World War I,[76] military doctrine and wartime experience clearly pointed to aerial observation, supplemented by photography, as the major contribution of the Air Service to the Allied victory. In fact, observation planes made substantial contributions to gaining air superiority as well as in gathering intelligence. It was the sheer size of the American aerial effort, in all of its applications, that swung the balance in favor of Allied air power. American military planners were wrong to discount the contributions of pursuit and bombardment aircraft; army aviators were wrong to underestimate the genuine contributions of aerial observation to intelligence gathering and to artillery-fire control.

Aerial Bombardment

The Air Service gained some valuable experience in interdictional attack upon German lines of transportation and supply. During the Meuse-Argonne offensive, aerial bombardment and strafing of enemy troop reserves concentrated on roads and in wooded areas disrupted the flow of personnel to the front. A series of bombing missions against Bayonville in September and October 1918 killed over 250 German soldiers and wounded 750 others. Major secondary roads leading to the St. Mihiel front were regularly bombed and strafed once the offensive was launched. British and French aviators concentrated upon night bombardment of Longuyen, Conflans, Metz, and Sablons during the St. Mihiel offensive. Their failure to neutralize those transportation centers reportedly caused General Pershing to limit bombardment of railroads and centers during the Meuse-Argonne campaign. In retrospect, Pershing's decision, based upon his assumption that railroad interdiction had been overemphasized, does not seem as flawed as it did to the Air Corps Tactical School in 1937 and 1938. Bombardment behind enemy lines exacted a heavy toll in Air Service casualties, and it had been shown difficult to destroy railroad tracks and bridges for any significant period of time. The most lasting damage resulted from derailing or exploding troop and supply trains operating on a strategically important railroad line.[77]

If targeting was a critical factor in interdictional bombing, it was even more determinative in long-range strategic bombing. During the German bombardment offensive against London, with Zeppelins and Gotha bombers, the greatest benefit to the German war effort was the British decision to withdraw fighters from France to provide for the defense of London. On the other hand, more valuable and more vulnerable targets were close at hand. On August 11, 1918, German aerial bombardment of a motor pool and lumber yard at Calais junked vast quantities of desperately needed spare parts, motor cars, ambulances, and tractors. All 55 airplane raids in England destroyed an estimated £1,434,526 in property; the monetary loss from the Calais raid was estimated at £1,250,000, and the tactical result was to render the transportation situation of the Allies seriously deficient.[78] Occurring near the end of the Ludendorf offensive, the loss of ground mobility must have had an immense impact upon the ground war in France.

Clearly, the impact of aerial bombardment cannot be judged by the simple calculation of property destruction. National morale and public opinion were driving factors in Germany's continuing its aerial offensive against the English cities. German Zeppelin raids seemed to be irresistible, since defensive fighters were unable to reach the airships which easily exceeded their maximum operating altitude of 16,000 feet. One of the last Zeppelin raids, carried out over Hull on August 21, 1917, was staged at 20,000 feet to avoid British fighters. However, at such a height identification of targets was difficult, and high wind velocities carried the airships off their course. Darkness and the blacked-out British landscape confused their navigation. When in the spring of 1917 the Germans shifted to raiding with Gotha G-IV bombers, they retained the advantage of higher operating altitudes than those of

British fighters. The Gothas also boasted greater maneuverability and speed than the immense Zeppelins. Only with a greater concentration of defensive fighters could the British hope to protect their cities against German bombardment.[79]

To a badly shaken British public, it seemed as if the nation was helpless and unable to prevent aerial attack. The first daytime Gotha attack on London occurred at 11:35 A.M., just as the streets began to be crowded with lunchtime crowds. Seventy-two bombs were dropped within a one-mile radius of Liverpool station, killing 162 people and wounding 432 others. As these raids continued, two of the best combat squadrons were recalled from France to counter them.[80] Ultimately the German need for aircraft on the Western Front, coupled with improved British fighter and anti-aircraft defense, stopped German aerial bombing in England. During the last Gotha raid, on May 19–20, 1918, thirty-four German bombers crossed the English Channel. Anti-aircraft artillery fire shot three out of the sky, and three more were destroyed by defending fighters.[81] By October 1917 the War Cabinet had adequate opportunity to evaluate the demoralizing impact that aerial attack had upon munitions workers. A group of DH-4 aircraft intended for shipment to Russia was diverted to the aerodrome at Ochey, near Nancy in France. Designated the 41st Bombing Wing, this group of airplanes was the forerunner of the Independent Air Force that would ultimately be charged with strategic bombardment of German industrial targets.[82]

Strategic bombardment had widespread diplomatic implications throughout World War I. American public opinion was deeply offended by the death of civilians—at Antwerp in August 1914 as well as in London. However, by August 1917 the British prime minister's Committee on Air Organization and Home Defence against Air Attacks noted that "the side that commands industrial superiority and exploits his advantages in that regard . . . ought in the long run to win." This realization, coupled with public demands for reprisals against Germany, moved the cabinet and military planners into the task of establishing a strategic bombardment program.[83]

Building upon substantial Royal Naval Air Service (RNAS) experience with intermediate-range bombardment,[84] the British began a systematic study of strategic long-range bombardment. Lord Tiverton, a lieutenant in the Royal Navy, began his analysis with an innovative study designed to estimate the probable number of bombs each type of target would require before it was destroyed. Subsequently he prepared a list of German areas and industries that were most critical to the enemy's war effort. These closely paralleled the target lists earlier prepared by the RNAS. Finally he recommended that daytime bombing was preferable to attacks at night. Not only was the navigation more satisfactory in daytime, but day bombers could operate with fewer crew members and therefore heavier bomb loads. Tiverton's September 1917 report identified the Verdun-Toul sector as the best staging area for strategic bombardment raids. It would permit the Allies to attack all four target areas, and thus compel the Germans to disperse their defensive fighters if the industrial centers were to be protected.[85]

British conceptual thought on strategic bombardment stressed continuous attack on a given target, and identified those targets that were particularly vulnerable to aerial attack. These included railroads while in operation, concentrations of railroad rolling stock in yards, and railway maintenance shops. Enemy aviation facilities and supply dumps were also good targets. Finally, factories were suitable for aerial attack. A memorandum from the chief of the Imperial General Staff stressed the importance of continuous attack on enemy industrial targets. This was necessary to produce sustained anxiety, to interrupt production, and to undermine public confidence in defensive measures. An earlier memorandum from Royal Flying Corps headquarters pointed out that long-distance bombing should be coordinated with British air offensives elsewhere, so that German pursuit aircraft were distracted from attacking the bombing force.[86] Clearly, the wartime experience with interdictional bombing at the front, coupled with the British public's reaction to German aerial attacks on London and other cities, provided a strong national consensus in support of a strategic bombardment program.

Although Lt. Gen. Sir David Henderson had long insisted that the aviation needs of the Western Front should take priority over the establishment of an independent air force for strategic bombing, by July 1917 he had begun to see the need for a central air service planning staff. On August 17, 1917, Lt. Gen. Jan C. Smuts submitted a report that emphasized the importance of air power and the need for a long-range bombing force. Henderson's support for the Smuts report hinged upon the need for centralized direction of military flying. Both the cause of strategic bombardment and the pressure for a separate air service received further support when Rear Adm. Mark Kerr of the Royal Navy was appointed to the interservice Air Board. Kerr was a supporter of strategic long-range bombardment and wished this program to be carried out under the control of the Air Ministry.[87]

The British intention to begin a strategic bombardment campaign against German cities was revealed at a joint British, American, and French meeting held on December 22, 1917. The French representative, Gen. Maurice Duvall, objected that available resources were inadequate to conduct this campaign as well as to continue the Allied air effort over the front lines. Furthermore, Duvall questioned the wisdom of bombing German towns when it was so easy for the Germans to retaliate. Lt. Col. Edgar S. Gorrell, as officer-in-charge of Strategical Aviation, Zone of Advance, AEF, indicated American intentions to pursue a program similar to that proposed by Trenchard, but that official approval would have to emanate from General Pershing's headquarters. Subsequently, Trenchard and Gorrell had informal discussions about how American aviation personnel might be included in the British campaign until such time as they could mount a separate strategic bombardment unit. However, in the summer of 1918 the British bombing force was separated from the Royal Air Force field command in France, and made independent of the authority of Marshall Ferdinand Foch, the Allied commander-in-chief. Loyalty to Foch and the concept of unified command in France caused the AEF to decline joining the British Independent Force, and to continue development of their own strategic bombardment unit.[88] While American decisions appear to have been made in France, based upon adherence to Pershing's principle of unified command, they may well have been endorsed by Secretary of the Army Newton Baker, who was shocked at the thought of aerial bombardment of civilian populations, and directed the army chief of staff to inform the AEF that American bombardment should be directed at targets serving "obvious military needs."[89]

Close cooperation between the American Air Service and the British Independent Bombing Force was sharply limited by these command considerations. Much closer operational ties existed to the Royal Air Force in the field. Only thirty-six American officers served with the Independent Force during the course of hostilities. However, General Mitchell was able to call upon Independent Bombing Force squadrons for support in the initial phases of the September 1918 American offensive at St. Mihiel.[90]

The Independent Force generally remained aloof from the air-power emergency that existed as a consequence of the Ludendorff offensive in the spring of 1918. The bombardment campaign against German industrial centers continued in theory, but after the official establishment of the Independent Bombing Force on June 6, 1918, the limited range of the available aircraft reduced the number of industrial targets subject to attack. Instead, General Trenchard emphasized bombing enemy airdromes and aviation supply dumps. Bombardment raids were also staged against German rail centers and operating railroad lines. Trenchard's secondary target was German blast furnaces, which were easily identified by night-flying bombers.[91]

British strategic bombardment drew some German pursuit squadrons from the battlefront. Under optimum conditions, aerial bombardment of rail centers and railroad lines interdicted the movement of troops and supplies to the front, and in this sense the Independent Force made substantial contributions to the Allied effort on the ground. One of the most productive of these attacks took place on July 16, 1918, when bombs dropped on the station at Thionville exploded a munitions train and six ammunition trucks. The blast and subsequent fire killed or wounded eighty-three persons. As a general rule, attacks on railroad stations were not this successful because both the buildings and the track beds were of brick construction. When German industrial targets were bombed, the factories were slightly damaged, but the greatest benefit was the loss of morale and productivity of the workers who often refused to return to work for fear of a subsequent attack.[92]

By November 1918, British tactical practice recognized the value of pursuit escort for bombardment aircraft. For deep penetrations into German territory, the fighter escort was expected to be double the number of bombing planes. Utilizing nighttime bombardment, the Independent Bombing Force benefited from Germany's lack of a night fighter and was generally unopposed during strategic long-range operations. The success of these bombing raids was determined by aerial photographs subsequently taken of the target area.[93]

The U.S. Air Service and Strategic Long-Range Bombardment

Although Gen. Billy Mitchell had begun to study strategic long-range bombardment in the early months of American participation in the war, Maj. Edgar S. Gorrell's study, "Strategical Bombardment," dated November 28, 1917, was the first comprehensive American treatment of the topic. Gorrell viewed aerial bombardment as the best method of breaking the trench war deadlock that existed on the Western Front, and he warned that the Germans were already developing aircraft to undertake a serious offensive in the air. That attack would include destruction of Allied industrial capacity. Hence it was essential that a bombing plan be developed that would destroy German chemical factories active in producing munitions. Another target should be the Mercedes engine factories, and the industry devoted to building the Bosch magneto. Both of these essential industries were located in the city of Stuttgart.[94]

Comparing the German army to the point of a drill, Gorrell argued that

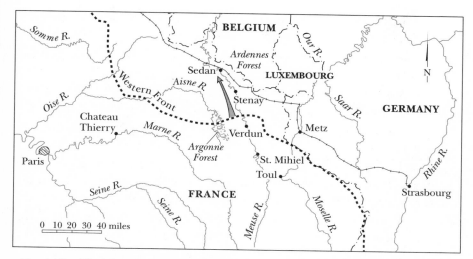

Map 4. The Allied drive through the Argonne Forest toward Sedan. With its railroad line of supply threatened, Germany negotiated an armistice to be effective on November 11, 1918.

the drill shank supporting the army was the nation's industrial and commercial capacity. He continued: "The object of strategical bombing is to drop aerial bombs upon the commercial centers and the lines of communications in such quantities as will wreck the points aimed at and cut off the necessary supplies without which the armies in the field cannot exist." Adopting the "general division made by English experts," he proposed that the geographical areas of Dusseldorf, Cologne, and Mannheim-Ludwigshafen be considered the primary industrial targets. When sufficient aircraft became available, the air attack could be expanded to include some feints in the direction of Karlsruhe and Rastadt. Finally, munitions works in the Saar Valley might be attacked when weather conditions precluded longer flights. Echoing the Tiverton report, Gorrell advocated basing strategic-bombing aircraft in the Toul area, thereby gaining maximum dispersal of defending German fighters.[95]

The lack of nighttime bombing aircraft required that the United States begin with daylight raids, supplementing them with night bombardment as suitable planes were delivered to operational units. Navigational skills would have to be enhanced before long flights into Germany might be successful, and an adequate supply of aerial bombs, hopefully stored in underground ammunition dumps, would be a priority. In addition, adequate shelter for airplanes was an important factor in extending their operational life beyond eight days. Recalling Mexican Punitive Expedition experience, Gorrell urged that pilots and observers be given vigorous training in the topography of Germany, thereby avoiding the danger of becoming disoriented or lost on bombardment missions. Like British airmen, Gorrell stressed the need for a concentrated effort against a single target. The groups from various Allied bases would attack at short intervals, thereby providing continuous bombardment that would wreck the industrial target and demoralize its workmen.[96]

Gorrell's 1917 plan called for cooperation with the Allies, since both France and Britain had expressed interest in launching a strategic bombardment campaign. Of the two, it appeared that only Britain had the capacity to do so, but the French were strong in their support and would lend such assistance as was available to them. Of course, Gorrell in 1917 could not anticipate the establishment of the British Independent Bombing Force, and the altered command relationships that would restrict American cooperation with British air commanders. His 1917 plan was submitted to the chief of Air Service, AEF, and subsequently received General Pershing's positive endorsement.[97]

On January 2, 1918, Gorrell drew up a detailed scenario for phasing in a strategical aviation unit. He anticipated that a single officer working alone would require fourteen months before the administrative details were completed and an adequate analysis of British experience and operational systems could be made. However, if an efficient staff were assembled, the strategic-bombing activity might be in place by June 1918. Shortly thereafter, Gorrell, promoted to lieutenant colonel, was assigned to AEF headquarters for this purpose, and Col. Ambrose Monell, former president of the International Nickel Company, was placed in command of the Strategical Section of the Air Service, Zone of Advance. Working with Monell was British Wing commander Spencer Grey, of the Royal Naval Air Service. Grey was considered one "the world's greatest authority on questions dealing with aerial bombardment," according to Gorrell.[98]

It rapidly became clear that American industrial production of aircraft would never meet the projected aircraft production schedules. Wing commander Grey became discouraged and left his work with the American headquarters. Colonel Monell discovered that the Allied supply of pursuit aircraft was inadequate to staff a strategic pursuit component, and that the Handley Paige bomber would prove difficult to produce in sufficient numbers to stage long-range attacks on Germany in 1918. As a result, Air Service strategy shifted to accommodate the shorter range of the DeHavilland

DH-4, then being assembled in France from American-built components. In retrospect, Gorrell commented that there were two great faults with the original plan: (1) too much optimism was felt for the Air Production Program, and (2) failure to coordinate with the General Staff, AEF, due to Air Service inexperience, resulted in a lack of mutual cooperation in launching and planning for strategic bombardment aviation.[99] Along with these planning oversights, the establishment of the British Independent Air Force as a separate command from the Allied ground forces made American participation more difficult.

Sensitive to the American command objections to the U.S. strategic bombardment unit being separate from the AEF Air Service, Gorrell's group changed the name of the unit to GHQ, Air Service Reserve.[100] A cosmetic name change did not allay all objections. When in May 1918 the American bombardment units were ready to assist British Independent Force bombers with night bombardment missions, Major General Patrick notified General Pershing's headquarters of this development. Despite Pershing's prior approval of Gorrell's strategic bombardment plan, the general's chief of staff cautioned that cooperation should not separate American bombardment forces from their place as an "integral part of the American Expeditionary Forces." Furthermore, it was directed that "the higher officers among our bombing personnel be impressed with the importance of the principle of the concentration of the effort of each arm, and of the coordination of all efforts, to a common tactical end. It is therefore directed that these officers be warned against any idea of independence and that they be taught from the beginning that their efforts must be closely coordinated with those of the Air Service and with those of the ground army." Cooperation with the British was to be limited, particularly when American ground forces required bombardment support, which would be directed from AEF headquarters.[101]

Doubtless viewed as a sharp command reversal at the time of its issuance, Pershing's reaction in retrospect seems to have been a product of three factors: (1) the Air Service had already proven difficult to command, given the Foulois-Mitchell disagreements and prewar breaches of command relationships by aviation personnel, (2) Allied experience demonstrated the value of interdictional bombardment, but strategic attacks on enemy industrial targets were as yet of questionable value (they were also impolitic, given army secretary Baker's opposition), and (3) the broader aims of Allied cooperation were being undermined by the British Independent Bombing Force, and the United States was committed to unified command in France.

A limited survey of American strategic bombing, completed after the Armistice, reflected that American bombardment targets were interdictional in nature — railroad stations, railroad yards, troop concentrations, and bridges. All of these targets were within sixty-five miles of the principal bases located at first at Amanty and later at Maulan. For all practical purposes, the American "strategic" bombardment effort was interdictional bombing at a slightly greater distance than had been customary.[102] However, the British campaign had been more ambitious, and within the limited area surveyed, their aerial bombardment killed 641 persons and wounded an additional 1,262. Material damage in Germany and occupied territory was estimated at 35,449,190 German marks; when added to indirect costs and loss of production, the impact was calculated at 72,563,723 marks. However, the British bombing campaign was faulted by the American surveyors in four particulars:

(1) There was no predetermined program to destroy those industries most vital to maintaining German armies in the field.

(2) Bombing was extremely inaccurate, particularly when compared to Royal Naval Air Service success against submarines.

(3) Attacks were directed at strategic towns, rather than the military objectives within those areas. Bombing for morale effect alone was not a productive use of air power.

(4) Failure to bomb a target continuously permitted quicker repair of the destroyed facility; it also failed to destroy the target permanently.[103]

The American survey team came down strongly in favor of unified theater command, commenting, "there can exist no such force as a separate or independent bombing force."[104]

Conclusion

The abrupt end of the First World War on November 11, 1918, left more questions than the years of combat had answered. That proved to be especially true of strategic long-range bombardment. Major General Patrick in his "Final Report" noted that while an Allied night-bombing group had not been organized, Allied experience indicated that the morale impact of nighttime aerial bombing was substantial. That was also true of daylight attacks, which had the added value of drawing enemy aircraft away from the front lines and into defensive positions.[105] However, given the great expectations that strategic bombardment engendered, the overall accomplishments were minimal. Major General Foulois observed that "although the plans for strategic air operations were fully developed by June, 1918, their actual execution was only partially started prior to the cessation of hostilities."[106]

Uncertainty about the accomplishments of strategic long-range bombardment in the immediate postwar years was firmly based upon the inconclusive nature of the wartime experience. In point of fact, at the Armistice even the much-hailed British Independent Bombing Force was still equipped with obsolete aircraft and had fielded only nine bombardment squadrons and one fighter squadron. The original projections had been to employ between 40 and 104 squadrons in this effort to destroy German industry.[107]

In addition, British air commanders had surrendered to the public clamor to avenge the aerial bombardment of London. Thus the bombing that the Independent Force accomplished (like the tactical bombardment by Air Service units) was against towns, and not against military and industrial targets within those localities. Writing his multivolume study of British aviation in World War I, historian H. A. Jones pointed out the error in targeting: "The art of air warfare is mainly a question of choice of the right targets at the right time. The temptation to dissipate effort will invariably be great. The commander or Government most successful in resisting sentimental or similar motives . . . whose choice of objectives is governed to the greatest extent possible by pure military considerations" was most likely to succeed.[108]

There are bits and pieces of evidence that would suggest the Air Service was persuaded early in the war that their primary contribution to the Allied effort in the air should be in terms of strategic bombardment. A December 1917 memorandum prepared by Headquarters, Royal Flying Corps, commented, "Apart from the necessary local work for their own Army which will require an organization of fighting, artillery, photographic, reconnaissance, and short distance bombing squadrons similar to our own and the French, . . . [American assistance] will be of especial value for bombing operations in Germany."[109] Whether or not this plan was revealed to American airmen is not clear, but we do know that in August 1918, an American pilot, Henry W. Dwight, wrote his mother that he and his unit were flying with Liberty engines, "probably to be used for bombing." Patrick's "Final Report" admitted that while some 160 bombing missions had been completed by American squadrons, the war ended before they were ready for strategic air warfare.[110]

Recent historical study, as well as Army War College teaching in the 1930s, occasionally suggests that had the First World War continued into

1919, the Central Powers would have been overwhelmed by an aerial blitz-krieg.[111] To a limited degree the threat of Allied predominance in the air over the battlefield may have led to the Armistice, and to that extent the success of the Allies may have been due to air power — or its potential expansion with American industrial and military assistance. However, even the limited use of strategic bombardment had created command difficulties between the Americans, the French, and the British. The production of modern aircraft in the United States was still sometime in the future, and as we have noted patent litigation on the part of the Wrights could easily have slowed that aircraft production effort in spite of the existence of the patent pool.[112] Even without patent litigation, aircraft production in the United States was far below Allied expectations.

There was precious little in the U.S. Army's World War I experience with strategic long-range bombardment that would justify its adoption as a doctrine upon which future warfare might safely depend. In the 1930s this divergence between the potentialities of World War I air power, and its actual accomplishments were well recognized. Lawrence S. Kuter, lecturing to the Air Corps Tactical School in the postwar period, pointed out that the First Bombardment Group in France had not been trained or equipped to bomb accurately, and their planes were easily destroyed because of their wood construction and the flammability of gasoline tanks that were kept under pressure during flight. They were certainly not the bombardment group anticipated in Gorrell's 1917 memorandum.[113]

On the other hand, the war had verified the great value of aerial observation, by both balloons and airplanes, and the great contributions that photographic reconnaissance could make to military intelligence. Upon this point there was general agreement between the General Staff, General Pershing, and the Air Service. Testifying before the House Committee on Military Affairs in 1919, Brigadier General Mitchell stressed the need for observation aircraft and balloons to serve with each army division. When asked about the command of observation units, he stated that observation aircraft should be assigned to the army and navy commanders and stay with those units. In his "Final Report," Major General Patrick noted the exceptionally valuable service that aerial observation and photography had made to the war effort; he added that in the future Air Service officers should be trained in the work of the other arms, and also be more knowledgeable of General Staff tactical planning. Both would facilitate more effective operations by the pilots and observers.[114]

The importance of some tactical lessons would be overlooked in the Air

Service's analysis of what had happened during the twenty months that the United States had been at war, and the eight months that the Air Service experienced combat. At the outset of American aerial participation, General Mitchell at Chateau-Thierry demonstrated the tactical advantage of concentrating aircraft to gain air superiority over the battlefield. Earlier, Major Gorrell identified the critical need for accurate evaluation of targets that had genuine military significance, a skill that was equally as necessary in tactical support of ground forces as it was in strategic bombardment contexts. These and other lessons would lie fallow until historical study or doctrinal development rediscovered them.

One example of the value of historical study is the perspective of historian Lee Kennett, who views American participation in a new and more favorable light. First of all, when the United States entered the war, the tempo of the air war had reached its highest point, with a commensurate rise in casualties. Kennett observes that 75 percent of French aviation casualties occurred during the last two years of the war. Thus the AEF Air Service found itself involved in the high point of aerial combat from the very first weeks of its operations. Secondly, the depletion of German supplies and equipment generated serious logistical problems for enemy units. When the United States entered the war with fresh troops and vast quantities of matériel, the blow to German morale was substantial. American potential, as much as, if not more than, American combat units present in the field, greatly accelerated German willingness to negotiate an armistice.[115]

For better or for worse, the First World War did not teach what the airmen wanted to hear — that their weapon was the key to future military victory. It did confirm the immense value of the Air Service to the army's combat operations and, by doing so, it tied army aviation more closely to the ground force command structure than the Air Service officers accepted. An Indian army officer attached to the U.S. Army Air Service during the war wisely predicted that the army flyers would have a hard struggle against misunderstanding, and might be hard-pressed to retain their place within the fighting organizations of the U.S. Army.[116] Doctrine in the 1920s stressed the close interrelationship between military aviation and the information-gathering function: "The Air Service aids the Infantry, helps adjust Artillery, assists in keeping the staff informed, destroys the enemy air service by using machine guns and bombs, assists in deciding actions on the ground, and prevents the enemy air service from rendering similar assistance to the hostile forces."[117] Major Milling cautioned that the stabilized trench warfare of World War I was responsible for giving undue emphasis to artillery fire direction. In his opinion, observation was the most important function of the Air Service during the war.[118] It was in the 1930s and 1940s, with the ambiguities of World War I well behind them, that army aviators began to embrace Giulio Douhet's long-range strategic bombardment views. Feeling that they had been denied the opportunity to demonstrate this offensive use of air power in the First World War, army airmen simultaneously began to develop both strategic-bombardment doctrine and the aircraft needed to put that conceptual thought into practice.[119]

American military planners recovering from the shock of pre-1917 unpreparedness in the air would continue to be alert to the need to maintain military and naval air services that were competitive with those of other nations. In his 1919 testimony before a congressional committee, Maj. Benjamin D. Foulois (now reduced to his permanent grade) stressed the need to encourage civil aviation. Planes designed for sport racing might support an industry that in wartime could convert to construction of pursuit aircraft. Bombing planes could be developed by manufacturers who in peacetime constructed aircraft designed to carry mail and cargo. Brigadier General Mitchell echoed those sentiments and stressed the need to have a reserve flying program as well as a large base in civil aeronautics from which wartime pilots could be acquired.[120]

To this extent, World War I was a prologue to the future growth of the Air Service, the Air Corps, and the U.S. Air Force. It was also an epilogue to the confusions, dissensions, and eclecticism of the early years of army aviation. Gradually, army professionalism began to draw military aviators out of the clubby civilian atmosphere of the Aero Club of America, the Aeronautical Society, and the militia and volunteer "reserve" units. The disappointments, casualties, and mistakes of World War I chastened the exuberance of army flyers who once basked in public adulation even as their flying colleagues perished in unsafe airplanes that belonged in museums rather than in the air. World War I aviation generals reverted to being captains and majors once more, and the peacetime Air Service began a new era of its history. It would be a time dominated for a decade by the ambivalent legacy of the First World War — a tension between a fantasy of what could have been, and the grim recollection of what actually happened.

Appendix

Chronology of Significant Events

March 1906
United States patent is issued to Wright brothers.

August 1, 1907
Aeronautical Division of Signal Corps established.

June 1908
Aeronautical Society of New York, subsequently Aeronautical Society of America, is established.

September 1908
Army acceptance tests of Wright flyer take place at Fort Myer, Virginia; they end when the airplane crashes, killing Lt. Thomas E. Selfridge and injuring Orville Wright.

1908–9
Aeronautics, periodical publication of Aero Club of America, inaugurates a section of "Army News" in each issue.

February 1909
Herring-Curtiss company is formed.

March 4, 1909
William Howard Taft is inaugurated.

June–July 1909
Successful trials of Wright flyer are held at Fort Myer; Wright military flyer is accepted by army.

January 3, 1910
Preliminary injunction issued in *Wright Co. v. Herring Curtiss Co.*; injunction is subsequently dissolved on procedural grounds.

September 1911
Commencement of the Turco-Italian War in Tripoli and Libya

March 1912
House Committee on Military Affairs issues a report detailing European progress in military aviation.

August 1912
Balkan Wars begin.

August 10–24, 1912
    Combined National Guard maneuvers in Connecticut demonstrate the
    importance of aerial observation.
September 15, 1912
    Signal Corps flying officers participate in and serve as officials for Fourth
    International Gordon Bennett Airplane Meet, Chicago, Illinois.
October 1912
    Lt. Henry H. Arnold wins Clarence M. McKay Trophy for airmanship.
November 11, 1912
    French army military maneuvers
March 4, 1913
    Woodrow Wilson is inaugurated.
August 12–16, 1913
    House Military Affairs Committee holds hearings on the Second Hay Bill.
January 1914
    British army transfers its dirigible airship to the navy and announces its intention
    to emphasize airplane flying.
January 13, 1914
    U.S. Court of Appeals for Second Circuit affirms decision upholding the
    Wrights' patent.
July 18, 1914
    Second Hay Bill is enacted into law, creating the Aviation Section of the Signal
    Corps and altering restrictive personnel policies concerning army aviators.
August 1, 1914
    First World War begins in Europe.
May 15, 1915–June 1917
    German naval Zeppelins and Gotha bombers stage night raids on London and
    some other British cities.
October 18–November 18, 1915
    Lt. Col. Lewis E. Goodier court-martial is held in San Francisco; Goodier is
    reprimanded.
November 1915
    General Staff issues a supplement to army doctrine recognizing the
    reconnaissance value of aircraft, as well as a combat role to gain air superiority
    for observation purposes.
February 12–April 24, 1916
    Military board appointed by army chief of staff to look into administration of
    Signal Corps Aviation Section. As a consequence, Brig. Gen. Scriven is
    reprimanded, and Lt. Col. Samuel Reber is reprimanded and relieved of
    command of the Aviation Section.
February 12–July 10, 1916
    General Staff investigating committee, chaired by Col. Charles W. Kennedy,
    appointed to consider organization and management of Aviation Section. Its
    recommendation for a central agency within the army to control aeronautics is
    rejected by the chief of staff's office, but Secretary of War Newton D. Baker issues

instructions that the chief of the Aviation Section report directly to the chief of staff and secretary of war, with the Aviation Section remaining within the Signal Corps.

March 5–June 3, 1916

National Defense Act of 1916 is introduced, debated, passed by Congress, and signed into law by President Wilson.

March 15, 1916

Punitive Expedition, under the command of Brig. Gen. John J. Pershing, enters northern Mexico in pursuit of Pancho Villa.

March 19–30, 1916

First Aero Squadron attempts night flight to join Punitive Expedition's headquarters; of eight planes in squadron, none reaches headquarters without making intermediate stops.

April 17, 1916

Reprimand of Lt. Col. Goodier is confirmed by President Wilson.

April 19, 1916

Last JN-3 in service with the First Aero Squadron crashes after a photo-reconnaissance mission.

March, August 1916

Congress passes urgency appropriations for army aviation.

June–September 1916

Battle of the Somme provides insight into the value of aerial observation, close ground support, artillery-fire direction, and air superiority.

September 1916

Wright Company merges into Wright Martin Aircraft Company.

April 6, 1917

United States declares war on Germany, Austria, and Turkey.

July 24, 1917

Manufacturers' Aircraft Association forms a patent pool for cross-licensing of airplane production in the United States.

October 1917

First Aero Squadron arrives in France for training with underpowered French observation planes.

May 18, 1918

96th Aero Squadron cannibalizes parts from French Breguet 14 B-2 bombers and stages bombardment missions against railroad targets for two weeks.

Ca. June 20, 1918

Under the direction of Col. Billy Mitchell, American squadrons are moved by air to counter the German attack in the area of Chateau-Thierry.

August 26, September 22, 1918

Mitchell assembles an overwhelming force of American and Allied airplanes and achieves air superiority over the St. Mihiel salient during the battle.

November 11, 1918

Armistice ends First World War.

Notes

USAFAL   Special Collections Division, U.S. Air Force Academy Library, Colorado Springs, Colorado

WB/LC   Wright Brothers Papers, Library of Congress

WIC/LC   Captain Washington I. Chambers Collection, Library of Congress

INTRODUCTION

1. Among the many Mahan editions, the one most appropriate to our time period is *The Influence of Sea Power upon History, 1660–1783*, 24th ed.

2. The manuscript papers of Capt. Washington I. Chambers, the first director of naval aviation, are at the Library of Congress Manuscript Division. They provide exhaustive evidence of the disadvantages Navy aviators faced within the Navy itself and with Congress. Unfortunately, Captain Chambers's papers have not as yet been researched to provide a full account of these difficulties.

3. The standard work on the international law of aerial bombardment in this period remains Royse, *Aerial Bombardment*.

4. John T. Greenwood asserts that lack of appropriations prevented the army from implementing changes in tactics, medical service, and transportation recommended by army officers who observed combat in the Russo-Japanese War: "American Military Observers," 500–502.

CHAPTER ONE

1. Historian Bill Robie identified the Aero Club of America as the "focal point of American flying activities throughout the early days of airplane, balloon, glider, and dirigible development." It and its successor, the National Aeronautical Association, were responsible for licensing dirigible and airplane pilots until 1916; Robie, *For the Greatest Achievement*, xiv, 55–56. Cooke, *U.S. Air Service in the Great War*, notes Army–Aero Club connections at pp. 3–4. The bicycle, automobile, and ballooning origins of British military aviation are traced in Driver, *Birth of Military Aviation*, 1–84.

2. The definitive work on ballooning is Crouch, *The Eagle Aloft*, which details initial American contacts with European balloon activity (dating from 1783), and discusses at length the Civil War activities of Thaddeus S. C. Lowe, at pp. 13–30, 56–70, and 335–415.

3. Ibid., 391–92, 396–403, 412–15.

4. Baldwin's balloon tethers were caught by trees, within reach of small arms and artillery fire. Troops in the vicinity were exposed to heavy Spanish fire and bombardment; they included 1st Lt. John J. Pershing and volunteer Lt. Col. Theodore Roosevelt. Ibid., 522–27.

5. The chief signal officer, Brig. Gen. Adolphus W. Greely, in conjunction with William A. Glassford and Thomas S. Baldwin, established an army balloon section in 1891 and proceeded to gather information for the purchase of a spherical balloon. Ibid., 519–22.

6. Crouch, *Dream of Wings*, 255–93, provides an excellent discussion of the Langley experiments and the army's decision to fund them.

7. K-*WB*, 147–49, 150, 157–58; F-*WBA*, 53; CL-*AGW*, 143; Milling, "A Short History," 9–10, AFHRA; TL-*NA*, 3; Holley, *Ideas and Weapons*, 26.

8. It is impossible to overstate the importance of the Aero Club of America to the early history of aviation. The discussion that follows has been taken from newspaper and magazine references as well as from the official magazines of the Aero Club, *Aeronautics* (hereafter cited *A*), *Flying* (hereafter cited *F*) and *Aerial Age Weekly* (hereafter cited *AAW*); see also Robie, *For the Greatest Achievement*, 2–3, 9, 10, for early activities of the Aero Club of America. For the earliest membership lists, reliance has been placed upon the bulletins issued annually and now on deposit in the E. L. Jones Collection (hereafter cited Jones/AFHRA). For a more extensive discussion of the Aero Club of America, see Herbert A. Johnson, "The Aero Club of America and Army Aviation, 1907–1916," *New York History*, 65 (1985): 374–95.

9. Cuneo, *German Air Weapon*, 10; Raleigh, *War in the Air* (hereafter R-*WA*), 120–21.

10. Frank, "American Air Service," 75.

11. *Aero Club of America* (New York: Douglas Taylor & Co., 1910), 7. The objectives in the certificate of incorporation as a membership corporation parallel those in the constitution of the Aero Club of America, printed in the 1907 yearbook, 6–7. These and other Aero Club yearbooks are in Jones/AFHRA.

12. CL-*AGW*, 63; Robie, *For the Greatest Achievement*, 38.

13. McMinn, "Memories of Grover Loening," 204; Knabenshue persisted in his work with balloons, and in May 1913 he and Walter Brookings flew their 150-foot dirigible over Los Angeles; *A* 12 (1913): 192; the senior Lahm, Frank S., was a businessman with offices in Paris. *Aero Club of America* (New York: Blanchard Press, 1913), 47.

14. *A* 3, no. 6 (1908): 13; *A* 4, no. 1 (1909): 13; *A* 5 (1910): 141, 206; *Aero Club of America*, 1913, ii–iv, 39, 48; K-*WB*, 270.

15. CL-*AGW*, 63; *Aero Club of America*, 1913, 45, 46; K-*WB*, 268–70; *A* 3, no. 2 (1908): 28; *A* 4, no. 3 (1909): 168; *A* 5 (1910): 165.

16. *A* 3, no. 1 (1908): 28; *A* 4, no. 2 (1909): 88; *A* 4, no. 3 (1909): 168; *A* 5 (1910): 165; *A* 6 (1910): 175; FG-*WBA*, 47; Looseleaf Chronology, Jan. 13, 1908, Notebook 5, Jones/AFHRA.

17. *A* 6 (1910): 87. The Air University Library, Maxwell AFB, Alabama, contains a complete set of *Aeronautics*, and the observations are based upon a study of that collection. In February 1914, *Aeronautics* became the official magazine of the more technically oriented Aeronautical Society of America; *A* 14 (1914): 76.

18. *A* 4, no. 3 (1908): 3–4; *A* 4, no. 1 (1909): 5–6; *A* 6 (1910): 39.

19. *NYT*, Jan. 31, 1909, part 2, p. 1. The Senate committee subsequently reduced the appropriation to $250,000. Ibid., p. 4; Beaver, *Newton D. Baker and the American War Effort*, 57.

20. *A* 1, no. 2 (1907): 41; *A* 3, no. 5 (1908): 28; *A* 3, no. 5 (1908): 27; *A* 4, no. 2 (1909): 73, 91; *A* 5 (1910): 238; *A* 6 (1910): 26, 33–34, 199; *NYT*, Feb. 7, 1909, part 4, p. 1; Apr. 13, 1909, 3; Aug. 5, 1910, 3; *F* 1 (1912): 11–12, 19. In February 1909, Cortlandt Bishop, the future president of the Aero Club of America, conducted a course on aeronautics at the West Side YMCA in New York City. *NYT*, Feb. 14, 1909, part 4, p. 2. On Loening, see Oral History Interview, Grover Loening, Sept. 18, 1969, Special Collections Division, USAFAL. Bill Robie discusses the Junior Aero Club at

length and identifies the club's guiding power as Miss E. Lillian Todd of Staten Island; *For the Greatest Achievement*, 47–49.

21. *NYT*, Jan. 16, 1907, 11; ibid., Aug. 23, 1910, 6; TL-*NA*, 9; *A* 5 (1909): 178; Loening interview, 4–5; Andrew Drew, "The Missouri Signal Corps in Aeronautics," *A* 8 (1911): 146.

22. CL-*AGW*, 67, 71, 219; Hennessy, "United States Army Air Arm," *USAF Historical Study No. 98* (hereafter H-AAA), 61.

23. CL-*AGW*, 67, 71, 219; H-AAA, 61. The trophy was donated by Clarence H. Mackay, a member of the Aero Club of America, to recognize outstanding achievement by a military aviator; Arnold was the first recipient. Ibid., 71–72; [Chief Signal Officer], *Report to the Secretary of War, 1913* [Oct. 10, 1913], 47.

24. U.S. House, *Aeronautics in the Army: Hearings before the Committee on Military Affairs*, 7.

25. Paul W. Clark, "George Owen Squier," 56–57, 77, 89, 95; Squier, "Present Status of Military Aeronautics," *A* 3, no. 5 (1908): 10–11, which abstracts a longer paper published as "Present Status of Military Aeronautics, 1908" in the December 1908 issue of the *Journal of the American Society of Military Engineers*, p. 1614; Allen, "Military Aeronautics," 155. See also Grahame-White and Harper, *Aeroplane in War*, 117–18.

26. *A* 8 (1911): 158–59; *A* 10 (1912): 165; *A* 11 (1912): 147. General Allen served as chief signal officer until 1912. The navy was equally aware of the value of Aero Club support. See TL-*NA*, 12.

27. Foulois, "Why Write a Book?," 2:60–62; H-AAA, 62, 63; *F* 2 (1913): 5; *A* 14 (1914): 104.

28. At least part of the difficulty seems to have been a dispute over the club's attitude toward heavier-than-air experimentation. Among the seceding group were Stanley Beach, Gutzon Borglum, William F. Whitehouse, Hudson Maxim, and Peter Cooper Hewitt. Hatch, *Glenn Curtiss*, 139; Studer, *Sky Storming Yankee*, 139. See also *A* 3, no. 1 (1908): 28, 31; *A* 4 (1908): 115. Dues for the Aeronautical Society were set at the low rate of $10 per annum to attract new members, and by November 1908, the Aeronautical Society held its first flying exhibition in the Bronx. *A* 3, no. 4 (1908): 13; *A* 4, no. 2 (1908): 114–15; *A* 6 (1910): 101. The choice of a name seems to have been governed by the British group, the Aeronautical Society of Great Britain, established in 1866 for scientific research and revived in 1897. R-*WA*, 43–44. The 1908–10 schism is discussed in Robie, *For the Greatest Achievement*, 50–52.

29. *A* 6 (1910): 101.

30. Robie, *For the Greatest Achievement*, 65–66.

31. Ibid., 94.

32. Chambers to Skerrett, Sept. 5, 1912, Container 22 (Robert G. Skerrett), WIC/LC.

33. Hobart Bishop Hankins, editor of *Fly* magazine, to Capt. Washington I. Chambers, Container 8 (*Aeronautics* magazine), WIC/LC; A. B. Gaines Jr. to Grover C. Loening, Oct. 30, 1913, GCL/LC.

34. *A* 10 (1912): 141,

35. Agreement of Apr. 8, 1910, Container 8 (Aero Club), WB/LC; Robie, *For the Greatest Achievement*, 50–52, 64.

36. Lt. T. G. Ellyson to Captain Chambers, Aug. 16, 1912; W. R. Cross, Chairman of Aero Club Contest Committee, to Chambers, Aug. 20, 1912; Chambers to Cross, Aug. 22, 1912: all in Container 14 (T. G. Ellyson), WIC/LC. Lt. Alfred A. Cunningham to Chambers, Sept. 2, 1912, Container 19 (Naval Airplanes), WIC/LC. Israel Ludlow to Alan R. Hawley, Mar. 5, 1915; Capt. Mark Bristol to Israel Ludlow, Mar. 6, 1915, Container 29 (Feb.–July 1915), MB/LC.

37. Foulois to Wright Brothers, June 30, 1912, Container 27 (Foulois), WB/LC.

38. E. L. Jones to Chambers, Oct. 21, 1913, Container 8 (*Aeronautics* magazine), WIC/LC. Lee S. Burridge informed Captain Chambers that Brigadier General Allen, Col. Samuel Reber, and Capt. Charles deF. Chandler "all say they cannot spare time to address the Aeronautical Society." Burridge to Chambers, Jan. 9, 1912, Container 8 (Aeronautical Society), WIC/LC.

39. E. L. Jones to R. S. Woodward, Mar. 12, 1913; Hobart Bishop Hankins to Capt. Washington I. Chambers, Mar. 13, 1913; Chambers to Hankins, Mar. 15, 1913; Jones to Chambers, Mar. 18, 1913; all in Container 8 (*Aeronautics* magazine), WIC/LC. See also G. T. Bindbeutel to Chambers, Mar. 22, 1913, Container 7 (Aerial Age), WIC/LC.

40. Ernest L. Jones to Chambers, Nov. 15, 1913, Container 8 (*Aeronautics* magazine), WIC/LC.

41. For example, see speeches of Congressmen Ames, Feb. 9, 1912, *CR*, 48, part 2, 1891–92; James Mann, Feb. 9, 1912, ibid., part 2, 1891; William G. Sharp, Jan. 8, 1912, ibid., part 1, 735, and Sharp, Aug. 1, 1912, ibid., part 10, 10007.

42. On the Hardwick Bill, see *CR*, 48, part 1, 736; part 4, 3832; part 9, 9266, part 10, 10245–247, 10264. See also U.S. House, *Military Aviation*, House Document 718, passim, and "Status of Army Officers in Aviation Service (H.R. 17256), July 18, 1912," House Report 1021, 62d Cong., 2d Sess. (Washington: Government Printing Office, 1912), passim.

43. For legislative history of the Hay Bill, see "Efficiency of the Aviation Service of the Army (H.R. 5304)," House Report 132, 63d Cong., 2d Sess. (Washington: Government Printing Office, 1913); "Purchase of Lands for Aviation School," Senate Report 925, 63d Cong., 3d Sess. (Washington: Government Printing Office, 1915). The major document is U.S. House, *Aeronautics in the Army: Hearings before the Committee on Military Affairs* . . . (hereafter referred to as *Aeronautics in the Army*). This document is conveniently reprinted in Maurer Maurer, ed., *The U.S. Air Service in World War I* (hereafter cited as MM-*AS*), 2:3–17. For a useful summary, see "Organization of Military Aeronautics," AAF Historical Studies, No. 25, 13–14, 18–19.

44. *Aeronautics in the Army*, 10, 20, 32.

45. Testimony of Lt. Henry H. Arnold, in ibid., 91; General Scriven, in ibid., 8; Captain Beck, in ibid., 40; FG-*WBA*, 105–6; Interview, Oct. 23, 1956, BDF/USAFAL; see also McClendon, "Question of Autonomy," 36, 38–39; [Greer], *Development of Air Doctrine*, USAF Historical Documents No. 89, 3; Milling, "A Short History," 30, AFHRA.

46. Chandler and Lahm were of the opinion that the Hay Committee hearings

increased interest in aviation on the part of the higher officers of the Signal Corps, and that they provided an opportunity to present Congress with comparative statistics on military aviation. CL-*AGW*, 257–58. On the other hand, Foulois subsequently expressed the opinion that the extensive discussion of Aviation Section personnel severely limited the attention directed toward the development and procurement of aircraft. Foulois, "Why Write a Book?," 2:125, 126. For quoted passages in committee reports, see House Report 132, 63d Cong., 2d Sess (Dec. 12, 1913), 4, and Senate Report 576, 63d Cong., 3d Sess. (June 2, 1914), 2.

47. "We have just heard that Hay has been 'kicked upstairs' and all of us are delighted — anything to get rid of him as chairman of House Mil[itary Affairs] Committee." Major Allen to Dora Allen, July 20, 1916, Container 10, 1916, Allen Papers, Library of Congress.

48. Hofstadter, *Age of Reform*, 135, 167–73.

49. Arnold, *Global Mission*, 40, 42; Goldberg, *History of the United States Air Force*, 7; FG-*WBA* 3 (1916): 111, 173; McClendon, "The Question of Autonomy," 40. One example of Aero Club heavy-handedness occurred in connection with the 1911 International Aviation Meet. Rather than asking navy captain Chambers to attend on behalf of navy aviation, they sent requests directly to President Taft and the secretary of the navy, bypassing both Chambers and his superior officers. Timothy Woodruff to Secretary George von L. Meyer, Sept. 11, 1911; Rudolph Forster, acting secretary to President Taft, to Secretary Meyer, Sept. 11, 1911; Timothy Winthrop to Chambers, Sept. 13, 1911; Beekman Winthrop to Woodruff, Sept. 14, 1911: all in Container 7 (Aero Club of America), WIC/LC.

50. Chambers to Wood, n.d. [ca. 1911–13], Container 7 (Aero Club of America), WIC/LC.

51. Burridge to Chambers, Mar. 12, 1912, Container 8 (Aeronautical Society), WIC/LC.

52. Kruckman to Chambers, May 28, 1912, Container 8 (Aeronautical Society), WIC/LC. Aero Club officials launched "mail barrages" to persuade congressmen to support the Aero Mail Bill in December 1913, only to have the bill introduced two days early and defeated before the letters arrived. Henry Woodhouse to Chambers, Dec. 29, 1913, Container 7 (Aero Club of America), WIC/LC.

CHAPTER TWO

1. Corn, *Winged Gospel*, vii–viii (quotation at vii).

2. Ibid., 2–9; the tests and Selfridge's death are described well in Alfred F. Hurley and William C. Heimdahl, "The Roots of Army Aviation," in Nalty, *Winged Shield, Winged Sword*, 1:12–14.

3. Goldman, *Rendezvous with Destiny*, 133–36; Hofstadter, *Age of Reform*, 186–98.

4. Ernest L. Jones, a prominent aviator and manufacturer, claimed that Custis was the first aeronautics reporter. Jones was the longtime editor of *Aeronautics*, the house organ of the Aero Club of America. Looseleaf Chronology, vol. 5, June 1, 1908, Jones/AFHRA; *A* 3, no. 1 (1908): 13; *A* 4 (1909): 88; CL-*AGW*, 53, 197. For a survey of aviation reporting, see Oscar G. Draper, "Popular Education in Aviation," *F* 1, no. 6 (1912): 30.

5. *A* 4 (1909): 88.

6. *A* 3, no. 4 (1908): 5; Hall, *Hudson and Fulton*, 60; TL-*NA*, 6.

7. *Collier's Weekly* (hereafter *CW*) 44, no. 15 (1910): 3; ibid. 51, no. 6 (1913): 7.

8. Pringle, *Roosevelt Biography*, 370–71, 374–75; *CW* 46, no. 19 (1911): 10.

9. This survey is based upon a cursory review of each issue between 1906 (volume 37) and 1914 (volume 52). Each photograph, article, editorial statement, or aviation-related advertisement has been counted. Undoubtedly many allusions hidden in the text of articles and pieces of fiction have been overlooked.

10. Maxim quotation in *CW* 42, no. 25 (1909): 15–16; quotation from Palmer in ibid. 43, no. 15 (1909): 9.

11. *CW* 46, no. 1 (1910): 21–22 (quotation at 22).

12. *CW* 45, no. 11 (1910): 19–20, 24–25; *CW* 46, no. 8 (1910): 9. An article by Elmer Roberts, "The Cavalry of the Air," anticipated the use of Zeppelins for scouting purposes on land and sea; it also stressed transportation of personnel and materiel by dirigibles, and noted Germany's growing interest in airplanes. *CW* 43, no. 25 (1909): 20–26.

13. *CW* 48, no. 1 (1911): 19; *CW* 48, no. 3 (1911): 23.

14. *CW* 44, no. 25 (1910): 5; *CW* 45, no. 8 (1910): 9; *CW* 46, no. 9 (1910): 31.

15. *CW* 50, no. 33 (1913): 27.

16. Volumes 51 (1906) through 66 (1914) were surveyed; see note 11, above.

17. On pacifism in editorial views, see *Century Magazine* 56 (1909): 474–75; *CW* 57 (1910): 952–53. Stedman's article is in *CW* 55 (1908): 18–26; in February 1909, *Century* published Henry B. Hersey's article warning of the aerial menace to the United States in any future war; *CW* 55 (1909): 627–30. The Wright article is in *CW* 54 (1908), 641–650; Post's narrative is in *CW* 59 (1911): 451–70.

18. *Atlantic Monthly* 108 (1911): 420.

19. "Congress and Military Aeronautics," *Scientific American* 100 (1909): 130; an earlier editorial commented adversely on committee action reducing the appropriation; see "Government Aid in the Development of Aeronautics," ibid. 98 (1908): 238–39. Evidence of Beach's service as aviation editor is in *A* 4 (1908): 106.

20. The discussion that follows is based upon an examination of *National Geographic Magazine* from volume 14 (1903) through volume 25 (1914). For 1912 subscriptions, see ibid. 33 (1912): 274.

21. *National Geographic* 14 (1903): 219–31; and ibid., 19 (1908): 35–52; by far the most useful is Bell's "Aerial Locomotion: With a Few Notes of Progress on the Construction of an Aerodrome" 18 (1907): 1–34. The Wrights' banquet is reported at ibid. 21 (1911): 267–84. Maj. Gen. Adolphus Greely, the former chief signal officer who single-handedly saved balloon and dirigible navigation in the Army, was an associate editor of *National Geographic*.

22. Kipling, *With the Night Mail*, ii, 70.

23. Wells, *The War in the Air*, 5; McFarland, "When the Airplane Was a Military Secret," 81.

24. Ibid., 81.

25. Ibid., 112.

26. R-*WA*, 158–59; McFarland, "When the Airplane Was a Military Secret," 77.

Growing concern about the range and carrying capacity of German Zeppelins is treated exhaustively in Gollin, *Impact of Air Power*, esp. 9–10, 53–60, 100, and 223–24, concerning public panics about supposed Zeppelin sightings and official reactions. Haldane was a prime mover in War Department development of balloons and airplanes; Driver, *Birth of Military Aviation*, 188–203.

27. *NYT*, July 5, 1908, part 3, p. 2; ibid., part 5, p. 9; *Proceedings of the United States Naval Institute* 36 (1910): 1190.

28. Quotation in clipping collection, Looseleaf Chronology, ca. May 6, 1908, vol. 5, Jones/AFHRA. Lieutenant Colonel William A. Glassford, a veteran balloonist in the Signal Corps, concurred in this view. "Aeronautics and War," *A* 8 (1911): 12–14.

29. Gollin, *No Longer an Island*, 315–52.

30. Quoted from Hartig, "Evolution of Air Force Public Relations," 8–9.

31. Clark, "George Owen Squier," 129, 147.

32. *NYT*, Oct. 11, 1908, part 3, p. 1.

33. Aaron Norman in *The Great Air War* notes that from 1910 to 1914 there was more aviation-oriented literature in Germany than in any other country. This may perhaps account for the popular enthusiasm and financial support for the Zeppelin program. On Foulois and the San Diego accidents, see FG-*WBA*, 113.

34. Squier, "Advantages of Aerial Craft," 18; *NYT*, Sept. 20, 1908, part 2, p. 6; Squier, "Present Status of Military Aeronautics," *Journal of the American Society of Military Engineers* 3 (1908): 1612. The U.S. Navy was not far behind; see *NYT*, Mar. 8, 1908, part 5, p. 10, and *United States Naval Institute Proceedings* 38 (1911): 163–203.

35. *NYT*, Oct. 6, 1910, 4.

36. *Army and Navy Journal* 44 (1907): 1348; Clark, "George Owen Squier," 131; Milling, "A Short History," 15, AFHRA; *A* 1, no. 4 (1907): 10; ibid, 7 (1911): 97; U.S. House, *Aeronautics in the Army*, 37; CL-*AGW*, 87–90; H-AAA, 47.

37. CL-*AGW*, 200–201; *CW* 47, no. 19 (1911): 11; Oral History Interview, General Carl Spaatz, Sept. 27, 1968, 4–5, USAFAL. The British publicity campaigns of George Holt Thomas and Claude Graham-White, which included exhibition flying, may have served as models for American activity. See Driver, *Birth of Military Aviation*, 130–38.

38. Benjamin D. Foulois, "Why Write a Book?," 2:22; Oral History Interview, General Benjamin D. Foulois, Jan 20, 1960, 71, USAFAL.

39. H-AAA, 45.

40. H-AAA, 33, 45, 57, 71; *A* 8 (1911): 213; *A* 13 (1913): 110, 112, 184, 216; *A* 14 (1914): 58; Looseleaf Chronology, vol. 5, Sept. 17, 1908, Jones/AFHRA.

41. *CW* 42, no. 2 (1908): 11; *CW* 45, no. 1 (1910): 9; *CW* 47, no. 24 (1911): 15; *CW* 48, no. 1 (1911): 19; *CW* 48, no. 8 (1911): 9.

42. Ibid. 50, no. 6 (1912): 8.

43. Foulois, "Why Write a Book?," 2:22; R-*WA*, 230–31. Of course public reactions are not predictable. When in 1908 Count Zeppelin's airship was destroyed in the presence of a large crowd, the audience burst into a chorus of "Deutschland uber Alles," and promptly circulated a subscription list to build another Zeppelin. Cuneo, *German Air Weapon*, 53.

44. Glassford, "Aeronautics and War," *A* 8 (1911): 14.

CHAPTER THREE

1. Scriven, *Service of Information*, 21, 23, 62, 76; *Field Service Regulations, 1914*.

2. Mitchell served on the general staff from 1913 to the summer of 1916, when he was assigned as acting chief of the Aviation Section of the Signal Corps. He remained in the Aviation Section thereafter, and was certified as a junior military aviator in September 1917. Hurley, *Billy Mitchell*, 15–21.

3. American newspapers also reported that Bulgarian forces had used aerial bombardment against Turkish troop formations during the Balkan Wars. *F* 3, no. 3 (April 1914): 73; *F* 3, no. 4 (May 1914): 124. In June 1914, *Flying* commented that the Turco-Italian and Balkan Wars provided "indiscussionable proof" of the value of military aviation. *F* 3, no. 5 (June 1914): 135–36. On Italian tactics and Giulio Douhet's early stress on command of the air, see *Origin of Air Warfare*, trans. d'Orlandi, 147, 149–50, 213.

4. Beeler, *History of the Italian-Turkish War*, 15, 31–34, 48; *Origin of Air Warfare*, 166, 167–72; *F* 1, no. 12 (Jan. 1913): 10.

5. *Origin of Air Warfare*, 50–51, 169–71, 175–76, 192–94; Beeler, *History of the Italian-Turkish War*, 54, 62–63; *F* 1, no. 12 (Jan. 1913): 11–12; *F* 2, no. 5 (Nov. 1913): 5–6. While awaiting a bomb-dropping device, the fliers dropped pamphlets on the Turkish army encampments, urging the troops to surrender. Beeler, 54.

6. *Origin of Air Warfare*, trans. d'Orlandi, 161, 173; Beeler, *History of the Italian-Turkish War*, 34, 78. These conditions were not unlike those that destroyed the First Aero Squadron during the Mexican Punitive Expedition in 1916.

7. *F* 2, no. 1 (1913): 8. Woodhouse emphasized the reconnaissance advantages of aircraft in his article.

8. *Origin of Air Warfare*, 184.

9. Ibid., 213–14.

10. "Prizes for Military Aeroplanes" (editorial), *Scientific American* 105 (1911): 402; "Aeroplane in War" (editorial), *Scientific American* 108 (1913): 574; *United States Naval Institute Proceedings* 38 (1912): 377–79, 803; *F* 2, no. 2 (Mar. 1913): 8. Congressman William G. Sharp, a perennial proponent of expanded military aviation, called the House of Representatives' attention to the Turco-Italian War by commenting, "You know what terrible havoc those men up in the air created." *CR*, 48, part 10, 10008 (Aug. 1, 1912).

11. *A* 13 (1913): 206; Frank, "American Air Service," 24–25; *F* 2, no. 4 (Mar. 1913): 16, 17; *F* 3, no. 3 (Apr. 1914): 73; Ford, *Balkan Wars*, passim; Schurman, *Balkan Wars*, passim.

12. General Allen to Chief of Staff, Aug. 5, 1909, WCD-C:5599-1, RG 165, NA; Captain Chandler to Adjutant General, Sept. 4, 1910, WCD-C:6188-1, RG 165, NA.

13. Précis of Military Events, Aug. and Sept. 1910, Oct. 1910, Feb. 1911, Mar. 1911, May 1911, Dec. 1912, Aug. 1913, in WCD-C:6165-3, 6165-4, 6165-5, 6165-9, 6164-10, 6165-12, 6165-31, 6165-43, 6165-46: all in RG 165, NA.

14. Précis of Military Events, Aug, 1910, Oct. 1910, Nov. 1910, Jan. 1911, May 1911, June 1911, Sept. 1912, Apr. 1913, WCD-C:6165-2, 6165-5 through 6165-8, 6165-12, 6165-13, 6165-28, 6165-35: all in RG 165, NA. The Lewis machine gun was fired from an airplane "with great accuracy" in Nov. 1913, WCD-C:6165-42, ibid.,

and the receiving War College office noted that the gun was already known to the U.S. Army.

15. Précis of Military Events, Mar. 1911, Feb 1914, WCD-C:6165-10, 6165-47, ibid.

16. Memorandum, Mar. 12, 1912; report, Mar. 12, 1913, Mar. 26, 1913, Jan. 11, 1914, WCD-C:7031-6, 7031-10, 7031-12, 7031-22, ibid.

17. Squier to War College Division, May 2, 1913, and Apr. 30, 1914, WCD-C:7811-1, 7031-30; Précis of Military Events, Nov. 1913, WCD-C:6165-42: all in RG 165, NA.

18. Formed in 1909 with Aero Club, aircraft manufacturers, and military officer members, the Advisory Committee on Aeronautics took an active role in supervision of governmental aviation activity. Henderson's suggestion is reported in Squier to War College Division, Apr. 30, 1914, WCD-C:7031-30, ibid. See also Précis of Military Events, Feb. and Apr. 1911, WCD-C:6165-9 and 6165-11, ibid., relaying details concerning the British Advisory Committee on Aeronautics.

19. Report, June 1910, and Report, Aug. 12, 1912, WCD-C:5599-3 and 5599-10, ibid.

20. Shartle to War College Division, Sept. 2, 1912, WCD-C:6652-14, ibid. In June 1913 the German government prohibited the sale of the Schutte-Lanz airship to foreign countries, and presumably discouraged German manufacturers from seeking external plants for manufacturing airships of the rigid type. On the other hand, as late as Apr. 29, 1914, German authorities assured the American attaché in Berlin that they would supply airplanes to the United States. Bornstad to War College Division, June 14, 1913, and Langhorne to War College Division, Apr. 29, 1914, WCD-C:6652-20 and 6652-40, ibid.

21. Shartle to War College Division, Apr. 26, 1912; Bornstad to War College Division, June 14, 1913; Major George T. Langhorne to War College Division, Oct. 27, 1913, and May 7, 1914, WCD-C:6652-6, 6652-20, 6652-26, 6652-43: all in ibid.

22. "Report of Brigadier General Tasker H. Bliss," 3, 5, 6–7, 15–17, 25, 33, 44–45.

23. Report on Maneuvers, by Lt. Col. T. Bentley Mott, Nov. 11, 1912, WCD-C:7017-7, RG 165, NA.

24. Harlow, *Theodore Roosevelt*, 161; Beale, *Roosevelt and the Rise of America*, 24, 35, 181; Pringle, *Roosevelt Biography*, 116; *NYT*, Feb. 11, 1908, 1, and Apr. 23, 1908, 1; Looseleaf Chronology, vol. 5, Jones/AFHRA.

25. Greenwood, "American Military Observers," 503–4.

26. Roosevelt's attitude toward military lobbying is documented by his adverse comments on Marine Corps–Congressional ties; Butt, *Letters*, 184.

27. *AAW* 3 (1916): 358.

28. Although the Wright medals were presented by President Taft, the Aeronautical Society of America was responsible for the planning and guest list. Butt, *Taft and Roosevelt*, 1:115–16, 158–59, 2:507; *NYT*, Sept. 8, 1910, 4; *A* 4 (1909): 191; *NYT*, Sept. 10, 1910, 4.

29. Butt, *Taft and Roosevelt*, 1:236; one of the principal objections to the General Staff Corps was its resemblance to the German General Staff organization.

30. Ibid., 1:157.

31. Coletta, *Presidency of Taft*, 4; Butt, *Taft and Roosevelt*, 1:7; Anderson, *William Howard Taft*, 227. Taft's friends and advisers did not share these attitudes. William Pitt Trimble, a close friend, was president of the Aero Club of Seattle; Secretary of the Navy Truman H. Newberry was president of the Aero Club of Washington; and Secretary of War Jacob Dickinson had been enthusiastic about flying since he attended the French military maneuvers in 1910. *A* 4 (1909): 86, 88; *NYT*, Dec. 10, 1910, 6.

32. *F* 2, no. 2 (Mar. 1913): 18.

33. *AAW* 3 (1916): 358.

34. See [Chief Signal Officer], *Report to the Secretary of War, 1912*, 24, for comparative figures.

35. Glassford, "Our Army and Aerial Warfare," 21.

36. *NYT*, Feb. 11, 1908, 1; Squier's biographer claims that both General James Allen and Captain Charles DeF. Chandler were enthusiastic for lighter-than-air development; Squier was undecided and inclined toward heavier-than-air work. Clark, "George Owen Squier," 132. Representative Hull, a regular Republican, was a Civil War veteran who had a son in the regular army. The son later became judge advocate general for the American Expeditionary Force in World War I.

37. *A* 2, no. 5 (1908): 3; *NYT*, July 13, 1908, 3.

38. *NYT*, Jan. 23, 1909, 1; *CR*, 43, part 2, 1618–20.

39. [Chief Signal Officer], *Report to the Secretary of War, 1909*, 28.

40. *NYT*, Oct. 21, 1910, 1; quotation in CL-*AGW*, 183; Goldberg, *History of the United States Air Force*, 6.

41. [Chief Signal Officer], *Report to the Secretary of War, 1909*, 28; Ibid., 1910, 24.

42. Milling, "A Short History," 19, 20, AFHRA; CL-*AGW*, 187; [Chief Signal Officer], *Report to the Secretary of War, 1911*, 23; *CR*, 46, part 1, 1020, 1023–24. In the same year, the U.S. Navy received $25,000 for aviation activities. Sitz, "A History of U.S. Naval Aviation," 5.

43. *CR*, 49, part 4, 3276–78. Representative Sharp was among the leading advocates of aviation in Congress; he had been commended for his work by the Aero Club of America. In Oct. 1914 he was confirmed as ambassador to France. *F* 1, no. 16 (Jan. 1913): 19; *F* 3, no. 9 (Oct. 1914): 265; quotation in *F* 2, no. 2 (Mar. 1913: 6.

44. *A* 12 (1913): 98; *A* 14 (1914): 74; *A* 15 (1914): 9; Kuter, "An Air Perspective," 12. In 1914 the House Military Affairs Committee cut the army aviation appropriation, leaving the flyers with $300,000. Representative Keifer's comment is quoted in Holley, *Ideas and Weapons*, 32.

45. Memoranda of June 8, 1912, and Sept. 23, 1912, for Chief of Staff; Brigadier General James Allen to Chief of Staff, Oct. 12, 1912: all in RG 165, V (Reports), 8980, NA.

46. Holley, *Ideas and Weapons*, 8, 9; "Organization of Military Aeronautics," Army Air Forces Historical Studies, No. 25, 9–10; Legislation Relating to the Air Corps Personnel and Training, 1907–39, file 101–39, p. 51, AFHRA.

47. See generally, "Organization of Military Aeronautics," AAF Historical Studies

No. 25, 7–8; Legislation Relating to Air Corps, 3–4; and U.S. House, *Military Aviation*, H. Doc. 718, 73.

48. Hay, *Report from Committee on Military Affairs*, 1; U.S. House, *Military Aviation*, House Document 718, 2; *CR*, 48, part 3, 3125; *CR*, 48, part 4, 3831. Congressman Hull, the former chair of the committee, was denied the Republican nomination for reelection in 1911, and James Hay succeeded him.

49. *CR*, 48, part 4, 3831.

50. Mott, *Military Attaché*, 109. A West Point classmate of General Pershing, Mott had several attaché tours in Paris; he attended the French military maneuvers in the summer of 1912 (24, 307). For the Hay Committee inquiries, see U.S. House, *Military Aviation*, 5–6, 17, 32.

51. U.S. House, *Military Aviation*, 55, 59–61.

52. Ibid., 3; *CR*, 49, part 3, 1627. The years 1912 and 1913 witnessed congressional debate over airmail routes to be established in Alaska. Although this aroused some public attention, it did not become significant until 1915 and 1916, when the aeronaut constituency opened old wounds in the airmail debate by publicly denouncing antiaviation congressmen. These matters will be discussed at greater length in Chapter 8, below.

53. "Organization of Military Aeronautics," AAF Historical Studies No. 25, 14–15, 18–19.

54. See Memoranda of Dec. 9, 1912, and Feb. 15, 1913, WCD-C:7615-3, 7615-4, RG 165, NA.

55. McClendon, "Question of Autonomy," 27–29, AFHRA. Colonel Scriven informed Foulois that Captain Beck guided Congressman Hay in drafting the first Hay bill. Foulois, "Why Write a Book?," 3:122.

56. McClendon, "Question of Autonomy," 31; "Organization of Military Aeronautics," AAF Historical Studies No. 25, 13–15; [Greer], *Development of Air Doctrine*, USAF Historical Studies No. 89, 1, 2.

57. Foulois felt that the second bill contained the same "revolutionary" features as the first one. Foulois, "Why Write a Book?" 3:122.

58. "Organization of Military Aeronautics," AAF Historical Studies No. 25, 10, 12, 13, 17.

59. The committee roster is printed in *Aeronautics in the Army*, 2.

60. Ibid., 6–8, 21–25, 46–49; Henry Breckinridge to James Hay, Aug. 18, 1913, Reports, V, 6519, and WCD-C: 7616-8, both in RG 165, NA.

61. *Aeronautics in the Army*, 25, 49.

62. Beck was the son of a retired general officer. His testimony supporting separation is in ibid., 37–38, 44.

63. Ibid., 51, 70. Foulois's quote is on p. 51.

64. Ibid., 88; McClendon, "Question of Autonomy," 35–36; "Organization of Military Aeronautics," AAF Historical Studies No. 25, 15–16.

65. [Chief Signal Officer], *Report to the Secretary of War, 1913*, 57.

66. "Organization of Military Aeronautics," AAF Historical Studies No. 25, 18–19; McClendon, "Question of Autonomy," 38–39.

67. An Act to Increase the Efficiency of the Aviation Service of the Army, and for Other Purposes, July 18, 1914, 63d Cong, 2d Sess., 38 Stat. 514–16.

68. Section 2, ibid., at 515, made permanent a provision in the 1912 appropriation act which permitted variations from the earlier restrictions upon tours of duty. See 37 Stat. 704, at 505, and 31 Stat. 748, at 755; see also the discussion of the Manchu law in chapter 7, below.

69. 38 Stat. 514, at 516. The provisions for the redetailing of proficient aviators, as well as the requirement of a certifying board, were retained in the National Defense Act of 1916. 39 Stat. 166, at 174–75.

70. 38 Stat. 514, at 516.

71. CL-*AGW*, 257–58; Foulois, "Why Write a Book?," 3:125–26.

72. Memorandum of Col. John Biddle for Chief of Staff, May 15, 1914, WCD-C:7615-11, RG 165, NA. This memorandum suggested that if HR 5304 passed, a volunteer supplement of the Aviation Section would be authorized. However, even without such specific legislation, the Volunteer Bill enacted Apr. 25, 1914, would provide sufficient authority to supplement aviation personnel. For this reason, no action need be taken to establish volunteer aviation troops, whatever fate might await HR 5304.

73. Ultimately the Hay Bill, amended to delete the sections providing for a separate aviation corps, was approved by the War Department, which recommended presidential signature. Breckinridge to President Woodrow Wilson, July 17, 1914, in Reports, V, War College Division, 8516, RG 165, NA.

CHAPTER FOUR

1. It is unfortunate that the American historians' fixation on the work of the Air Corps Tactical School after World War I has obscured the achievements of earlier years. However, Walter Raleigh, writing of Britain in this period, points out that "almost all the uses of aircraft which later became commonplaces of the war were exemplified in the French maneuvers of 1911." R-*WA*, 178.

2. Scrivener, "Military Use of Balloons and Dirigibles," 8–10; Parkinson, "Politics, Patents and Planes," 6–16; for European developments, see Hildebrandt, *Airships*.

3. In the August 1913 Hay Committee hearings, and in the 1914 and 1915 *Reports of the Chief Signal Officer*, the high command continued to emphasize the airplane's reconnaissance value. *Aeronautics in the Army*, 24, 63; [Chief Signal Officer], *Reports*, 1914, 4, and 1915, 6.

4. CL-*AGW*, 229; H-AAA, 62–63.

5. H-AAA, 92; [Chief Signal Officer], *Report to the Secretary of War, 1913*, 49, 54; CL-*AGW*, 254–55.

6. H-AAA, 45, 53; Milling, "A Short History," AFHRA, 21–22, 36; Bissell, *Brief History of the Air Corps*, 14. Foulois had mentioned aerial photography in his 1907 thesis, "Tactical and Strategical Value," 5.

7. "Military Aviation" (War College Division), 12–13. Aerial reconnaissance had been stipulated in *Field Service Regulations, 1914*, 13, 16.

8. H-AAA, 5; Parkinson, "Politics, Patents and Planes," 11–12. For use of artil-

lery fire direction balloons at Ladysmith in the Boer War, see Hildebrandt, *Airships*, 164–65.

9. "Our Army and Aerial Warfare," *A* 2 (1908): 20; Scriven, "Some Considerations," 8; [Chief Signal Officer], *Report to the Secretary of War, 1911*, 24, 25; "Military Aviation" (War College Division), 6, 20, 25–27.

10. CL-*AGW*, 237–38; Frank, "American Air Service," 79; H-AAA, 72; [Chief Signal Officer], *Report to the Secretary of War, 1913*, 45; *Aeronautics in the Army*, 127; Milling, "A Short History," 26, AFHRA; Clark, "George Owen Squier," 345–46. The French maneuvers of Mar. 1912 demonstrated the value of aerial artillery registry; Von Keler, "Military Supremacy of the Air." As early as June 1912, American military and naval circles were aware of the French maneuvers and the air-power uses demonstrated there. *United States Naval Institute Proceedings* 38 (1912): 804.

11. Holley, *Ideas and Weapons*, 15, contains an analysis of the difficulties in adopting new weapons systems.

12. Lawrence Paszek observed that little was done before World War I to develop combat airplanes in the American Army. Paszek, "Wright Pushers to Stratojets," 115. In light of what follows, that judgment may be subject to reconsideration; both at the experimental and the theoretical level, American aviators were quite active in the field. The problem was discussed before the Aero Club of America in Feb. 1909 and discussed pro and con in aviation books. *NYT*, Feb. 14, 1909, 2; Berget, *Conquest of the Air*, 260; Grahame-White and Harper, *Aeroplane in War*, 213. French thought was reported to Congress in Jan. 1912. U.S. House, *Military Aviation*, House Document No. 718, 24. A British report submitted to the Technical Sub-Committee on Imperial Defense seemingly parroted Foulois's 1907 thesis — that the battle for control of the air would precede the advance of ground forces — and concluded there was a need for armed airplanes. R-*WA*, 175–76; see also Bannerman-Phillips, "Grenadiers of the Air," 214–15, 229–30; and Von Keler, "Military Supremacy of the Air."

13. Beeler, *History of the Italian-Turkish War*, 54, 62–63; *Origin of Air Warfare*, trans. d'Orlandi, 169–71, 192–93; *Military Aviation*, House Doc. 718, 64–65. The Balkan War campaigns and German military preparations are discussed in *A* 13 (1913): 206; and *Aeronautics in the Army*, 89.

14. CL-*AGW*, 87–89, 206, 276; H-AAA, 45, 53–54, 105; *Aeronautics in the Army*, 102; Milling, "A Short History," 22, AFHRA; U.S. House, *Military Aviation*, House Doc. 718, 70–71; Goldberg, *History of the United States Air Force*, 6; *A* 8 (1911): 96; *A* 9 (1911): 39–40, 54; *A* 11 (1912): 84; *A* 13 (1913): 24, 72. For a similar French emphasis on precision bombing, see Von Keler, "Military Supremacy of the Air."

15. Allen, "Military Aeronautics," 156. A similar sentiment was expressed in Spaight, *Aircraft in War*, 8–9. General Allen's views may have been shaped by H. G. Wells's *War in the Air*, and also by Lt. Col. George P. Scriven's report on the defenses of Corregidor. Scriven stated that under continuous dirigible attack the fortress would be "pounded to rubbish and the members of the harassed garrison reduced to fiddle strings." George P. Scriven, "Some Considerations," 11, 16.

16. K-*WB*, 204, note 1.

17. Clark, "George Owen Squier," 150. A similar emphasis upon strategic bomb-

ing of industrial and transportation targets was expressed by Sir Hiram Maxim to the Aeronautical Society of America in Mar. 1909. *NYT*, Mar. 21, 1909, part 4, p. 2.

18. Scriven, "Some Considerations," passim.

19. *Aeronautics in the Army*, 77, 85. General Hurley has noted Mitchell's familiarity with Squier's publications, and that Squier forwarded aviation books to Mitchell when the younger officer was assigned to the general staff. Hurley, *Billy Mitchell*, 145. Squier and Mitchell became acquainted during the laying of the Alaskan telegraph lines by the Signal Corps.

20. *Aeronautics in the Army*, 89, 102.

21. Milling, "A Short History," 3, AFHRA; Squier, "Present Status of Military Aeronautics," 1613. Lt. Col. William A. Glassford claimed that aerial bombing would have no more than a temporarily frightening effect. "The Future of Military Aeronautics," *A* 5 (1911): 84. On the carrying capacity of airplanes and need for a bombardier, see Hearne, *Airships in Peace and War*, 104; and Glenn H. Curtiss's comment in *A* 7 (1913): 49. Cuneo claims that Germany did not create an adequate defense against rear area bombardment from the air because she felt enemy forces would use dirigibles and airplanes solely for reconnaissance and observation; she did not place any deterrent value upon the Hague Convention. Cuneo, *German Air Weapon*, 37.

22. "Tactical and Strategical Value," 7–8; on July 23, 1910, while leaving command of the Department of the Lakes, Maj. Gen. Frederick Dent Grant commented, "Airplanes can now be used for reconnaissance. It will not be long, I imagine, before they may be used in offensive operations." *NYT*, July 24, 1910, part 2, p. 1; in 1912, the *United States Naval Institute Proceedings* (38 [March]: 377–79) observed that since historically no commander would permit the enemy a free view of his positions, it was inevitable that there should be aerial combat and in "a very short time would see one side in possession of complete command of the air, and therefore able to get all the information it required without allowing the enemy to get any."

23. CL-*AGW*, 89–90, 222–23; *A* 10 (1912): 26; *A* 11 (1912): 115; *Aeronautics in the Army*, 85; Goldberg, *History of the Air Force*, 7; [Chief Signal Officer], *Report*, 24.

24. *A* 11 (1912): 115; Hagedorn, *Leonard Wood*, 2:176. After the first successful firing of a rifle from an airplane in 1910, one of the most enthusiastic aviation opponents on the General Staff produced a mathematical equation that proved that continuous firing would upset stability in flight! Norman, *Great Air War*, 20.

25. "Military Aviation," 13; *Field Service Regulations, 1914*, 13, 16, 19.

26. Significantly, the *Field Service Regulations, 1914*, 19, 198, printed an extract from the bombardment provisions of the Second Hague Convention, but made no mention of aerial bombardment as an activity of military aviation. They did mention that dirigibles, then unavailable in U.S. inventories, were capable of carrying explosives and machine guns.

27. Weigley, *American Way of War*, 192. Undoubtedly some segments of the public questioned whether long-range strategic bombardment was in keeping with a "defense only" preparedness posture. This inhibited the development of the long-range bomber in the 1930s. Watson, *United States Army in World War II*, 35–36.

28. *Field Service Regulations, 1914,* "corrected to July 1, 1917," reprints verbatim the 1914 provisions concerning the aero squadron's activities.

29. Holley, *Ideas and Weapons,* 31.

30. The continuing viability of the separation issue after 1914 is obvious from the fact that in 1915 the aeronautical editor of the *New York Tribune* and *Aerial Age Weekly,* Gordon Bruce, endorsed separation of the Aviation Section from the Signal Corps. McClendon, "Question of Autonomy," 41.

31. FG-*WBA,* 118, 186–97.

32. Note, for example, Congressman Sharp's statement in debate that Capt. Paul Beck of the Aeronautical Division had discussed a proposal to increase hazard pay with Sharp, and the officer had approved the proposal. *CR,* 49, part 3, 1637 (Jan. 16, 1913).

33. The Wood-Ainsworth controversy is well covered in secondary works. See Beaver, *Newton D. Baker and the American War Effort,* 10; Coletta, *Presidency of Taft,* 201, 204; Carter, *Creation of the American General Staff,* 61; Hagedorn, *Leonard Wood,* 2:96–97, 100, 107, 112–15, 120–23; Hewes, *From Root to McNamara,* 15, 25; Huntington, *Soldier and State,* 182, 298; and Stimson and Bundy, *On Active Service,* 32, 35–38. Interesting primary material appears in the published papers of Major Archie Butt, aide to Presidents Taft and Roosevelt. Butt, *Taft and Roosevelt,* 1:236; 2:464, 780–81; and his *Letters,* 41.

34. Hagedorn, *Leonard Wood,* 2:87–88; [Chief Signal Officer], *Report to the Secretary of War, 1912,* 29, and *Report to the Secretary of War, 1913,* 69.

35. Anderson, *William Howard Taft,* 91; CL-*AGW,* 33; H-AAA, 57. Significantly, Secretary of War Elihu Root, in conjunction with the establishment of the General Staff Corps in 1902–3, also supported the Dick Bill, which revitalized the National Guard. Jessup, *Elihu Root,* 1:267–68.

36. Hewes, *Root to McNamara,* 21.

37. CL-*AGW,* 54; Looseleaf Chronology, Apr. 1908, vol. 5, Jones/AFHRA.

38. *A* 10 (1912): 43. Foulois wrote to the Wright brothers that this was the biggest job he had yet been given in the army. He was in charge of the Signal Corps and Engineer activities of the National Guard, and was given permission to continue his flying at the College Park flying field. He encouraged the Wrights to make an airplane available to a recently organized militia detachment in the Ohio National Guard. Foulois to Wright Brothers, Dec. 2, 1911, Container 27 (Foulois), WB/LC.

39. *NYT,* Sept. 10, 1910, 3; H-AAA, 78.

40. Delano was an officer in the Aero Club of America. Reber to Loening, Mar. 4, 1914; Loening to Reber, [Mar. 1914]; and announcement, June 16, 1913, Container 1, GCL/LC. See also announcement on Provisional Aviation Brigade, Jan. 23, 1913, Container 8 (Aero Club), WB/LC.

41. H-AAA, 78.

42. *A* 7 (1910): 186; 14 (1914): 120; *NYT,* Sept. 10, 1910, 3; H-AAA, 54, 78; Hagedorn, *Leonard Wood,* 2:112; Van Vleet, Pearson, and Van Wyen, *United States Naval Aviation,* 10; Robert J. Collier to Orville Wright, [ca. Spring 1916], Container 18 (Collier), WB/LC; Announcement on U.S. Aeronautical Reserve, ca. 1910, Con-

tainer 8 (Aeronautical Reserve), and Office of the Secretary of the Navy to John Firth, Feb. 17, 1911, Container 16 (Harry Harkness), both in WIC/LC.

43. *A* 4 (1908): 119; *A* 7 (1910): 186.

44. Scriven, "Military Use of Balloons and Dirigibles," 8–10, 17–39; CL-*AGW*, 3–75. In 1915 the effective range of small-arms fire was 4,000 feet, and the use of balloon guns forced balloons and airplanes to 6,000 feet, from which height it was impossible to identify small detachments of ground troops. "Military Aviation," 12. The best general study of balloons in America is Crouch, *Eagle Aloft*; a good survey of early Army balloon activity is in Cooke, *U.S. Air Service in the Great War*, 4–7; see also the discussion in chapter 2, above.

45. Hildebrandt, *Airships Past and Present*, 143; Milling, "A Short History," 4, AFHRA; *A* 1, no. 6 (1907): 21; Glassford, "Our Army and Aerial Warfare," 18–21; *NYT*, Dec. 3, 1908, 8, and June 3, 1909, 1; Allen, "Military Aeronautics," 156; Report of First Lieutenant Frank P. Lahm to Chief Signal Officer, July 17, 1908, in Looseleaf Chronology, vol. 5, Jones/AFHRA; Clark, "George Owen Squier," 150.

46. The report has now been declassified.

47. Manuscript thesis, July 9, 1908, U.S. Army Military History Institute, Carlisle Barracks, Pa. Foulois's recollection of his school tour may be found in Oral History Interview, Jan. 20, 1960, 1–3, 5, 6, USAFAL.

48. FG-*WBA*, 59, 68; this duplicates an earlier memoir giving the date of the event as June 1909; Foulois, "Why Write a Book?," 2:23. The Hay Committee testimony is in *Aeronautics in the Army*, 53.

49. In Dec. 1907 the *New York Times* reported the army was "looking beyond" the dirigible to the "more scientific airplane." *NYT*, Dec. 10, 1907, 8, and May 9, 1909, 11. An English observer in 1910 reached the same conclusion. Hearne, *Airships in Peace and War*, 65.

50. CL-*AGW*, 105; H-AAA, 19; *A* 13 (1913): 96.

51. *NYT*, Oct. 11, 1908, part 3, p. 1; Oct. 25, 1908, part 2, p. 20; and June 1, 1909, 8. *Report of the Chief Signal Officer, 1909*, 28. In April 1908 a larger Zeppelin, with an estimated cruise speed of 47 miles per hour and a range of 1,500 miles, was reported; *NYT*, Apr. 28, 1908, 1. The *London Daily Mail*, in August 1908, reported that British planners remained skeptical about the use of either airplanes or airships in warfare; clipping in Looseleaf Chronology, vol. 5, Jones/AFHRA. See also Allen, "Aeronautics in the U.S. Signal Corps," 17.

52. *Report of the Chief Signal Officer, 1909*, 4.

53. Ibid.; Clark, "George Owen Squier," 150.

54. *NYT*, June 28, 1908, part 5, p. 8; Allen, "Military Aeronautics," 156.

55. *Report of the Chief Signal Officer, 1913*, 63; *Report of the Chief Signal Officer, 1914*, 6; Driver, *Birth of Military Aviation*, 210–38; the author also argues that Haldane's unwillingness to support private airplane manufacturers crippled the British aviation industry.

56. Coletta, *Presidency of Taft*, 201; it has also been pointed out that as secretary of war, Taft was more concerned with the administration of the Philippine Islands, and left the War Department matters to subordinates, resulting in factions within

the army and the civilian leadership of the department. Anderson, *William Howard Taft*, 13.

57. Coletta, *Presidency of Taft*, 130, 201; Pringle, *Life and Times of Taft*, 2: 603–8; Anderson, *William Howard Taft*, 86, 88.

58. *CR*, 43, part 2, 1618; *NYT*, June 28, 1908, part 5, p. 7; *Report of the Chief Signal Officer, 1912*, 22; Grahame-White and Harper, *Aeroplane in War*, 65.

59. *Aeronautics in the Army*, 161; Gollin, "Anticipating Air Attack," 199. For British acceptance of this cost conclusion, see Cuneo, *The Air Weapon*, 141; Grahame-White and Harper, *Aeroplane in War*, 45–46.

60. *NYT*, June 28, 1908, part 5, p. 8, and Aug. 3, 1909, 3; R-*WA*, 171–72; Bannerman-Phillips, "Grenadiers of the Air," 215; *CR*, 46, part 2, 1023.

61. Berget, *Conquest of the Air*, 10; Bannerman-Phillips, "Grenadiers of the Air," 262; Chambers, "Airplane — Dirigible," 745; Dienstbach and MacMechan, " 'Fallacy' of the Dirigible," 10.

62. Some of these matters are discussed in "Is the Aeroplane Practical for Scouting?" *Scientific American* 119 (1908): 166; Berget, *Conquest of the Air*, 258; and "The Dirigible in Warfare," reprinted in *Aeronautics in the Army*, 144; see also *NYT*, Nov. 20, 1907, 8; Aug. 5, 1908, 4; Sept. 17, 1908, 4; Dec. 2, 1908, 1; and Dec. 23, 1908, 1, suggesting that Zeppelins renewed interest in smaller, lighter-than-air craft. *NYT*, Sept. 27, 1909, 5 (French accident with *Republique*); *United States Naval Institute Proceedings* 38 (1912): 351.

63. Royse, *Aerial Bombardment*, 36–39, 65–67, 117.

64. Poolman, *Zeppelins over England*, 29; *NYT*, Aug. 4, 1907, part 5, p. 7; Crutcher, "Military Possibilities of Aeroplanes," 107; Cuneo, *German Air Weapon*, 124; Gollin, "Anticipating Air Attack," 198–99. See also Hearne, *Airships in Peace and War*, 80–81; and Bannerman-Phillips, "Grenadiers of the Air," 214–15, 229.

65. *CR*, 99, part 3, 3277.

66. In 1890 Lt. William A. Glassford was sent to Europe to report on military use of captive balloons, and the army purchased a stationary balloon shortly thereafter. Lieutenant Foulois's 1907 thesis recognized the use of free flying balloons during the siege of Paris in 1870. Manual, Technique of Balloon and Airship Operations, Air Corps Tactical School, Langley Field, Va., Jan. 1, 1928, 25, copy in Hannibal Collection, USAFAL; Foulois, "Tactical and Strategical Value," July 9, 1908, 8, U.S. Army Military History Institute, Carlisle Barracks, Pa. See also Wieczorek, "Military Value of Balloons," 14–16.

67. George O. Squier, "The Present Status of Military Aeronautics," *Journal of the American Society of Military Engineers* 3 (1908): 1614. However, the army did contract with Thomas S. Baldwin to deliver two spherical balloons at the same time it was to accept his dirigible for testing in the summer of 1908. *NYT*, June 25, 1908, 5.

68. American experience with captive balloons at the battle of Kettle's Hill near San Juan, is discussed in Harlow, *Theodore Roosevelt*, 175; Vandiver, *Black Jack*, 201; and Glassford, "Our Army and Aerial Warfare," 19. Both Theodore Roosevelt and John J. Pershing were among the troops subjected to heavy enemy fire because of the presence of a captive observation balloon near their units. See also Scrivener, "Military Use," 43–48; and Cuneo, *German Air Weapon*, 19.

69. *NYT*, July 31, 1910, Part 2, p. 5; *Report of the Chief Signal Officer, 1912*, 22; *Aeronautics in the Army*, 30; see also *F 2* (1913): 29.

70. Bids on the first dirigible contract had been sluggish, but the contract was awarded to Thomas S. Baldwin of California, despite a more expensive but perhaps superior bid of Peter Cooper Hewitt. Baldwin's dirigible was accepted on Aug. 16, 1908. *NYT*, Feb. 9, 1908, part 2, p. 5; Feb. 16, 1908, part 2, p. 8; Feb. 25, 1908, 1; July 13, 1908, 3; and Aug. 16, 1908, part 2, p. 3; *CR*, 99, part 3, 3277. See also H-AAA, 16.

71. *NYT*, Sept. 19, 1908, 6, and June 2, 1909, 6; Cuneo, *German Air Weapon*, 151, 155.

72. See the articles by Carl Dienstbach and T. R. MacMechan: "The Aerial Battleship," *McClure's Magazine* 33 (1909): 343–54, at 346–47, 349–50; "The 'Fallacy' of the Dirigible," 10–11; and "The Greyhounds of the Air," *Everybody's Magazine* 27 (1912): 191–304, at 302–3. By way of contrast, the scientific magazines recognized the extent of German and French airship construction. See "Government Aid in the Development of Aeronautics" 238–39.

73. *NYT*, Dec. 10, 1908, 5; Jan. 20, 1909, 1; Jan 31, 1909, part 2, p. 1; and Feb. 3, 1909, 3; *CR*, 93, part 2, 1630–31, 1632, 1635, 1636, 1637–38, 1640, and 96, part 2, 1021.

74. *CR*, 96, part 2, 1021.

75. Germany's decision was also due to a decrease in confidence over the reconnaissance capability of dirigibles. While Britain retained her emphasis on airplanes, she nevertheless attempted to balance her aerial forces with airships after 1912. Von Hoeppner, "Germany's War in the Air," 1, 3, Air University Library, Maxwell AFB, Alabama; Cuneo, *The Air Weapon*, 22; Grahame-White and Harper, *Aeroplane in War*, 64; R-*WA*, 75; Gollin, "Anticipating Air Attack," 199.

CHAPTER FIVE

1. The Hamilton quotation is in Hatch, *Glenn Curtiss*, 187.

2. Wilbur Wright to M. Hevesy, Jan. 25, 1912, McFarland, *Wright Papers*, 2:1035.

3. McFarland, *Wright Papers*, 1:269 (n. 3), 469 (n. 5), 2:1128; McFarland, "Wilbur and Orville Wright: Seventy-five Years After," in Hallion, *Wright Brothers*, 24; Hatch, *Glenn Curtiss*, 130; K-*WB*, 49, 69–71, 81–82; Zollman, "Patent Rights in Aircraft," 218; Worrel, "Wright Brothers' Patent," 1512–13.

4. Crouch, *Bishop's Boys*, 372–75, 379–80; Howard, *Wilbur and Orville*, 278; Roseberry, *Glenn Curtiss*, 130–31.

5. Crouch, *Bishop's Boys*, 235, 400–402; Howard, *Wilbur and Orville*, 151–52.

6. Studer, *Sky Storming Yankee*, 87–88, 94, 96, 100–102, 103–4; Hatch, *Glenn Curtiss*, 130; K-*WB*, 136–37, 146, 242–43, 290–91.

7. Studer, *Sky Storming Yankee*, 111; an assertion to the contrary is in K-*WB*, 280–91. Wright biographer Fred Howard noted that Orville Wright was reluctant to permit Lieutenant Selfridge to accompany him in the 1908 army acceptance flights; Wright feared that Selfridge would make mental notes that would benefit the Aerial Experiment Association. Howard, *Wilbur and Orville*, 271. On the other hand,

Dr. Tom D. Crouch provides strong evidence that the AEA received extensive information from the Wrights in December 1908, *Bishop's Boys*, 352–54.

8. K-*WB*, 290–91. The evidence leaves little room for doubt that the AEA knew of the Wright brothers' control system by early 1908, and their successful flight of the "June Bug" in June 1908 reinforces this supposition.

9. This and the prior paragraph are based upon the discussion in Howard, *Wilbur and Orville*, 308–11, 314, 316, 329; see also Crouch, *Bishop's Boys*, 400–402. Unfortunately for Curtiss, he had not yet seen the back of the nefarious Augustus Herring; at the time of Curtiss's death on July 23, 1928, litigation against him by Herring's heirs remained unsettled, but judgment had been entered against Curtiss. Curtiss considered his affiliation with Augustus Herring the greatest mistake of his life. For a careful discussion of the formation of Herring-Curtiss, and Curtiss's view of the bankruptcy and litigation, see Roseberry, *Glenn Curtiss*, 152, 157, 160, 164, 168, 179, 189–90, 237–38, 241–45, 254, 257, 433, 453–54.

10. Affidavit of Orville Wright, 1920, in *Wright Aeronautical Company v. United Aircraft Engineering Corp.*, Container 81, WB/LC; Harry A. Toulmin to Wright Brothers, May 19, 1904, Folio Toulmin, Container 51, ibid. See the discussion at Crouch, *Bishop's Boys*, 253–55, 316–17.

11. Crouch, "Aeronautics in the Pre-Wright Era," in Hallion, *Wright Brothers*, 25; Spearman, *John Joseph Montgomery*, 118; Wilbur Wright to Octave Chanute, Jan. 8, 1904, McFarland, *Wright Papers*, 1:412–13; Octave Chanute to Ernest L. Jones, Aug. 26, 1909, ibid., 2:913. The basic facts may be studied in ibid., 1:335–36, 346, and 2:723–24; see also K-*WB*, 166–67; McFarland, "Wilbur and Orville Wright," in Hallion, *Wright Brothers*, 25–26; Charles H. Gibbs-Smith, "The Wright Brothers: Their Influence," in ibid., 32; Wright, *How We Invented the Airplane*, 63.

12. Orville Wright reported this to Octave Chanute on Jan. 29, 1910, adding that they had avoided a public refutation of the statement. McFarland, *Wright Papers*, 2:984. See also Crouch, *Bishop's Boys*, 253–55, 276–77.

13. Wilbur Wright to Octave Chanute, Aug. 28, 1906, and Chanute to Wilbur Wright, Aug. 31, 1906, McFarland, *Wright Papers*, 2:723–24. Wright brothers to Editor, *Scientific American*, Mar. 14, 1912, ibid., 2:1040; *A* 10 (1912): 100. See discussion and sources cited at note 11, above.

14. This involved a demonstration of the warping technique by twisting the two ends of a long cardboard box in opposite directions; this was claimed to have been the manner in which the Wrights initially discovered the use of wing twisting to secure lateral stability.

15. K-*WB*, 112; McFarland, *Wright Papers*, 1:417, 498; Worrel, "Wright Brother's Patent," 1512, 1514, 1516.

16. Worrel, "Wright Brothers' Patent," 1517–18. On these various implications, see §1021 in William Robinson, *Law of Patents*, 3:250.

17. Worrel, "Wright Brothers' Patent," 1518. The fixed wing-aileron arrangement was characteristic of the Curtiss aircraft designs.

18. McFarland, *Wright Papers*, 1:481, 482.

19. Plaintiff's brief on motion for preliminary injunction, *Wright Aeronautical Co.*

v. Handley Paige, Ltd., Dec. 3, 1920, Container 81; Harry Toulmin to Wright brothers, Mar. 5, 1908, Folio Toulmin, Container 53: both in WB/LC.

20. Orville Wright, affidavit draft, *Wright Aeronautical Corp. v. United Aircraft Engineering Corp.*, ca. 1920, Container 81, WB/LC; Howard, *Wilbur and Orville*, 319.

21. The patent litigation is well summarized in Crouch, *Bishop's Boys*, 411–17, 423, 440–43.

22. Howard, *Wilbur and Orville*, 327.

23. Ibid., 234–38.

24. McFarland, *Wright Papers*, 2:907, 909, 911; *Wright Co. v. Herring Curtiss Co.*, 177 Fed. 257, at 260–61 (1910); Hatch, *Glenn Curtiss*, 128–30, 144, 176–77, 180, 184–86; K-*WB*, 288, 293; Studer, *Sky Storming Yankee*, 98. The litigation is well summarized and carefully analyzed in Roseberry, *Glenn Curtiss*, 345–62.

25. *Wright Co. v. Herring-Curtiss Co.*, 204 Fed. 587–614, at 603, 605, 607 (W.D.N.Y. 1913). The case was affirmed on appeal; see per curiam opinion at 211 Fed. 654–55 (2d Cir. 1914). Hatch, *Glenn Curtiss*, 232.

26. 204 Fed. 587, at 607.

27. Ibid., 608–12.

28. Subsequent to his 1910 decision, Judge Hazel must have been disconcerted by the reversal of Judge Charles Hough, sitting in the Southern District of New York. Hough decided that a patent for a motor car was of "pioneering" status, only to be reversed by the Circuit Court of Appeals for the Second Circuit. *Electric Vehicle Co. v. C. A. Duerr & Co.*, 172 Fed. 923 (Cir. Ct., N.Y., 1909), reversed by *Columbia Motor Car Co. v. C. A. Duerr & Co.*, 184 Fed. 916 (Cir. Ct. Appeals, 1911). Quotations from the 1913 Hazel opinion are in 204 Fed. 587, at 605, 606.

29. *Boyden Power-Brake Co. v. Westinghouse*, 170 U.S. 537, at 561–62 (1898) This was a 5–4 Supreme Court decision that turned upon whether the invention was "pioneering." The majority held the invention entitled to liberal construction, but that it was not of "pioneering" quality. In 1912 it was held that to be a pioneering invention, the theory expounded in the patent application had to be put to use; *Manhattan Book Casing Machine Co. v. E. C. Fuller Co.*, 274 Fed. 964, at 969 (1912).

30. 211 Fed. 654, at 655 (Cir. Ct. App., 2d Cir., 1914); quotation in McFarland, *Wright Papers*, 2:1073.

31. The first actions, filed in 1910, were against aviators Louis Paulhan and Claude Grahame-White. The Grahame-White litigation, based on a 1910 exhibition flight at Belmont Park, N.Y., was settled for $17,000 in May 1911. Wilbur Wright indicated displeasure that his attorneys had permitted Grahame-White to pay so little in settlement of damages. On July 5, 1914, Grover Loening wrote Orville Wright that there was resentment that the Wright Company waited until flying events took place, and then decided whether to sue. Toulmin to Wright brothers, Jan. 2, 1910, Feb. 18, 1910, May 13 and 26, 1911, Folio Toulmin, Container 53; and Folio Loening, Container 38, WB/LC. See also Howard, *Wilbur and Orville*, 347; and Crouch, *Bishop's Boys*, 418–19.

32. On the matter of securing jurisdiction of foreign exhibition fliers, and of suing their promoters and managers, see Toulmin to Wright brothers, Dec. 18 and 19, 1909, Feb, 19, 1910, Folio Toulmin, Container 53, WB/LC.

33. At this time the U.S. circuit courts were the initial trial courts for many actions, but they were held by U.S. district judges, sitting either singly or in association with other district judges. Appeals from circuit court decisions were taken to the circuit court of appeals for the appropriate circuit; from the circuit courts of appeal, cases could, in most instances, be appealed to the Supreme Court of the United States or reviewed by writ of error in the Supreme Court.

34. *Wright Co. v. Paulhan*, 177 Fed. 261–71 (Cir Ct., S.D.N.Y., 1910); Eubank, "Aeronautical Patent Law," 145. The quoted material is in 177 Fed. 261, at 264.

35. See the negotiations conducted on behalf of the Wrights with the Aero Corporation, Ltd., in Container 75, WB/LC.

36. See the litigation papers, ca. 1920, in Container 81, WB/LC. By way of defense, the British government pleaded that Crown settlement of a patent infringement action in 1914 included the right to manufacture, use, and sell aircraft within the United States under the terms of the American, as well as the British, patent.

37. Col. Samuel Reber to Orville Wright, Jan. 14, 1914, and Wright to Reber, Jan. 17, 1914, Folio Reber, Container 46, WB/LC.

38. In the years 1909–12, the patent litigation was the greatest drain on the Wright brothers' time, with Wilbur assuming most responsibility for this activity. Crouch, *Bishop's Boys*, 447; Toulmin to Wright Company, Jan. 22, 1910, and Wright Company to Toulmin, Container 53, WB/LC.

39. Container 81, WB/LC.

40. Dr. Roseberry, Glenn Curtiss's biographer, asserted that after their 1910 success with litigation, the Wrights withdrew from active work with the Wright Company, and planned to emphasize experimentation. "As matters turned out, they devoted most of their time instead to prosecuting the patent infringement activities." Roseberry, *Glenn Curtiss*, 230.

41. Loening to Orville Wright, June 22, 1913, Aug. 1 and 15, 1913, Jan. 10, 1914, Folio Loening, Container 38, WB/LC. There is some uncertainty whether Loening joined the Wright firm in June 1912 or June 1913; the correspondence indicates that he began work with the Wrights in June 1912, but perhaps that was in an unpaid capacity. His 1935 memoir states that he began in 1912; his 1968 memoir states 1913. Grover Loening, *Our Wings Grow Faster*, 30–31, 38–39; Loening, *Take Off into Greatness*, 54–55.

42. Loening to Orville Wright, Jan. 1914 (?), Folio Loening, Container 38, WB/LC; Herbster to Capt. Mark Bristol, Dec. 7, 1915, Container 30, MB/LC.

43. Loening to Wright, Folio Loening, Container 38, WB/LC; Reber to Wright, Oct. 22, 1913; Loening to Reber, Dec. 6, 1913; Reber to Wright, Dec. 30, 1912; Reber to Wright, Jan. 7, 1914; Wright to Reber, Feb. 3, 1914: all in Folio Reber, Container 46, WB/LC. A Wright Company official, Albert Freedman, notified Orville Wright that he was going to San Diego to placate the officers in charge of army aviation; Jan. 9, 1914, Folio Freedman, Container 27, WB/LC. See discussion at Crouch, *Bishop's Boys*, 458–59; see also Loening, *Our Wings Grow Faster*, 47.

44. Affidavit, Jan. 12, 1915, in *Wright Company v. Curtiss Aeroplane Company*, Container 76, WB/LC.

45. Transcript, Oral History Interviews with Frank P. Lahm, Nov. 14, 1959, and

Nov. 15, 1962, AFHRA. There was also widespread preference for Curtiss control systems over those of the Wrights, which continued to use levers while Curtiss utilized a wheel-based system. Crouch, *Bishop's Boys*, 436–37.

46. Statistics in Loening, *Take Off into Greatness*, 67; stalling comment in Loening, *Our Wings Grow Faster*, 47; author's examination of the original Wright flyer, and models of the Wright B and Wright C flyers, in the National Aeronautics and Space Museum, Washington, D.C., on Sept. 16, 1997.

47. "Chronology of Events," 18, 27, 31, Jones/AFHRA; Sitz, "History of U.S. Naval Aviation," Technical Note No. 18, Series of 1930, 6; *Chronicle of the Aviation Industry*, 16. In December 1914, a former Wright Company mechanic informed Loening that Wright was still working on a flying boat. Hermann Schier to Loening, Dec. 13, 1914, Container 1, GCL/LC.

48. Loening to Milling, June 15, 1914, Container 1, GCL/LC; Loening spent the following year working for the government at the San Diego flying field. Two Wright Company mechanics joined him, one having been fired by Wright after the other resigned. Apparently there was an effort to recruit Loening once more, subsequent to Orville Wright's sale of the Wright Company to a syndicate of businessmen in 1914. See Lt. Col. Samuel Reber to Loening, July 13, 1914; Alpheus F. Barnes to Loening, July 27, 1914; Herman Schier to Loening, Dec. 13, 1914; Charles Nellis to Loening, Dec., 15, 1914; A. B. Gaines Jr. to Loening, Oct. 6, 1915: all in Container 1, GCL/LC.

49. Loening, *Our Wings Grow Faster*, 44–46; Loening, *Take Off into Greatness*, 56.

50. Chambers to Wright, May 25, 1912, Container 17; Reber to Wright, Nov. 25, 1913, Folio Reber, Container 46: both in WB/LC. See also my discussion in chapter 3, above.

51. McFarland, *Wright Papers*, 2:1087 (n. 10); Loening, *Take Off into Greatness*, 114.

52. There is considerable dispute over whether the Langley airplane as reconstructed was an exact replica of the 1903 model that crashed. For a discussion of the 1903 Langley "flight," and the subsequent Smithsonian effort to prove Langley "first," see Crouch, *Bishop's Boys*, 261–72, 484–501; and Robie, *For the Greatest Achievement*, 331. See also Crouch, *Bishop's Boys*, 171–80, 219–28, arguing that while the Wrights had access to Langley's computations, they refused to rely upon them.

53. Loening, *Take Off into Greatness*, 83–84.

54. McFarland, *Wright Papers*, 2:962, 982, 1087–88; K-*WB*, 309–10; Studer, *Sky Storming Yankee*, 324–25, 368; Crouch, *Bishop's Boys*, 419–21, 484–501, 526–29.

55. Studer, *Sky Storming Yankee*, 207, 217.

56. Ludlow to Chambers, Dec. 31, 1914, Container 7, Aero Club of America, WIC/LC.

57. Crouch, *Bishop's Boys*, 162–63, 447–48, 455–56, 458, 461, 465.

58. Ibid., 461.

59. Ibid., 67–92. Crouch notes that Orville refused to speak to his sister after her marriage, and that their only contact thereafter was on her deathbed.

60. A French approach is documented in two letters, Counsellor Clause to William Jennings Bryan, July 31, 1914; and Maj. Edgar Russell to Secretary of War, Aug. 20, 1914: both in RG 111, General Correspondence, 1889–1917, #36009, NA;

see also Orville Wright to Capt. Charles DeF. Chandler, Dec. 29, 1911, McFarland, *Wright Papers*, 2:1031–32. A British manufacturer's inquiry came through the attaché in London, Maj. George O. Squier to War College Division, Jan. 15, 1913, RG 165, War College Division Correspondence, #7031-6, NA.

There is evidence that the army aviators took the initiative in improving the Wright flyer. On Sept. 1, 1910, Lieutenant Foulois informed the chief signal officer that he had equipped the Wright flyer with wheels, permitting it to land on rougher terrain, and eliminating the monorail, tower, and weights previously required for takeoff. Foulois to Chief Signal Officer, Sept. 1, 1910, Container 14, BDF/LC.

61. Jerome S. Fanciulli to Brig. Gen. James Allen, Nov. 29, 1910; Scriven to Commissioner of Patents, Feb. 14, 1913; Commissioner of Patents to Scriven, Feb. 18, 1913; and Scriven to Wright Co., Mar. 3, 1913: all in RG 111, General Correspondence, 1889–1917, #25857-2, #32295, NA.

62. Various patents for flying machines, #27490; Maj. Edgar Russell to Commissioner of Patents, Sept. 15, 1913, #33201; Lt. Col. Samuel Reber to Commissioner of Patents, #34176; see also Becker and Becker to Secretary of War, Apr. 12, 1910, #23889; and Brigadier General Allen to Commissioner of Patents, July 1, 1909, #21704: all in ibid.

63. Wright Brothers to Milling, Feb. 3, 1912; Milling to Wright Brothers, Mar. 5, 1912, Folio Milling, Container 40; Affidavits of Walter R. Brookins, Alpheus Barnes, and Roy Knabenshue, in *Wright Company v. Curtiss Aeroplane Co.*, Container 76: all in WB/LC. Statements of Lieutenants Foulois, Milling, Arnold, and Kirtland and Capt. Paul Beck in *Wright Company v. Claude Grahame-White*, ca. 1910, Container 76, WB/LC.

64. The Smithsonian Institution provided testimony and cooperated in Curtiss's reconstruction of the Langley flyer, all in an attempt to prove that Samuel P. Langley had preceded the Wright brothers in their 1903 flight. See Affidavit of Robert L. Reed, Smithsonian constructor, in *Wright Company v. Curtiss Aeroplane Company*, Container 75, WB/LC.

65. Loening to Orville Wright, ca. August 1913, Folio Loening, Container 38, WB/LC. Loening specifically identified Captain Chambers and Cmdr. John Towers as the two officers who continually preferred Curtiss aircraft. Perhaps the reason for the Wright Company's failure with flying boats was Orville Wright's refusal to copy the ideas of others. See Loening's comment on Wright's resistance to tractor airplanes; *Take Off into Greatness*, 57.

66. Affidavit of G. Ray Hall, ca. 1913, in *Wright Company v. Curtiss Aeroplane Co.*, Container 76, WB/LC.

67. Roseberry, *Glenn Curtiss*, 395–97, 401; Crouch, *Bishop's Boys*, 462. Although this tactic was good delaying strategy, we should point out that there were very significant differences between the AEA-Curtiss airplane of 1908 and the Wright flyer. See Roseberry, 142, for a helpful discussion of the mechanical differences. Quite clearly the holding that Wrights were "pioneers" is what decided the 1909–14 litigation in their favor.

68. Representative S. D. Fess of Ohio, speaking on H.R. 5326, July 4, 1917, *CR*, part 55, 5123–24.

69. Letter to Frank S. Lahm, Aug. 2, 1911, Frank P. Lahm Collection, AFHRA.

70. Capt. Paul W. Beck to Chief Signal Officer, Mar. 7, 1911, and letterhead, Burgess-Curtiss Co., 1913, RG 111, General Correspondence, 1889–1917, #25857-20, #32984, NA. Despite the Burgess-Curtiss claim of a license, the Wrights asserted in February 1914 that any aircraft delivered to the army after January 1913 were an infringement upon their patents. Orville Wright to Lt. Colonel Reber, Feb. 4, 1914, in McFarland, *Wright Papers*, 2:1075–76.

71. Wright Company to Lt. Colonel Reber, Feb. 11, 1914, RG 111, General Correspondence, 1889–1917, #34523, NA.

72. See the figures for army procurement in Table 1. Although Wright Company production faltered to the point of extinction, the personal prestige of Orville Wright persisted. In an undated letter, probably in the spring of 1916, magazine publisher Robert J. Collier was discussing the endowment of an aerial squadron to serve in Mexico. He reported to Orville Wright that Harry Payne Whitney was supportive of the effort, but that Whitney wanted Wright's views concerning the "patent situation" before he made his final decision. Undated letter (ca. spring 1916?), Folio Collier, Container 18, WB/LC.

73. K-*WB*, 269–71, 282, 285–86. The sales price was reportedly $1.5 million; Crouch, *Bishop's Boys*, 465.

74. Mitchell, "Pooling of Patents," 5, Jones/AFHRA.

75. *F* 4 (1915): 737; *AAW* 3 (1916): 623; *AAW* 4 (1916–17): 381, 384, 690, 704, 723, 733; *Chronicle of Aviation Industry*, 17, 18; "Aeronautics: Patents, Monopolies, Agreements," 98–99, 104; Eubank, "Aeronautical Patent Law," 149; K-*WB*, 296; Hatch, *Glenn Curtiss*, 252–53; Studer, *Sky Storming Yankee*, 325; McFarland, *Wright Papers*, 2:1098; Robie, *For the Greatest Achievement*, 94–95; Roseberry, *Glenn Curtiss*, 360–62.

76. General Mitchell's 1935 testimony suggested that the monopolistic influence of the patent pool limited competition in the aviation industry, and that Congress should reinstate its program to buy out the pooled patent rights, thereby freeing competition in the American aviation industry. Mitchell, "Pooling of Patents," 3, 5–7, Jones/AFHRA.

77. Patrick, *Report*, in MM-*AS*, 1:81. Appropriations after 1914 fluctuated wildly. Naval aviation received $1 million in March 1915, and the army appropriation at the same time was $300,000. In September 1915 the army aeronautics appropriation was raised to $13,281,666. In 1914 the pressure of European orders induced nineteen new airplane manufacturing companies into the business. However, the quality standards and production capacity of many firms were deficient, as evidenced by the shoddy parts supplied to American military and naval flyers during the years 1914–17. *Chronicle of Aviation Industry*, 16, 17.

78. *CR*, 55, part 4, 5123–24.

CHAPTER SIX

1. Lt. Colonel Goodier testified that Curtiss fliers learned to fly by themselves, a civilian of the Curtiss Company providing only preliminary instruction in "grass

cutters," that is, in aircraft that did not leave the ground. Court-Martial Transcript (hereafter C-MT), 362–63.

2. Loening, *Our Wings Grow Faster*, 49.

3. The Goodier court-martial is not mentioned in the most recent official history of the air force. See Nalty, *Winged Shield, Winged Sword*, esp. 1:29–30. Interestingly, although Rebecca Raines reports the outcome of the court-martial in her Signal Corps branch history, she does not identify the Goodier revelations as originating in a criminal proceeding. Raines, *Getting the Message Through*, 166.

4. Cowan testified at the court-martial that when he arrived at San Diego, many of the younger pilots found it below their dignity to study engines, metallurgy, and other aspects of aeronautical engineering, subjects he believed were essential for pilots. He insisted upon this type of study, and, according to him, the aviators resented it. C-MT, 175–77.

5. Loening commented that "the whole scandal was amply aired in the newspapers." *Our Wings Grow Faster*, 59.

6. Foulois had been promised command of the newly formed First Aero Squadron and, as will be shown later, was suspected of pro–Signal Corps loyalties at this time.

7. Proceedings of a General Court-Martial held at San Francisco, California, Oct. 18, 1915, file JAGO 95565, 2 vols., microfilm A1773/1659, frames #0707–711, 0724, AFHRA (this source hereafter referred to as C-MP, followed by the frame number, and document page, if any.) The authorization for the Goodier court-martial was War Department Special Order 209, Sept. 8, 1915. Capt. Allen J. Greer, 16th Infantry, was the judge advocate for the prosecution. William Penn Humphreys, a civilian attorney from San Francisco, was defense counsel, and a military counsel was assigned to assist him. C-MP, frames #0822, 0824.

8. For Kirtland testimony, see C-MP, frames #0840, 0843–845, 0847, 0850, 0862, 0864, 0866, 0868, transcript pp. 18, 21–23, 25, 28, 40–41, 42, 44, 46; see also General Court-Martial #95565, Lt. Col. Lewis E. Goodier, General Order Apr. 26, 1916, transcript of trial, pp. 18–25, 28–30, in RG 153, NA.

9. C-MP, frames #0852, 0871, 0874, transcript pp. 30, 49, 52.

10. C-MP, frames #0870, 0873, transcript pp. 48, 51. Subsequently, Lieutenant Dodd testified that this conversation took place in the Aviation School officers' mess on Feb. 26, 1915, at about 12:30 P.M. However, the reference to Fort Sam Houston or Texas City did not form part of Dodd's answers. Dodd did recall Cowan suggesting that the officers appoint Foulois their spokesman, since he had already been promised command of the First Aero Squadron, and thus had nothing to gain or lose. Ibid., frames #0970–71, transcript pp. 148–49.

11. C-MP, frames #0855, 0886, 0890, 0894, 0895, 0897, transcript pp. 33, 64, 68, 72, 73, 75.

12. Ibid., frame #0901, transcript p. 79.

13. Ibid., frame #0906, transcript p. 84.

r14. Ibid., frames #0907, 0914, transcript pp. 85, 92; the quotation is on frame #0910, p. 88.

15. Ibid., frames #0939, 0942, 0950–951, transcript pp. 117, 120, 154, 126–27, quotation on frame #0961, transcript p. 139.

16. Ibid., frames #0940, 0868, 0975, 0979–980, transcript pp. 118, 147, 153, 158.

17. Ibid., frames #0097, 1003–4, 1007, 1010, 1028, transcript pp. 175, 181–82, 185, 188, 207, quotation on frame #1004, transcript p. 181.

18. Ibid., frames #988, 1024, 1025, 1035, 1038, transcript pp. 176, 203, 204, 213, 216, quotation on frame #1035, transcript p. 213. Earlier, Lieutenant Kirtland had testified that Patterson was certified as a junior military aviator when he had only 54 hours of flying time; Kirtland was certified a junior military aviator after he completed 912 hours. Ibid., frame #0880, transcript p. 59.

19. Ibid., frames #1013–15, 1023, 1054, 1085, transcript pp. 191–93, 202, 232, 264. The correspondence showed serious misfeasance on the part of Reber and Cowan; for example, on Feb. 25, 1915, Reber told Cowan to pad the list of pilots in the First Aero Squadron when such a list was requested by General Scriven. If necessary, Cowan was to put the names of aviation students in the report. See Exhibit 17, referred to in the judge advocate general's summary of the case for the secretary of war, Jan. 3, 1916; ibid., frame #0763.

20. On the inspections, see notes 28 and 29, below.

21. C-MP, frames #0998, 1000, transcript pp. 176, 178.

22. Cowan, ibid., frames #1306–308, transcript pp. 483–85; Reber, ibid., frame #1114, transcript, p. 291.

23. Ibid., frames #1041–43. transcript pp. 219–21.

24. Ibid., frames #0762, 0859, 0903, 0964–965, JAG summary, pp. 37, 81, 142, 143. Lieutenant Willis testified that it was general knowledge in the school that Cowan was "gunning for" Ned Goodier, mainly because of the banter over Wright and Curtiss airplanes. Ibid., frame #1176, transcript p. 353. On Taliaferro's record, see ibid., frames #1136–37, transcript pp. 313–14.

25. Letters, Reber to Cowan, Apr. 27, 1915; Cowan to Reber, May 14, 1915; Reber to Cowan, May 14, 1915; Reber to Cowan, Aug. 11, 1915, ibid., frames #1047, 1050, 1051, 1056, transcript pp. 225–27, 229, 234.

26. Ibid., frame #1338, transcript p. 564.

27. Ibid., frames #1147, 1150, 1152, 1154, 1155, 1298, 1300–303, transcript, pp. 324, 327, 329, 331–32, 475, 477–79, 480, 488.

28. Memorandum to Chief of Staff from Maj. Gen. W. W. Witherspoon, Chief, Mobile Army Division, General Staff, Mar. 6, 1914, in Reports, V, 9973, RG 165, NA; Whitehorne, *Inspectors General*, 49.

29. The Chamberlain investigation is documented in WCD-C: 7615-12, RG 165, NA; and in Reports, V, 9563, ibid. The general failure of the Signal Corps to comply with the recommendations persisted until well into World War I; see Whitehorne, *Inspectors General*, 49–50, 153–54. Portions of Chamberlain's reports, dealing with Wright aircraft, were forwarded to Orville Wright with the permission of the secretary of war. Wright to Secretary of War, Mar. 31, 1914, Reber to Wright, Apr. 7, 1914, Container 46, Reber, WB/LC.

30. Whitehorne asserts that the Chamberlain inspection was triggered by the

aviation activity being redesignated the Aviation Section of the Signal Corps. *Inspectors General*, 48–49. However, the redesignation occurred in July 1914, and Chamberlain was already on the scene in February 1914.

31. Testimony by Colonel Goodier, C-MP, frames #1188, 1190, 1268, 1274, 1277, transcript pp. 365, 367, 368, 445, 451. Captain Cowan testified that many of the motors supplied with the First Aero Squadron planes were found to be defective and rejected. In addition, Colonel Goodier noted that the Curtiss airplanes at the school were altered under the direction of Grover Loening; ibid., frames #1277, 1300, transcript pp. 454, 477.

32. Ibid., frames #1338–39, 1374, 1377, transcript pp. 515–16, 550, 553; quotation from military counsel on frame #1335, transcript p. 512.

33. Ibid., frames #1425–27, transcript p. 601–3.

34. Baker to Wilson, Apr. 14, 1916, ibid., frame #0775.

35. Ibid., frames #0768–769, 0776–777, 0780–782, 08128.

36. Reber to Cowan, Feb. 17, 1913, and Feb. 25, 1916, Court-Martial, Exhibits, General Court-Martial #95565, RG 153, NA. The quotation is from the February 25 letter.

37. Memorandum of Jan. 30, 1916; Reber to Cowan, May 24, 1915: both in ibid.

38. Memorandum of Jan. 30, 1916, re memos of Feb. 25, 1913, and early summer 1913, Cowan to Reber, in ibid.; quotation in Reber to Cowan, Feb. 16, 1915, ibid.

39. Memorandum of Jan. 30, 1916, ibid.

40. See the testimony of Lieutenant Jones: "I considered Captain Foulois as a man very wishy-washy; I considered him a man afraid of responsibility, afraid of the Signal Corps; that he was very anxious to get command of the first aero squadron, and thereby have his nest feathered. . . . I thought that his position was due entirely to the fact that he catered to the Signal Corps. He was very, very much afraid of the Signal Corps." C-MT, 79.

41. Henry H. Arnold, Report on Artillery Spotting, Nov. 6, 1912, file 168.65-38, AFHRA; Oral History Interview, Frank P. Lahm, Nov. 24, 1959, AFHRA.

42. Navy Lt. Victor Herbster to Chambers, Dec. 31, 1912, Container 16, WIC/LC; Reports on Accident, Sept. 7 and 9, 1915, Lt. Byron C. Jones and Maj. A. J. Rowley, Container 34, BDF/LC. On Loening's experiences, see *Our Wings Grow Faster*, 47–49, 50–51, 63, and *Take Off into Greatness*, 67. See also Loening to Cowan, May 7, 1915; Dodd to Cowan, May 20, 1915; Loening to Cowan, Sept, 15, 1914, and Apr. 14, 1915: all in Container 2, GCL/LC. For Foulois's efforts, see Order No. 14, Signal Corps Aviation School, July 20, 1914; Orders for Inspection and Flight Preparation, Signal Corps Aviation School, Feb. 1, 1914: both in Container 34, BDF/LC.

43. McClendon, "Question of Autonomy," 42–44; "Organization of Military Aeronautics," 20; *AAW* 2 (Feb. 28, 1916): 365. Senator James E. Martine, of New Jersey, traveled to the North Island Aviation School in the first part of 1916 and reported that he was pleased with what he saw there; *CR*, 53 (1916), part 12, 11530.

44. Quotations in Chamberlain, *Investigation of the Aviation Service* (S. Rep. 153), 1–3, 4; "Organization of Military Aeronautics," 22–23.

45. Memorandum to War College Division, General Staff Corps, Feb. 12, 1916, in Reports, War College Division, V, 12360, RG 165, NA.

46. *AAW* 2 (1916): 365; *AAW* 3 (1916): 80, 173; *F* 5 (1916): 163. Reber, the son-in-law of retired Lt. Gen. Nelson A. Miles, was injured by a fall in his home on Apr. 3, 1916, allegedly caused by strain over the army investigation. Squier's recall from Europe was requested on Mar. 21, 1916, WCD-C: 7015-100, RG 165, NA.

47. A statistical list of Aeronautical Division and Aviation Section officers up to and including 1917, prepared by Mr. James N. Eastman Jr., former chief of the Historical Research Branch, AFHRA, provides this information concerning Cowan and Patterson. Photocopy in the author's possession.

48. Chief of Staff to War College Division, Apr. 24, 1916; Memo, General Scriven to Adjutant General, Apr. 27, 1916: both in WCD-C: 9520–1, 9520–6, RG 165, NA. Memos, Chief of Staff to War College Division, Apr. 24, 1916, and Apr. 26, 1916, Reports, V, 12659, RG 165, NA.

49. Foulois to Maj. John McA. Palmer, Apr. 30, 1916; Palmer to Foulois, May 6, 1916; Foulois to Palmer, May 16, 1916: all in WCD-C:9520-18, RG 165, NA.

50. Dargue statement, May 11, 1916; Milling statement, May 23, 1916; testimony of Frederick W. Barker, president of Aeronautical Society of America, May 23 and June 1, 1916; WCD-C: 9520-14, 9520-16, 9520-18, RG 165, NA. Lt. Colonel Squier testified that the commanding officer of a flying school would preferably be a flying officer, but it was not necessary that he be so. American military attachés reported that in the British forces, aviation forces were always commanded by flying officers. This echoed the memorandum submitted to the chief of staff on the first Hay Bill on Feb. 15, 1913. WCD-C: 9520-18; Major S. L. H. Slocum to War College Division, Mar. 9, 1912, WCD-C: 7031-1, ibid.; Memo for Chief of Staff on H.R. 28728, Feb. 15, 1913, Reports, War College Division, V, 8516, RG 165, NA.

51. Board of Officers, Report, May 2, 1916; Kirtland to Kennedy, May 26, 1916: both in WCD-C: 9520-18, RG 165, NA.

52. Memo, Brig. Gen. M. M. Macomb to Chief of Staff, May 31, 1916, Reports, War College Division, V, 12659, RG 165, NA.

53. Report of Committee on Aviation, June 30, 1916, WCD-C: 9520-18, RG 165, NA.

54. Bliss to Secretary of War, July 7, 1916, Reports, War College Division, V, 12659, RG 165, NA.

55. Ibid. General Bliss later served as chief of staff during the First World War.

56. Squier went on to become chief signal officer during World War I.

57. See the discussion in Hurley, *Billy Mitchell*, 16–18.

58. See General Patrick's "Final Report," in MM-*AS*, 1:52, 65.

59. The accounts of the relationship between Foulois and Mitchell are far from clear. For Foulois's side of the story, see FG-*WBA*, 155–60, 172–74, quotation on 174; for Mitchell's version, see Hurley, *Billy Mitchell*, 31–35. Hurley suggests that if more experienced officers had been available, Pershing would likely have fired both of them (34). The Foulois-Mitchell and Mitchell-Lahm tensions are described in Cooke, *U.S. Air Service*, 80. See also Whitehorne, *Inspectors General*, 192–94.

60. Patrick, *United States in the Air*, 25 (quotation is on 85–86 and dates from 1921).

61. FG-*WBA*, viii, 182. The two had apparently clashed earlier over proposed

legislation establishing new flying fields, causing Mitchell to seek a new assignment. FG-*WBA*, 139–41. Actually, Mitchell had three weeks' enlisted service before his father's influence gained him a second lieutenant's commission in the First Wisconsin volunteer regiment in 1898. Hurley, *Billy Mitchell*, 3.

62. Mitchell, *Memoirs*, 165; FG-*WBA*,, 159–60.

63. Mitchell, *Memoirs*, 174, 195; FG-*WBA*, 156–57; Frank, "American Air Service Observation," 244.

64. FG-*WBA*, 156–57.

65. Frank, "American Air Service Observation," 244.

66. Sec. 26, "An Act to Increase the Efficiency of the Permanent Establishment of the United States [Army?]," Feb. 2, 1901, 31 Stat. 748, at 755. When the General Staff was created in 1903, a similar limitation applied to officers detailed to the General Staff. Sec. 3, "An Act to Increase the Efficiency of the Army," Feb. 18, 1903, 32 Stat. 830, at 831. For a use of the term "Manchu law," see Henry T. Allen to Congressman James Hay, Dec. 23, 1913, Container 10, Folio 1913, Allen Papers, LC.

67. In a typescript report prepared by Foulois in 1924, there is mention of a conflict between Col. Raynal C. Bolling and Mitchell over supplies to the Zone of Advance, which was resolved by the replacement of Bolling by Col. Richard O. Van Horn. In the same report Foulois stated that he had heard from American Embassy sources that Mitchell was making derogatory remarks in French cafes and other public places concerning the administration of the Air Service. This confirmed reports Foulois had been receiving for six months prior to Mar. 18, 1918. Foulois, "Report: The Air Service," 168.68-6, Appendix A, pp. 12–13, Appendix D, p. 5, AFHRA.

68. Hurley, *Billy Mitchell*, 34.

69. These rank, age, and marital-status qualifications were sharply criticized in September 1915 by the chief signal officer, Brig. Gen. George P. Scriven, *Report to the Secretary of War, 1915*, 9, 10. They were also criticized in the General Staff's statement of air doctrine, "Military Aviation," 17. In 1919 congressional hearings, General Mitchell asserted that detailing line officers to aviation duty prevented the development of military careers in aviation. U.S. House, *United States Air Service*, 62.

70. Col. F. Fraser Hunter, an Indian army officer assigned to the U.S. First Army, in his "Report of Air Service," AFHRA, 15, commented that there was little liaison or cooperation between the U.S. Army and its Air Service before October 1918. There may be exaggeration in the comment, but the fact that it was made at all suggests that Air Service officers were not easy to work with at the army staff level.

CHAPTER SEVEN

1. Letter of Nov. 17, 1916, Container 30 (1916), MB/LC.

2. See chapter 8, below.

3. J-*WA*, 2:76–77; Morison, *War on Great Cities*, 25; Cuneo, *The Air Weapon*, 30–31. Norman, *Great Air War*, 331, incorrectly states that the Germans failed to exploit the dirigible in the first weeks of the war for long-range reconnaissance. Subsequent to these German attempts to use Zeppelins over the front lines, they sent a dirigible to

scout the defenses at the fortress of Verdun, and it was also shot down. Horne, *Price of Glory*, 68; von Hoeppner, "Germany's War in the Air," 11.

4. The Germans, on the other hand, did not spot the British advance to Mons because airplane reconnaissance did not extend that far, and the high command refused to authorize the use of Zeppelins. While Germany had done some work with aerial reconnaissance of troop movements, official doctrine had not accepted the practice, and it was only after the first six months of the war that airplane observation was used effectively. Von Hoeppner, "Germany's War in the Air," 3, 6–7.

5. R-*WA*, 299–301, 304, 312–313, 316–20; Horne, *Price of Glory*, 201. Aerial reconnaissance was not always used or available as needed. See J-*WA*, 2:130, concerning British ground forces failing to exploit weak points in enemy defenses during the battle of Loos when those conditions could have been spotted from the air. There is some question as to whether aerial reconnaissance detected the change of the line of German advance. Cuneo, *The Air Weapon*, 68, 72.

6. R-*WA*, 332–33, 335, 338; Vandiver, *Black Jack*, 154; von Hoeppner, "Germany's War in the Air," 14. Remarkably, British accomplishments in aerial intelligence were achieved without formal coordination between the British air service and the intelligence sections. Not until late 1916 were intelligence groups attached to the R.F.C. squadrons on a permanent basis. J-*WA*, 3:314–16.

7. J-*WA*, 3:338, 441. According to Sam Hager Frank, the Germans distrusted the value of aerial reconnaissance, and the French had let their capabilities in this area decline after 1912; "American Air Service Observation," 25–30. By this point the U.S. Army had also recognized the value of aerial photointelligence and had begun work on a suitable camera for that purpose. Chief Signal Officer, *Report to the Secretary of War, 1912*, 24; Grahame-White and Harper, *Aeroplane in War*, 127; von Hoeppner, "Germany's War in the Air," 14, 72. Woodward was of the opinion that Germany led in aerial photography; *Britain and the War*, 356.

8. J-*WA*, 2:91; Woodward, *Britain and the War*, 358. Apparently the Germans relied upon cavalry reconnaissance during their initial attack through Belgium, and only when the front lines stabilized did they employ aerial observation. Neumann, *German Air Force in the Great War*, 133.

9. Horne, *Price of Glory*, 53–54.

10. J-*WA*, 2:172, 196–97, 208–9, 225, 273–74, 291; Farrar-Hockley, *The Somme*, 93, 112, 126, 146, 162–63; Frank, "American Air Service Observation," 59–60. It also was the case that reconnaissance by airplanes had alerted the Germans of the likelihood of a forthcoming offensive. Cuneo, *The Air Weapon*, 237–38. The German air commander noted that allied artillery spotting was so efficient that it aided barrages that "literally annihilated the German artillery"; von Hoeppner, "Germany's War in the Air," 51.

11. J-*WA*, 2:291.

12. Farrar-Hockley, *The Somme*, 112; J-*WA*, 2:225.

13. Farrar-Hockley, *The Somme*, 76–77, 80; J-*WA*, 2:83, 172, 208; Woodward, *Britain and the War*, 362; Cuneo, *The Air Weapon*, 239–40.

14. See Farrar-Hockley, *The Somme*, 152; and J-*WA*, 2:146–48. Allied air superi-

ority and its significance in denying German reconnaissance opportunities was noted in U.S. aviation literature in September 1916; *F*5 (1916): 352.

15. Norman, *Great Air War*, 102; J-*WA*, 6:553.

16. The details of this industrial contest have been set forth elsewhere. See J-*WA*, 2:136, 150, 161, 162–63, 394; 3:260, 263, 265–66; 6:28, 556–57.

17. J-*WA*, 2:150.

18. On the principles of concentration, see J-*WA*, 2:465; 3:400; Frank, "American Air Service Observation," 46; Farrar-Hockley, *The Somme*, 152; and Woodward, *Britain and the War*, 359.

19. The development of an offensive strategy of pursuit operations was a product of French experience at Verdun and discussions in the winter and spring of 1915–16 between French aviation leaders and British officers, particularly Brig. Hugh Trenchard. Horne, *Price of Glory*, 203–7; R-*WA*, 327–28, 412, 414; J-*WA*, 2:164–65, 269–71, 323–25. For German policies, see Neumann, *German Air Force*, 137, 221; and Norman, *Great Air War*, 103–7. The depressing effect Allied air power had upon German ground forces is discussed in J-*WA*, 2:269–71, 323–24. General von Hoeppner indicated that by August 1916, German air commanders had succeeded in obtaining local air superiority by a concentration of forces, and that the barrage tactics had been discontinued; "Germany's War in the Air," 54; see also Cuneo, *The Air Weapon*, 245, 259–61, 268–69, esp. 283–84.

20. J-*WA*, 3:399; Middleton, *Air Warfare*, 67, 92–93.

21. J-*WA*, 2:296–97.

22. Ibid., 165, 258. On defensive tactics and the use of fighter escort with observation aircraft, see ibid., 2:156–58; 4:553, 555; and Woodward, *Britain and the War*, 358. In the spring of 1916, the French provided the observers in their airplanes with machine guns and concentrated their pursuits to do the maximum damage to German fighters. Norman, *Great Air War*, 102. German reconnaissance patrols were forced to fly at high altitudes to avoid allied defenses, both on the ground and in the air. Neuman, *German Air Force*, 38; von Hoeppner, "Germany's War in the Air," 17–25. A manuscript history by Gen. Henry H. Arnold, written in about 1950, notes that formation flying in a "V" format was introduced in the fall of 1915 and used effectively to gain air superiority over the fortress at Verdun and during the battle of the Somme in the summer of 1916; Arnold, "History of the Air Force," file 168.2-8, AFHRA (document is not paginated).

23. Mitchell, *Memoirs*, 105–6; Appendix 3 to "Report: Misunderstanding . . . Air Service and the Ground Troops," AFHRA; and "Military Aviation," 13.

24. J-*WA*, 2:118, 181, 434; Woodward, *Britain and the War*, 361; Norman, *Great Air War*, 330.

25. J-*WA*, 2:94–95, 104, 117–18, 133–34; Slessor, *Air Power and Armies*, 124; Cuneo, *The Air Weapon*, 248–49; J-*WA*, 2:133–34.

26. J-*WA*, 2:326–34. Air Marshal Slessor believed that the main function of interdictional bombing was to keep enemy aircraft away from the front lines; hence the deeper the interdictional bombardment, the more satisfactory would be the results. Slessor, *Air Power and Armies*, 126–27.

27. Bissell, *Brief History of the Air Corps*, 5; Holley, *Ideas and Weapons*, 137. There are

numerous examples of strategic bombardment causing the diversion of air power from combat zones. Von Hoeppner, "Germany's War in the Air," 42; Cuneo, *The Air Weapon*, 361–62; J-*WA*, 5:127 (for 1917–18). Air Marshal Slessor pointed out that the aerial defense of London was a political and humanitarian necessity, but it was not militarily essential. Slessor, *Air Power and Armies*, 17.

28. The various attacks are discussed in detail in J-*WA*, 2:97, 99–100, 350; and 3:104–5, 115, 120, 129–39, 185–86, 222, 226–27, 232.

29. J-*WA*, 3:69.

30. Ibid., 71, 88.

31. Two solid scholarly discussions are Poolman, *Zeppelins over England*, republished as *Zeppelins Against London* (New York: John Day Co., 1961); and Douglas Robinson, *Zeppelin in Combat*. See also Charlton, *War over England*; Brandenfels, *Zeppelins over England*; Morison, *War on Great Cities*; Whitehouse, *Zeppelin Fighters*; and Rawlinson, *Defense of London*.

32. J-*WA*, 3:145–46, 243–46; Poolman, *Zeppelins over England*, 10; Robinson, *Zeppelin in Combat*, 345–46.

33. Robinson, *Zeppelin in Combat*, 247. Jones questions the effectiveness of aerial bombardment after June 13, 1917; at that time a surprise daylight attack by Gotha bombers caused more casualties than the entire Zeppelin campaign; J-*WA*, 6:1; see also Woodward, *Britain and the War*, 374–75. By way of contrast, a night attack on St. Pancras station did extensive damage and caused considerable loss of life, but the trains continued to run without interruption. Morison, *War on Great Cities*, 164.

34. Morison, *War on Great Cities*, 28–29, 108, 110, 114, 172–73; J-*WA*, 3:149, 213; Neumann, *German Air Force*, 124–25; Woodward, *Britain and the War*, 371–73.

35. The best mode of attack was from the underside of the rear of the Zeppelin, firing with incendiary bullets into the gas bag. Incendiary bullets and explosive ammunition became available in June and July 1916. R-*WA*, 343–44, 389–90, 395–401, 431, 447; J-*WA*, 2:350–53, 443–44; 3:99–100, 122–25, 132–33, 154, 161, 164, 168, 180, 183, 215–16, 224–25, 238; Middleton, *Air Warfare*, 138–39; Morison, *War on Great Cities*, 100–101; Spaight, *Aircraft in War*, 48–49.

36. Woodward, *Britain and the War*, 363–64.

37. R-*WA*, 343–44, 431, 447; J-*WA*, 2:451–53; 3:278–79; 6:98, 99, 118; Spaight, *Aircraft in War*, 47. Mitchell, *Memoirs*, 109. In addition to the Royal Flying Corps activity, the Royal Naval Air Service established No. 3 Wing at Luxeuil, France, with strategic bombardment as its mission. J-*WA*, 6:118.

38. Spaight, *Aircraft in War*, 47; Mitchell, *Memoirs*, 109.

39. Patrick, "History of the Air Service," 2. Concerning 1917, Billy Mitchell wrote, "The American regular army and navy knew nothing of up-to-date war and refused to be taught"; *Memoirs*, 9. Professor Holley notes correctly that censorship concerning military aviation in Europe was very strict, and that the belligerents uniformly denied requests to observe the front lines. He then concludes, incorrectly, that the Signal Corps was largely ignorant of developments; *Ideas and Weapons*, 36.

40. "Military Aviation," passim.

41. Chief Signal Officer, *Report to the Secretary of War, 1915*, 14.

42. Loening to Wright, Aug. 14, 1915, Container 2, GCL/LC.

43. Chambers to Austin, Oct. 5, 1914, Container 7, WIC/LC.

44. Ibid.

45. Royse, *Aerial Bombardment*, 63; Weigley, *Towards an American Army*, 200; Frank, "American Air Service Observation," 112; Greenwood, "American Military Observers," 113.

46. Squier, "Report of Military Attaché," 14:7, 30; Clark, "George Owen Squier," 220, 221–26. Squier reported a Royal Service Institution discussion of airplane employment doctrine, and specifics concerning the capabilities of British bombing aircraft, 205. See also Squier to War College Division, Nov. 30, 1914, WCD-C: 7015-79, RG 165, NA.

47. Squier, "Report on Military Attaché," 8:2, 3, 6–10, 11; 12:6, 10.

48. Ibid., 2 (no pagination); 9:2–3, 5, 7.

49. Ibid., 7:13–14; 12:8.

50. Ibid., 12:7.

51. Ibid., 12:2.

52. Ibid.

53. Clark, "George Owen Squier," 205, 228, 230, 240–41, 249. Cooke, *U.S. Air Service*, 7–8, discusses Squier's work as an attaché.

54. "Military Aviation," passim.

55. Ibid., 6. The chief signal officer's recommendation that pursuit aircraft be authorized equipment for an aviation squadron was adopted and incorporated in the statement of military policy on Nov. 1, 1915. Memorandum for Chief of Staff, Nov. 1, 1915, War College Division, General Correspondence, V, 9965, RG 165, NA.

56. "Military Aviation," 7–9.

57. Ibid., 12.

58. Ibid., 13.

59. Ibid., 14–15.

60. Statement of Henry A. Wise-Wood, resigning in protest from the Naval Consulting Board on Dec. 22, 1915, printed in *F* 4 (1915): 809.

CHAPTER EIGHT

1. A letter from Lt. Commander Mustin to Capt. Mark Bristol, dated June 17, 1914, indicated that flying at Veracruz was dangerous. Rain frequently added to the weight of the air frames, and the engines were less efficient in hot weather. The navy pilots were always flying at full power to sustain themselves in the air. Luckily there was only one accident. Container 29, Jan.–June 1914, MB/LC.

2. Eisenhower, *Intervention*, 82, 89, 105, 119, 122, 125; Clendenen, *U.S. and Villa*, 82–98.

3. Van Fleet and Armstrong, *United States Naval Aviation*, 10–11; TL-*NA*, 41–43. Quirk, *Affair of Honor*, provides a good overall summary of the diplomatic situation but does not mention the use of naval aviation.

4. Clendenen, *U.S. and Villa*, 91, 98, 110–113; Eisenhower, *Intervention*, 148–150, 166.

5. Clendenen, *U.S. and Villa*, 36–41, 42, 45–46, 57.

6. However, Villa continued his policy of expelling Spaniards, and First Chief Carranza supported his actions regarding them. Ibid., 74–76, 78–79.

7. Ibid., 103.

8. On DuVal West, see ibid., 155, 158–59; on the various battles, see ibid., 166, 170, 210–11, 214. See also Eisenhower, *Intervention*, 191.

9. Clendenen, *U.S. and Villa*, 176.

10. Ibid., 180–91, 214–16, 218–19; Eisenhower, *Intervention*, 191.

11. Military historian Clarence Clendenen advances the interesting hypothesis that Villa's failure was due to a well-directed pro-Carranza propaganda campaign. The determining factor for President Wilson and the American people was the view that Villa was really a representative of the "interests" — international bankers and rich industrialists. Carranza thus became the darling of the extreme liberals, including the influential journalist Lincoln Steffens. Finally the newly established State Department Division of Mexican Affairs was distinctly anti-Villa in its views. While Clendenen is very persuasive, he seems to discount the impact of Villa's early defeats, as well as his clumsy maneuvering in Mexican political conventions in 1914 and 1915. *U.S. and Villa*, 195–206.

12. Ibid., 239–40; Eisenhower, *Intervention*, 224.

13. Clendenen, *U.S. and Villa*, 241.

14. Eisenhower, *Intervention*, 230–31. In reviewing the history of the March 10 order, Clendenen missed the amendment of the order which included the capture of Villa as part of the expedition's mission. He thus claimed that Pershing had succeeded — Villa's band *was* broken up — but that there had been no direction to capture Villa. *U.S. and Villa*, 251.

15. Clendenen, *U.S. and Villa*, 256–57; Eisenhower, *Intervention*, 236–38, 241–43. For a general history of the Punitive Expedition, see Herbert Mason, *Great Pursuit*.

16. On Pershing's early career, see Smythe, *Guerrilla Warrior*. In addition to his military experience, Pershing reportedly was far more tactful and diplomatic than the department commander, Maj. Gen. Frederick Funston. Eisenhower, *Intervention*, 234–35. Pershing had also served as governor of the Moro Province in 1911. Birtle, *U.S. Army Counterinsurgency*, 162.

17. Smythe, *Guerrilla Warrior*, 232. Pershing's use of airplanes for reconnaissance was included in his instructions and formed a part of the 1915 statement of doctrine by the General Staff. Thomas and Allen, "Mexican Punitive Expedition," 4, 5, 15; "Military Aviation," 12.

18. Hines, "First Aero Squadron," 191.

19. Wiser, "Pershing's Mexican Campaign," 437. The First Aero Squadron arrived at Columbus a few hours before the departure of the expedition. It had been carried on trucks, and the planes had to be reassembled for flight. Eisenhower, *Intervention*, 239.

20. War College Division to Chief of Staff, Feb. 18, 1915; Memoranda, War College Division to Chief of Staff, July 29, 1915–Nov. 19, 1915; Memorandum for Adjutant General on Captain Foulois Report, ca. Nov. 1915: all in Reports, V, 8980, RG 165, NA. The situation is also referred to in an Oral History Interview, Maj. Gen.

Benjamin D. Foulois, Dec. 1965, pp. 22–23, USAF Oral History Program Interview #766, AFHRA. The grounding of the JN-3s on General Funston's orders is documented by letters of Maj. A. J. Browley, Sept. 7, 9, 1915; Major General Funston to Adjutant General, Sept. 13, 1915; and a memorandum on operations showing planes grounded for engine trouble, dated July 26, 1915–Nov. 19, 1915: all in Container 34, BDF/LC.

21. Foulois to Commander, Fort Sam Houston, Mar. 10, 1916, in folio Signal Corps Aviation School, Administration, Container 34, BDF/LC.

22. Hines, "Mexican Punitive Expedition," 150. Foulois, from past experience flying in Texas, was also aware that the lifting quality of air in Texas, due to density, pressure, and humidity, was less than it was in the mid-Atlantic states. Foulois to Chief Signal Officer, May 3, 1910, Container 34, BDF/LC; Foulois to Wilbur Wright, May 25, 1910, Container 27, WB/LC.

23. It is interesting that Gorrell, one of the pilots, recalled Pershing's message to be "airplanes were urgently needed at Casas Grande," rather than the less emphatic "immediately." Gorrell, "Riding Boots," 25.

24. FG-*WBA*, 126–27.

25. Toulmin, *Pershing in Mexico*, 50; Gorrell, "Riding Boots," 30; Nuhn, "Mexican Punitive Expedition," AFHRA, 62–66.

26. Lt. J. E. Carberry to Capt. A. S. Cowan, Jan. 26 and May 14, 1915, Container 34, BDF/LC.

27. *F*4, no. 12 (Jan. 1916): 819, 831–32; FG-*WBA*, 116–17; Bissell, *Brief History of the Air Corps*, 14–15; "Men and the Machines," 4:30; Nuhn, "Mexican Punitive Expedition," AFHRA, 69.

28. Herbert Mason, *Great Pursuit*, 109.

29. Gorrell, "Riding Boots," 26.

30. Mason, *Great Pursuit*, 109–15, Clendenen, *Blood on the Border*, 316–17; Nuhn, "Mexican Punitive Expedition," AFHRA, 102; Gorrell, "Riding Boots," 30; Hines, "First Aero Squadron," 191.

31. Nuhn, "Mexican Punitive Expedition," AFHRA, 103; Gorrell, "Riding Boots," 27–30; Hines, "First Aero Squadron," 191.

32. Toulmin, *Pershing in Mexico*, 22–23: Hines, "First Aero Squadron," 192.

33. "History of the Air Force," 168.2-8, AFHRA.

34. Memorandum, Benjamin D. Foulois, July 9, 1916, Container 34, BDF/LC.

35. Foulois, "Report"; Herbert Mason, *Great Pursuit*, 111–12; Clendenen, *Blood on the Border*, 317.

36. Nuhn, "Mexican Punitive Expedition," AFHRA, 120–21; Hines, "First Aero Squadron," 193; Elser, "Pershing's Mexican Campaign," 438, 442–43; *AAW* 3 (1916): 116. For reconnaissance on April 10, 1916, see Vandiver, *Black Jack*, 630. The need for accurate intelligence is noted in Thomas and Allen, "Mexican Punitive Expedition," 15.

37. Clendenen, *U.S. and Villa*, 264; Eisenhower, *Intervention*, 249. Villa had been shot in the leg, very likely by one of the "volunteers" pressed into service with his band, and, following his battle with Carrancista force, Villa fled to Guerrero on March 28.

38. Hines, "Mexican Punitive Expedition," 180–87; Clendenen, *U.S. and Villa*, 267; Eisenhower, *Intervention*, 275.

39. Vandiver, *Black Jack*, 622; Smythe, *Guerrilla Warrior*, 232; Thomas and Allen, "Mexican Punitive Expedition," chap. 2, p. 4.

40. Nuhn, "Mexican Punitive Expedition," AFHRA, 114; Thomas and Allen, "Mexican Punitive Expedition," chap. 5, p. 5. Courier duty for airplanes had been proposed in 1912 and 1914. Grahame-White and Harper, *Aeroplane in War*, 111–12; Spaight, *Aircraft in War*, 8.

41. Henry Allen to Dora Allen, Apr. 18, 1916, Container 10, Allen Papers, LC. Pershing wisely felt that dispersing the airplanes would decrease their effectiveness and increase supply problems. Hines, "Mexican Punitive Expedition," 153.

42. Smythe, *Guerrilla Warrior*, 240; Herbert Mason, *Great Pursuit*, 211–12; Clendenen, *U.S. and Villa*, 278–81; Eisenhower, *Intervention*, 295–97.

43. Tompkins, *Chasing Villa*, 149, 167; O'Connor, *Black Jack Pershing*, 125; Foulois, "Report," 2; Thomas and Allen, "Mexican Punitive Expedition," 145–46; Elser, "Pershing's Mexican Campaign," 444; Toulmin, *With Pershing*, 47; Hines, "First Aero Squadron," 191.

44. Foulois, "Report," 3, 4; Nuhn, "Mexican Punitive Expedition," AFHRA, 134–35.

45. Apparently some aerial mosaics were made before the crash. Foulois, "Report," 8, 9.

46. Herbert Mason, *Great Pursuit*, 145–46. What was left of the squadron left Mexico on April 22, 1916. Nuhn, "Mexican Punitive Expedition," AFHRA, 137, 165–66.

47. Smythe, *Guerrilla Warrior*, 232, 233; FG-WBA, 134; Herbert Mason, *Great Pursuit*, 116. Gorrell claimed that although he had given no interviews, his experiences in the desert on March 19–30 were published within twenty-four hours of his return. Gorrell, "Riding Boots," 9. On Bowen's statement, see *AAW* 3 (April 1916): 86.

48. Henry Allen to Dora Allen, Apr. 14, 1916, Container 10, Allen Papers, LC; Squadron Order No. 24, May 10, 1916, Box 34, BDF/LC; Hines, "Mexican Punitive Expedition," 173; Oral History Interview, Benjamin D. Foulois, Dec. 1965, USAF Oral History Program Interview #766, file K239.0512-766, pp. 25–27, AFHRA.

49. Nuhn, "Mexican Punitive Expedition," AFHRA, 127–32, 177–78, 218–19; Bissell, *Brief History of the Air Corps*, 16; "Organization of Military Aeronautics," 24. Sawyer, "Viva Villa," 60, 74; Foulois, "Report," Appendix, 10; Smythe, *Guerrilla Warrior*, 233; *AAW* 3 (1916): 24.

50. Chief Signal Officer, *Report to the Secretary of War, 1916*; Oral History Interview, Benjamin D. Foulois, Dec. 1965, USAF Oral History Program Interview #766, K239.0512-766, p. 24, AFHRA.

51. Tompkins, *Chasing Villa*, 113; Foulois, "Report," 3, 4.

52. Vandiver, *Black Jack*, 670–71; Paszek, "Wright Pushers to Stratojets," 114; Frank, "American Air Service Observation," 82–83. See also Maurer, "1st Aero Squadron," 208–9.

53. Nuhn, "Mexican Punitive Expedition," AFHRA, 68, 176, 125–26, 176; "Men

and the Machines," 28. Samuel T. Moore inaccurately claims a court-martial by Cowan triggered the Goodier court-martial and subsequent Senate investigations; *U.S. Airpower*, 43–44. On the Goodier court-martial, see chapter 6, above.

54. *AAW* 3 (1916): 83.

55. Clendenen, *U.S. and Villa*, 293–95, 314; Eisenhower, *Intervention*, 307.

56. Birtle, *U.S. Army Counterinsurgency*. 207.

57. Ibid.; Eisenhower, *Intervention*, 239, 307. It would be pure speculation to consider the impact upon officers in Pershing's command. However, it is useful to consider that at least three World War II generals served as lieutenants in the Punitive Expedition—George S. Patton, James Lawton Collins, and Henry H. "Hap" Arnold.

58. Clark to Foulois, Apr. 29, 1916; Dargue Statement, May 11, 1916; Foulois to Maj. John McA. Palmer, May 16, 1916: all in WCD-C: 9520-18, RG 165, NA.

59. Memorandum for Adjutant General on HR 14341, May 6, 1916, WCD-C: 7112-17, RG 165, NA; Henry Allen to Dora Allen, Aug. 4, 1916, Container 10, Allen Papers, LC; General Scriven visited the Punitive Expedition's camp at Campo Dublan, on Nov. 18, 1916, Henry Allen to Dora Allen, Nov. 19, 1916, ibid.

60. *CR*, 53, part 1, 494; part 3, 2860; part 4, 3835–36. Chamberlain, *Investigation of the Aviation Service* (S. Rep. 153), 1–4.

61. *CR*, 53, part 5, 4253; part 8, 7420. U.S. House. H. Rep. 369, 1.

62. *AAW* 2 (1916): 365; ibid. 3 (1916): 47, 111; see the discussion in chapter 6 concerning "personal" letters between Reber and Capt. Arthur S. Cowan.

63. Cowan to Reber, Apr. 10, 1914, printed in Chamberlain, *Investigation* (S. Rep. 153), 3.

64. *AAW* 2 (1916): 365.

65. Raines, *Getting the Message Through*, 166–68. Raines points out that Glassford was relieved from command of the Aviation School after still another inspector general's inquiry in early 1917.

66. *AAW* 3 (1916): 83. It should noted that General Foulois was incorrect in his memoirs; he claimed that Reber was removed before, rather than after, the Mexican Punitive Expedition. FG-*WBA*, 124–25.

67. It is possible that press coverage protected the aviators from disciplinary action arising from the press leaks. *Aerial Age Weekly* reported on May 1, 1916, that "the aviators have been muzzled again. It is reported some are to be 'reprimanded' for talking." *AAW* 3 (1916): 210.

68. Hines, "First Aero Squadron," 195; *Literary Digest* 52 (1916): 1769; *AAW* 1 (1915): 13. Hawley was president of the Aero Club of America in 1915.

69. *AAW* 3 (1916): 25.

70. "Our Unpreparedness Revealed by Villa," 883, 884.

71. FG-*WBA*, 136; Oral History Interview, Benjamin D. Foulois, Jan. 20, 1960, p. 63, BDF/USAFAL; Holley, *Ideas and Weapons*, 53.

72. Sawyer, "Viva Villa," 67.

73. Ibid., 63.

74. A good introduction to the antecedents and provisions of the National Defense Act is in Matloff, *American Military History*, 366–68; see also Raines, *Getting the*

Message Through, 151–52. Amended by the National Defense Act of 1920, these bills governed army organization until 1950; Matloff, 407–11.

75. *CR,* 53, part 5, 4495–96. The conference committee recommended that 114 first lieutenants be authorized for the Aviation Section, and this number was enacted into law. Ibid., part 9, 8378.

76. Ibid., 53, part 5, 5075 (both Thomas and Works).

77. Ibid., 5073.

78. Ibid. Senator Chamberlain's figures were wrong, but the thrust of his comment was quite accurate.

79. Ibid., part 7, 6367.

80. General Correspondence, General Staff, V, 12270, RG 165, NA.

81. Subsequent to the enactment of the National Defense Act, the War College Division requested military attachés to report on the organization of military aviation in their host countries, since it was "contemplated to ask Congress to create a separate aviation corps." Form letter, Secretary of War College Division to Attachés, Aug. 24, 1916, WCD-C: 9520–28, RG 165, NA.

82. *AAW* 3 (1916): 469; *AAW* 4 (1917): 181. In December 1916, the magazine editorially commented that the American public, since the Villa raid, had awakened to the fact that having fostered the work of Langley, the Wrights, and Curtiss, the United States lagged behind the aviation work being done in even the smallest of nations. *AAW* 4 (1916): 301.

83. Container 30, 1916, MB/LC.

84. Conference Committee Report to the House, May 20, 1916, *CR,* 53, part 9, 8378, 8379, 8395; Act of June 3, 1916, National Defense Act, 39 Stat. 166, at 174–75. The statute also authorized the appointment of civilian pilots in the grade of aviator, such appointments to be made if suitable military officers could not be detailed for flying duty. 39 Stat. 166, at 175. Since certification of pilots under the International Federation of Aeronautics (F.A.I.) rules was no longer required, Alan Hawley of the Aero Club (which administered F.A.I. business in the U.S.), made a formal protest to the Signal Corps on Aug. 11, 1916. Captain Milling advised Lt. Colonel Squier that the army's requirements exceeded those of the F.A.I., but that the service manual would be amended to provide that the F.A.I. certificate would be made available to qualifying officers. WCD-C: 9520–26, RG 165, NA.

85. Conference Committee Report, May 20, 1916, *CR,* 53, part 9, 8379; 39 Stat. 166, at 175.

86. Testimony of Brig. Gen. George P. Scriven and Lt. Col. Samuel Reber, Jan. 18, 1916, in U.S. House, *Increase the Efficiency,* 1:320, 322.

87. Lt. Col. George O. Squier, statement, May 29, 1916, WCD-C:9520-18, RG 165, NA; Tasker H. Bliss, Assistant Chief of Staff, to Judge Advocate General, July 3, 1916; Adjutant General to Judge Advocate General, July 12, 1916; Report, Proposal for Separate Aviation Corps, Aug. 12, 1916: all in WCD-C: 9520–24, ibid.

88. The debate on the National Guard and modified Continental Army plan was extensive. The flavor can be distilled from *CR,* 53, part 5, 4303–7, 4315, 4318, 4333–34, 4340–41, 4355, 4419, 5357–58; *CR,* part 6, 5368, 5372–73, 5583, 5587, 6026; *CR,* part 7, 6357, 6371; *CR,* part 8, 7594, 7600–601; and *CR,* part 9, 8395. See

also U.S. House, H. Rep. 297, 4–9. Secondary materials on the issue include good surveys by Link, *Wilson and Progressive Era*, 179–88; and Blum, *Wilson and Politics of Morality*, 122. For more detailed consideration, see Baker, *Wilson Life and Letters*, 6:31–32; Houston, *Eight Years in Wilson's Cabinet*, 1:66–67, 177–78 (illustrating Garrison's solitary commitment to the Continental Army plan); Walworth, *Woodrow Wilson*, 2:46–47. Although the General Staff supported the Continental Army plan, the Chiefs of Staff did not necessarily do so. See Palmer, *Washington, Lincoln, Wilson*, 315. Tumulty, *Woodrow Wilson as I Knew Him*, 238, indicates that Gen. Leonard Wood suggested the plan to Garrison; Gen. Tasker H. Bliss opposed the plan. See Hagedorn, *Leonard Wood*, 2:174; and Palmer, *Bliss, Peacemaker*, 108.

89. A U.S. Aeronautical Reserve was launched in September 1910 as a consequence of Aero Club interests in military flying. In March 1911 Aero Club member Robert J. Collier lent the Army Aviation Section an airplane for flying when all army airplanes were undergoing repairs. In 1915 the Aero Club launched the National Aeroplane Funds, a public subscription that raised $400,000 to train National Guard and Naval Militia pilots and to establish coastal landing fields. Robie, *For the Greatest Achievement*, 80–82, 89, 91.

90. U.S. House, *Increase the Efficiency*, 1:317, 321, 322–23.

91. Alan Hawley to Lt. Colonel Squier, May 27, 1916; Frederick W. Barker, statement, June 1, 1916: both in WCD-C: 9520-18, RG 165, NA; General Scriven to Adjutant General, June 30, 1916; War College Division to Chief of Staff, July 28, 1916; Gen. Hugh Scott to Adjutant General, July 29, 1916: all in WCD-C: 9520-19, RG 165, NA.

92. U.S. House, *Increase the Efficiency*, 1:326, 328–29, 332, 338–40.

93. Foulois, "Report," 10; "Men and the Machines," 78.

94. "Men and Machines," 26–27; there had been earlier evidence of propeller malfunctions in adverse climatic conditions. *A* 7 (1910): 41; U.S. House, *Aeronautics in the Army*, 139. The navy was experimenting with propellers in December 1916; U.S. House, *Status of Aviation*, 529. The commencement of quality control in aviation contracting began with the appointment of a Technical Advisory and Inspection Board in 1916; Alfred F. Hurley and William C. Heimdahl, "Roots of U.S. Military Aviation," in Nalty, *Winged Shield, Winged Sword*, 1:31.

95. As the bad news arrived, *Aerial Age Weekly* commented on May 15, 1916, "[T]he Mexican expedition brought out the shocking conditions of the Army Aero Corps and the public and the press have expressed their disgust in no uncertain terms. But the truth about the Navy is not yet known—. . . ." *AAW* 3 (1916): 262.

EPILOGUE

1. Vandiver, *Black Jack*, 720, 749–50. The Foulois quotation is at FG-*WBA*, 179. A 1913 article reprinted in the *Congressional Record* asserted that five years would be required for the United States to overtake Germany in military and naval airships and airplanes; *CR*, 41, part 4, 3277–78. *Aerial Age Weekly* pointed out that while the Wilson administration in October 1915 recommended $6 million to expand the military and naval aviation programs, a total of $7.5 million was needed for the army alone, and the navy and militia establishments required $5 million each; *AAW* 2

(1915): 77. Charles Seymour unfairly blamed Secretary of War Newton Baker for taking half measures, citing his lack of administrative ability and his commitment to pacifism; *Wilson and the World War*, 117–18; see also *History of the U.S. Signal Corps*, 98–100.

2. In 1915 Lt. Col. Samuel Reber, then in charge of the Aviation Section of the Signal Corps, observed that the United States, having been the first to fly, was now at the "tail of the procession" (quoted in "Military Aviation," 15–17); and in 1918 Maj. Gen. George O. Squier agreed that from 1908 through 1916, U.S. Army aviation had stood still for lack of money and had been far surpassed by European nations ("Aeronautics in the United States," 4, USAFAL).

3. Historian Maurer Maurer, introducing his monumental collection of World War I Air Service documents, noted that the United States made little progress in building its air power before April 1917, and that even observation planes then in the inventory were inadequate by European standards. MM-*AS*, 2:vii.

4. Discussing the aerial bombardment of London, a historian has suggested that fewer citizens were killed by the raids than died annually in traffic accidents, and that less property was destroyed by the bombing than that which was ruined by the ravages of rats. De Weerd, *Wilson Fights His War*, xx.

5. Squier, "Aeronautics in the United States," 63, USAFAL.

6. Kennett, *First Air War*, 226.

7. Ibid., 43, 219. The extensive and time-consuming program of establishing training facilities and educating aviation personnel is detailed in Cooke, *U.S. Air Service*, 17–34.

8. See discussion of General Pershing's attitude in Norman, *Great Air War*, 491.

9. Hurley, *Billy Mitchell*, 22–27. Professor Weigley argues that it is unclear how much Mitchell was influenced by General Trenchard. Rather, he contends that Mitchell moved from advocacy of interdictional bombardment to strategic long-range bombardment of cities over the period 1917–19. Weigley, *American Way of War*, 225–26. The difference in interpretation seems to focus upon ambiguities in Trenchard's doctrinal thinking in 1917, and whether Trenchard was as "middle of the road" as Hurley presents him. There is certainly some inconsistency in Trenchard's behavior. For example, he joined General Henderson in urging that Field Marshall Haig protest the diversion of aircraft from the French front to carry out the Royal Naval Air Service's strategic bombardment offensive in 1916. Neville Jones, *Origin of Strategic Bombing*, 91.

10. Mitchell, *Memoirs*, 146.

11. Ibid., 28–30; Holley, *Ideas and Weapons*, 46–48.

12. Mitchell, *Memoirs*, 30–31. Professor Holley notes this division of military opinion concerning strategic bombardment. He suggests that even Henderson's broad view of interdictional bombardment went far beyond the views of most military thinkers of the day. Holley, *Ideas and Weapons*, 54–55, 58. Holley points out that once the Bolling Mission ended, there was no formal American group for the surveillance of European developments of aircraft and tactics (61). Henderson's views had been radically changed by the World War I experience. In 1912 he was an advocate for reconnaissance use of aircraft. However, the aerial bombardment work

of the Royal Naval Air Service, and the interrelationships between reconnaissance, bombardment, and air combat, were well established by 1917. Neville Jones, *Origins of Strategic Bombing*, 128, 204; Finney, "Early Air Corps Training," 156.

13. Hurley, *Billy Mitchell*, 32–33; Holley, *Ideas and Weapons*, 137.

14. Gorrell, "Future Role of American Bombardment Aviation," 2, 3–9, 15, 16, AFHRA; a variant copy was printed in Gorrell, "American Proposal for Strategic Bombardment," 102–7. The full text, with helpful notes, is at MM-*AS*, 2:141–51.

15. See the relevant portion of Gorrell's "History," reprinted in MM-*AS*, 2:152–57.

16. Patrick, "Final Report," in MM-*AS*, 1:103–4. In addition to training by French and British schools, sixty-five American pilots were given advanced bombardment training at Foggia, Italy, for service with Italian units in Caproni bombers over Austrian lines. Patrick, "History of the Air Service," 19, 20, 23.

17. "Final Report," in MM-*AS*, 1:6–7; Major Milton F. Davis, who commanded an instruction center at Issoudon, pointed out that there was duplication in training when pilots arrived at Issoudon, but that actual work with combat aircraft was unavailable until they joined their units at the front. Duplicative training was also criticized by Capt. Frederick W. Zinn, Chief of the Personnel Section, Zone of Advance. Ibid., 4:41, 311–12.

18. MM-*AS*, 4:319, 322–23, 325, 329–30. When war was declared on April 6, 1917, only 65 U.S. Army officers had flying training, and even fewer had flown in Mexico. In July 1917 the United States began to send 100 cadets to France without preliminary flying training, in the hope that Allied flying schools might accommodate them. They didn't. Ibid., 1:93, 96. Col. Frank Lahm also identified gunnery training as a bottle neck, and was critical of American plans to depend on Allied instruction. Ibid., 4:16–17.

19. 1st Lt. H. F. Bott to "Chick," July 9, 1918, "Unit Not Specified," World War I Research Project, U.S. Army Military History Institute, Carlisle Barracks, Pa. The Milling comment on delays is in MM-*AS*, 4:8. Kennett suggests that while there was resentment against flying units and their personnel, ground forces were quick to resent any seeming neglect by the air services. He quotes a French poulu message to French Escadrille C 51 "We infantrymen here in our holes watch you all the time. We see everything you do. You are our gods, our protectors. When a day passes and we don't see you, we are like children whose mamma hasn't given them any desert" (*First Air War*, 155).

20. Lahm's comments are in MM-*AS*, 4:196–98; the slow process of training and introducing American balloon companies into combat is described in Cooke, *U.S. Air Service*, 45–50. Historian Eileen Lebow points out that difficulties in developing equipment, coupled with the need to train balloon-company personnel, were the cause of these delays. The first companies to come on line arrived in the Toul Sector in January and February 1918, and then their work was hampered by the assignment of commanding officers who knew nothing about balloon operations. Lebow, *A Grandstand Seat*, 4, 13, 17–18, 62–63.

21. MM-*AS*, 4:142, 160–61, 203; Kennett, *First Air War*, 26. Lebow argues that despite the communication difficulties, stationary balloon observation was recog-

nized, by the army as well as by the enemy, to be the most effective means of targeting. A single veteran balloon observer could regulate the fire from six to twelve artillery batteries simultaneously. Lebow, *A Grandstand Seat*, 117, 127, 147.

22. Milling, "A Short History," 50, AFHRA; Squier, *Aeronautics in the United States*, 8, 18, 20.

23. Goldberg, *History of the Air Force*, 16; Patrick, "Final Report," in MM-*AS*, 1:60–61.

24. Patrick, "Final Report," in MM-*AS*, 1:65–66.

25. Ibid., 85–87.

26. Ibid., 59–60, 88. Historian Aaron Norman asserts that the Armistice found four good combat planes of American design ready for production; *Great Air War*, 9.

27. Professor Holley points out that the so-called Ribot cable obscured the doctrinal basis upon which the French were proceeding — that strategic bombardment should be given a priority. When it arrived, the U.S. Joint Army-Navy Board applied its quite different doctrinal assumptions, and started on a program to build reconnaissance and artillery liaison aircraft. Holley, *Ideas and Weapons*, 40–42, 43. There is a good summary of the aircraft production crisis and the postwar separation of the Air Service from the Signal Corps in Raines, *Getting the Message Through*, 194–200.

28. "Brief History of the Air Service," 10; Patrick, *United States in the Air*, 56. Professor Holley points out that the procurement of aircraft in the United States and abroad was complicated by U.S. aerial objectives shifting from observation to bombardment; *Ideas and Weapons*, 135, 136.

29. At the inception of the Ludendorff offensive, the Germans concentrated 730 aircraft in the sector marked for the initial offensive. The same massing tactics had been utilized before the German offensive against the French fortress at Verdun in 1916. Kennett, *First Air War*, 90, 208–9.

30. Hudson, *Hostile Skies*, 90–115; the evaluation of the Fere-en-Tardenois raid is based upon General Mitchell's memoirs, probably written in 1926 but published posthumously. Mitchell, *Memoirs*, 210, 213. The Germans achieved surprise before their Aisne-Marne offensive because high winds limited Allied aerial reconnaissance. However, as the German advance continued, the British used interdictional bombardment of railroad junctions and trains on the tracks as a way to halt the rapidity of the advance. J-*WA*, 4:397, 400, 408.

31. Hagood, *Services of Supply*, 297–98, 301–3, 313; Patrick, "History of the Air Service," AFHRA.

32. For a general discussion of these developments, see Hudson, *Hostile Skies*, 119–41.

33. Ibid., 131–32.

34. Ibid., 139–41.

35. FG-*WBA*, 177–78. Concentration of American air power is detailed in Cooke, *U.S. Air Service*, 121–26, 138–57.

36. Hudson, *Hostile Skies*, 144–95. Gen. Carl Spaatz later felt that bombardment was not very effective except that it increased ground-troop morale. He blamed poor bombsights and "darkness" for the lack of success. Spaatz, Oral History Interview, Sept, 27, 1968, p. 6, USAFAL. Lebow notes that balloon observation facilitated the

use of a "creeping barrage" in the opening phases of the St. Mihiel offensive (Sept. 21, 1918). Lebow, *A Grandstand Seat*, 122.

37. Hudson, *Hostile Skies*, 258–95, covers the Meuse-Argonne aerial effort; the material on the "Lost Battalion," a contingent of the 308th Infantry Regiment that had advanced too rapidly and was cut off behind enemy lines, is in ibid., 255–68. See also the discussion in Frank, "American Air Service Observation," 357–58, and Cooke, *U.S. Air Service*, 160–99.

38. For "balloon busting," difficulties in communicating with troops, long-range reconnaissance, and bombardment strategy, see Frank, "American Air Service Observation," 262–65, 269–79. General Mitchell used 300 aircraft in two formations for the Oct. 9, 1918, attack on German troop reserves at Damvillers-Wavrille; he used five squadrons in the October 18 attack on the strategic highway town of Bayonville, in which 250 enemy troops were killed and 700 wounded. Ibid., 272–73, 275.

39. Ibid., 265, 271–73.

40. Ibid., 302–4.

41. Memorandum B, "Example of Enemy Preparations for an Offensive in Flanders," Air Photo Officer, 2nd British Army, July 1918, typescript, pp. 1–3, 5, Headquarters AEF, Conger Manuscripts Collection, U.S. Army Military History Institute, Carlisle Barracks, Pa. An interesting variation between German and Allied observation was that the Germans did their reconnaissance in the morning hours, while Allies used the afternoon and early evening hours. This was due to the location of the sun behind the observation aircraft, which made them more difficult to locate. "Report: Misunderstanding . . . ," 3, Appendix 3, p. 8, AFHRA. See also Cooke, *U.S. Air Service*, 55–73.

42. On the importance of aerial observation to both sides, see Middleton, *Air Warfare*, 62–63; Mitchell, *Memoirs*, 28; J-*WA*, 4:299, referring to early spotting of German counteroffensive; and General Patrick's "Final Report," which referred to night reconnaissance providing Allies with advance knowledge of Ludendorff's offensive in July 1918, in MM-*AS*, 2:48, 81. In June 1917, Orville Wright noted that "if the enemy's eyes can be put out—it will be possible to end the war." Letter, June 21, 1917, to C. M. Hitchcock, *Wright Papers*, 2:1105. Use of air observation to detect potential enemy attack is discussed in Frank, "American Air Service Observation," 61–62; for German views see Neumann, *German Air Force*, 131–33; von Hoeppner, "Germany's War in the Air," 61. The Germans provided continuous aerial observation after their infantry attacked, with pursuit protection assigned to the observation aircraft. "Organization of German Air Service," 192, Hannibal Collection, USAFAL.

43. Von Hoeppner, "Germany's War in the Air," 10. On the St. Mihiel reconnaissance, see the section of Patrick, "Final Report," MM-*AS*, 1:259–66.

44. Vandiver, *Black Jack*, 945.

45. Patrick, "Final Report," MM-*AS*, 1:269–73.

46. "Brief History of Air Service," 16.

47. MM-*AS*, 1:275–80.

48. The DeRam automatic plate camera was in production in the United States and France by the war's end, as was an improved British camera. In addition, the

Salmson two-seater observation plane was in use by American units, and it proved far more satisfactory than the English DeHavilland DH-4. Patrick, "History of the Air Service."

49. Frank, "American Air Service Observation," 258; J-*WA*, 4:269; "Organization of German Air Service," 165, Hannibal Collection, USAFAL. Report, Henry to Chief of Air Service, Mar. 7, 1918, p. 14.; and Report of Major Kerr to Chief, Intelligence, Feb. 1918: both in Headquarters AEF, Conger Manuscripts, U.S. Army Military History Institute, Carlisle, Pa. The long-range German gun incident is in Haemin, *Aerial Photography*, 43–46.

50. Middleton, *Air Warfare*, 72; Memorandum B, pp. 6, 7, Headquarters AEF, Conger Manuscripts Collection, U.S. Army Military History Institute, Carlisle, Pa. Lee Kennett comments on the value of aerial photography of trench activity; *First Air War*, 37–38.

51. "Report on the Organization and Operation of Intelligence 'A,' at the British II Army," Sept. 18–29, 1918, p. 6, Headquarters AEF, Conger Manuscripts, U.S. Army Military History Institute.

52. Frank, "American Air Service Observation," 64; Squier, *Aeronautics in the United States*, 44; some valuable information on photointelligence and its interpretation is in MM-*AS*, 4:157–60, 214–17, 292–98. Lee Kennett opines that aerial observation was the major contribution that the air services made to the war effort; *First Air War*, 31, 37–38, 220.

53. Cooke, *U.S. Air Service*, vii–viii.

54. "Tactical History of Corps Observation," in MM-*AS*, 1:193–95.

55. "First Corps Observation," in ibid., 1:206–15.

56. Ibid., 1:218; see also Frank, "American Air Service Observation," 355–56; and "Brief History of the Air Service," 18.

57. MM-*AS*, 1:228–29; for liaison difficulties, see also Frank, "American Air Service Observation," 258–59, 267–68.

58. MM-*AS*, 1:242–43.

59. Ibid., 1:247–48, 251–52, 255.

60. J-*WA*, 4:218–19, 299, 359–60; "Organization of German Air Service," 166–67, Hannibal Collection, USAFAL. On the ranging and fire-direction methods, General Mitchell seems to contradict Jones. See Mitchell, *Memoirs*, 114.

61. J-*WA*, 4:185, 6:501; "Organization of German Air Service," 159, 169, 191.

62. MM-*AS*, 4:169.

63. 2d Lt. Fred E. D'Amour, in MM-*AS*, 4:171–72.

64. American balloon companies were able to move their balloons and equipment from the St. Mihiel salient to the Meuse-Argonne region in a period of twelve hours. Lebow, *A Grandstand Seat*, 135. At the end of the war, General Pershing's report mentioned all of the combat arms and the service units, including the airplane squadrons, but not the balloon service. Ibid., 169.

65. See MM-*AS*, 1:325–39.

66. See General Patrick's comments in MM-*AS*, 1:33.

67. J-*WA*, Appendix, 16; von Hoeppner, "Germany's War in the Air," 111, 118;

"Report: Misunderstanding . . . ," 3; Hunter, "Report of Air Service," 401–21, AFHRA.

68. We have already noted Gen. Billy Mitchell's concentration of American and Allied aerial units as a preliminary to the St. Mihiel offensive. See notes 34 and 35, above. See also J-*WA*, 4:349–50, quoting General Foch on Apr. 1, 1918; von Hoeppner, "Germany's War in the Air," 74, 92, 103; and "Organization of German Air Service," 193.

69. "Organization of German Air Service," 193; J-*WA*, Appendix, 14.

70. See Patrick, "Final Report," MM-*AS*, 1:43–44, for bombers and Spad fighters inflicting heavy damage on German pursuits; for Salmson observation planes outdistancing Fokker D-VII pursuits at high altitude, see ibid., 272; for gunnery advantages of observation and bombing planes, see ibid., 263.

71. General Foch estimated that Allied planes outnumbered German aircraft by the ratio of three to one. J-*WA*, 4:349–50. Jones earlier commented that German technological advance in fighter aircraft in the spring of 1917 forced the Royal Flying Corps to provide heavy fighter escort to all reconnaissance and bombing aircraft during the battle of Arras. Ibid., 3:238.

72. First Pursuit Group Diary, July 30, 1918, 88, Langley AFB, Va.

73. Memorandum of Maj. James Logan, Aug. 10, 1916, in WCD-C: 6652–76, RG 165, NA; J-*WA*, 6:443–44, and Appendix, 89; "Organization of German Air Service," 190. For a statement of the aggressive policy in postwar tactical study, see "Notes on the Characteristics, Limitations and Employment of the Air Service," 5. General Patrick's "Final Report" clearly set forth the U.S. Air Service's view—that pursuit aircraft were primarily to destroy enemy airplanes, not to escort friendly observation planes. MM-*AS*, 1:34.

74. Holley, *Ideas and Weapons*, 137, 173–74.

75. Milling, "Strategic and Tactical Use of Aircraft," 215, 216, U.S. Army Military History Institute, Carlisle Barracks, Pa.

76. Wilson, *Wings of the Dawn*, 67–68.

77. Frank, "American Air Service Observation," 346, 331, 372; "History of First Pursuit Wing," 2, 4, 5, 16, 21; Patrick, "Final Report," MM-*AS*, 1:31, 39. British interdiction of transportation facilities prevented a German artillery unit from being resupplied with ammunition and thus slowed the German advance at Warfusele-Abancourt in March 1918; J-*WA*, 4:339. Kuter, "American Airpower," 9–10, 25–26, AFHRA. For effective strikes at railroad trains on tracks, see First Pursuit Group Diary, (Oct. 3, 1918), 126–27. British officers debated whether Somme bridges should be attacked in August 1918, arguing instead that rail lines were critical. J-*WA*, 6:452, 461–62. Air Marshal Slessor seems to have had the last word by outliving his opponents in the debate. He argued that the railroads could have been destroyed if air attacks had been concentrated on them rather than on enemy air forces! Slessor, *Air Power and Armies*, 131.

78. J-*WA*, 6:430; Neville Jones, *Origins of Strategic Bombing*, 128; Woodward, *Britain and the War*, 366.

79. J-*WA*, 5:19, 22–23, 42–43, 56–57, 101–2.

80. Ibid., 4:134–35, 152–54; 5:26–27, 30; Neville Jones, *Origins of Strategic Bomb-*

ing, 131; Norman, *Great Air War*, 419–26; Morison, *War on Great Cities*, 116. Another London attack on July 7, 1917, directed at the city and East End, killed 54 persons and injured 190; J-*WA*, 5:36.

81. Morison, *War on Great Cities*, 133–34, 140; J-*WA*, 5:128–30; 6:425–26. Georg P. Neumann stated that the lack of bombing aircraft with sufficient operating altitude caused Germany to abandon daytime bombing operations; *German Air Force*, 159. See also the discussion of strategic bombardment of England in Kennett, *First Air War*, 42–43, 58–60, supporting the argument that the destructive impact of aerial bombardment was overestimated.

82. J-*WA*, 5:90–91.

83. Walworth, *Woodrow Wilson*, 2:12; *F* 3, no. 9 (1914): 270; J-*WA*, Appendix, 11.

84. The RNAS had conducted several tests of aerial bombardment prior to American entry into the war. In the fall of 1916, fifty-six RNAS bombers staged a successful raid on Obernsdorf, Germany, with the loss of nine aircraft. RNAS planners targeted chemical works and explosive plants as their first priority, munitions factories as their second, and iron foundries as their third. Geographically, they targeted factories in the following priorities: (1) the Mannheim-Ludwigshafen group, (2) the Main group, (3) the Cologne group, and (4) the Saar-Lorraine-Luxembourg group. The Saar-Lorraine area proved to be the only target within easy reach, and it was bombed frequently by British and French bombing units. Neville Jones, *Origins of Strategic Bombing*, 59, 107–9, 113–15, 123–24, 212.

85. Ibid., 143–45.

86. J-*WA*, 4:279, Appendix, 26; Memorandum, December 1917, printed in J-*WA*, Appendix, 91.

87. J-*WA*, Appendix, 5; Neville Jones, *Origins of Strategic Bombing*, 135, 138, 140, 151.

88. Gorrell, "American Proposal for Strategic Bombing," 114–15; Gorrell, "History of the Strategical Section," 24, AFHRA, printed in MM-*AS*, 2:152–53; Neville Jones, *Origins of Strategic Bombing*, 147–48; Kennett, *First Air War*, 56.

89. Beaver, *Newton D. Baker*, 169.

90. "Brief History of the Air Service," 24, 25, AFHRA; MM-*AS*, 1:37. Gen. Mason Patrick recalled a conversation with Gen. Sir Hugh Trenchard in June 1918, during the course of which Trenchard stated that he did not seek an independent status for the Independent Bombing Force, but that it had been forced upon him; Patrick, *United States in the Air*, 22.

91. J-*WA*, 4:284; 6:132–38; Neville Jones, *Origins of Strategic Bombing*, 142; Woodward, *Britain and the War*, 375; Holley, *Ideas and Weapons*, 137–38.

92. Jones, 6:118, 123–24, 140–41, 141–53, 157. Lee Kennett estimates that of 141 British and French attempts to destroy railway stations, only three were successful; *First Air War*, 51.

93. Hunter, "Report of Air Service," 2, 11, AFHRA; Mitchell, *Memoirs*, 126.

94. Gorrell's study is printed in MM-*AS*, 2:141–57; the materials discussed are on pp. 141–43.

95. Ibid., 143 (quotation), 145–46.

96. Ibid., 146–48, 150. As early as March 1915, army aviators recognized the

need for nighttime and foul-weather navigation by compass. In September 1915 a British bombardment attack flew above the clouds by compass for seventy minutes, before descending directly on the enemy target. Lt. John E. Carberry to Capt. Benjamin D. Foulois, Mar. 4, 1915, Container 34, BDF/LC; J-*WA*, 2:250–61.

97. MM-*AS*, 2:151. "History of the Strategical Section," 3; and Kuter, "American Airpower": both at AFHRA.

98. The material is based upon an extract from Gorrell's 1919 "History of the Strategical Section, A.E.F.," reprinted in MM-*AS*, 2:153–55.

99. Ibid., 155–57. The factory at Romorantim, France, was operated as Air Service Production Center No. 2, and was staffed largely by American mechanics.

100. Ibid., 156.

101. Discussion in ibid., 191–92, quotations on p. 192.

102. See editorial note on the bombing survey, MM-*AS*, 4:365, 367.

103. Damage estimates are in ibid., 4:500; the critique is on p. 501.

104. Ibid., 502.

105. Patrick, "Final Report," in MM-*AS*, 1:39, 43, 45, 48. Historian Neville Jones echoes this evaluation; *Origins of Strategic Bombing*, 196–98.

106. FG-*WBA*, 180.

107. J-*WA*, 6:164, 173.

108. Ibid., 6:427–28.

109. Ibid., Appendix, 91.

110. Quotation in MM-*AS*, 1:17; and see Maurer's comment in ibid., 2:vii. Dwight's letter is in Box 1, Henry W. Dwight Papers, Special Collections Division, USAFAL.

111. Woodward, *Britain and the War*, 376 (written in 1968); Course at the Army War College, 1930–31, p. 2, U.S. Army Military History Institute, Carlisle Barracks, Pa.

112. Cooke, *U.S. Air Service*, viii.

113. Kuter, "American Airpower," AFHRA. Gen. Carl Spaatz echoed these sentiments in a 1968 oral history interview, commenting that 1918 theory was far ahead of aircraft capability; Spaatz, Oral History Interview, Sept. 27, 1968, Special Collections Division, USAFAL.

114. U.S. House, *Army Reorganization*, 908, 921; Patrick, "Final Report," in MM-*AS*, 1:47. Maurer also comments that General Pershing felt the sole function of aviation was to assist the ground forces, and that most of the army, including the air service, agreed with him; ibid., 2:vii, ix. It was estimated that the air service flew 3,790 hours during the Chateau Thierry campaign, 3,593 hours in the seven-day campaign at St. Mihiel, and 18,500 hours between September and November 11, 1918, in the Argonne-Meuse offensive. "Brief History of the Air Service," 13, AFHRA. The conclusion in regard to the priority of aerial observation corresponds with the view expressed by Professor Holley, *Ideas and Weapons*, 159.

115. See Kennett, *First Air War*, 83–84, 215–16.

116. Hunter, "Report of Air Service," 19, AFHRA.

117. "Notes on the Characteristics, Limitations and Employment of the Air Service," 3.

118. Milling, "Tactics of the Air Forces in War," U.S. Army Military Institute, Carlisle Barracks, Pa.; see also Course at the Army War College, 1930–31, ibid.

119. See Wilson, *Kitty Hawk to Sputnik to Polaris*, 142.

120. U.S. House, *Army Reorganization*, 926, 941–42; Mitchell's comments are in U.S. House, *United Air Service*, 44–45.

Bibliography

MANUSCRIPT AND ARCHIVAL COLLECTIONS

Carlisle Barracks, Pennsylvania
U.S. Army Military History Institute
  Army War College Papers
    Course at Army War College, 1921–23, G-3, #229-16
    Course at Army War College, 1930–31: Report of Committee No. 5. Subject:
      "Employment and Organization of Army Aviation and Anti-Aircraft
      Defense," #373-5.
    Foulois, Benjamin D. "The Tactical and Strategical Value of Dirigible Balloons
      and Dynamical Flying Machines." Thesis, deposited in Army War College
      Library, July 9, 1908.
    Milling, Thomas DeW. "Strategic and Tactical Use of Aircraft." Lecture at the
      Army War College, May 5, 1922. #215-216.
    ——. "Tactics of the Air Forces in War." Lecture at the Army War College,
      November 27, 1923. #275A-16.
    Patrick, Mason M. "The Air Service." Lecture at the Army War College, April
      25, 1922. #228-44.
  Conger Manuscript Collection
    Headquarters, American Expeditionary Forces
    Squier, George O. "Report of Military Attaché on the British Army in the
      Field," [November 16, 1914, to January 2, 1915].
  World War I Research Project: Air Service
    Box: Unit Not Specified
    Box #1, Regimental Squadrons 1–199
    Box #2, Aero Squadrons 200 Up

Langley Air Force Base, Hampton, Virginia
Headquarters, First Tactical Fighter Wing
  First Pursuit Group Diary, mimeographed

Maxwell Air Force Base, Montgomery, Alabama
Air Force Historical Research Agency
  Arnold, Henry H. "History of the Air Force, 1950." Typed manuscript. File 168.2-8.

Burge, Vernon L. "Early History of Army Aviation." Typescript. File 168.65011-4.

[Foulois, Benjamin D.] "Report of Operations of the First Aero Squadron, Signal Corps, with the Punitive Expedition, U.S.A. for the Period March 15 to August 15, 1916." File 168.6501-7A.

Futrell, Robert F. "Development of Aeromedical Evacuation in the USAF, 1909–1960." File 101-23.

——. "Ideas, Concepts, Doctrine: A History of Basic Thinking in the United States Air Force, 1907–1964." File 101-139.

General Information on Bombing. n.d. [1921?] File 248.222-10B.

[Goodier, Lewis E.]. "Proceedings of a General Court-Martial convened at San Francisco, California, October 18, 1915." 2 vols. File JAGC No. 95565. Microfilm, file A 1773/1659.

Gorrell, Edgar S. "The Future Role of American Bombardment Aviation." n.d. [1917?]. Typescript. File 248.222-78.

——. "History of the Strategical Section, A.E.F."; American Expeditions. File 167.401-1.

——. "Why Riding Boots Sometimes Irritate an Aviator's Feet." *U.S. Air Service* 17, no. 10 (Oct. 1932): 24–30.

"History and Development of Army Aeronautics," vol. 1. File 167.401-11.

"History of the First Pursuit Wing, St. Mihiel Operation (1918)." File 167.4017-3.

Hunter, F. Fraser. "Report of Air Service, First Army, American Expeditionary Force, France, Nov. 16, 1918." File 167.401-21.

Elmer L. Jones Collection

Bulletins of the Aero Club of America

"Chronology of Events Showing the Development of the Inventions and Discoveries of Glenn H. Curtiss with Reference to the Aeroplane, Hydroaeroplane and Flying Boat, 1904–1913." Breed, Abbott & Morgan, Attorneys at Law, 32 Liberty Street, New York, N.Y. File 168.653-4.

Looseleaf Chronology [of aviation events], vol. 5

Mitchell, William. "Pooling of Patents: Testimony before the House of Representatives Committee on Patents, Monday, February 11, 1935" (pamphlet). File 168.6549.

"Procurement of Aircraft." File 168.65413-12.

"Separate Air Force." Typescript. 2 vols. File 168.6541-10.

Frank P. Lahm Collection, File 167-601-25

Lahm, Frank P. "The Wright Brothers as I Knew Them." [ca. 1940]. Mimeographed. File 167.6-1.

Legislation Relating to the Air Corps Personnel and Training Programs, 1907–1939. File 101-39.

Milling, Thomas DeW. "A Short History of the United States Army Air Service, 1861–1917." [ca. 1925?]. File 167.401-11A.

Morriss, James M. "The Organizational Development of the Air National Guard

from Inception to World War II." Typed draft, August 1961. USAF Historical
Archives, Research Studies Institute, Maxwell Air Force Base, Alabama.

Nuhn, Perry A. "The Mexican Punitive Expedition and the United States Army
Aviation Section." Thesis 880-68, Air Command and Staff College, Maxwell
AFB, Alabama, 1968.

Patrick, Mason M. "History of the Air Service, Services of Supply, A.E.F." [ca.
1919]. USAF Historical Division Archives. File 167.401-14A.

"Report: The Air Service, American Expeditionary Forces (1917–1918)."
Prepared by Lt. Col. Benjamin D. Foulois, 1924, for use by Gen. John J.
Pershing in his book *My Experiences in the World War*. Typescript. File 168.68-6.

"Report: Misunderstanding between the Air Service and the Ground Troops."
August 1918. File 167.404-2.

Air University Library

Von Hoeppner, Ernst W. "Germany's War in the Air." Typescript translation by
J. Hawley Larned, [ca. 1920].

U.S. Air Force Academy, Colorado Springs, Colorado

U.S. Air Force Academy Library

Henry W. Dwight Papers

Benjamin D. Foulois Papers

Hannibal Collection of Manuals and Pamphlets

Hugh Johnson Knerr Papers

Laurence S. Kuter Lecture. "American Airpower — School Theories versus World
War Facts." Air Corps Tactical School, Maxwell Air Force Base, Alabama,
1937–38.

Lafayette Escadrille Papers

William Mitchell Papers

"Organization of the German Air Service." [May 1919]. Mimeographed, G-2,
Headquarters, AEF

George O. Squier Papers

Squier, George O. "Aeronautics in the United States at the Signing of the
Armistice." An Address before the American Institute of Electrical
Engineers, January 10, 1919.

Washington, D.C.

Library of Congress

Henry Tureman Allen Papers

Henry S. Breckinridge Papers

Mark Lambert Bristol Papers (Naval Historical Foundation Collection)

Washington Irving Chambers Papers (Naval Historical Foundation Collection)

Benjamin D. Foulois Papers

James Hay Papers

Grover C. Loening Papers

Mason Patrick Papers

Wilbur and Orville Wright Papers

National Archives
 Records of the Chief Signal Officer. Record Group 111.
  General Correspondence, 1889–1917.
 Records of the War Department, General and Special Staffs. Record Group 165.
  War College Division. General Correspondence, 1903–1919.
  War College Division, Entry V. Reports.
 Records of the War Department, Judge Advocate General. Record Group 153.
  General Court-Martial #95565, Lt. Col. Lewis E. Goodier. General Order April
   26, 1916. Transcript of Trial.

ORAL HISTORY INTERVIEWS

All of the following interviews were conducted by historians assigned to oral-history
collection duties by the Air Force Historical Research Agency (or its predecessor
units) and by members of the Department of History at the United States Air Force
Academy. A substantial number of interviews were conducted at the research
center, or at the academy, when the interviewee visited those installations.

Maxwell Air Force Base, Montgomery, Alabama
Air Force Historical Research Agency
 Benjamin D. Foulois, December 1965, Interview #766
 Frank P. Lahm, November 24, 1959, and November 15, 1962

U.S. Air Force Academy, Colorado Springs, Colorado
U.S. Air Force Academy Library
 Benjamin D. Foulois, January 20, 1960
 Ben J. Johnson, November 12, 1973
 Grover Loening, September 18, 1969
 Edward V. Rickenbacker, October 31, 1967
 Carl Spaatz, September 27, 1968, and March 15, 1974

NEWSPAPERS AND PERIODICALS

Aerial Age Weekly, vols. 1–3 (1915–17)
Aeronautics, vols. 1–14 (1907–15). Volume 1 of this series is entitled *American
 Magazine of Aeronautics.*
Army and Navy Journal, vols. 44, 45 (1907)
Atlantic Monthly, vols. 99–118 (1907–16)
Century Magazine, vols. 51–71 (1906–16)
Collier's: The National Weekly, vols. 37–52 (1906–14)
Flying, vols. 1–5 (1912–16)
National Geographic Magazine: An Illustrated Monthly, vols. 14–25 (1903–14)
New York Times, January 1907–April 1917
Proceedings of the United States Naval Institute, vols. 33–38 (1907–12)

Air Corps Tactical School. *Manual, Technique of Balloon and Airship Operation.* Air Corps Tactical School, Langley Field, Virginia, Jan. 1, 1928. Copy in Hannibal Collection, U.S. Air Force Academy Library.

Bissell, Clayton. *Brief History of the Army Air Service and Its Late Development.* Fort Monroe: Coast Artillery School Press, 1926. Copy in Air Force Historical Research Agency, Maxwell Air Force Base, Alabama, file 248.211-61Z.

"Brief History of the Air Service, American Expeditionary Forces." Mimeograph. AEF. History Division, Information Group, War Department, Office of the Director of the Air Service, July 1, 1920. Copy in Air Force Historical Research Agency, Maxwell Air Force Base, Alabama, file 167.401-14.

Carter, William Harding. *Creation of the American General Staff: Personal Narrative of the General Staff System of the American Army.* 68th Cong., 1st sess. S. Doc. 119. Serial 8254. Washington: Government Printing Office, 1924.

[Chamberlain, Senator George E.]. *Report: Investigation of the Aviation Service, United States Army,* to accompany Senate Joint Resolution 65. 64th Cong., 1st sess., Feb. 21, 1916. S. Rep. 153. Serial 6897.

[Chief Signal Officer]. *Reports of the Chief Signal Officer, U.S. Army to the Secretary of War, . . .* Washington: Government Printing Office, 1909–19.

Field Service Regulations, United States Army, 1914. War Department, Office of the Chief of Staff. Washington: Government Printing Office, 1914. Corrected to July 1, 1914.

Field Service Regulations, United States Army, 1917. War Department, Office of the Chief of Staff. Washington: Government Printing Office, 1917. Corrected to April 15, 1917.

[Greer, Thomas H.]. *The Development of Air Doctrine in the Army Air Arm, 1917–1941.* USAF Historical Studies, no. 89. U.S.A.F. Historical Division, Research Studies Institute, Air University, Maxwell AFB, Montgomery, Alabama, 1955.

[Hennessy, Juliette A.]. *The United States Army Air Arm, April 1861 to April 1917.* USAF Historical Studies, no. 98, U.S.A.F. Historical Division, Research Studies Institute, Air University, Maxwell AFB, Montgomery, Alabama, May 1958.

Hay, James. *Report from the Committee on Military Affairs, Amending H.R. 448, Calling for Information Relating to the Development of Military Aviation in the United States and Foreign Countries.* 62d Cong., 2d sess., [Mar. 26, 1912]. H. Rep. 450. Serial 6135. House Reports, vol. B.

McClendon, R. Earl. "The Question of Autonomy for the United States Army Air Arm, 1907–1945." Mimeograph, 1950. Air University Documentary Research Study. Documentary Research Division, Air University Library, Maxwell AFB, Montgomery, Alabama.

Matloff, Maurice. *American Military History.* Rev. ed. Washington: Government Printing Office, 1973.

"Military Aviation." Prepared by the War College Division, General Staff Corps, as a supplement to the "Statement of a Proper Military Policy for the United States" [1915]. Washington: Government Printing Office, 1916.

"Notes on the Characteristics, Limitations and Employment of the Air Service." Prepared by the Training and Operations Group, Director of Air Service, May 1920. Air Service Information Circular 1, no. 72 (June 12, 1920).

"Organization of Military Aeronautics, 1907–1935 (Congressional and War Department Action)." Army Air Forces Historical Studies no. 25, mimeograph. Historical Division, Assistant Chief of Staff, Intelligence, 1944.

[Patrick, Mason M.] "Final Report of the Chief of Air Service, A.E.F., to the Commander-in-Chief, American Expeditionary Forces." Air Service Information Circular 2, no. 180 (1921).

Perry, Robert E. "Command of the Air." An address before the American Academy of Political and Social Science, Philadelphia, April 29, 1916. Printed May 9, 1916. (64th Cong., 2d sess. S. Doc. 689. Serial 7125. Senate Documents, vol. 12.)

"Report of Brigadier General Tasker H. Bliss, U.S. Army, Commander of Maneuvers and Chief Umpire, Connecticut Maneuver Campaign, August 10–12, 1912." Printed, but not published. Copy in U.S. Army Military History Institute, Carlisle Barracks, Pennsylvania.

[Ryan, John P.] "Report of the Bureau of Aircraft Production, John D. Ryan, Director." Washington: Government Printing Office, 1918.

Scriven, George P. *The Service of Information, United States Army*. Signal Corps Circular 8, 1915. Washington: Government Printing Office, 1915.

——. "Some Considerations Affecting the Defense of Corregidor against Aerial Attack," Oct. 4, 1910. Typescript. Photostat from National Archives, File S.C. #29662, in Air Force Historical Research Agency, Maxwell AFB, Base, Montgomery, Alabama. File 167.04.

[Sitz, W. H.]. "A History of U.S. Naval Aviation." Technical Note no. 18, 1930 series. Navy Department, Bureau of Aviation. Washington: Government Printing Office, 1930.

——, comp. "A History of U.S. Naval Aviation." April 1925. Technical Note no. 160, Navy Department, Bureau of Aeronautics. Washington: Government Printing Office, 1925.

Simpson, Albert R., ed. *The World War I Diary of Col. Frank P. Lahm, Air Service, A.E.F.* Maxwell AFB, Montgomery, Alabama: Historical Research Division, Aerospace Studies Institute, Air University, 1970.

Thomas, Robert S., and Inez V. Allen. "The Mexican Punitive Expedition under Brigadier General John J. Pershing, United States Army, 1917–1918." Mimeograph. Washington: Office of the Chief of Military History, 1954.

U.S. Army. "Air Service Operations." Information Services, Air Service, U.S. Army, June 18, 1919. Prepared under the direction of Lt. Col. Edgar S. Gorrell. Copy in Air Force Historical Research Agency, file 167.4–7.

U.S. Army. "Army Aviation Service." *Senate Report on H.R. 4304*. 63d Cong., 2d sess., June 2, 1914. S. Rep. 576. Serial 6553. Senate Reports, vol. 2.

U.S. Congressional Record, vol. 43 (60th Cong., 2d sess., Dec. 7, 1908–Mar. 4, 1909) through vol. 56 (65th Cong., 2d sess., Dec. 3, 1917–Sept. 20, 1918).

U.S. House. 64th Cong., 1st sess., n.d. H. Rep. 297. Serial 6903. House Reports, vol. 1, Miscellaneous.

U.S. House. 64th Cong., 1st sess., Aug. 2, 1916. H. Rep. 1076. Serial 6905. House Reports, vol. 3.

U.S. House. 64th Cong., 2d sess., [Feb. 8, 1917]. H. Doc. 2043. Serial 7243. House Documents, vol. 117.

U.S. House. 65th Cong., 1st sess., Sept. 24, 1917. H. Rep. 161. Serial 7252. House Reports, vol. 1.

U.S. House. Committee on Military Affairs. 64th Cong., 1st sess., [March 16, 1916]. H. Rep. 369. Serial 6904. House Reports, vol. 2.

U.S. House. *Aeronautics in the Army: Hearings before the Committee on Military Affairs, in Connection with H.R. 5304.* 63d Cong., 1st sess., [Aug. 12, 14, 15, 16, 1913]. Washington: Government Printing Office, 1913.

U.S. House. *Army Appropriations Bill, Conference Report.* 63d Cong., 3d sess., [Feb. 27, 1915]. H. Rep. 1462. Serial 6766.

U.S. House. *Army Appropriations Bill, Conference Report.* 63d Cong., 3d sess., [Mar. 2, 1915]. H. Rep. 1488. Serial 6766.

U.S. House. *Army Reorganization: The Air Service: Hearings before the Committee on Military Affairs.* 66th Cong., 1st sess., part 19. Washington: Government Printing Office, 1919.

U.S. House. *Aviation School and Training Grounds for the Signal Corps of the United States Army.* 64th Cong., 1st sess., Feb. 14, 1916. H. Doc. 687. Serial 6971. Washington: Government Printing Office, 1916.

U.S. House. "Efficiency of the Aviation Service of the Army." 63d Cong., 2d sess., n.d. H. Rep. 132. Serial 6558. House Reports, vol. 1.

U.S. House. *Expenditures in the War Department — Aviation.* 66th Cong., 2d sess., [Feb. 16, 1920]. H. Rep. 637. Serial 7652. Washington: Government Printing Office, 1920.

U.S. House. *Increase of the Signal Corps.* 65th Cong., 1st sess., n.d. H. Rep. 97. Serial 7252. House Reports, vol. 1.

U.S. House. *Military Aviation.* 62d Cong., 2d sess., [April 26, 1912]. H. Doc. 718. Serial 632. House Documents, vol. 14. Washington: Government Printing Office, 1912.

U.S. House. *Status of Army Officers in Aviation Service.* 62d Cong., 2d sess., [July 18, 1912]. H. Rep. 1021. Serial 6133. House Reports, vol. 5.

U.S. House. *The Status of Aviation in the United States: Statements of Charles D. Walcott and Henry D. Souther to the Committee on Naval Affairs of the House of Representatives, Dec. 7, 1916.* Washington: Government Printing Office, 1916.

U.S. House. *To Increase the Efficiency of the Military Establishment of the United States: Hearings before the Committee on Military Affairs.* 64th Cong., 1st sess., Jan. 6–Feb. 11, 1916. 2 vols. Washington: Government Printing Office, 1916.

U.S. House. *Transportation of Mail by Aeroplanes.* 63d Cong., 2d sess., [Dec. 10, 1913]. H. Rep. 126. Serial 6558. House Reports, vol. 1.

U.S. House. *United Air Service: Hearings before a Subcommittee of the Committee on Military Affairs*. 66th Cong., 2d sess. Washington: Government Printing Office, 1919.

U.S. Senate. 65th Cong., 2d sess., [April 6, 1918]. S. Rep. 380. Serial 7304. Part 1.

U.S. Senate. *Preparedness for National Defense*. 64th Cong., 1st sess., n.d. S. Doc. 442. Serial 6952. Senate Documents, vol. 42, Documents of a Public Nature, 2.

U.S. Senate. *Purchase of Lands for Aviation School*. 63d Cong., 3d sess., [Jan. 26, 1915]. S. Rep. 925. Serial 6762. Senate Reports, vol. 1.

U.S. Senate. *Reorganization of the Army: Hearings before the Subcommittee of the Committee on Military Affairs*. 66th Cong., 1st sess., part 20, n.d. Washington: Government Printing Office, 1919.

U.S. Senate. [*Views of the Minority*]. 65th Cong., 2d sess., April 6, 1918. S. Rep. 380. Serial 7304. Part 2.

BOOKS, ARTICLES, THESES, AND DISSERTATIONS

"Aeronautics: Patents, Monopolies, Aircraft Manufacturers Cross-Listing Agreement." *Air Law Review* 7 (1936): 98–115.

"Aeronautics in War." *Scientific American* 99 (1908): 38.

"Aeroplane in War." *Scientific American* 108 (1913): 574.

Allen, Brig. Gen. James. "Aeronautics in the U.S. Signal Corps." *American Magazine of Aeronautics* 2, no. 1 (1908): 16–17.

———. "Military Aeronautics." *Aeronautics* 6 (1910): 155–58.

Anderson, Donald F. *William Howard Taft: A Conservative's Conception of the Presidency*. Ithaca, N.Y.: Cornell University Press, 1973.

Arnett, Alex Mathews. *Claude Kitchen and the Wilson War Policies*. Boston: Little, Brown & Co., 1937.

Arnold, Henry H. *Global Mission*. New York: Harper & Brothers, 1949.

Baker, Ray Stannard. *Woodrow Wilson: Life and Letters*. Vol 4: *President, 1913–1914*; Vol. 5: *Neutrality, 1914–1915*; Vol. 6: *Facing War, 1915–1917*; Vol. 7: *War Leader, April 6, 1917–February 28, 1918*. Garden City, N.Y.: Doubleday, Doran & Co., 1931, 1935, 1937, 1939.

Bannerman-Phillips, H. "Grenadiers of the Air: Exploits in Bomb-Dropping from Flying Machines." *Scientific American* 107 (1912): 214–15, 229, 262.

Beale, Howard K. *Theodore Roosevelt and the Rise of America to World Power*. Baltimore, Md.: Johns Hopkins University Press, 1956.

Beaumont, Andre. "Aeroplane in Naval Service." *Scientific American* 105 (1911): 384, 397.

Beaver, Daniel R. *Newton D. Baker and the American War Effort, 1917–1919*. Lincoln: University of Nebraska Press, 1966.

Beeler, William H. *The History of the Italian-Turkish War*. Annapolis, Md.: Advertiser-Republican, 1913.

Bell, Alexander Graham. "Preparedness for Aerial Defense: An Address Delivered before the National Convention of the Navy League of the United States,

Washington, D.C., April 10–13, 1916." Pamphlet no. 73, Navy League of the United States. Washington: Navy League of the United States, 1916.

Berget, Alphonse. *The Conquest of the Air*. New York: G. P. Putnam's Sons, 1909.

Bigelow, Donald N. *William Conant Church and the Army and Navy Journal*. New York: Columbia University Press, 1952.

Birtle, Andrew J. *U.S. Army Counterinsurgency and Contingency Operations Doctrine, 1860–1941*. Washington: Center for Military History, U.S. Army, 1998.

Blum, John Morton. *Woodrow Wilson and the Politics of Morality*. Boston: Little, Brown & Co., 1956.

Brandenfels, Treusch von Buttlar, Baron. *Zeppelins over England*. Translated by Huntley Paterson. New York: Harcourt Brace & Co., 1932.

Buerhig, Edward H. *Woodrow Wilson and the Balance of Power*. Bloomington: Indiana University Press, 1955.

[Butt, Archibald W.] *The Letters of Archie Butt: Personal Aide to President Roosevelt*. Edited by Lawrence F. Abbott. Garden City, N.Y.: Doubleday, Page & Co., 1924.

——. *Taft and Roosevelt: The Intimate Letters of Archie Butt*. 2 vols. Garden City, N.Y.: Doubleday, Doran & Co., 1930.

Carnahan, Burrus M. "The Law of Air Bombardment in Its Historical Context." *Air Force Law Review* 17, no. 2 (Summer 1975): 39–60.

Chambers, Capt. W[ashington] Irving. "Airplane — Dirigible." *United States Naval Institute Proceedings* 38 (1912): 745.

——. "Aviation Today and a National Aerodynamic Laboratory." *Aeronautics* 11 (1912): 157–62.

Chandler, Charles D., and Frank P. Lahm. *How Our Army Grew Wings: Airmen and Aircraft before 1914*. New York: Ronald Press, 1943.

Charlton, Lionel E. *War over England*. London: Longmans, Green & Co., 1936.

Chronicle of the Aviation Industry in America, A: A Salute to the Aviation Industry. Cleveland: Eaton Manufacturing Company, 1948.

Churchill, Allen. *Over Here!: An Informal Recreation of the Home Front in World War I*. New York: Dodd, Mead & Co., 1968.

Clark, Paul W. "Major General George Owen Squier: Military Scientist." Ph.D. diss., Case Western Reserve University, 1974.

Clendenen, Clarence C. *Blood on the Border: The United States Army and the Mexican Irregulars*. New York: Macmillan, 1969.

——. *The United States and Pancho Villa: A Study in Unconditional Diplomacy*. Ithaca, N.Y.: Cornell University Press, 1961.

Coffman, Edward M. "The American Military Generation Gap in World War I: The Leavenworth Clique in the A.E.F." In *Command and Commanders in Modern Warfare*, 2d enlarged ed. Edited by William Geffen. Washington: Government Printing Office, 1971.

Coletta, Paolo E. *The Presidency of William Howard Taft*. Lawrence: University Press of Kansas, 1973.

"Congress and Military Aeronautics." *Scientific American* 100 (1909): 130.

Cooke, James T. *The U.S. Air Service in the Great War, 1917–1919*. Westport, Conn.: Praeger, 1996.

Cooper, John Milton, Jr. *The Vanity of Power: American Isolationism and the First World War, 1914–1917*. Westport, Conn.: Greenwood Press, 1969.

Corn, Joseph J. *The Winged Gospel: America's Romance with Aviation, 1900–1950*. New York: Oxford University Press, 1983.

Cronon, E. David. *The Cabinet Diaries of Josephus Daniels, 1913–1921*. Lincoln: University of Nebraska Press, 1963.

Crouch, Tom D. *The Bishop's Boys: A Life of Wilbur and Orville Wright*. New York: W. W. Norton, 1989.

———. *A Dream of Wings: Americans and the Airplane, 1875–1905*. New York: W. W. Norton, 1981.

———. *The Eagle Aloft: Two Centuries of the Balloon in America*. Washington: The Smithsonian Institution Press, 1983.

Crutcher, Philip. "Military Possibilities of Aeroplanes." *Scientific American* 99 (Aug. 1908): 107 (Correspondence).

Cuneo, John R. *The Air Weapon, 1914–1916*. Vol. 2 of *Winged Mars*. Harrisburg, Pa.: Military Service Publishing Co., 1947.

———. *The German Air Weapon — 1870–1914*. Vol. 1 of *Winged Mars*. Harrisburg, Pa.: Military Service Publishing Co., 1942.

Devlin, Patrick, Baron. *Too Proud to Fight: Woodrow Wilson's Neutrality*. New York: Oxford University Press, 1975.

De Weerd, Henry A. *President Wilson Fights His War: World War I and the American Intervention*. New York: Macmillan, 1968.

Dienstbach, Carl, and T. R. MacMechan. "The 'Fallacy' of the Dirigible." *Aeronautics* 11 (1912): 10–11.

Drew, Andrew. "The Missouri Signal Corps in Aeronautics." *Aeronautics* 8 (1911): 145–46.

Driver, Hugh. *The Birth of Military Aviation: Britain, 1903–1914*. Woodbridge, Eng.: The Boydell Press, 1997.

Eisenhower, John S. D. *Intervention!: The United States and the Mexican Revolution, 1913–1917*. New York: W. W. Norton, 1993.

Elser, Frank B. "General Pershing's Mexican Campaign." *Century* 99 (1920): 433–47.

Eubank, John A. "Aeronautical Patent Law." *Dickinson Law Review* 56 (1952): 143–57.

Farrar-Hockley, A. H. *The Somme*. Philadelphia: Dufour Editions, 1964.

Finnegan, John P. *Against the Specter of a Dragon: The Campaign for American Preparedness, 1914–1917*. Westport: Greenwood Press, 1974.

Finney, Robert T. "Early Air Corps Training and Tactics." *Military Affairs* 20 (1956): 154–61.

Ford, Clyde S. *The Balkan Wars: Being a Series of Lectures Delivered at the Army Service Schools, Fort Leavenworth, Kansas*. Fort Leavenworth: Press of the Army Schools, 1915.

Foulois, Benjamin D. "Why Write a Book?" *Air Power Historian* 2 (1955): 17–35, 45–69; 3 (1956): 114–37.

Foulois, Benjamin D., and C. V. Glines. *From the Wright Brothers to the Astronauts*. New York: McGraw-Hill, 1968.

Frank, Sam Hager. "American Air Service Observation in World War I." Ph.D. diss., University of Florida, 1961.

Freud, Sigmund, and William C. Bullitt. *Thomas Woodrow Wilson, Twenty-eighth President of the United States: A Psychological Study*. Boston: Houghton Mifflin, 1967.

Garrison, Lindley M. "Aircraft as a Military Asset." *Flying* 3 (1914): 133.

Geffen, William, ed. *Command and Commanders in Modern Warfare*. 2d ed. Washington: Government Printing Office, 1971.

Gill, C. C. *What Happened at Jutland: The Tactics of the Battle*. New York: George H. Doran, 1921.

Glassford, William A. "Aeronautics and War." *Aeronautics* 8 (1911): 12–14.

———. "Our Army and Aerial Warfare." *American Magazine of Aeronautics* 2, no. 1 (1908): 18–21.

Goldberg, Alfred, ed. *A History of the United States Air Force, 1907–1957*. Princeton, N.J.: D. Van Nostrand, 1957.

Goldman, Eric F. *Rendezvous with Destiny: A History of American Reform*. New York: Random House, 1956.

Gollin, Alfred, "Anticipating Air Attack—in Defense of Britain." *Aerospace Historian* 23, no. 4 (1976): 197–201.

———. *The Impact of Air Power on the British People and Their Government, 1909–14*. Stanford, Calif.: Stanford University Press, 1989.

———. *No Longer an Island: Britain and the Wright Brothers, 1902–1909*. Stanford, Calif.: Stanford University Press, 1984.

Gorrell, Edgar S. "An American Proposal for Strategic Bombing." *Air Power Historian* 5, no. 2 (1958): 102–17.

———. "Why Riding Boots Sometimes Irritate an Aviator's Feet." *U.S. Air Services* 17, no. 10 (October 1932): 24–30.

"Government Aid in the Development of Aeronautics." *Scientific American* 48 (1908): 238–39.

Grahame-White, Claude, and Harry Harper. *The Aeroplane in War*. Philadelphia: Lippincott, 1912.

Greene, Francis V. *The Present Military Situation of the United States*. New York: Charles Scribner's Sons, 1915.

Greenwood, John T. "The American Military Observers of the Russo-Japanese War (1904–1905)." Ph.D. diss., Kansas State University, 1971.

Guinn, Paul. *British Strategy and Politics, 1914 to 1918*. Oxford: Clarendon Press, 1965.

Haemin, Graver. *Aerial Photography: The Story of Aerial Mapping and Reconnaissance*. New York: Macmillan, 1972.

Hagedorn, Hermann. *The Bugle That Woke America: The Saga of Theodore Roosevelt's Last Battle for His Country*. New York: John Day Co., 1940.

———. *Leonard Wood: A Biography*. 2 vols. New York: Harper & Brothers, 1931.

Hagood, Johnson. *The Services of Supply: A Memoir of the Great War*. Boston: Houghton Mifflin, 1927.

Hall, Edward H. *Hudson and Fulton*. New York: Hudson-Fulton Celebration Commission, 1909.

Hallion, Richard P., ed. *The Wright Brothers: Heirs of Prometheus*. Washington: Smithsonian Institution Press, 1978.

Harbaugh, William H. *Power and Responsibility: The Life and Times of Theodore Roosevelt*. New York: Farrar, Straus & Cudahy, 1961.

Harlow, Alvin P. *Theodore Roosevelt: Strenuous American*. New York: Julius Messner, 1943.

Hartig, John L. "The Evolution of Air Force Public Relations." M.A. thesis, American University, 1956.

Hatch, Alden. *Glenn Curtiss: Pioneer of Naval Aviation*. New York: Julius Messner, 1942.

Hearne, R. P. *Airships in Peace and War*. London: John Lane, 1910.

Hewes, James E., Jr. *From Root to McNamara: Army Organization and Administration, 1900–1963*. Washington: Government Printing Office, 1975.

Hildebrandt, A[lfred]. *Airships Past and Present*. London: Archibald, Constable & Co., 1908.

Hines, Calvin W. "First Aero Squadron in Mexico." *American Aviation Historical Society Journal* 10 (1965): 190–97.

————. "The Mexican Punitive Expedition of 1916." M.A. thesis, Trinity University, 1961.

History of the U.S. Signal Corps, by the Editors of the Army Times, A. New York: G. P. Putnam's Sons, 1961.

Hofstadter, Richard. *The Age of Reform: From Bryan to F.D.R*. New York: Alfred A. Knopf, 1955.

Holley, Irving B., Jr. *Ideas and Weapons: Exploitation of the Aerial Weapon by the United States During World War I*. New Haven, Conn.: Yale University Press, 1953.

Homze, Edward L. "The Luftwaffe's Failure to Develop a Heavy Bomber before World War II." *Aerospace Historian* 24, no. 1 (1977): 20–26.

Horne, Alistair. *The Price of Glory: Verdun 1916*. New York: St. Martin's Press, 1963.

Houston, David F. *Eight Years with Wilson's Cabinet, 1913–1920*. 2 vols. Garden City, N.Y.: Doubleday, Page & Co., 1926.

Howard, Fred. *Wilbur and Orville: A Biography of the Wright Brothers*. New York: Alfred A. Knopf, 1987.

Huidekoper, Frederic Louis. *The Military Unpreparedness of the United States: A History of American Land Forces from Colonial Times until June 1, 1915*. New York: Macmillan, 1916.

Huntington, Samuel P. *The Soldier and the State: The Theory and Politics of Civilian-Military Relations*. Cambridge, Mass.: Harvard University Press, 1957.

Hurley, Alfred F. *Billy Mitchell: Crusader for Air Power*. New ed. Bloomington: Indiana University Press, 1975.

Ironside, Sir Erwin. *Tannenberg: The First Thirty Days in East Prussia*. Edinburgh: William Blackwood & Sons, 1928.

Irving, John. *The Smoke Screen of Jutland*. New York: David McKay Co., 1967.

"Is the Aeroplane Practical for Scouting?" *Scientific American* 69 (September 1908): 166.

Jessup, Philip C. *Elihu Root*. 2 vols. New York: Dodd, Mead & Co., 1938.

Johnston, R. M. *Arms and the Race: The Foundations of Army Reform*. New York: The
     Century Company, 1915.
Jones, H. A. *The War in the Air*. Vols. 2–6. Oxford: Clarendon Press, 1928–37.
Jones, Neville. *The Origins of Strategic Bombing: A Study of the Development of British Air
     Strategic Thought and Practice up to 1918*. London: William Kimber, 1973.
Kelly, Fred C. *The Wright Brothers*. New York: Harcourt, Brace & Co., 1943. (A later
     edition is entitled *The Wright Brothers: A Biography Authorized by Orville Wright*. New
     York: Farrar, Straus & Young, 1950.)
Kennett, Lee. *The First Air War, 1914–1918*. New York: The Free Press, 1991.
Kipling, Rudyard. *With the Night Mail: A Story of 2000 A.D.* New York: Doubleday,
     Page & Co., 1909.
Knox, Sir Alfred. *With the Russian Army, 1914–1917*. New York: E. P. Dutton & Co.,
     1921.
Kuhn, Perry R. "The Mexican Punitive Expedition and the United States Army
     Aviation Section." Thesis 880-68, Air Command and Staff College, Air
     University, 1968.
Kuter, Laurence S. "An Air Perspective in the Jet Atomic Age." *Air University
     Quarterly Review* 8, no. 2 (1956): 2–17.
Lebow, Eileen F. *A Grandstand Seat: The American Balloon Service in World War I*.
     Westport, Conn.: Praeger, 1998.
Legg, Stuart. *Jutland: An Eye-Witness Account of a Great Battle*. New York: John Day Co.,
     1966.
Link, Arthur S. *Wilson: Campaigns for Progressivism and Peace, 1916–1917*. Princeton,
     N.J.: Princeton University Press, 1965.
———. *Wilson: The Struggle for Neutrality, 1914–1915*. Princeton, N.J.: Princeton
     University Press, 1960.
———. *Wilson the Diplomatist*. Baltimore, Md.: Johns Hopkins University Press, 1967.
———. *Woodrow Wilson and the Progressive Era, 1910–1917*. New York: Harper & Row,
     1954.
Loening, Grover. *Our Wings Grow Faster*. Garden City, N.Y.: Doubleday, Doran & Co.,
     1935.
———. *Take Off into Greatness: How American Aviation Grew So Big, So Fast*. New York:
     G. P. Putnam's Sons, 1968.
Long, Arthur S. *Wilson: Confusions and Crises, 1915–1916*. Princeton, N.J.:
     Princeton University Press, 1964.
McFarland, Marvin W. "When the Airplane Was a Military Secret: A Study of
     National Attitudes before 1914." *Air Power Historian* 2 (October 1955): 70–82.
———, ed. *The Papers of Wilbur and Orville Wright*. 2 vols. New York: McGraw Hill
     Book Co., 1953.
McMinn, Robert E. "Memories of Grover Loening." *Aerospace Historian* 23 (1976):
     202–6.
Mahan, Alfred T. *The Influence of Sea Power upon History, 1660–1783*. 24th ed.
     Boston: Little, Brown & Co., 1914.
Mason, Herbert M., Jr. *The Great Pursuit*. New York: Random House, 1970.

Maurer, Maurer. "The 1st Aero Squadron, 1913–1917." *Air Power Historian* 4 (1957): 207–14.

———, ed. *The U.S. Air Service in World War I.* 4 vols. Washington: Government Printing Office, 1978–79.

"Men and the Machines, 1913–1915, The: A Chronological Treatise on the Growth of Air Power." *Air Power Historian* 3 (1956): 171–78; 4 (1957): 25–33, 76–86.

Middleton, Edgar C. *Air Warfare of To-day and of the Future.* London: Constable & Co., 1918.

Military Order of the Carabao. *The Carabao's First Seventy Years, 1900–1970.* Washington: Military Order of the Carabao, 1970.

Mitchell, William. *Memoirs of World War I.* New York: Random House, 1960.

Moore, Samuel T. *U.S. Airpower: The Story of American Fighting Planes and Missiles from Hydrogen Bags to Hydrogen War Heads.* New York: Greenberg, 1958.

Morison, Frank (pseud.). [Albert H. Ross]. *War on Great Cities.* London: Faber & Faber, 1937.

Morrow, John H., Jr. *Building German Airpower, 1909–1914.* Knoxville: University of Tennessee Press, 1976.

Mott, T. Bentley. *Twenty Years as Military Attaché.* New York: Oxford University Press, 1937.

Nalty, Bernard C., ed. *Winged Shield, Winged Sword: A History of the United States Air Force.* 2 vols. Washington: Government Printing Office, 1997.

Neumann, Georg P., comp. *The German Air Force in the Great War.* Translated by J. E. Gurdon. London: Hodder & Stoughton, 1920.

Norman, Aaron. *The Great Air War.* New York: Macmillan Co., 1968.

O'Connor, Richard. *Black Jack Pershing.* Garden City, N.Y.: Doubleday & Co., 1961.

Origin of Air Warfare, The: I Primo Voli Di Guerra Nel Mondo. 2d ed. Translated by Renato d'Orlandi. Rome: Historical Office of the Italian Air Force, 1961.

"Our Unpreparedness Revealed by Villa." *Literary Digest* 52 (1916): 883–86.

Ovitt, S. W., ed. *The Balloon Section of the American Expeditionary Forces.* New Haven, Conn.: S. W. Ovitt, 1919.

Palmer, Frederick. *Bliss, Peacemaker: The Life and Letters of General Tasker Howard Bliss.* Freeport: Books for Librarians Press, 1934. Reprint. Freeport, N.Y.: Books for Libraries Press, 1970.

———. *John J. Pershing: General of the Armies.* Harrisburg: Military Services Publishing Co., 1948.

Palmer, Henry R., Jr. "Lighter-than-Air Flight in America, 1784–1910." *Journal of the American Aviation Historical Society* 24 (1979): 162–86.

Palmer, John M. *Washington, Lincoln, Wilson: Three War Statesmen.* Garden City, N.Y.: Doubleday, Doran & Co., 1930.

Parkinson, Russell J. "Politics, Patents and Planes: Military Aeronautics in the United States, 1863–1907." Ph.D. diss., Duke University, 1963.

Paszek, Lawrence J. "Wright Pushers to Stratojets." *Airpower Historian* 10, no. 4 (October 1963): 111–17.

Patrick, Mason M. *The United States in the Air.* Garden City, N.Y.: Doubleday, Doran & Co., 1928.

Poolman, Kenneth. *Zeppelins over England*. London: Evans Brothers, 1960.

Pringle, Henry F. *The Life and Times of William Howard Taft*. 2 vols. New York: Farrar & Rinehart, 1939.

———. *Theodore Roosevelt: A Biography*. Rev. ed. New York: Harcourt Brace & Co., 1955.

"Prizes for Military Aeronautics." *Scientific American* 105 (November 1911): 402.

Quirk, Robert E. *An Affair of Honor: Woodrow Wilson and the Occupation of Vera Cruz*. New York: W. W. Norton, 1967.

Raines, Rebecca R. *Getting the Message Through: A Branch History of the U.S. Army Signal Corps*. Washington: Center of Military History, 1996.

Raleigh, Walter. *The War in the Air*. Vol. 1. Oxford: Clarendon Press, 1922.

Rawlinson, Alfred. *The Defense of London, 1915–1918*. 3d ed. London: Andrew Melrose, 1924.

Robie, Bill. *For the Greatest Achievement: A History of the Aero Club of America and the National Aeronautical Association*. Washington: Smithsonian Institution Press, 1993.

Robinson, Douglas H. *The Zeppelin in Combat: A History of the German Naval Airship Division, 1910–1915*. London: G. T. Foulis & Co., 1962.

Robinson, William C. *The Law of Patents*. 3 vols. (Boston: Little, Brown & Co., 1890).

Roseberry, C. R. *Glenn Curtiss: Pioneer of Flight*. Syracuse, N.Y.: Syracuse University Press, 1991.

Royse, Morton W. *Aerial Bombardment and the International Regulation of Warfare*. New York: H. Vinal, 1928.

Saunders, Hilary St. G. *Per Ardua, the Rise of British Air Power, 1911–1939*. Oxford: Oxford University Press, 1945.

Sawyer, Robert K. "Viva Villa." *Military Review* 41, no. 8 (August 1961): 60–75.

Scheer, Reinhard. *Germany's High Sea Fleet in the World War*. London: Cassell & Co., 1920.

Schurman, Jacob G. *The Balkan Wars, 1912–1913*. Princeton, N.J.: Princeton University Press, 1914.

Scrivener, John H. "The Military Use of Balloons and Dirigibles in the United States, 1793–1963." M.A. thesis, University of Oklahoma, 1963.

Segre, Claudio G. "Douhet in Italy: Prophet without Honor." *Aerospace Historian* 26 (1979): 69–80.

Seymour, Charles. *American Neutrality, 1914–1917*. New Haven, Conn.: Yale University Press, 1935.

———. *Woodrow Wilson and the World War: A Chronicle of Our Own Times*. New Haven, Conn.: Yale University Press, 1921.

Showalter, Dennis E. *Tannenberg: Clash of Empires*. Hamden, Conn.: Archon Books, 1991.

"Signal Corps Vision of Air Power, A." *Signals* 4 (1949): 20–21.

Simonson, Gene R. "The Demand for Aircraft and the Aircraft Industry, 1907–1958." *Journal of Economic History* 20 (1960): 361–82.

Sinclair, James A. *Airships in Peace and War*. London: Rich & Cowan, Ltd., 1934.

Slessor, J. C. *Air Power and Armies*. London: Oxford University Press, 1936.

Smith, Daniel M. *Robert Lansing and American Neutrality, 1914–1917*. Berkeley: University of California Press, 1958.

Smythe, Donald. *Guerrilla Warrior: The Early Life of John J. Pershing*. New York: Charles Scribner's Sons, 1973.

Snyder, Thomas S. "Cadet Pilot Training at Chanute Field during the Great War." *Aerospace Historian* 25 (1978): 31–35.

Solibakke, Richard C. "The First Successful Government Contract for 'One (1) Heavier-than-Air Flying Machine.' " *Public Contract Law Journal* 8 (1976): 195–204.

Spaight, James M. *Aircraft in War*. London: Macmillan & Co., 1914.

Spearman, Arthur D. *John Joseph Montgomery, 1850–1911: Father of Basic Flying*. Santa Clara. Calif.: University of Santa Clara, 1967.

Squier, George O. "The Advantages of Aerial Craft in Military Warfare." *American Magazine of Aeronautics* 2, no. 1 (1908): 17–18.

——. "Aeronautics in the United States at the Signing of the Armistice, November 11, 1918: An Address to the American Society of Electrical Engineers, January 10, 1919." Reprint, possibly from vol. 11, *Professional Memoirs, Corps of Engineers, U.S. Army* (1920).

——. "The Present Status of Military Aeronautics." *Professional Memoirs, Corps of Engineers, U.S. Army* 1 (December 1909): 1612–14.

——. "The Present Status of Military Aeronautics in the United States." *Aeronautics* 3, no. 5 (1908): 10–11.

Stimson, Henry L., and McGeorge Bundy. *On Active Service in Peace and War*. New York: Harper & Brothers, 1947.

Studer, Clara. *Sky Storming Yankee: The Life of Glenn Curtiss*. New York: Stackpole & Sons, 1937.

Tedder, Lord. *Air Power in War*. London: Hodder & Stoughton, 1948.

Terry, Jay T. "The Evolving Law of Aerial Warfare." *Air University Review* 27, no. 1 (November/December 1975): 22–37.

Tompkins, Frank. *Chasing Villa: The Story behind the Story of Pershing's Expedition into Mexico*. Harrisburg: Military Service Publishing Co., 1934.

Toulmin, Harry A. *With Pershing in Mexico*. Harrisburg: Military Services Publishing Co., 1935.

Tumulty, Joseph P. *Woodrow Wilson as I Knew Him*. Special Literary Digest ed. Garden City, N.Y.: Doubleday, Page & Co., 1921.

Turnbull, Archibald, and Clifford L. Lord. *History of United States Naval Aviation*. New Haven, Conn.: Yale University Press, 1949.

Vandiver, Frank E. *Black Jack: The Life and Times of John J. Pershing*. College Station: Texas A & M University Press, 1977.

Van Vleet, Clarke, and William J. Armstrong. *United States Naval Aviation, 1910–1980*. Washington: Deputy Chief of Naval Operations–Air Warfare, 1981.

Van Vleet, Clarke, Lee M. Pearson, and Adrian O. Van Wyen. *United States Naval Aviation, 1910–1970*. 2d ed. Washington: Government Printing Office, 1970.

Von Keler, Theodore M. R. "Military Supremacy of the Air." *Scientific American* 107 (December 1912): 550; 108 (January 1913): 6.

Walworth, Arthur. *Woodrow Wilson.* 2 vols. New York: Longmans, Green & Co., 1958.

Watson, Mark S. *United States Army in World War II.* Vol. 6 of *Chief of Staff: Prewar Plans and Preparation.* Washington: Government Printing Office, 1950.

Weigley, Russell F. *The American Way of War: A History of United States Military Strategy and Policy.* New York: Macmillan, 1973.

——. *Towards an American Army: Military Thought from Washington to Marshall.* New York: Columbia University Press, 1962.

Weinstein, Edwin A. *Woodrow Wilson: A Medical and Psychological Biography.* Princeton, N.J.: Princeton University Press, 1982.

Wells, H[arold] G. *The War in the Air.* 1908. Reprint. London: Collins Clear Type Press, 1921.

Whitehorne, Joseph W. A. *The Inspectors General of the United States Army, 1903–1939.* Washington: Office of the Inspector General and Center for Military History, 1998.

Whitehouse, Arch. *The Zeppelin Fighters.* Garden City, N.Y.: Doubleday, 1966.

Wieczorek, George A. "The Military Value of Balloons." *Aeronautics* 2, no. 2 (1908): 14–16.

Wilson, Eugene E. *Kitty Hawk to Sputnik to Polaris.* Barre, Mass.: Barre Gazette, 1960.

——. *Wings of the Dawn: A Study of Airpower as a Contribution to Civilization.* Hartford, Conn.: Eugene Wilson, 1955.

Wiser, Frank B. "General Pershing's Mexican Campaign." *Century* 99 (1920): 433–47.

Woodhouse, Henry. "Aeronautics and the War." *Flying* 3, no. 8 (September 1914): 229–33, 251–52.

——. "Growing Wings." *Collier's Weekly* 50, no. 8 (1912): 14–15, 33–34, 36.

Woodward, Sir Llewellyn. *Great Britain and the War of 1914–1918.* London: Methuen & Co., 1967.

Worrel, Rodney K. "The Wright Brothers' Pioneer Patent." *American Bar Association Journal* 65 (1979): 1612–18.

Wright, Orville. *How We Invented the Airplane.* Edited by Fred C. Kelly. New York: Davis McKay Co., 1988.

Zollman, Carl. "Patent Rights in Aircraft." *Marquette Law Review* 2 (1927): 216–21.

Index

tion unit, 210–11; and training personnel, 187–89, 209; in World War I, 184, 207, 211

Airships, 87; and coastal defense, 50; and explosive hydrogen, 50; ground fire vulnerability of, 45; manufacturers of, 50, 87; naval uses of, 79, 154; and transportation, 79. *See also* Dirigibles; Zeppelin airships

Air superiority, 6, 69, 71, 145, 155, 185; and artillery survival, 153; and centralized control, 193; and concentration of forces, 146, 201; offensive advantage of, 202–3; and reconnaissance, 71, 145, 193, 292; and target selection, 146; and technological development, 45; and Veracruz incursion, 157; in World War I, 191, 201–3. *See also* Combat, aerial; Command and control

Allen, Henry T., 168, 170

Allen, James, 20, 37–38, 47, 56, 62, 63, 56, 69, 79, 81, 88

American Aerodrome Company, 93

American Expeditionary Force, air organization, 186

Angle of attack, wing, 98, 128

Angle of incidence, 98, 128

Army, 66, 82, 110, 134–35; arms and branches of, 2; and Board of Fortifications and Ordnance, 12; and foreign intelligence, 24; and Langley experiments, 12, 54

Army aviation: divisional assignment of, 154; and exhibition flying, 5, 40–41; factions within, 116; and flying safety, 116, 127–29, 181; and World War I, 185; and Wright Company, 107, 108, 116, 127, 140

Army-Navy relationship, 109

Arnold, Henry H., 19, 40, 61, 63, 131, 165

Artillery: and counter-battery fire, 196, 197, 200; and "creeping barrage," 153, 193; and doctrinal over-

emphasis, 215; fire direction, 4, 44–45, 57–58, 67–69, 70, 143–45, 152–53, 197; and radio communication, 68, 145, 199; and training defects, 188–89, 194, 198–200; in World War I, 189, 197–201

Atlantic Monthly, 33

Attaché reports, 43, 47–52, 56, 58, 68, 140, 151–56, 186

Aviation progress, 105, 107, 140, 152

Aviation Section, 3, 6, 139, 141, 171, 175–79; establishment of, 24, 43, 61–63; and independence, 134; and military discipline, 26; morale in, 116, 140, 184; obsolete airplanes in, 152; and Wright Company, 100–101, 107. *See also* Aeronautical Division; Air Service

Baker, Newton D., 132, 134, 139, 162, 170, 178, 180, 207

Baldwin, Thomas S., 14

Balkan Wars (1912–13), 44, 47, 69

"Balloon busting," 194

Balloonists, training, 188–89

Balloon navigation: and artillery fire direction, 79; and Civil War, 11–12; and communication to ground, 79; and ground fire, 67, 79; and hovering ability, 67, 79; and Spanish-American War, 12; and sport ballooning, 12–13, 87; and World War I, 137, 198, 200

Balloons, free flying. *See* Airships

Balloons, stationary, 89, 155, 194; and American Civil War, 67; and attracting enemy fire, 79; congressional neglect of, 86, 188–89; and moving front warfare, 79, 86, 194, 201; and trench warfare, 79, 89, 189, 201; and weather conditions, 79

Beachey, Lincoln, 173

Beck, Paul W., 20, 25, 61, 62, 63

Bell, Alexander Graham, 15, 33–34, 92, 96

Bishop, Cortlandt F., 15, 18, 92–94

Martin Aircraft Company, 107
Masculinity, 38
Maxim, Hudson, 97
Meuse-Argonne Offensive, 194–95,
199, 203
Mexican Punitive Expedition, 6–7, 110,
141, 152, 156, 157–72, 191, 209–10;
climatic conditions, 165; command
and control, 168–69; morale, 168–
69; motorized transportation, 172;
preparedness movement, 181; press
censorship, 169; propeller warping,
165, 170; reconnaissance, 166–67,
169; significance of, 175; terrain, 166
Military aviation: and European prog-
ress, 43; and Progressivism, 9
"Military Aviation" (publication), 140,
147, 151, 154–56, 157, 162
Military intelligence. *See* Attaché reports
Military policy, 6, 140
Military tradition, 20
Milling, Thomas deW., 19, 61, 68, 98,
104, 108, 122, 133, 188, 215
Mitchell, William ("Billy"), 44, 63, 70,
126, 135–38, 150, 156, 184, 185,
191–96, 201, 214, 216
Mobility, air, 165, 191
Monell, Ambrose, 210
Monopoly, 99
Mott, T. Bentley, 51, 59–60
Murray, Arthur, 119, 127

National Advisory Committee on Aeronautics (U.S.), 49, 108, 114
National Defense Act (1916), 4, 6–7,
175–81; and Aviation Section personnel, 178; and reserve provisions, 180–
81; Signal Corps in, 177
National Geographic, 33–34
National Guard, 20, 59, 64, 66, 74–75,
180–81; and Aero Club of America,
76; and aero squadrons, 76–77; and
army pilots, 74, 138, 139, 180; and aviation units, 20, 64, 181; and Continental Army plan, 180; flight training for,

75; and maneuvers in 1912, 20, 51, 57,
68; and National Defense Act (1916),
political significance of, 75, 180–81;
and reserve military pilots, 181
National preparedness, 1, 6, 9, 66
Naval aviation, 8, 22–23; and aeronaut
constituency, 27; and Curtiss connec-
tions, 108, 110; and Squier report,
153; and Veracruz incursion, 158–59;
and Wright airplanes, 101–2. *See also*
Chambers, Washington I.
Naval funding, 8, 55
Naval militia, 74
Naval supremacy: and Zeppelins, 33
Navigational instruments, 189
"New Army," 74, 76
Newspapers: as aviation sponsors, 30;
and pro-aviation press, 171, 174;
World War I reports in, 141
New York Times, 85, 86, 87
New York World, 169
Nicholls, Sam J., 178
Nicolson, William, 128
Night flying, 164

Observation. *See* Reconnaissance
Offensive tactics, 147
"Old Army," 74

Palmer, John, 133
Patent applications, 107–8
Patent jam, 114
Patent pool, 114–15, 214
Patrick, Mason, 114, 136, 151, 189,
190, 192, 211, 212, 214. *See also*
"Final Report"
Patterson, William L., 122–23, 126,
128, 130, 132, 133
Paulhan, Louis, 99–100, 104
Peace: and air power, 29, 33, 70
Pershing, John J., 6, 135, 136, 138,
161–72, 184–214 passim; and inde-
pendent U.S. sector, 192; and military
aviation, 167, 204; and Philippines,
123, 131, 162

Wilson, Woodrow, 54, 129, 139, 157–59, 175

Winder, Charles B., 75

"Winged Gospel," 29, 162

Wing warping, 98, 102–3

Wise-Wood, Henry A., 21, 23, 27

With the Night Mail, 34–35, 56

Wolcott, Charles, 178

Wood, Leonard, 71, 74–76

Woodhouse, Henry, 20, 46, 61, 151

Works, John Downey, 177

World powers: funding of aviation by, 55

World War I, 65–66; American entry into, 174, 185, 215; American pilots in, 1–2; and attaché reports, 6, 141; evaluation of, 184, 214; and General Staff Corps, 141; land warfare in, 141; and postwar analysis, 213–16; rising tempo of, 215; and temporary promotions, 138;

World War II, 2, 196, 202, 216

Wright, Orville, 14, 97, 99, 104, 105, 106–7, 113–14, 115, 151

Wright, Wilbur, 14, 77, 90, 94, 106, 113

Wright Aeronautical Company, 101. *See also* Wright brothers

Wright B biplane, 40–41, 117

Wright brothers, 53, 70, 92–93, 105, 106, 140; and Aeronautical Division, 23, 100–101; and airplane design, 5, 116; and clothing, 32; and control system, 91; first flight of, 1; and glider experiments, 91, 94; and hard bargaining, 100–101; litigation strategy of, 100; and military acceptance trials, 29; and patent litigation, 5, 9, 34, 90–115, 101, 113, 128. *See also* Wright, Orville; Wright, Wilbur

Wright C flyer, 102, 104, 117

Wright Company, 104; and army aviation, 107, 117; and capitalization, 110; and engineering, 111–12; and government procurement of airplanes, 110; navy aviation and, 101–2, 108; neglects designing, 90, 111; neglects manufacturing, 90, 101, 110; and patent enforcement, 110; and pilot training, 116, 128; and pusher and tractor engines, 101, 111; and refinancing, 107, 113–14; and seaplanes, 108. *See also* Wright brothers

Wright Company v. Herring-Curtiss, 97–99, 105, 106, 108

Wright flyer (1903), 105

Wright patent: and attemps to purchase in U.S., 96; British requirement for use of, 95; and combination of control elements, 91–92; and earlier patents, 97–98; and file wrapper estoppel, 95; and France, 96; and Germany, 93–94, 96; and litigation, 90; and pioneering invention, 95, 97; and prior disclosure, 92–94; and public opinion, 99, 106

Zahm, Albert F., 18, 105

Zeppelin airships, 49–50, 81–83; and bombardment, 50, 79; cost-effectiveness of, 83; and Farman, 83; and ground fire, 50, 84, 142; lift capacity of, 69; limitations of, 84, 149, 204; and London bombardment, 4, 148–50, 204; longevity in flight of, 37, 155; range of, 69, 155; and reconnaissance, 50, 84, 142; secrecy concerning, 88

Zero defects, 1